STRESS, SOCIAL SUPPORT, AND WOMEN

Edited by

Stevan E. Hobfoll
Department of Psychology
Tel-Aviv University

● HEMISPHERE PUBLISHING CORPORATION
A Subsidiary of Harper & Row, Publishers, Inc.
Washington   New York   London

DISTRIBUTION OUTSIDE THE UNITED STATES
McGRAW-HILL INTERNATIONAL BOOK COMPANY
Auckland   Bogotá   Guatemala   Hamburg   Johannesburg   Lisbon
London   Madrid   Mexico   Montreal   New Delhi   Panama   Paris
San Juan   São Paulo   Singapore   Sydney   Tokyo   Toronto

STRESS, SOCIAL SUPPORT, AND WOMEN

1 2 3 4 5 6 7 8 9 0   E B E B   8 9 8 7 6 5

This book was set in Press Roman by Hemisphere Publishing Corporation. The
editors were Christine Flint Lowry and Marybeth Janney; and the typesetter
was Shirley J. McNett
Edwards Brothers, Inc. was printer and binder.

Library of Congress Cataloging in Publication Data
Main entry under title:

Stress, social support, and women.
    (The Series in clinical and community psychology)

    Includes bibliographies and index.
    1. Stress (Psychology) 2. Stress (Psychology)
3. Women—Psychology. 4. Adjustment (Psychology)
5. Women—Services for. I. Hobfoll, Stevan E., date.
II. Series.
BF575.S75S7739   1985   155.9   84-27967
ISBN 0-89116-404-9
ISSN 0146-0846

This book is dedicated to the loving memory of my mother, Anita Grace Hobfoll: artist, musician, career woman, family woman, and above all individualist. Often in my travels or standing before some work of art I see the world through eyes I know to be hers.

Contents

V

BEREAVEMENT AND OLD AGE

CONCLUSION

Contributors

CAROL S. ANESHENSEL, University of California at Los Angeles, Los Angeles, California, USA

ELIZABETH A. BANKOFF, Northwestern University, Evanston, Illinois, USA

JAY A. BEHRMAN, University of Utah, Salt Lake City, Utah, USA

VERONICA J. DARK, University of Utah, Salt Lake City, Utah, USA

BARTON J. HIRSCH, University of Illinois, Urbana, Illinois, USA

STEVAN E. HOBFOLL, Tel Aviv University, Ramat Aviv, Israel

CHRISTINE A. HODSON, Alameda County Hall of Justice, Hayward, California, USA

JOSEPH J. LEON, California State Polytechnic University, Pomona, California, USA

MARGARET W. LINN, University of Miami School of Medicine, Miami, Florida, USA

ROGER E. MITCHELL, Stanford University and Veteran's Administration Medical Center, Palo Alto, California, USA (currently: Psychological Consultation Center, University of Rhode Island)

ELLEN OSTROW, University of Maryland, College Park, Maryland, USA

STEPHEN C. PAUL, University of Utah, Salt Lake City, Utah, USA

CYNTHIA S. RAND, Johns Hopkins University School of Medicine and Baltimore City Hospitals, Baltimore, Maryland, USA

JULIAN RAPPAPORT, University of Illinois, Urbana, Illinois, USA

ROBIN J. RENDERS, University of Illinois, Urbana, Illinois, USA

LIBBY O. RUCH, University of Hawaii at Manoa, Honolulu, Hawaii, USA

ZAHAVA SOLOMAN, Tel Aviv University, Ramat Aviv, Israel

CATHERINE H. STEIN, University of Illinois, Urbana, Illinois, USA

BETH E. VANFOSSEN, University of New York, Brockport, New York, USA

MARY L. S. VACHON, Clarke Institute of Psychiatry, Toronto, Canada

BRIAN L. WILCOX, University of Virginia, Charlottesville, Virginia, USA

Preface

In recent years women have experienced rapid changes in every aspect of their lives. Challenging a male-dominated society, women have demanded more rights, wages, and status at work, and in the home and social environment. There has been a consequent increase in attention to the special needs of women and heightened awareness of issues relevant to women in such diverse areas as medical service delivery, law enforcement, treatment of the elderly (most of whom are women), and provision of emergency shelter.

This book is concerned with the stressors women undergo from adolescence to old age and the resources, especially interpersonal resources, women use to cope with these stressors. There follows a series of chapters that address the use of social support as a resource for coping with stressful life events that confront women in a variety of contexts during their life span. The chapter authors, most of them women and all of them deeply concerned in their work with women's issues, address their subject matters as psychologists, sociologists, epidemiologists, and health practitioners. Many of the issues are emotionally charged, which demands that the theories, interpretation of the results, and design of the studies be examples of high-quality empirical social-science research. Many of the points made should be even more convincing due to the high standards of the researchers involved.

A central goal of this volume, which is addressed in almost every chapter and is the central topic of the final chapter, is to draw implications from research on social support for clinical and other interventions as they concern women. A second goal, which is related to the first, is to encourage new research in the area of social support, and to suggest methodological and theoretical directions this research might take. This second goal is also highlighted in the final chapter.

Following an ecological life-span approach developed in the introductory chapter, this volume proceeds along the life course of women, addressing the problems women normally confront or are threatened with in each life stage. Special issues, not necessarily age related, are placed according to the approximate chronological order in which they generally occur.

First, stressors occurring among adolescent and young adult women are addressed. Next, research on career, marriage, and family stressors is presented.

Two special issues that follow are women's coping with violent assault and women's health concerns—including giving birth and breast cancer. The closing section presents the adjustment of women to widowhood and finally, old age. Following this an attempt is made to summarize major points regarding methodology, theory, and applications.

The volume is divided into five sections, and an Introduction. In the Introduction I present the case for the study of stress among women. The introduction develops an ecological, life span perspective of the interaction of individual, stressors, and coping resources—focusing on social support.

The first of the five sections is on "Developmental Issues in the Adjustment of Women." Barton Hirsch and Robin Renders discuss the development of social relationships in a case study of an adolescent female. The benefits and stressfulness of establishing adolescent friendships are explored here in depth. The second chapter is written by Ellen Ostrow, Stephan Paul, Veronica Dark and Jay Behrman. This chapter explores the effects of social support among college women within the traditional Mormon environment of the University of Utah. Implications for preventive university intervention utilizing social support strategies are discussed as a product of their needs assessment for these women, many of whom were found to be challenging their traditional family and religious roles. In the third chapter Cathy Stein and Julian Rappaport present their findings on the adjustment of graduate student wives, many of whom are supporting their husbands through school, and raising children. This chapter is placed in a developmental framework wherein many of these women are adjusting to being separated from their families for the first time, and to having and caring for their first child. In this chapter the authors combine quantitative and qualitative analysis, highlighting sense of family obligation as a value related to the use and utility of social support.

The second section of the volume is entitled "Career, Marriage and Family Stressors." Dr. Vanfossen writes on the role of spouse support on depression in women. Her research emphasizes the importance of both intimacy, and perhaps more important, equity of spouse support for women. Next, Zahava Solomon, now a major in the Israeli Defense Forces in charge of mental health research, presents her research on the mothers of young children exposed to the radiation leak at Three Mile Island. In a control group field study, she analyzes the effect of supportive social interactions on women who felt both themselves and their young children threatened by the dangerous effects of radiation.

Carol Aneshensel then presents a longitudinal study of the effect of social support on depression among women who are experiencing employment, marriage, and parenting role strain. The final chapter in this section, by Brian Wilcox, concerns the effectiveness of social support in the divorce process. As a community psychologist, Dr. Wilcox relates his work to an ecological perspective and this chapter considers the fit of personal and social resources through different stages of the divorce process.

Section 3 is entitled "Violence Toward Women." Libby Ruch together with Joseph Leon present research to establish a model to explain the determinants of the impact of rape on women. Type of social support offered by intimate males who may be unsympathetic or themselves indirectly blamed by virtue of being men is one of the important factors they examine. Drs. Ruch and Leon attempt to explain within a general theoretical model the potential benefit of social support in helping these women reestablish trust and repair a sense of depleted self worth. Roger Mitchell and Christine Hodson present a related chapter on women's coping with being violently assaulted within marriage and "love" relationships. They examine this betrayal of trust and the effect social support and coping strategies play for battered women. The fact that women most in need of support may have the least social support, and may lack the skills to utilize help and ability to actively address their problem, is investigated. Personal values and attitudes of significant others are also addressed in this chapter.

Women's Health is the topic of section 4. In the first chapter Cinthia Rand explores the question of the use of nurse midwives as medical practitioners who may provide greater social support to women who are giving non-medically complicated births. The discussion of change of preference by women from fulfillment of emotional needs to fulfillment of medical necessities during problem deliveries illustrates both the ecological fit and lack of fit of social support when needs are altered from an emotional orientation to a task orientation which social relationships cannot fulfill. The next chapter by Mary Vachon, herself a nurse, discusses the impact of breast cancer on women. Dr. Vachon presents theoretical and empirical material in analyzing the similarities and differences of loss of the breast to loss of spouse and the effect social support has in each of these traumatic processes.

The final section is entitled "Bereavement and Old Age." Elizabeth Bankoff explores the personal and structural characteristics related to the provision of peer support to women following death of their spouse. This is a somewhat different perspective than most of the other chapters, as it emphasizes the question of what characteristics are related to acquiring peer support rather than the question of the effect of peer support. Margaret Linn then discusses the impact of social support on elderly women who live independently. Dr. Linn has in her past research addressed cultural issues in the support process in the multi-ethnic environment of Miami, Florida. Her chapter presents a picture of the changing role of women—in particular how this affects elderly women. She emphasizes the special physical, emotional, economic and safety needs of these women who occupy a niche in our culture which will be occupied by an increasing percentage of the population.

Following this section, I present a final chapter organizing the implications for research and applications suggested by the contributors to this volume. The utility of social support as an element in intervention efforts and attempts at environmental change are discussed. Suggestions for future research and methodological issues are also discussed along with concluding remarks. The intervention and research strategies are placed within an ecological model which expands on the dimension of time when considering the support process, and a cognitive approach for the investigation of social support is detailed.

This volume has been organized to provide a comprehensive life span perspective concerning the ecology of women's lives. Hopefully the reader will find that it approaches this goal.

The volume is recommended for upper-level and graduate courses and for use by mental health professionals. It should be particularly valuable for courses in women's studies, community psychology, social psychology, social work, and life-span development that emphasize a research orientation. The book is written in a fashion, however, that those readers naïve to social science methodology and statistics are spared wading through numbers and tables if they so desire.

I would like to thank Charles D. Spielberger and Irwin G. Sarason for their assistance as consulting editors to this series. Fred Begell, Christine Flint Lowry, Kate Roach, and Marybeth Janney of Hemisphere Publishing Corporation were also very helpful throughout the development of this volume.

I would also like to thank Gerald Caplan and Perry London for encouraging my work and so freely sharing with me their time and ideas. Norman Milgram and Yona Teichman were also very helpful and provided insightful comments regarding chapters that I wrote for the volume.

My wife, Ivonne, herself an active clinical psychologist, has always provided me with the support I need. She combines career and family, love and affection in a way that allows me to meet my own needs as a husband, father, and academician.

Stevan E. Hobfoll

INTRODUCTION

1

The Ecology of Stress and Social Support among Women

Stevan E. Hobfoll
Tel Aviv University

If the 1960s were often termed the "Age of Anxiety," then the 1970s and 1980s entered us into the "Age of Stress" ("Stress", 1983). Established cultural norms and ways of thinking that emerged from the postwar years were challenged in the 1960s and began to be remolded in the 1970s. Civil rights, antiwar and women's issues were addressed heatedly. Often cited as having begun with the 1973 Arab Oil Embargo, economic strains have been felt worldwide, and employment problems emerged in the place of the, perhaps nostalgically remembered security and serenity of the 1950s. Women's roles in the family and the marketplace altered rapidly and radically, to no small part because of demands they made. No other issue could affect more lives, for more people from different walks of life, races, or socioeconomic groups. While the quest for the rights and privileges of women was not so apparent on the streets, serious challenges have been occurring nevertheless at the home and workplace, among career women, and female factory workers alike, and among mothers, daughters, and sisters. Women themselves have experienced a private struggle even with the questions "who am I?", "who do I want to be?" and "how do I want others to respond to me?"

There is a need at the present time to explore how women cope with stressors that affect their lives. Social support is one of the most important resources in this coping process. Careful study of this topic will hopefully provide new information that can be exploited for developing new intervention strategies in the treatment of women, establishing prevention programs, encouraging healthy work and family environments, and in effecting the slow process of societal change. If medical services, for example, are to be tailored to meet the special emotional needs of women giving birth, physicians, hospital administrators, and federal funding agencies will need to be advised in terms of clear, well-thought-out applied research, which makes a strong case for change. Change is expensive, stressful, and thus at least, in part, justifiably resisted. As change often affects the vested interests of one group in order to enhance the interests of another group, it is also resisted for sometimes unjustifiable reasons. Good research is a powerful tool in the armamentarium of the change agent.

I would like to thank Perry London and Norman Milgram for their helpful comments on this chapter.

A LIFE SPAN, ECOLOGICAL APPROACH

Research on stress and coping has tended to be atheoretical and without clear models. This is the nature of science in any new area of research and without idea-directed observation it would be difficult to devise theories and models (Kuhn, 1970). In order to organize this area of research an ecological model related to a life span approach was seen as a fundamental step toward greater understanding. The purpose of this chapter is to present such a perspective.

Women and Stress

The question of "why a volume such as this should address women separately from men?", other than separation for the sake of interest or simplification, can be answered in what I see as a convincing manner by emphasizing an ecological approach. An ecological perspective includes individuals as they interact with their environment. It implies that the biological, psychological, sociological, and physical aspects of the life space should be considered not separately, but as a constellation. Women are born and develop biologically different than men, they are usually socialized differently than men, they not surprisingly have different psychological traits than men (as a group) and experience different role demands in the family, workplace, and society in general.

Each of these differences are equally true for men, and, of course, research on stressors impinging on men and social support is being carried out. However, beyond these differences women also are confronted with two stressors that men are not, or at least not to the same extent. The first, mentioned earlier, is rapid change. The adaption of organisms to a changing ecology is the greatest of challenges. Many species, even great and strong, become extinct during such periods. Other species thrive in the changed conditions, emerging often in the place of others or in newly created niches. The world of women has changed markedly in the past 20 to 30 years, and rapidly in the last 10. Women have always worked—working women have always worked hard, but work and professional alternatives have broadened tremendously in recent years. Women, more than ever, are working in almost every field and every level of expertise and authority (Smith, 1979).

The second stressor special to women is that they have entered a world away from the home, a world that has traditionally been dominated by men. This has especially been true in terms of positions of control and power. Even with the increase and variety of jobs held by women the concentration of women are still performing "women's work", being employed in the clerical, health care (not including physicians), education (not including higher education), domestic and food service industries (Smith, 1979). Not surprisingly, the positions held by men have been more richly rewarded and are accompanied by more of the "extras" so sought after—the expense account, travel, the key to the executive bathroom, and now tennis courts (Barret, 1979), and even jobs that have the protection of unions (Hunt, 1982). As in the civil rights movement, the introduction of women into the corridors of decision making and power, and for more minorities and women merely getting equal pay for equal work at all levels, has caused conflict (Barret, 1979).

This is stressful on a number of counts. It is stressful because "taking ground" requires more energy than "defending ground." It is stressful because women have often not had the mentors or been privy to membership in "old boys" networks that aid in job promotion and day-to-day "jostling" at the workplace. It is stressful because while boys had played aggressive, competitive sports and men were idealized as heroes playing the same sports on television resulting in aggressiveness, competitiveness, and dominance (Maccoby & Jacklin, 1974), girls were absent from such rituals, or participated as spectators or cheerleaders. Competitiveness among women was not rewarded, and often was punished (Maccoby & Jacklin, 1974).

Ecologies are products of interaction. For women these changes outside the home should have been accompanied by changes in the home. As the chapter in this volume by Vanfossen (Chap. 5) indicates, this has not necessarily occurred. Instead, women have tended to become worker by day and housewife by night. Instead of other family members changing their responsibilities and dividing the work parcel at home, these tasks have been left to wives and mothers (Vanfossen, 1981; Yogev, 1981). The work of men outside of the home is still viewed more seriously. So the working woman is an adjunct. She is paid less, has less responsibility at work, and not surprisingly is expected to and expects to move when her husband's job requires (Barret, 1979).

An ecological perspective also demands attention to biology. For women, this draws the focus to a number of potential stressors that are different from those experienced by men. The first class of these are strictly biological. Girls experience greater developmental change in regard to secondary sexual characteristics during adolescence than do boys, requiring adjustment in self-concept and body image. Women get pregnant and give birth, both potentially exhilarating and stressful events. Women are at higher risk than men for breast cancer, and if cancer is found, often have to live with removal of one or both breasts. This has profound implications for their view of self and sense of sexuality (Child, Barry, & Bacon, 1965). Finally, women tend to live longer than men, and so are more likely to be widowed and be alone during their old age.

The second class of biologically related stressors are a product of the interaction of biology and environment. These include limitations placed on women because of their biology, either justifiably (pregnant women shouldn't be exposed to repeated radiation), or unjustifiably. Women tend to be physically smaller than men, become pregnant, and menstruate. Over and above some degree to which any difference may incur limitations (and advantages), these characteristics are often used against women in justifying preference for selection, advancement, and giving responsibility to men (Barret, 1979). While a woman may lose a few months work postpartum for two children, her husband may lose 10 years of productivity due to a coronary infarction and is at greater risk for alcoholism (Gomberg, 1974).* While events may be actuarially determined, those related to men are seldom a factor considered in job decisions. In general, employers do not consider empirical or criterion-based information in selection or advancement (an exception being, for example, the United States mail service requiring mail

---

*A number of European countries and Israel allow 3–6 months of paid maternity leave (national insurance funded) and up to a year unpaid maternity leave, in which the woman's position must be held for her return.

carriers to be capable of lifting a given weight; U.S. Department of Labor, 1969; Fullerton & Byrne, 1977).

Violence against women is also related to the interaction of biology and environment. Women are both at a disadvantage to protect themselves against a physical assault perpetrated by a man, and are selected as objects for violence in the case of rape. The courts and police have become more sensitive to rape victims and more punitive of rapists, to an increasing extent viewing the crime as the severe violence it is and not a mere sexual faux pas ("Rape", 1983). Nonetheless a peaceful evening stroll alone for anyone in most American cities and many European cities is a bygone dream—the reality is a nightmare for women.

Women and Caring

As a product of biology, in part, and to a great extent socialization practices, women tend to be different psychologically than men (Maccoby & Jacklin, 1974). While there are many such differences noted in the literature, I wish to expand on one set of characteristics, related to women's social self, which I see as an advantage, especially as related to social support. Women are more sensitive than men to social interactions, they develop closer and more extensive social networks, and are more giving in these relationships (Belle, 1982; Eisenberg & Lennon, 1983; Jourard, 1971; Wheeler & Nezlock, 1977). In an insightful series of studies and theoretical discussions Kessler and his colleagues (Kessler, McLeod, & Wethington, 1985) have shown that women care more about what occurs to those around them. Women, Kessler finds, include more individuals within the network of persons about whom they say, "what happens to you is important to me." Of course, this increases their vulnerability to psychological distress as the potential for experiencing negative recent life events increases with the size of their social network. However, can the world be imagined as a place without this caring?

This sensitivity to others and greater emotionality is often interpreted, rather one-sidedly as a problem, because one of the consequences of these traits is that women as a group tend to be more depressed than men and because they come to therapy more frequently than men for psychological concerns (Al-Issa, 1982). However, men are more likely to display characterological disorders and to "act out." Sociopaths seldom come for treatment on their own volition. Women seem more comfortable in seeking help, and in caring for others enough to want to help. They also develop the intimate social networks in which social support takes place. This caring, however, as noted above has a cost (Kessler et al., 1985).

Women and Social Support

Social support has been found in a great number of studies to have a positive effect on mental and physical health (Brown, Brolchrain, & Harris, 1975; Cobb, 1976; Dean & Lin, 1977; Hirsch, 1980; Nucholls, Cassel & Caplan, 1972; Vanfossen, 1971; Wilcox, 1981). The previous discussion leads us to why social support may be an especially germane topic to the study of coping among women. Again the ecology of women's lives can be used as a framework to address this question. Viewed from this perspective women's living space must be considered in the context of their personalities, values, the values of others around them, and the availability of support and other coping resources. In addition, the type of stressor must be evaluated in the context of an interaction with each other of these variable domains.

As follows from the previous discussion, women are more likely to seek help than men when they feel they need it. Women seem to discuss feelings more easily and already in adolescence develop more intimate relationships with other young women than do adolescent boys (Maccoby & Jacklin, 1974). As Kessler et al. (1985) have noted, this is accompanied by a sense of caring of what goes on in the lives of friends and family, beyond the nuclear family. These are essentially the two ingredients of social support, the "give and take" of intimate, sharing relations. Mutuality or reciprocity of support giving is a key ingredient in successful supportive relations (Caplan, 1974; Hobfoll, 1985).

After establishing such relationships, the question to be asked is "do women need social support more than men?" Both men and women have been found to benefit from quality supportive social interactions, especially intimate ones (Brown et al., 1975; Pearlin et al., 1981). For the sake of discussion let us assume that both sexes can derive great benefit from love, caring, physical help, and good advice. However, men it will be argued have an edge on women, as they have on one hand the nurturant female providing them support and have social approval for their provider role. Women, on the other hand, may actually receive social rejection for whatever role they adopt. In addition, women are left with spouses and boy-friends who feel less comfortable in nurturant roles, who probably have great demands outside of the family, and who expect primarily to be recipients of nurturance.

Vanfossen (1981; Chap. 5) has shown that employed women are in double jeopardy compared to men. Having gone to work they can now be stressed in two worlds, whereas men are more affected by the work world alone. Employed wives were also more likely to provide expressive support than their spouses, were more upset by parenting problems and in general were more stressed by a lack of support or conflict in the home than were husbands. Men were found, on the other hand, to be more sensitive to problems in the workplace than were women. It appears that for women, social support at home and affirmation for their role whether in or outside the home would be ecologically consistent with their needs. For men, social support at the workplace might be more appropriate, but this may be true because women are meeting their needs at home.

Aneshensel (Chap. 7) argues that both the working woman and the housewife experience stressors due to the role versus reward character of their lives. House-wives may receive support from their spouses and others due to their role conformity, but may feel that they do not receive esteem from these same others. The employed woman may feel both lack of support at home for her career and lack of support at work for her advancement. In both cases, women who receive affirmation for whom they are and what they do experienced less psychological strain than women who did not receive such support (Aneshensel, Chap. 7). Men also need such support, but as a group they are less likely to feel their role devalued, and they are more likely, since they are not challenging any cultural norms, to be supported for their behavior. Unemployed men may also have increased needs for social support due to their being placed in a role that is incongruous with traditional sex-role expectations.

Divorced women may also have greater social support needs than divorced men, and be in a situation that limits receipt of the same. During divorce both men and women experience great distress and can benefit from supportive social interaction. Following divorce women usually receive child custody and generate lower incomes than their former spouses. Both factors make instrumental support such as assistance with child care, shopping, home repair, and emotional support highly desirable for divorced women. Dating and finding a sexual partner, two important sources of social support and enjoyment, may prove more difficult for single mothers than for their former husbands, as children limit social time and baby-sitters add an additional expense on the budget. As custody laws become more liberalized this may change to some extent.

As victims of violence, women are also in need of social support. Ruch and Leon (Chap. 9) discuss the special needs of victims of rape for emotional support over a long period following the attack. Battered women, in addition to needing emotional support and advice, often need instrumental support such as physical protection, financial assistance for legal fees and physical shelter for themselves and for their children. This may be seen as a radical alteration of their ecological niche. As social support has been seen as effective because it provides messages regarding self-worth (Caplan, 1974), it may be a critical determinant of recovery from the psychological trauma experienced by raped or battered women.

Women who experience rape or battering are in some ways similar to women who have had a breast removed or who are widowed. Each of these experiences are especially common to women, and likely have sexual consequences. In each case, peer support may be expected to be especially helpful. Women who have experienced these traumas may have a certain empathy for other women for whom these are recent experiences (Bankoff, Chap. 13). They may also be perceived as understanding by victims, while men or women who have not been through "it" may be seen as (and may, in fact, be) naive. Self-help groups may also receive training in counseling skills, making them ideal preventive inter-ventionists.

To summarize this discussion, women and men are both often placed in stressful life conditions. Women may feel more comfortable than men, however, with establishing and exploiting social ties when they experience difficulties. Women are sensitive to stressors both in the home and workplace, while role expectations may limit the social support they receive whether home or employed. In addition to role conflict, women also often experience a number of life events, that men either do not, or are much less likely to experience. For these events social support may be a key resource due to the negative impact these events have on well-being. Peer support may in such cases be especially helpful, as those who have experienced such events may be empathic and perceived by victims as understanding.

Ecological Congruence

In two recent papers (Hobfoll, 1985); Hobfoll, Kelso, & Peterson, in press) I have presented a model of what I have called "ecological congruence" as a mechanism for understanding the potential contribution of various resources, especially social support, in the coping process. Rather than accepting a priori that a given resource is appropriate merely because we have labelled it a "resource," this model requires placing the potential resource in an ecological framework in which it may be evaluated and understood. Social support, or any resource for that matter, may or may not have a positive effect for a given individual or group, and the very term "social support" is misleading as it implies a priori a supportive effect from social interactions.

The general model can be stated in the following mapping sentence that emphasizes various dimensions inherent in all social ecologies (Figure 1). The dimensions are: resource, need, strain, time, values (of self and others), and perception. These dimensions are seen as a constellation in which there is a given resource-individual-situation fit that determines the "valence of effect."

As may be noted in Figure 1, individuals have a variety of potential resources at their disposal. Within each resource category there are furthermore different types and qualities of each potential strength, i.e., different personality resources or types of social support. Following the mapping sentence, these potential resources may have positive, negative, or no effect on reducing strain (Strain Dimension). This effect will be determined by the extent to which the particular resource, or combination of resources (Resource Dimension) which are recruited meet, do not meet or interfere (Valence of Effect) with the task or emotional demands placed on the individual (Need Dimension).

Demands change over time in relation to the event and differ in regards to the person's place in the life span (Time Dimension). Elderly women have different needs following divorce than do young women. Both groups have different needs during, immediately following, and one year after the divorce. The resources may further vary in their effectiveness in relation to the personal values of the individual regarding the event ("it's okay for someone in our family/in our society to be divorced") (Values dimension). These values may even be expressed as outright constraints, as for example, in Israel where the man has to grant his wife the divorce, in some religions where divorce is granted only on pain of excommunication or ostracization from the community, and in some states' abortion laws. Finally, the individual's own perception of what constitutes threat, support, personal needs, existent cultural values, etc. is a critical axis on which objective events acquire personal meaning (Perception Dimension). To illustrate how the model of ecological congruence can be employed the following example is given.

In a recent study by Perry London and myself (Hobfoll & London, in press) personality resources of self-esteem and sense of mastery, and social support resources (Resource Dimension) of intimacy with friends and family and amount of actual support received during the current period were studied in respect to psychological distress—state depression and anxiety (Strain Dimension), among women whose loved ones were mobilized during the first week of the recent Lebanon War (June, 1982). The event was perceived as ecologically being a crisis with little warning time (Time Dimension). The elapsed time since the event was seen as critical in limiting the recruitment and receipt of social support (Time X Resource interaction). Cultural norms suggested women would be expected to perform their role functions, but expressions of emotions were assumed to be acceptable, suggesting that social support, if obtainable, would be willingly requested and offered (Values Dimension). Israelis are aware of the real threats of war and have been to enough war-related funerals to have no delusions about potential outcome.

Evaluating these factors it was predicted that women with greater personality resources would experience less distress than women possessing lesser personality

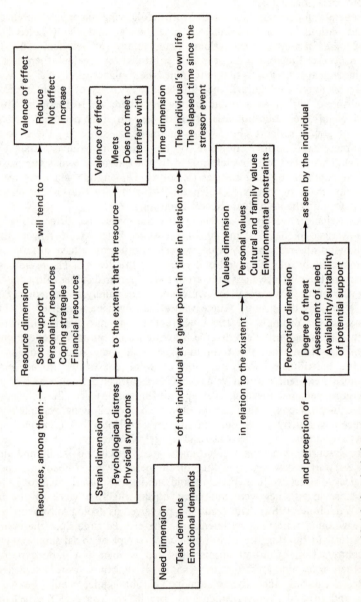

Figure 1 Model of ecological congruence.

resources. It was further predicted that greater social support would also be related to less psychological distress. Due to the lack of time, however, personality resources were expected to be more effective in this situation than social support resources.

The first and last hypotheses were confirmed. While women in general had extremely elevated state depression and anxiety, women who had greater self-esteem and mastery were less likely to experience severe psychological distress. These measures of self-esteem and mastery were shown to be trait measures that were not affected by crisis events (Hobfoll & Walfisch, 1984; Pearlin, Lieberman, Menaghan, & Mullan, 1981). However, social support was actually found to have a negative impact on psychological distress. Women who had greater intimacy with friends and who reported receiving greater amounts of support during the events were more state anxious and state depressed than women who had less intimate friends and who received less actual support. Intimacy with family was not related to distress.

Upon debriefing it became evident why social support would actually increase strain. Women reported that friends generated "rumor mills", which usually disseminated horrifying rumors (e.g., "they're not broadcasting the real number of dead", or "the lack of information is because hundreds have been killed like in '73" [Yom Kippur War]). Furthermore, friends were often experiencing the identical event and could find no other topic to discuss. The more friends women possessed and the more they sought out and received "support", the more likely they were to be part of the "pressure cooker" process. Women who were distressed probably also sought out more support. More isolated individuals, with a strong sense of self-esteem and mastery coped better and by not being part of the "pressure cooker" process, may actually have experienced less stressors—social support having in this case become itself a stressor. Before debriefing we had expected social support to be emotionally supportive when, in fact, the content of intimate social interactions was itself stress producing.

The model of ecological congruence may also facilitate comparison across studies. Until now the level of comparison between studies has been global. So, all stressors, mediated by all social interactions, for all persons and groups, across any time period have been compared. This is based on the assumption that either the effect of social support is so pervasive that its effect is felt in the same manner in all conditions, or that the conditions themselves have a limited effect on the process. This has caused much consternation when reviewers have been unable to explain, for example, why some investigations verified a stress-buffering effect of social support, whereas others have found only a direct effect. Having no model to organize their thinking the scientist and practitioner is awash in the sea of infinite explanations. Any model, no matter how complex, limits the number of possible operating mechanisms. An incorrect model can be rejected and a partially correct model can be improved upon. The absence of a model, however, prevents even the ability to limit the universe of possibilities.

The absence of an organizing system also leads to a second related problem. If, for example, the ecology of the event is assumed not to be a major factor, then differences between studies are attributed to weaknesses in methodology alone. It is not the conditions that account for differences, but faulty measurement. Consequently, differences between studies can be "explained away," instead of being explained.

Comparing the women during war study discussed above to a second longitudinal investigation of a crisis event concerning women within 24 hours prior to biopsy for suspected cancer and 3 months later for those not having cancer (Hobfoll & Walfisch, 1984), it was found that in both studies personality resources had an advantage over social support resources in preventing psychological distress during the immediate stages of the threatening event. The studies are comparable in relation to time, type of stress (sudden and not of the individuals' doing), values (acceptable to receive support), groups (women who are neither very old or very young), type of strain measured, and need (emotional support and help with children). These trends will, of course, need to be verified by further comparison to like studies.

If trends can be found for similar ecologies, trends may also be teased from investigations that have some common aspects. Pearlin et al. (1981) in a discussion of the effect of social support immediately following crisis showed evidence to suggest that the effect of social support may, in part, be to bolster self-esteem that is depleted as time elapses and the acute stressor becomes chronic. Consequently, social support may have greater value for coping with chronic stressors than acute stressors. This clarifies the findings in the acute stressor studies of women during war and prior to biopsy. Each of the studies have examined psychological strain, considered self-esteem and social support resources, and evaluated events that require emotional support.

Future research will need to verify or challenge these early findings. However, it is suggested that application of the model of ecological congruence encourages attempts, as in these cases, to identify the effectiveness of specific resources in relation to different ecologies, and to follow a program of study within an organized system rather than carrying out "question-based" studies that have typified this field.

CONCLUSIONS

This chapter emphasized the special stressors impingent on women from adolescence through old age. An ecological perspective was seen as guiding research and application of social support for women during stressful periods in their lives. A model of "ecological congruence" that emphasizes the person-situation fit of social support and other coping resources was presented. This model emphasizes that biological, cultural, need, time, and perception dimensions must be considered in order to understand and predict the potential effect of natural or professional intervention—the application of resources.

To the extent that the model proposed above is considered relevant to the study of stress and resource utilization, research and interventions will need to be both multi-modal and interdisciplinary. Intervention or examination aimed at a single mode implies that other modalities may be ignored, temporarily set aside, or held constant. However, the interactive nature of ecologies, if such expression is more than a catch-phrase, implies that a number of interrelated entities must be addressed simultaneously. Affecting one dimension of the ecology inevitably affects each of the others. These reverberations along the ecosystem are often surprising in outcome, especially if the ecology has not been carefully considered.

If different aspects of the individual and her environment are to be studied or affected, professionals with varied backgrounds will need to work together.

Individual professionals will likewise need to widen their scope. For an understanding of the ecology of women, mental health professionals will need to sharpen their knowledge of economics, therapists will need to acquire community organizational skills, and activists will have to learn to develop job training programs aimed at making women more employable in more highly paid occupations.

The complexity of an ecological approach may at first appear so cumbersome as to motivate an avoidance response and a clinging to simpler models. However, researchers and interventionists have, in fact, been developing multidimensional models related to their work in the general area of stress and social support with considerable success. While complexity for complexity's sake alone is antithetical to science, it is believed that this model will have heuristic and additional explanatory value and more closely approaches the reality that individuals face.

REFERENCES

Al-Issa, I. (1982). Gender and adult psychopathology. In I. Al-Issa (Ed.), *Gender and psychopathology* (pp. 84–103). New York: Academic.

Barret, N. S. (1979). Women in the job market: Occupations, earnings and career opportunities. In R. E. Smith (Ed.), *The subtle revolution* (pp 31–62). Washington, DC: The Urban Institute.

Belle, D. (1982). The stress of caring: Women as providers of social support. In L. Goldberger & S. Breznitz (Eds.), *Handbook of Stress; Theoretical and clinical aspects* (pp 496–505). New York: Free Press.

Brown, G., Bhrolchrain, M., & Harris, T. (1975). Social class and psychiatric disturbances among women in an urban population. *Sociology, 9,* 225–254.

Caplan, G. (1974). *Support systems and community mental health: Lectures on concept development.* New York: Behavioral.

Child, I. L., Barry, H., III, & Bacon, M. K. (1965). Sex differences: A cross-cultural study of drinking. *Quarterly Journal of Studies on Alcohol,* Supplement No. 3.

Cobb, J. (1976). Social support as a moderator of life stress. *Psychosomatic Medicine, 38,* 300–314.

Dean, A., & Lin, N. (1977). The stress buffering role of social support: Problems and prospects for future investigation. *Journal of Nervous and Mental Disease, 165,* 403–417.

Eisenberg, N., & Lennon, R. (1983). Sex differences in empathy and related capacities. *Psychological Bulletin, 94,* 100–131.

Fullerton, H. N., & Byrne, J. J. (1977). Length of working life for men and women. In 1970 U.S. Department of Labor, Bureau of Labor Statistics, Special Labor Force Report No. 187. Washington, DC: U.S. Government Printing Office.

Gomberg, E. S. (1974). Women and alcoholism. In V. Franks & V. Burtle (Eds.), *Women in therapy: New psychotherapies for a changing society* (pp. 169–190). New York: Brunner-Mazel.

Hirsch, B. J. (1980). Natural support systems and coping with recent life changes. *American Journal of Community Psychology, 7,* 453–468.

Hobfoll, S. E., & London, P. (In press). The relationship of self concept and social support to emotional distress among women during war. *Journal of Social and Clinical Psychology.*

Hobfoll, S. E., & Walfisch, S. (1984). Coping with a threat to life: A longitudinal study of self-concept, social support and psychological distress. *American Journal of Community Psychology, 12,* 87–100.

Hobfoll, S. E. (1985). The limitations of social support in the stress process. In I. G. & B. R. Sarason (Eds.). *Social support: Theory, research, and applications* (391–414). The Hague: Martinus Nijhof.

Hobfoll, S. E., Kelso, D., & Peterson, W. J. (in press). When are support systems, support systems? A study of skid row. In S. Einstein (Ed.), *Drugs and alcohol use: Issues and factors.* New York: Plenum.

Hunt, J. (1982). A woman's place is in her union. In J. West (Ed.), *Work, women and the labor market.* (pp. 154-171). London: Routledge & Kegan Paul.

Jourard, S. (1971). *The transparent self.* New York: Van Nostrand.

Kessler, R. C., McLeod, J. D., & Wethington, E. (1985). The costs of caring: A perspective on the relationship between sex and psychological distress. In I. G. Sarason & B. R. Sarason (Eds.). *Social Support: Theory, research, and applications* (491-506). The Hague: Martinus Nijhof.

Kuhn, T. S. (1970). *The structure of scientific revolutions,* 2nd ed. Chicago: University of Chicago Press.

Maccoby, E., & Jacklin, C' N. (1974). *The psychology of sex differences.* Stanford, CA: Stanford University Press.

Nucholls, K. B., Cassel, J., & Kaplan, B. H. (1972). Psychosocial assets, life crisis and the prognosis of pregnancy. *American Journal of Epidemiology, 95,* 431-441.

Pearlin, L. I., Lieberman, M. A., Menaghan, E. G., & Mullan, J. T. (1981). The stress process. *Journal of Health and Social Behavior, 22,* 337-356.

Rape: The sexual weapon. (1983, September 5). *Time,* pp. 37-39.

Smith, R. E. (1979). The movement of women into the labor force. In R. E. Smith (Ed.), *The subtle revolution.* (pp. 1-29). Washington, DC: The Urban Press.

Stress: Can we cope? (June 6, 1983). *Time,* pp. 44-52.

U.S. Department of Labor, Women's Bureau (1969). Facts about women's absenteeism and labor turnover. Washington, DC: Government Printing Office.

Vanfossen, B. E. (1981). Sex differences in the mental health effects of spouse support and equity. *Journal of Health and Social Behavior, 22,* 130-143.

Wheeler, L., & Nezlock, J. (1977). Sex differences in social participation. *Journal of Personality and Social Psychology, 35,* 742-754.

Wilcox, B. L. (1981). Social support, life stress and psychological adjustment: A test of the buffering hypothesis. *American Journal of Community Psychology, 9,* 371-387.

Yogev, S. (1981). Do professional women have egalitarian marital relationships? *Journal of Marriage and the Family, 43,* 865-871.

I

DEVELOPMENTAL ISSUES IN THE ADJUSTMENT OF WOMEN

I

2

The Challenge of Adolescent Friendship: A Study of Lisa and Her Friends

Barton J. Hirsch
Robin J. Renders
University of Illinois at Urbana–Champaign

A glance at the table of contents for this volume reveals much about the state of research on adolescent friendship and social support. Every chapter but this is concerned with adults or those about to enter adulthood (e.g., college students). The absence of other chapters on school-age adolescents testifies quite accurately to the continued neglect of this developmental period among those who conduct research on social support.

While psychologists and other social scientists tend to pay little attention to adolescents under most circumstances, this "benign neglect" is particularly difficult to justify with respect to the study of friendship and social support (cf. Adelson & Doehrman, 1980). Friendships in adolescence have long been thought to have an intensity that may be unequaled (Berndt, 1982; Douvan & Adelson, 1966). These social relationships also have important mental health consequences (Hirsch & Reischl, 1985). In a national study comparing preadolescents and adolesents referred to clinics with a matched sample of nonreferred children (Achenbach & Edelbrock, 1981), no other symptoms differentiated the groups more clearly than did disturbances in peer relations (Hartup, 1983). Some investigators have also found that adult psychiatric patients are best differentiated from controls on the basis of adolescent, rather than preadolescent, interpersonal behavior (Watt, Fryer, Lewine, & Prentky, 1979).

It would be difficult to understand adolescence without studying adolescent friendships. Friendships are tied to major developmental tasks of the period. For example, the need to develop new kinds of life involvements and social identities is generally considered fundamental to adolescent development (e.g., Conger & Peterson, 1984; Douvan & Adelson, 1966; Erikson, 1963). At school, they must acquire knowledge of specific content areas, develop work skills, establish more mature relationships with nonparental authority figures, and lay the basis for formulating post-high school vocational plans. With family members,

This case study is drawn from a larger investigation of adolescent development, social networks, and mental health. Funding was provided via an individual NIMH National Research Service Postdoctoral Fellowship, held at the Stanford University Social Ecology Laboratory, with additional funding provided via NIMH MH16744 and an NIMH New Investigator Research Award in Prevention.

they must develop or maintain valued relationships based on greater independence and changing interests and values. Friends can positively and negatively affect the ability of adolescents to achieve these objectives by means of modeling, advice, and encouragement (Hirsch, 1981). There are also important developmental changes with friends themselves: Adolescents must learn to share a variety of new activities, perspectives, and emotions, and explore alternative forms of closeness and conflict at both dyadic and group levels (Hirsch, 1985).

While research has been conducted on adolescent friendships (Berndt, 1982), mostly on qualities deemed important in a best friend, few links have been made between these studies and other aspects of personality or mental health. Correspondingly, there has been little attention to developmental considerations among the few existing studies of adolescent social support (Burke & Weir, 1978; Cauce, Felner, & Primavera, 1982).

This chapter focuses on two critical issues in understanding social support and friendships, issues that are salient throughout the life span: How are friendships initiated and deepened? What kinds of social competences are expressed at different stages of friendship development? These issues are fundamental not only to our basic theoretical understanding of friendship and social support, but also to our ability to design preventive and therapeutic social network interventions. If we are going to initiate programs to develop stronger, more supportive social networks, we need to study how people go about developing such networks on their own, in the natural environment. What different strategies are utilized? What accounts for success and failure? What problems need to be faced? Unfortunately, few studies with any age group have addressed these issues.

In this particular report, we employ a case-study approach, a methodology which has proven quite useful in early stages of developing other research and clinical domains. This approach permits us to take fullest advantage of a semi-structured interview format. In contrast to more typical survey research, we can explore much more fully the rich qualitative data which otherwise is often unreported in statistically-oriented presentations.

Lisa, the subject of our chapter, had just turned thirteen when we interviewed her for the first time towards the end of the seventh grade. She was very psychologically minded and verbally articulate, attractive, and extremely poised. Lisa was eager to talk about her friendships, of which she had many. Indeed, her interviewer at times thought that she could "write a book" about how to develop a social network. We can thus explore in considerable detail and concreteness some issues that are involved in developing a social network.

In returning to interview her for a second time one year later, it was not altogether surprising, though it was unexpected, to discover that she had skipped the eighth grade, advancing from the seventh to the ninth. This promotion was based on Lisa's social abilities rather than her academic performance, though she was a good student. We thus were able to interview her during two important school transitions, transitions that can often be extremely stressful (e.g., Cauce et al., 1982; Hirsch, 1985). Indeed, this period may encompass more change than any other in life (cf. Newcomb, Huba, & Bentler, 1981).

In addition to the two interviews conducted with Lisa, information is presented that was obtained from an interview with her boyfriend, Aaron, and a close friend, Debbie. Both were interviewed at the time of Lisa's initial interview.

The use of multiple informants has been rare in support research. This format enables us to address important issues from a variety of perspectives.

LISA

Lisa was the leader of a tightly structured group at the time of the first interview. She was apparently quite active socially and popular at school. She listed more than the maximum number of friends allowed on a questionnaire on which she was to indicate members of her social network. She later stated, "These are my *best* friends. I have a thousand *friends.*" Most of the people she listed as her closest friends were also leaders of groups independent of Lisa's group.

The distinction of leaders and followers among her friends was a natural one for Lisa to make. She described herself as having been a leader since she was very young, and went on to say that it had caused her tremendous trouble throughout her life. For example, she had experienced conflicts with teachers when she left people out of her group, and at times felt she was held responsible for the behavior of individuals within the group: "everytime the group does something wrong it's always blamed on me and that is really terrible. That really bugs me." Although Lisa was aware of the security obtained by belonging to a group and enjoyed being able to decide the group's activities, by the time of the second interview she remarked that she was "glad to get rid of being the leader of a group.... You get slapped in the face. These people would do what you wanted them to do and you never thought about it, and then they turned around and they all said 'No.' " We shall see that there were additional, more subtle costs to attaining her position.

In addition to her own personal experience with social relationships, Lisa had exposure to more formal views on interpersonal relationships from several sources. Lisa had taken a special course with counselors at her school on peer counseling, and several close family friends were professionals in this area. In addition, she stated she liked to read about young people's problems such as drug abuse and changes in life.

Let us consider how she developed her network by considering some specific relationships.

Helen

Helen had been one of Lisa's closest friends for many years. The manner in which Lisa became friends with her illustrates one of her favorite strategies: the use of a "stepping stone."

Lisa (L): I met her when I was in third grade. She hated me and I wanted to be her friend *real bad,* and for third and fourth grade she totally ignored me. And in the fifth grade she kind of gave me a chance. And I gave her my best side and she liked me and starting the end of fifth grade we started [becoming friends] . . . I invited her to a home party, a party we had here, and she liked that, and she invited me to go to the movies with her, and I invited her to spend the night at my house and then we talked and then we got to know each other. . . .

Interviewer (I): When you wanted to become friends, but it didn't work out, did you try to become friends with her?

L: Uh Huh.

I: You offered to do things with her?

L: Yes. I asked her to come over. She made up excuses.

I: So what do you think? Did you do something different that last time? What was different about the situation that she came?

L: I was older. And I was in her class again . . . and people liked me. So then I guess she thought, "Oh, I guess she's O.K." And I made friends with one of her best friends. And so then I invited her *and* her best friend to come to a party. Her best friend couldn't come, which I was glad of, but she [Helen] came anyway.

I: When you invited her best friend, was that partly a technique to get her [Helen] to come?

L: Yes. Yes. Very much so.

I: Out of curiosity, is that other person on your list [of friends] now?

L: No.

Lisa's basic approach in winning Helen's friendship involved a meeting through a mutual friend followed by increasingly personal and reciprocal invitations. Lisa was aware of the importance of being accepted by mutual friends, especially since Helen had rejected her previous overtures toward friendship. The two friends quickly moved from the group activity of the party to dyadic but indirect contact at the movies to a much more intensely personal interaction at Lisa's home.

Lisa reported that problems developed in her relationship with Helen shortly after they became friends. Lisa explains that initially Helen was much more popular than she was. She goes on to say, "Then I met her and she was kind of a stepping stone—and now you could say I'm higher than she is. Now I'm more popular and have more friends." Lisa reports that their friendship became more difficult for Helen as Lisa became more popular; however, Lisa stated that the discrepancy in social status was not a problem for her. While some friendship remained between them, they were now in different schools and rarely saw each other.

The development of this friendship is remarkable in several ways. Lisa doggedly pursued Helen's friendship despite 2 years of rejection. Clearly, becoming friends with Helen was an important goal. She developed a plan of action that she carefully followed and that eventually proved effective. This plan involved using another friend as a vehicle to approach Helen. This certainly has some implications for intervention efforts, as making friends with the friends of one's friends—or, to use network terminology, gaining access to the second-order zone—is a clear potential intervention strategy. While this proved a successful maneuver in this instance, it may not have been without its own cost. We may wonder what happened to the friend who was used as the intermediary and then, apparently, was cast aside. An emerging issue in this context will be how to make use of one's contacts and friendships without "using" and abusing these people in the process.

Finally, we see Lisa distinguishing between two major stages of friendship. The first stage is the entry stage, beginning the relationship. The second stage involves developing and intensifying the relationship. She saw the first stage as involving largely superficial, at times even artificial contact. The second stage was the more personal and honest involving more individual contact and self-disclosure.

Different strategies were seen to be needed for each stage, as we shall see more clearly in discussing Lisa's friendship with Debbie and Aaron.

Debbie

At the time of the first interview, Lisa ranked Debbie among her closest friends. In describing the course of their friendship, we shall again see the importance of a mutual friend as a bridge between two people who previously were not friends with each other, except that in this instance, it is the mutual friend who persuades Lisa to become friends with Debbie. We shall also be introduced to the importance of popularity or social status to Lisa and the effect this has on her friendships.

Interviewer: How about Debbie? When did you meet her?

L: Sixth grade. I didn't like her at all. A real nerd . . . she was a brain and knew everything . . . and I guess I didn't give her a chance. That automatic out, you know. Everybody, no matter whether they want to or not, does that. Making quick judgments.

I: . . . in sixth grade she was hanging out with Jeanne. Then, in a way, you were forced to spend more time with her . . . so how did you work that out, because at first you didn't care for her.

L: Well, I said to Jeanne, "How could you like her?" Jeanne told me about her . . . that she's a nice person, that her family is a lot like mine, she has the same views on a whole lot of things. She is just normally a really sweet person that I could be friends with . . . very nice.

I: Then you said, well, we'll try it out . . . were you friendly towards her?

L: Yes.

I: How were you friendly towards her?

L: I was just nice to her and she ate lunch with us and I talked with her and then I invited her somewhere. . . .

I: When you first started to become friends with her, how much status did she have then?

L: None. She still has no status at school. People want to know why I'm friends with her.

I: Does that bother you?

L: Yes. I mean there are times that I just want to kill myself because I'm embarrassed to be with her and that she's one of my very best friends.

Here we see differences in social status serving not only as a barrier to becoming friends, but acting as a threat to the friendship even after the formation of what Lisa considers a close relationship. This tends to call somewhat into question Lisa's attempt to relegate status considerations merely to the beginning of relationships; this should be borne in mind when we return to a consideration of Lisa's perspectives on friendship and social skills later in the paper.

For her part, Debbie also did not like Lisa when they first met. She felt Lisa was "stuck up" and noted that she hung out with the sixth graders. Debbie comments that they came to know each other in the sixth grade because the older kids were gone and they were the only ones left. As their friendship developed, they went to movies together, played sports, and visited at each other's houses. Debbie reports that Lisa disclosed more personal information than she, and further commented that Lisa was the only one of her friends with whom she had any problems. For example, she did not enjoy sports activities with Lisa as much as her other friends because she thought Lisa cheated and was a poor sport when she lost. They also had disagreements when Lisa copied from others' papers during tests and then seemed to act superior when she got a higher grade.

There seemed to be some friction in this relationship as well as some discrepancy in the friends' reports of their closeness. Debbie predicted they would drift apart when they got into high school because Lisa would become friends with other people who would not necessarily like her. She acknowledged that there was already some distancing between them as Lisa was making new friends with some eighth graders. Debbie seemed displeased with aspects of Lisa's behavior, whereas Lisa was more concerned with the difference in their status at school.

Aaron and Friends

Aaron had been Lisa's boyfriend for one month at the time of the first interview. He was a year older and perceived as popular by Lisa. She stated that she had a crush on him most of that year and had broken up with another boyfriend because she liked Aaron. Their relationship commenced when Lisa asked him to a Sadie Hawkins dance. Though Aaron described their relationship as an "impossible dream" come true and hoped they would stay together for a long time, Lisa questioned how well they were getting along and how long they would be together. She also liked some other boys and felt somewhat constricted by her relationship with Aaron.

Aaron was not Lisa's first boyfriend, as she reports having two boyfriends the year before. In many ways, her relationship with Aaron was very much like her relationship with any other friend.

Interviewer: When you go out with Aaron, what do you do?
L: Movies, or out to lunch, usually out to lunch. Or just ride our bikes or talk, or he comes and helps me take care of the animals, or something like that.
I: So in a lot of ways it's doing things together that you do with anyone else?
L: Yeah. Just like a friend . . . in a lot of ways.
I: But it's also clear that it's a boyfriend/girlfriend thing.
L: Yeah.

She sees Aaron every day at school, but infrequently on weekends, which she primarily spends with her other friends. It is interesting that heterosexual activity at this early stage is quite informal, and probably does not require the level of social skills that Lisa possesses. We may speculate that in later years, when dating has become more formal and ritualized, greater social skills are required. Many adolescents with poorer social skills may not begin getting involved in dating until they are older, at which time they may need much more social skill and self-confidence than they would have at an earlier stage. Thus, we may speculate that those with good social skills who start "going out" early may have it doubly easy, while those with poorer social skills who begin "going out" later may have it doubly hard.

When Lisa became friends with Aaron, she also became acquainted with his group of friends. She identified this group of people as those she most wanted to be closer with at that point in time. Lisa described her approach to Aaron's friends as follows: "I have to watch what I say more—make sure it's the right thing, make sure you're witty and funny . . . have to act more mature. I put in this 'tape.' I have a really childish side and another side that is mature. And I can make either one come out. I say to myself, 'now it's time to be . . .'." When asked how these new friendships would be affected if she and Aaron broke up, she replied, "I've made it with them. I made friends with them all. Now I don't need him anymore. Literally, you know, I'm there." Though Lisa had been attracted to Aaron for some time and emphasized that she had not "used" him, she was clearly aware of the social advantages associated with their friendship.

Lisa's persistence in pursuing a desired relationship is evident with Aaron as well as Helen. She maintained her interest in him throughout the year and considered ways in which she could make her feelings known to him. However, her interest in him had already begun to diminish at the time of the interview. It also seems that part of Aaron's appeal was, again, the entry he provided to a new group of friends. Once she was in contact with the desired friends, she was able to put her strategy for initiating friendships into motion, as she did with Helen. This strategy involved selective presentation of those aspects of herself which she viewed as most consistent with the target group of friends.

While with Aaron's friends, older than she, the proper strategy was to act mature and witty, in general Lisa was of the opinion that being a Pollyanna was the best way to initiate friendships and be seen as attractive by others. However, first you had to have the opportunity, because "if you wore the wrong thing, and you looked the wrong way, and you weren't good looking, people aren't going to give you the first chance that the other person has. And I don't agree with that, but that's just the way it is."

Given this entree, she would then show her good side, her Pollyanna: "I'm good at being nice to people. I'm good at showing my good side. I'm good at being open and accepting. I show the good things I have, like 'life is beautiful' and all that kind of stuff, you know [laughs]." Even with her social skills, the stepping stone remains of importance on occasion: "Even though I am a very outgoing person, I am very tense in situations where there's a group of people that I really want to be a part of and I have no way of getting into it . . . because here they are and I'm all by myself instead of having a friend to say 'Hey, guys, this is Lisa,' I would have to say 'Hey, I'm Lisa.' " While she often would not be comfortable providing her own introduction, once the initial contact is made she appears to have little trouble in taking further initiative, as is evident in the description of all three friendships.

Fortunately, real friendships do finally seem to emerge after all this concern with status and stepping stones. Getting to know others, she finds that they are often quite different than the fronts that they, like herself, had presented initially. When "you get close to people . . . it matters who you are," and Lisa felt one of her strengths was being accepting of other people. For Lisa, the most important thing in a friendship is "being together one-on-one. That's very important. Alone with the person and talking to the person; that would be the main thing. And the least important is just getting together with a group of people, or going to a movie together. I mean because [in that case] there's no real personal "whatever" in there, because you're not having to be with a person, having to make conversation without having some entertainment." As Debbie validates, Lisa does indeed open up and self-disclose. However, as is also evident in Lisa's relationship with Debbie, she is not always able to put aside considerations such as comparative social status.

FOLLOW-UP INTERVIEW

The follow-up interview allows a look at the further development of some of Lisa's important friendships. At the time of the second interview one year later, Lisa informed the interviewer that she had skipped the eighth grade and was now in high school. Lisa stated that her teachers and guidance counselors suggested the grade advancement because of her social maturity. She expressed her immediate response to the idea of changing schools as follows: " . . . when this opportunity came up, it was like freedom—being able to escape what I would have to go through there. . . . They [her classmates in seventh grade] all thought [that] I thought I was really great because I had these older friends . . . I didn't have many friends in the seventh grade at the time. Socially, I didn't want to stay at [junior high school], because all of my friends were eighth graders [now going to high school]." She later stated that she had problems with her old friends when she became friends with the eighth graders. They felt she just wanted to be popular.

Lisa went on to say that she had made all new friends since she arrived at the high school as she had decided she did not want to be friends anymore with the eighth graders (now ninth graders) whom she had befriended last year. They had changed at the high school and she now considered them to be "burn-outs." These changes in turn prompted major changes in her social life. She described herself as less popular than before, but " . . . very well-known. A lot of people know who I am. I have a lot of acquaintances, but not a lot of good friends." Her two closest friends were both more popular than she was. At this time Lisa seemed more aware of the importance of the quality of friendships and less concerned with simply having large numbers of friends.

Lisa was doing better academically than she had in the seventh grade, and stated her biggest problem was feeling insecure about the number of friends she had. She said, "I need to be able to relax and say 'Kathy and Barbara are my good friends, and I have all these other people I can go to . . . '" Her group now consisted of about five friends who were not close to each other. She said she had purposely made an effort to be less "cliquey" this year by keeping her friends in different worlds. Lisa identified her friends as reflecting different aspects of her own personality. She felt she was able to show her "true side" to the friend who was most like herself. Other friends were associated with, respectively, the "false side," her "mothering side," a mature side (talking about the future), and a silly side. In this manner she embedded several of her social identities in her social network. Overall, Lisa felt she had changed greatly during the time of this transition, stating, "I can't relate to the person I was a year ago. I used to play a lot of games with people." At this time Lisa seemed more aware of the importance of the quality of her friendships.

Changes in Friendship

Lisa reports that she did not talk with Debbie at all during the past year. She explains, "When I went to [the high school], I had to start a new life. I thought since I was at [the high school], I should concentrate on those people. I think they felt I deserted them [her close friends from last year]." This is consistent with her philosophy about making new friends which she expressed during the initial interview as follows: "Something I think about in my mind as being O.K. . . . I take things as a conquest or something I have to work on, a problem. If a relationship is working fine, I need my energy to go into another relationship. I'll let it sit for awhile. I'll know it's there and she'll know it's there."

As previously stated, Lisa disapproved of some of the activities of the group of friends she made through Aaron. Although they played a role in her decision to advance to high school, she decided she no longer wished to be friends with them. Lisa reported that she had also ended her relationship with Aaron shortly after the first interview because she was no longer interested in him. She had a new boyfriend, John, who she felt was more of the leader in their relationship. Of this new relationship, Lisa states, "We have two different expectations about our relationship. More than John himself is the role he fills in my life that will be absent when he's gone . . . somebody to give you support and warmth."

In sum, Lisa went through many changes between the first and second interviews. Her group of closest friends was completely changed. Although she was able to draw successfully on her skills in making new friends, she seemed to have less control over her social environment than in the past. Thus, it is not surprising that Lisa's primary concern during this transition had to do with the number of friends that she had. However, the social stress of the transition may be one of the factors that prompted the personal growth that she reported was evident in her new friendships.

DISCUSSION

Perhaps the most striking feature of Lisa's conversations about her friends is the emphasis on the elaborate process of making friends. This may be partly due to the structure or demand characteristics of the interview, but it also seems to capture her characteristic style. The emphasis on making friends leads to a social network that may be stable in structure but is certainly everchanging in its constituents. Although Lisa was highly skilled in developing her social network, at times the size and complexities of the network seemed to exceed her control and thereby pose problems for her. The continued emphasis on making friends led the elaborate social network to become a problem in itself. It is important to acknowledge the potential for friendships to pose problems as well as serve as a resource for development and coping.

The focus on the development of Lisa's friendships suggests the range of social competencies that may be drawn upon in this arena. In particular, Lisa differentiated skills (and attributes) needed to initiate a relationship from those needed to enhance and deepen the relationship once it had begun. The importance of third-person intermediaries in the former process was particularly striking. It is interesting to note that of the 60 or so adolescents interviewed as part of this research project, the other adolescent for whom such "stepping stones" were recognized as being very important was also in a leadership position. This 7th grade boy indicated during a discussion of the possible advantages of denser (more interconnected) networks, that if you wanted to become friends with Jack, and were already friends with a friend of Jack's, Jack could then see that you treated friends well and would therefore be likelier to respond favorably to your own overtures. Certainly these two peer leaders, in their early adolescence, had some rather sophisticated insights about social processes. In turn, this raises other questions—e.g., was Lisa atypical in her social network maneuvers or was she just better able to recognize and articulate what is typically done?

Fine's (1981) description of preadolescent relationships seems applicable in part to this network. These earlier friendships are characterized by attempts to structure situations to control access to peers. The major concern is with self-presentation and the desired peer status. Although Lisa emphasized the importance of intimate self-disclosure in her friendships, commitment and loyalty to established relationships still seemed subordinate to the development of new relationships. Thus, Lisa's earlier friendships seemed to be fairly appropriate for her age. Adolescent friendships, on the other hand, are widely recognized for the emerging significance of trust, commitment, intimacy, and loyal support (Douvan & Adelson, 1966; Selman, 1981; Sullivan, 1953; Berndt, 1982). While Lisa was highly skilled in certain aspects of social relationships, whether she would be able to meet the challenge of adolescent friendship remained to be determined.

The relationship of social networks to the ecology of human development (e.g., Hirsch, 1985) is an intriguing question. Lisa was interviewed during two major school transitions—indeed, at the time of her entrance into adolescence. We have a picture of her social network from fifth grade or so into seventh and then ninth grade. Certain themes are clear. She seems almost preoccupied with building a certain kind of social network with the focus of her attention often on those a grade ahead of her. In part, this is seen by her friends as status climbing. On the other hand, it may be that she really did in some sense belong with this other group, in which she was finally placed in ninth grade. Upon being placed with this cohort, she seems less preoccupied with popularity and social status, focuses more on the intrinsic qualities of the friendship, and, to top it off, gets better grades.

The changes in Lisa are probably due to several factors. She seems to have achieved a better person-environment "fit" with this new cohort. Ongoing social development probably was important as well. There was also considerable physical growth from the time of the first to the second interview (we are uncertain whether the growth spurt had started prior to the first interview). Prior research suggests that there may also have been considerable cognitive development during this time (cf. Conger & Peterson, 1984). These varied factors may well have interacted; for example, the developmental changes may have enhanced her ability to fit in with her new classmates.

This chapter focused on describing and analyzing the development of several specific friendships. We discussed the strategies Lisa employed, both the positive and negative outcomes of her actions, as well as some ethical issues that may arise in implementing programs to build supportive social networks. We suggested that the study of friendship development involves a complex analysis of a person's goals, skills, history, and environment. Indeed, we briefly hinted at the complex developmental ecology that must ultimately be considered in order to fully understand the functions and course of social network relationships. Personal or environmental changes in the lives of any one or more individuals affects the interface of their diverse social ecologies—their relationship—challenging its adaptability.

The empirical study of adolescent friendship development is just beginning. The challenge to researchers and practitioners is to further our understanding of this specific topic while remaining sensitive to the broader developmental and ecological contexts of the "personal communities" we seek to understand or create.

REFERENCES

Achenbach, T., & Edelbrock, C. (1981). Behavioral problems and competencies reported by parents of normal and disturbed children aged 4 through 16. *Monographs of the Society for Research in Child Development, 46.* (1, Whole No. 188).

Adelson, J., & Doehrman, M. (1980). The psychodynamic approach to adolescence. In J. Adelson (Ed.), *Handbook of Adolescent psychology.* New York: Wiley.

Berndt, T. J. (1982). The features and effects of friendship in early adolescence. *Child Development, 5,* 1447–1460.

Burke, R., & Weir, T. (1978). Benefits to adolescents of informal helping relationships with parents and peers. *Psychological Reports, 42,* 1175–1184.

Cauce, A., Felner, R., & Primavera, J. (1982). Social support in high-risk adolescents: Structural components and adaptive impact. *American Journal of Community Psychology, 10,* 417–428.

Conger, J., & Petersen, A. (1984). *Adolescence and youth: Psychological development in a changing world* (3rd ed.). New York: Harper & Row.

Douvan, E., & Adelson, J. (1966). *The adolescent experience.* New York: Wiley.

Erikson, E. (1963). *Childhood and society* (2nd ed.). New York: Norton.

Fine, G. A. (1981). Friends, impression management, and preadolescent behavior. In S. R. Asher & J. M. Gottman (Eds.), *The development of children's friendships.* Cambridge: Cambridge University Press.

Hartup, W. (1983). Peer relations. In P. Mussen (Ed.), *Handbook of child psychology. Vol IV: Socialization, personality and social development* (4th ed.). New York: Wiley.

Hirsch, B. (1981). Social networks and the coping process: Creating personal communities. In B. H. Gottlieb (Ed.), *Social networks and social support.* Beverly Hills: Sage.

Hirsch, B. (1985). Social networks and the ecology of human development: Theory, research, and practice. In I. G. Sarason & B. R. Sarason (Eds.), *Social support: Theory, research and application.* The Hague: Martinus Nijhof.

Hirsch, B., & David, T. (1983). Social networks and work/nonwork life: Action-research with nurse managers. *American Journal of Community Psychology, 11,* 493–508.

Hirsch, B., & Reischl, T. (1985). Social networks and developmental psychopathology: A comparison of adolescent children of a depressed, arthritic, or normal parent. *Journal of Abnormal Psychology, 94,* 272–281.

Newcomb, M., Huba, G., & Bentler, P. (1981). A multidimensional assessment of stressful life events among adolescents: Derivation and correlates. *Journal of Health and Social Behavior, 22,* 400–414.

Selman, R. L. (1981). The child as a friendship philosopher. In S. R. Asher & J. M. Gottman (Eds.), *The development of children's friendships.* Cambridge: Cambridge University Press.

Sullivan, H. S. (1953). *The interpersonal theory of psychiatry.* New York: Norton.

Watt, N., Fryer, J., Lewine, R., & Prentky, R. (1979). Toward longitudinal conceptions of psychiatric disorder. *Progress in experimental personality research, 9,* 199–283.

Thoits, P. (1982). Conceptual, methodological, and theoretical problems in studying social support as a buffer against life stress. *Journal of Health and Social Behavior, 23,* 145–158.

3

Adjustment of Women on Campus: Effects of Stressful Life Events, Social Support, and Personal Competencies

Ellen Ostrow
University of Maryland

Stephen C. Paul, Veronica J. Dark
and Jay A. Behrman
University of Utah

Approximately 31 million American women and men are attending colleges or universities in this country. In the age group of women who are 18-19 years old, 39% are college students. This percentage decreases as age increases, but even in the 30-34 year age range 7% of women are still in college (National Center for Education Statistics, 1980). Thus, the population of women who are college students represents a significant proportion of the young women in America.

Developmental theorists propose that the college years constitute a psychologically significant time in the lives of young people (e.g. Chickering, 1969). For many, this period involves a transition from child to adult roles, during which time an autonomous identity is formed. College students face demands of independent living, new relationships with parents and peers, academic challenges, financial pressures, and the need for career decisions: stresses that have the potential for creating significant psychological distress (Dohrenwend & Dohrenwend, 1974). Therefore, the quality of adjustment to university life warrants concern.

Although the college population represents a somewhat select group of Americans in terms of relative economic advantage and basic intellectual competencies, its members are far from invulnerable to disorder. In fact, the college population has been portrayed as a high-risk group for the development of psychological difficulties. Epidemiological studies conducted on college campuses indicate that between 7 and 16% of students are handicapped by psychological adjustment problems (Reifler & Liptzin, 1969; Segal, 1966). Research conducted prior to 1966 indicated that 7-8% of undergraduates were seriously disturbed, another 20% were unable to make full use of their abilities, and "roughly one-third . . . appear(ed) to be disturbed seriously enough to give pause to a psychiatric evaluator . . . " (Segal, 1966, p. 357). These findings parallel those from epidemiological surveys of the general population that estimate the prevalence of functional disorder to be 16-25%, with another 13% showing severe, but undiagnosable psychological and somatic distress (Dohrenwend, et al., 1980).

Campus epidemiological research also has identified demographic subgroups that have higher rates of adjustment difficulties. In almost all studies conducted, higher rates of disturbance have been found among female than among male college students (e.g. Greenley & Mechanic, 1976). This discrepancy parallels similar findings for the general population in which women have been found to report more psychological and somatic symptoms (cf., McMullen & Gross, 1983). According to research on campus, women are also more likely than men to seek out and use available professional mental health assistance (Greenley & Mechanic, 1976; Reifler & Liptzin, 1969). This higher utilization of campus mental health facilities by women again corresponds with findings from research carried out in the general community (Gore, 1979; McMullen & Gross, 1983). Authors attempting to explain these sex differences have argued as to whether these prevalence rates reflect true differences in disturbance or a greater tendency among women to report distress (Gore, 1979; McMullen & Gross, 1983). There is reason to believe that women are more inclined to recognize and acknowledge emotional distress than men. It is more consistent with a feminine sex role to report being "sick." There is also evidence that men tend to underreport symptoms (McMullen & Gross, 1983) because being "sick" is considered feminine. Furthermore, the masculine sex role emphasizes success and self-reliance. Men tend to attribute difficulties to external factors, to overestimate their performance and to restrict self-disclosure, all of which preclude symptom recognition and help-seeking (Deaux, 1976).

Although demographic characteristics associated with disturbance and help-seeking on the campus have been identified, previous research has not examined psychological characteristics associated with membership in these high-risk groups. This chapter summarizes two studies taken from an extensive program of research investigating the roles of stressful life events, social support, and personal competencies in predicting adjustment on a university campus. While the two studies have addressed the functioning of men as well as women on our campus, this chapter will focus primarily on the information we have collected on the particular stressors that college women experience and the ways in which they use their personal competencies, informal sources of social support, and professionals to help them manage those stressors. In addition, we will draw some conclusions about the women we have studied in the college age group and make some suggestions about the types of interventions, especially preventive interventions, that our data suggest.

LIFE EVENTS, SOCIAL SUPPORT, COMPETENCIES, AND ADJUSTMENT

The relationship between the occurrence of stressful life events and the development of a variety of psychological difficulties has been documented extensively (Dohrenwend & Dohrenwend, 1974; Rabkin & Struening, 1976). Evidence indicates that life stress distributes itself differently in different contexts and that people vary in the extent to which they experience the same life events as stressful (Dohrenwend & Dohrenwend, 1974; Makosky, 1980; Perkins, Tebes, Joss, Lacy, & Levine, 1982). We took these findings into consideration in our studies and examined the distribution of stressful events among university students as a function of demographic groupings as well as examining the relationship of events to adjustment difficulties.

Many stressful life events are unavoidable. Given this, we set out to develop a strategy to identify factors that mediate the relationship between stressful life events and the development of symptoms. One set of promising mediating factors is personal competency. Research has consistently demonstrated a relationship between the possession of particular intrapersonal competencies and healthy adjustment (Beiser, 1971; Coelho, Hamburg, & Adams, 1974; Gesten, Cowen, & Wilson, 1979). In fact, mental health may be defined as the possession of those competencies needed to meet environmental demands. Competence was adopted as a central concept in our research program.

Although there is no single comprehensive formulation of critical competencies in the literature, a finite set of skills have consistently received attention. Poorer adjustment has been shown to be associated with a lack of problem-solving skills and, conversely, improvements in adjustment have been produced via problem-solving training (D'Zurilla & Goldfried, 1971; Gesten, Flores de Apodaca, Rains, Weissberg, & Cowen, 1978). Interpersonal competencies, including social and communication skills, have been found to be related to adjustment outcomes (e.g., Coelho et al., 1974; Lewinsohn, Mischel, Chaplin, & Barton, 1980). Planning and self-management skills have also been linked to adjustment (Beiser, 1971; Coelho et al., 1974).

Personal resources ordinarily constitute the first line of defense in the face of life stress (Veroff, Douvan, & Kulka, 1981). However, we live in a social world and often rely on others for support to bolster our own resources, particularly at times when our resources are depleted or inadequate. It appears that most people turn to informal sources of support in the face of a stressful event and not to mental health professionals (Gourash, 1978; Veroff et al., 1981). The effects of social support on adjustment have been documented repeatedly (Gottlieb, 1981; Mitchell, Billings, & Moos, in press), but the precise mechanisms by which these effects are exerted remain unclear.

Social support may affect adjustment independently and directly, perhaps by providing social integration, which then results in heightened self-esteem (Andrews, Tennant, Hewson, & Vaillant, 1978; Hirsch, 1981). Alternatively, social support may buffer a person from the effects of life stress (e.g., Barrera, Sandler, & Ramsay, 1981; Hirsch, 1980; Wilcox, 1981). In the second case, the quality of one's social ties would not influence adjustment until the occurrence of some stressful life change. In that event, the extent to which needed instrumental and emotional aid were available from one's social network would determine the ultimate effects of the stress on one's well being. Our research program has examined characteristics of social support systems associated with healthy and poor adjustment in college women as well as the factors influencing professional help-seeking.

The unique concerns of women on campus and the factors affecting their adjustment have received limited attention in the literature. Recently, the applicability to women students of both data and theory concerning college student development has been seriously questioned (Johnson & Scarato, 1979; Leonard & Collins, 1979). There is evidence that different criteria for adjustment are employed in evaluating women and men, both by others (Broverman, Broverman, Clarkson, Rosenkrantz, & Vogel, 1980) and by women themselves (Deaux, 1976;

Schaffer, 1980). Reporting distress, minimizing one's competence and asking for help are all congruent with a traditional feminine role, while denying discomfort, emphasizing one's skills and self-reliance are stereotypically masculine. Thus, culturally prescribed sex roles influence self-perceptions of symptoms (McMullen & Gross, 1983), expressions of personal competence (Deaux, 1976), and help-seeking preferences (Gross & McMullen, 1983). We believe our research helps to illuminate the nature of the adjustment of women to the university, the life stresses they encounter, and the extent to which their coping skills and social support systems influence their adjustment and help-seeking.

We will report findings gathered on women in two studies and attempt to relate what we found to intervention strategies on campus. The first study was an epidemiological survey carried out on a large random sample of students at the University of Utah. It was designed to measure the prevalence and distribution of psychological adjustment problems in that sample and to test hypotheses about the roles of stressful life events, social support, and personal competencies in predicting adjustment. Based on Dohrenwend's model of the stress-disorder process (Dohrenwend, 1978), we predicted that social support and personal competencies would interact with stressful events in ways that would buffer the negative effects of such stressors. In the second study, we gathered data on 44 clients receiving personal counseling in the University Counseling Center using the same measures employed in the initial epidemiological study. The responses of those clients on all of the measures were then compared with the responses of the total random sample, trichotomized into high, medium, and low adjustment groups.

UNIVERSITY OF UTAH EPIDEMIOLOGY STUDY: RISK AND FACTORS PRECIPITATING DISORDER

Survey Description

In the first study, an epidemiological survey instrument was mailed to 1,936 University of Utah students, representing a random sampling of 10% of the students enrolled for spring quarter, 1981. The survey package consisted of four instruments that measured demographic characteristics, global adjustment, personal competencies, and social support for coping with various life events. The following demographic variables were assessed: age, sex, residence, marital status, number of dependents, ethnic background, geographic and religious background, current religious participation, academic status and standing, major area of study, employment, source of financial support, participation in athletics and social organizations, career direction and certainty, and previous use of counseling.

The Bell Global Psychopathology scale was used to assess psychological adjustment (Schwab, Bell, Warheit, & Schwab, 1979). The Bell scale is a standardized measure that produces a global severity score and several subscale scores, including Depression, Anxiety, Phobias, Obsessive-Compulsiveness, and Serious Psychopathology. The instrument correlates highly with other widely used psychopathology measures including the Health Opinion Survey (HOS) and the Langner-22 Scale. There is some evidence that suggests that the Bell may more accurately estimate prevalence and severity of psychopathology in younger age groups (e.g., college students) than the HOS or Langner because of the emphasis that these latter instruments place on physical complaints (R. A. Bell, personal communication, 1981).

Negative life events and social support were assessed with the Social Support Questionnaire. This instrument is a mail survey adaptation of the Arizona Social Support Interview Schedule that has been used in a variety of studies of social support (Barrera et al., 1981). In contrast to the Arizona measure that assesses support independently of life events, the Social Support Questionnaire asks respondents to evaluate the social support they received during the occurrence of specific life stresses. Respondents are asked to: (a) name those people from whom they would seek six categories of social support (discussion of private feelings, material aid, advice and information, positive feedback, physical assistance, social participation) and to indicate if these persons are friends, family members, or professionals; (b) indicate which of ten categories of stressful life events (work, academic and financial difficulties, residence and school transitions, health problems, family and relationship conflicts, relationship terminations, death of someone close) culled from the items on the College Student Life Event Scale (Sandler, 1979) occurred for them since the beginning of the academic year; (c) indicate which of the people listed in each support category actually provided them with that kind of support for each stressful life event; and (d) provide qualitative ratings of support received for each category of stressful life event, including availability of and satisfaction with support, knowledge of how to communicate the need for support, and comfort in requesting it.

The Social Support Questionnaire permits measurement of total support network size, multidimensionality of relationships (i.e., persons providing multiple types of support), reciprocity of support, and those people in the respondent's network with whom they have experienced unpleasant disagreement (conflicted network size). A test-retest reliability study conducted with 149 general psychology students over a 3-week interval produced a reliability coefficient of .78 for the total number of stressful life events and coefficients ranging from .55-.82 for the occurrence of each of the 10 event categories. The reliabilities for the social support measures indicated that care must be exercised in interpreting the social network data. While the reliability for network size was acceptable (.71), that for other measures was lower, ranging from .43-.64.

Competencies were assessed using the Personal Competency Inventory that we developed. This instrument asks respondents to rate the extent to which they possess 30 competencies. The Personal Competency Inventory produces a separate score for each of four subscales and a total score. The Social subscale addresses abilities needed for building, maintaining, managing and improving interpersonal relationships, including communication, assertiveness, intimacy, and interpersonal problem-solving skills. The Personal subscale is concerned with self-maintenance, self-control, and affect management abilities. The Problem-Solving scale explores the components of effective problem solving, including problem recognition and definition, alternative exploration, and resource organization. Finally, the Functional subscale addresses basic skills essential for success in an academic setting, including computational, reading, writing, studying, and time-management skills. Test-retest reliabilities on 149 general psychology students over a 3-week period produced a correlation of .79 for the total score and a range from .61-.77 for subscale scores. A factor analytic study has provided initial validation for the scale and subscales (Poulton, Paul, & Ostrow, 1982).

Description of Respondents

The survey was completed by 1,036 participants (54%). Comparisons of respondents, nonrespondents, and the total university population indicated that the returning sample was demographically representative of those surveyed. Of the respondents, 55% were male and 45% female with a mean age of 25.5 years. The sample consisted of 26% freshmen, 18% sophomores, 19% juniors, 20% seniors, and 17% graduate students. The sexes distributed themselves approximately equally across the various years in school but the women (mean age = 26.6 years) were significantly older than the men (mean age = 24.5 years).* Both the women and men in the sample had average GPAs (2.8 on a 4.0 scale) and most had selected majors and careers.

Less than 10% of women and men were from nonwhite minority groups. The majority of the sample was unmarried (63.4%), while almost one third was currently married. Significantly more women (9.4%) than men (1.9%) were divorced or separated. Most students lived with some other person and approximately 25% of both men and women lived with their own children. Although 75% of the women were employed at least part time, women relied more on others for financial support than did men. Significantly more women (12.6%) than men (4.8%) relied on their spouses for financial support.

Westerners composed 79% of the sample and 60% came from Utah. A large percentage of the residents of the state are members of the Church of Jesus Christ of Latter Day Saints (LDS), or Mormons. More than a religion, the church constitutes an active social system. Family life is valued, families tend to be large, and people often marry at a young age. Young adults, especially young men, are expected to go on a proselytizing religious mission. Divorce and religious inter-marriage are strongly discouraged. The consumption of alcohol and cigarette smoking are forbidden. Church members participate in a complex social network. Home visits are made by lay clergy to offer support and spiritual guidance. Children attend religious school, members contribute a percentage of their income to a tithing system, and the church has its own social services. Reflecting this context, more than half of the survey sample reported coming from an LDS background. However, more men (57%) than women (47%) were currently affiliated with the church and women tended to be less active religious participants than men. It is striking that 10% of the men in the sample had spent the previous year on a religious mission while an equivalent proportion of the women had been homemakers.

Females and males differed in the extent of their athletic participation. Significantly more men than women participated in both organized and informal group athletics; 30% of the women said they never participated in sports, versus 19% of men.

In some respects, then, responding women closely resembled the "traditional" female stereotype. They were older than typical college coeds, many were or had been married. The primary activity reported by 10% during the previous year was being a homemaker and 26% were parents at the time of the survey, a finding

---

*The statistical analyses regarding findings reported in this chapter have been omitted to enhance readability. The analyses are available in other articles and papers that can be obtained by writing to the authors.

consistent with the national trend toward increasing numbers of older women returning to college (Chickering, 1981). It is worth noting that women, more than men in the sample, functioned outside the organized social structures of religion or athletics, and more women had experienced marital separation or divorce.

Prevalence of Adjustment Problems

The mean adjustment score on the Bell for respondents from the entire random sample was 27.1. This score reflects somewhat lower adjustment than that reported for the general community population in the Florida Health Study (M = 23.3) and far better adjustment than the mean (52.8) reported for a group of psychiatric inpatients and outpatients (Schwab et al., 1979). Consistent with other epidemiological research both on campuses and in the general population, responding women reported a significantly higher level of disturbance (M = 29.5) than did the men (M = 25.2). Of the total respondents, 13.7% scored at least one standard deviation above the sample mean, constituting a high-risk group. Seventeen percent of responding women fell in the defined high-risk group.

Demographic Predictors of Adjustment

As a set, the demographic variables accounted for approximately 15% of the variance in adjustment scores. Sex, age, year in school, marital status, religious participation and affiliation, participation in group athletics, previous career or academic counseling, and GPA contributed significantly to the prediction of adjustment in a multiple regression analysis.

Women consistently reported lower adjustment levels than men. Analyses indicated that, except for marital status, sex did not interact significantly with other demographic characteristics in predicting psychopathology. Greater maladjustment was reported among students who did not affiliate with any organized religion while active participants in religious activities showed better adjustment. Participation in group athletics was similarly associated with health. Married students fared best, divorced students worst, with this difference being most extreme for men.

Stressful Life Events

Financial difficulties were the most common of the stressful events reported among respondents (48%). Not surprising for a student population, more than 40% of men and women had experienced academic difficulties during the previous year. Relationship conflicts were also experienced by a large number of respondents (36%). A significantly greater proportion of women (40%) than men (32%) reported relationship and family conflicts and relationship terminations. Health problems were reported by more women (27%) than men (18%), a finding consistent with other research (McMullen & Gross, 1983). Also, more women had made school transitions (32%) than men (22%).

A multiple regression analysis indicated that the set of stressful life event categories accounted for approximately 15% of the variance in Bell adjustment scores. In descending order of importance, events significantly predicting adjustment were: 1) family conflict; 2) relationship termination; 3) academic difficulties;

4) health problems; 5) relationship conflict; and 6) work difficulties. The most commonly experienced events were not necessarily the ones that were the most predictive of adjustment difficulties. Life stresses associated with relationships had potent effects on adjustment and these events were also more likely to occur among women.

Social Support

The social support variables were entered into a multiple regression analysis predicting adjustment scores. The aggregate combination accounted for 12% of the variance in adjustment, with three variables making significant contributions: satisfaction, conflicted network ratio and availability of support. Satisfaction with support received was the most important contributor among the three significant variables for both women and men. Women in the sample reported having proportionately more people in their networks with whom they had unpleasant disagreements than men.

For both women and men, friends were the most popular source of support, with family being a close second. Consistent with other literature on help-seeking, natural support systems were preferred over professionals as sources of help in coping with stressful life events, regardless of the specific event (Veroff et al., 1981). However, a somewhat larger proportion of support providers to women (M = 7.1% of providers) were professionals than was the case for men (M = 5.3% of providers). This is consistent with other literature demonstrating a greater inclination on the part of women to seek professional assistance (McMullen & Gross, 1983).

Personal Competence

All four subscales of the Personal Competency Inventory contributed significantly to the prediction of adjustment in a multiple regression analysis. The Personal Competency Scales accounted for more adjustment variance (34.7%) than any other set of independent variables. The ordering of subscales in terms of importance was: 1) personal abilities; 2) problem-solving skills; 3) social competencies; and 4) functional-academic abilities. As students rated themselves as more highly competent, they also reported lower levels of psychological disturbance. There were no differences between women and men for total scores or scores on each of the four subscales in the inventory.

Independent Variable Interaction

Regression analysis was used to assess the additive and interactive effects of stressful life events, social support and personal competence on adjustment. In combination, personal competencies (Beta Weight = .785), negative life events (Beta Weight = .604), social support (Beta Weight = .112), and the interaction between personal competencies and social support (Beta Weights = .034) accounted for 39% of the variance in adjustment. Contrary to our expectation, social support did not interact significantly with stressful life events in predicting adjustment. Thus, social support exerted an independent effect on adjustment, and did not buffer the effects of stressful life events. It did, however, interact with personal competence. Increases in personal competencies were associated with a decrease in importance of social support in producing adjustment outcomes. More competent people were better adjusted, regardless of the social support they received. However, for less competent people, the presence or absence of an adequate social network was critical in determining their adjustment.

CLINICAL AND NORMATIVE SAMPLE COMPARISONS: CHARACTERISTICS OF HELP-SEEKERS

In our second study we compared the normative epidemiological sample to a sample of counseling center clients in order to examine the psychological characteristics of those people who seek help from professionals. Of the 44 clients who participated in the clinical sample, 26 were women and all were receiving personal counseling during the winter quarter, 1981-1982, at the University of Utah Counseling Center.

As we expected, counseling center clients were significantly more disturbed than students in the normative sample. The mean Bell score of 40.5 for the clinical sample was much higher than that reported for the random sample (M = 27.1). It was also higher than the general population mean in the Florida Health survey (23.3), but somewhat lower than that reported for the psychiatric inpatients and outpatients (52.8) in that study (Schwab et al., 1979).

Marital disruption was far more common among clients (25% divorced or separated) than among students in the random sample (5.3%). Clients tended to exist outside the mainstream of religious activity as well. Over half of the normative group claimed LDS church membership compared to only 22.7% of the clinical sample. Furthermore, 43.2% of counseling clients reported no religious affiliation, a figure that was disproportionate to the number of unaffiliated students in the normative sample (17.5%). Counseling center clients experienced significantly more negative life events than did respondents in the random sample, particularly relationship conflicts, work difficulties, residence transitions, and family conflict.

Comparisons of Well- and Poorly-Adjusted Nonclient Women and Female Clients

In order to further explore the variables associated with health, maladjustment, and help-seeking among women, we trichotomized the normative sample of women into high, medium, and low adjustment groups and compared these groups to the women in the clinical sample. Table 1 presents the means and standard deviations for all of the variables for the four groups of women.

Women who were clients in the counseling center reported more adjustment difficulties than women in the high and medium adjustment groups in the normative sample. The highest mean maladjustment score occurred among women who were not clients, but who were in the low adjusted normative group. Approximately 16% of the women in the normative sample reported strikingly high levels of adjustment problems, close to the levels found in the combined inpatient and outpatient sample in the Florida health survey (Schwab et al., 1979). Poorly adjusted women, both in and out of counseling reported twice as many stressful life events as the best adjusted group. The client and low adjustment groups were

Table 1 Trichotomized normative groups and clinical group women mean scores

	Normative high adjustment (n = 45)		Normative medium adjustment (n = 342)		Normative low adjustment (n = 82)		Clinical sample (n = 26)	
	M	SD	M	SD	M	SD	M	SD
Bell score	[11.2]	[2.91]	[26.7]	[6.27]	[51.1]	[10.26]	[41.2]	[16.93]
No. stressful life events*	[1.90]	[1.49]	[2.92]	[1.77]	[4.11]	[2.13]	[4.27]	[2.76]
Social support variables								
Network size*	11.49	3.35	11.68	4.44	10.37	4.34	12.25	3.85
Conflicted network size*	1.23	1.42	1.52	1.60	2.33	2.05	1.40	1.35
Conflicted network ratio*	.10	.11	.15	.24	.24	.22	.14	.15
Multidimensionality	7.20	2.86	6.81	2.83	6.66	2.54	7.25	2.73
Reciprocity	14.68	2.20	14.61	1.98	14.61	2.04	15.32	1.82
Satisfaction*	1.29	.42	1.44	.47	1.70	.45	1.53	.50
Availability*	1.33	.47	1.37	.43	1.67	.50	1.53	.48
Know how to communicate need*	1.26	.45	1.46	.49	1.69	.48	1.77	.59
Comfort in asking*	1.38	.43	1.61	.53	1.91	.49	2.01	.69
Person competency inventory								
Total PCI scale score*	129.59	11.30	115.97	11.75	99.82	14.61	104.55	17.83
Social*	38.95	4.06	35.11	4.69	29.08	6.02	30.86	7.52
Personal*	30.97	3.34	33.79	4.31	28.51	4.85	29.48	6.43
Problem solving*	26.41	2.88	24.02	3.34	20.60	3.93	21.96	4.92
Functional*	25.73	3.39	23.10	3.15	21.52	3.89	23.62	2.90

*Significant relationship between group and variable, $p < .01$.

significantly more likely to report academic difficulties, family and relationship conflicts, and relationship terminations.

Regardless of client status, women who were less well adjusted were less satisfied with the support they had received and found needed support to be less available. They indicated that they had more difficulty knowing how to ask for support and that they experienced more discomfort in making such requests. In addition, the low adjustment, nonclient group reported that their network relationships were characterized by more conflict.

Differences in personal competence levels also differentiated among the adjustment groups. Well-adjusted women rated themselves to be highly competent while maladjusted women reported themselves to be skill deficient. This was the case whether or not they had been recipients of counseling.

Well-adjusted women came primarily from advanced level classes while the more poorly adjusted women were from earlier class levels. The client group was distinguished by having significantly more disrupted marital histories than were present in the normative groups. For example, 31% of women who were clients were divorced or separated, compared to 2% of the well-adjusted women.

Religion also played a role in adjustment. Clients were more often religiously unaffiliated and they were not active religious participants. Although they were not necessarily the best adjusted individuals, LDS women were underrepresented among the client group. Higher degrees of religious participation, regardless of the religious group to which one claimed membership, were associated with better adjustment.

DISCUSSION

Our data are consistent with the results of epidemiological research conducted as long as 20 years ago (Segal, 1966). Of the students in our sample, 14% reported levels of psychological disturbance sufficient to place them in a "high-risk" category. Our findings also suggest that there are still significant numbers of students who do not seek treatment in spite of the fact that their reported levels of distress often exceed those of students receiving counseling.

Women constitute a group that seems to be at higher risk for the development of disorder. As noted earlier, sex-role stereotypes foster "sick role" behavior among women while limiting symptom recognition and help-seeking among men. The LDS emphasis on self-reliance may have exaggerated these typical inclinations in the present sample.

Several additional factors appear to place college women at greater risk than men for the development of psychological distress. Though they were equal in competence to men in terms of GPA, academic standing, progress in career decision-making, and Personal Competency Scores, there is reason to think this might be as much a liability as an asset. Success in an academic environment requires achievement striving, competition and aggressiveness, behaviors associated with a masculine sex role. Thus, being competent may elicit more sex-role conflict for women, and therefore more felt distress. There are numerous suggestions in the sex-role literature that women fear that competence and achievement will bring with them the loss of affection from others, especially men (Deaux, 1976; Horner, 1972; Locksley & Douvan, 1979). Feeling different, criticized and socially isolated may result from behaving inconsistently with a female stereotype. Such concerns seem particularly marked among women with more traditional sex-role ideologies (Deaux, 1976) and one would expect to find more such women in the LDS-dominated culture of Salt Lake City. Thus far, these variables have been neglected by developmental theorists (Gilligan, 1982).

The social environments of the women in the sample were more disrupted, also placing them at risk for disturbance. Women were more likely to experience stressful interpersonal events and reported more conflict in their social networks. As with other research, stressful events involving interpersonal relationships were both commonly experienced and predictive of disturbance and professional help-seeking (Houston, 1971; Perkins, Levine, Kraus, & Perrotta, 1980). Indeed, recent research on life event stress indicates that the most threatening life events are those involving interpersonal loss, deprivation or stress, and events that disrupt or threaten social ties (Eckenrode & Gore, 1981).

The importance of this result is augmented by the finding that having a greater proportion of network relationships marred by conflict was also associated with maladjustment, help-seeking, and being female. Women have been described as more focused on affiliative and relationship concerns than men (Deaux, 1976) and this may result in greater sensitivity to, and therefore reporting of, interpersonal conflict. Such conflict appears to take its toll as well, since stressful events involving the disruption of smooth interpersonal relationships and conflict with persons who were sources of support both accounted for a significant proportion of adjustment variance. Gourash (1978) noted that professional rather than informal sources of help are frequently sought to cope with the upset that arises from problems with network members. Indeed, it may require a dramatic disruption in such ties to finally drive one to seek professional help. This is suggested by the present finding that the one characteristic most clearly distinguishing recipients of counseling from other students, regardless of adjustment level, was having been divorced or separated.

Not only does divorce involve the loss of a primary relationship, but other social connections may be disrupted as well, one's social role may be lost, or ongoing social ties may restrict the development of a new social identity (Hirsch, 1981; Mitchell et al., in press). Again, the LDS context may have exacerbated the typical effects of divorce. The church's emphasis on marriage and family may place a divorced woman in the role of a deviant, a recipient of disapproval, and a social outcast.

The women in the present sample, particularly those in counseling, were not well integrated into ongoing social structures. They were less likely to be LDS church members and more likely to be religiously unaffiliated or nonparticipants in religious activities. They also avoided group athletics. Hirsch (1981) has emphasized the importance of establishing social identities through meaningful participation in one's social networks. To the extent to which college women lack access to social networks that provide opportunities for expression of and support for appropriate social identities, their mental health may suffer.

The role flexibility of network members may be particularly important for older women returning to school, perhaps in the aftermath of marital disruption. Hirsch (1980) has noted that during the occurrence of such life changes, the constricting norms of previously established networks may impede the development of new, more appropriate social roles. Older, returning women students are likely to feel isolated, lacking clear social identities, and be unprepared for the academic and interpersonal demands of the college environment. It might be particularly difficult for a divorced woman returning to school in pursuit of a career to develop a meaningful social identity within an LDS culture. The stress created by the combined transitions of divorce and reentry to school may be intensified in a culture that places such high value on traditional roles of wife and mother, leaving such women bereft of social identity and connectedness.

Gottlieb (Gottlieb & Todd, 1979) has emphasized that the distinctive quality of natural social support, as opposed to professional assistance, is its ready availability. Distressed women, both in and out of counseling, found such informal help to be unavailable. Why this would be the case is unclear and the concurrent measurement of variables in the present research does not permit observation of a process that may occur over time. Persons unable to access needed support may have alienated people in their network (Heller, 1979). Without premorbid assessments of social competence, we cannot rule out the possibility that social skill deficits independently contributed to distress and support deficiencies among women in the sample.

Even if one were competent enough to establish and maintain supportive relationships, requesting needed support can be a difficult process. The most disturbed women, in and out of counseling, reported being unsure of how to ask for support and being uncomfortable in making such requests. Again, the concurrent measurement of variables obscures a dynamic process. Social discomfort and symptomatology tend to act in mutually reinforcing ways. An individual who has difficulty communicating her needs for support may experience more social isolation and with this a loss of self-esteem and increased psychological distress. As this occurs, one's problems become magnified and comfort in sharing one's concerns with others diminishes even more.

Indeed, our findings suggest that more important than either the absence of life stress or presence of social support is the possession of critical personal competencies. Other researchers have noted that although most students encounter academic difficulties and interpersonal conflicts, some cope and grow while others succumb (Coelho et al., 1974). The current research supports the notion that such "invulnerable" female students possess effective problem solving, interpersonal, and self-maintenance skills. For such women, the presence or absence of social support mattered less for their adjustment.

Limitations of Current Studies

There are a number of limitations to the findings reported in this chapter that should be noted. Although the return rate was typical of research of this kind (e.g., Kraus, Perrotta, Perkins, & Levine, 1980) and respondents were demographically representative of the population, there is no way of knowing how nonrespondents might differ on the independent variables measured.

We feel cautious about drawing conclusions from the social support data. The reliabilities of the social support instrument overall were only moderate. We chose to measure only support received during the occurrence of stressful life events and, as a result, these variables cannot be considered to act independently, in spite of the absence of a significant interaction in the regression analysis. Additionally, it has been suggested that the relationship between social support and adjustment may vary depending upon whether these variables are measured concurrently or in a prospective design (Monroe, 1983).

The Personal Competency Inventory, like all of the instruments employed in these studies, is a self-rating instrument. Although clinical-normative comparisons and factor analytic data support the validity of the measure, the research did not include behavioral measures of competence. It is possible to interpret the results to mean that more disturbed individuals view themselves as less competent. The absence of measures of premorbid adjustment prevents the conclusion that less competent persons become more disturbed. Rather, it is possible that persons in distress come to view themselves as less competent. The concurrent measurement of independent and dependent variables in the present research raises this issue for all observed associations.

Currently, we are taking steps to improve and further validate the instruments employed in this study. In addition, we are collecting longitudinal data to permit measurement of incidence, rather than prevalence rates. This prospective methodology will also permit examination of causal hypotheses. Until these data are available, the present results must be treated as suggestive. Still, their consistency with so much other literature indicates they are not simply artifactual. Maladjusted female students and clients differed in systematic ways from well-functioning women and these differences were consistent with theoretically-derived predictions.

Intervention Directions

It seems reasonable to conclude that the necessity for primary prevention of disturbance on the campus is as critical as it was 20 years ago. Significant numbers of women are impaired and very few seek help even when it is from all appearances needed. The impracticality of a passive stance to well-developed pathology is clear. The possession of competencies and social resources predicted health in this (and other) research. In order to promote optimal adjustment, competencies should be taught and social resource access facilitated before life stress can take its toll.

Social support deficiencies have been shown to lead to one of two outcomes in students undergoing stress: they may become more isolated or seek professional help (Kraus et al., 1980). In our research, social network deficiencies were most common among women who were counseling center clients and disturbed women who did not seek counseling. Primary prevention efforts to increase the availability of needed support by teaching network members to be responsive to one another seem warranted. Network members might be encouraged to offer more help, rather than waiting to be asked. Additionally, potential recipients of support might benefit from interventions designed to make asking easier, both by increasing skills in communicating feelings and the need for help as well as by making the experience and expression of support needs acceptable.

The malevolent effects of the disruption of marital and community ties and the concomitant loss of social identity are clear, particularly when combined with entry into an environment requiring behaviors inconsistent with sex-role stereotypes and cultural expectations. This suggests the need to develop social network interventions for women to facilitate a sense of identity and belongingness. Primary prevention efforts to facilitate the formation of "personal communities" (Hirsch, 1981) may reduce the rate of disorder among women. Opportunities within these social networks for the recognition and reinforcement of achievement-related behaviors as well as more stereotypic social roles would be critical for the development of viable social female identities. Social support interventions involving older returning women students might enable such women to utilize one another as resources. In addition to focusing on the development of flexible roles and meaningful social ties, skills to meet the demands of academic and work environments could be taught.

The life stresses most predictive of maladjustment primarily involved interpersonal conflict. It may be that less socially skilled persons are more vulnerable to the occurrence of such events. Social abilities also affect the formation and maintenance of supportive relationships. Interpersonal problem-solving and communication skills are critical ingredients for a successful marriage and marital disruption was strongly associated with maladjustment and client status in the present research. Clearly, there is a need for proactive training in communication, conflict management, and other social skills needed to form and maintain supportive ties.

Interpersonal, self-maintenance, problem-solving, and functional-academic abilities are easily operationalized and taught. Universities might consider teaching critical competencies as part of the regular academic curriculum. The advantage of the present research strategy is its ability to identify those women most in need of assistance, particularly those who would not voluntarily seek help. It is to these women that preventive competency-based and social support interventions should be targeted.

REFERENCES

Andrews, G., Tennant, C., Hewson, D. M., & Vaillant, G. E. (1978). Life event stress, social support, coping style and risk of psychological impairment. *Journal of Nervous and Mental Disease, 166,* 307–317.

Barrera, M., Sandler, D., & Ramsay, T. (1981). Preliminary development of a scale of social support: Studies on college students. *American Journal of Community Psychology, 9,* 435–448.

Beiser, M. (1971). A study of personality assets in a rural community. *Archives of General Psychiatry, 24,* 244–254.

Broverman, I., Broverman, D., Clarkson, F., Rosekrantz, P., & Vogel, S. (1980). Sex-role stereotypes and clinical judgments of mental health. *Journal of Consulting and Clinical Psychology, 34,* 1–7.

Chickering, A. W. (1969). *Education and identity.* San Francisco: Jossey-Bass.

Chickering, A. W. (Ed.). (1981). *The modern American college.* San Francisco: Jossey-Bass.

Coelho, G. V., Hamburg, D. A., & Adams, J. E. (1974). *Coping and adaptation.* New York: Basic.

Deaux, K. (1976). *The behavior of men and women.* Monterey, CA: Brooks/Cole.

Dohrenwend, B. P., Dohrenwend, B. S., Gould, M. S., Link, B., Neugebauer, R., & Wunsch-Hitzig, R. (1980). *Mental illness in the United States.* New York: Praeger.

Dohrenwend, B. S. (1978). Social stress and community psychology. *American Journal of Community Psychology, 6,* 1–14.

Dohrenwend, B. S., & Dohrenwend, B. P. (Eds.). (1974). *Stressful life events: Their nature and effects.* New York: Wiley.

D'Zurilla, T. J., & Goldfried, M. R. (1971). Problem-solving and behavior modification. *Journal of Abnormal Psychology, 78,* 107–126.

Eckenrode, J., & Gore, S. (1981). Stressful events and social supports: The significance of context. In B. Gottlieb (Ed.), *Social networks and social support.* Beverly Hills, CA: Sage.

Gesten, C., Cowen, C., & Wilson, A. (1979). Competence and its correlates in young normal and referred school children. *American Journal of Community Psychology, 7,* 305–313.

Gesten, E., Flores de Apodaca, R., Rains, M., Weissberg, R., & Cowen, E. (1978). Promoting peer related social competence in school. In M. W. Kent & J. E. Role (Eds.), *The primary prevention of psychopathology: Vol. 3. Promoting social competence and coping in children.* Hanover, NH: University Press of New England.

Gilligan, C. (1982). *In a different voice.* Cambridge, MA: Harvard University Press.

Gottlieb, B. (Ed.). (1981). *Social networks and social support.* Beverly Hills: Sage.

Gottlieb, B., & Todd, D. (1979). Characterizing and promoting social support in natural settings. In R. Munoz, L. Snowden, & J. Kelly (Eds.), *Social and psychological research in community settings.* San Francisco: Jossey-Bass.

Gore, W. (1979). Sex differences in the epidemiology of mental disorder: Evidence and explanations. In E. Gomberg & V. Franks (Eds.), *Gender and disordered behavior.* New York: Bruner/Mazel.

Gourash, N. Help seeking: (1978). A review of literature. *American Journal of Community Psychology, 6,* 413–423.

Greenley, J., & Mechanic, D. (1976). Patterns of seeking care for psychological problems. In D. Mechanic (Ed.), *The growth of bureaucratic medicine: An inquiry into the dynamics of patient behavior and the organization of medical care.* New York: Wiley.

Gross, A., & McMullen, P. (1983). Models of the help-seeking process. In B. M. De Paulo, A. Nadler, & J. D. Fisher (Eds.). *New directions in helping, Vol. 2: Help-seeking.* New York: Academic.

Heller, K. (1979). The effects of social support: Prevention and treatment implications. In A. Goldstein & F. Kanfer (Eds.). *Maximizing treatment gains: Transfer enhancement in psychotherapy.* New York: Academic.

Hirsch, B. S. (1980). Natural support systems and coping with major life changes. *American Journal of Community Psychology, 8,* 159–172.

Hirsch, B. J. (1981). Social networks and the coping process: Creating personal communities. In B. Gottlieb (Ed.), *Social networks and social support.* Beverly Hills: Sage.

Horner, M. S. (1972). Toward an understanding of achievement related conflict in women. *Journal of Social Issues, 28,* 157–176.

Houston, B. K. (1971). Sources, effects, and individual vulnerability of psychological problems for college students. *Journal of Counseling Psychology, 18,* 157–165.

Johnson, M., & Scarato, A. M. (1979). A knowledge base for counselors of women. *The Counseling Psychologist, 8,* 14–16.

Kraus, S., Perrotta, P., Perkins, D., & Levine, M. (1980). *Student help-seeking in response to stressful life events.* Paper presented at the annual meeting of the Eastern Psychological Association, Hartford, CT.

Leonard, M. M., & Collins, A. M. (1979). Women as footnotes. *The Counseling Psychologist, 8,* 6–7.

Lewinsohn, P. M., Mischel, W., Chaplin, W., & Barton, R. (1980). Social competencies perception. *Journal of Abnormal Psychology, 89,* 203–212.

Locksley, A., & Douvan, E. (1979). Problem behavior in adolescents. In E. Gomberg & V. Franks (Eds.), *Gender and disordered behavior.* New York: Bruner/Mazel.

Makosky, V. P. (1980). Stress and the mental health of women: A discussion of research and issues. In M. Guttentag, S. Salasin, & D. Belle (Eds.), *The mental health of women.* New York: Academic.

McMullen, P., & Gross, A. (1983). Sex differences, sex roles, and health-related help-seeking. In B. M. DePaulo, A. Nadler, & J. D. Fisher (Eds.), *New directions in helping, Vol. 2: Help-seeking.* New York: Academic.

Mitchell, R., Billings, A., & Moos, R. (in press). Social support and well-being: Implications for prevention programs. *Journal of Primary Prevention.*

Mitchell, R., & Trickett, E. (1980). Social network research and psychosocial adaptation: Implications for community mental health practice. In P. Insel (Ed.), *Environmental variables and the prevention of mental illness.* Lexington, MA: DC Health.

Monroe, S. (1983). Social support and disorder: Toward an untangling of cause and effect. *American Journal of Community Psychology, 11,* 81–98.

National Center for Education Statistics (1980). Fall enrollment in colleges and universities (NCES 82-323). Washington, DC: U.S. Department of Education.

Perkins, D., Levine, M., Kraus, S., & Perrotta, P. (1980). *Correlates of life stress among college students.* Paper presented at the annual meeting of the Eastern Psychological Association, Hartford, CT.

Perkins, D., Tebes, J., Joss, R., Lacy, O., & Levine, M. (1982). *Big school, small school: Characteristics of life stress and help-seeking at three contrasting colleges.* Paper presented at the annual meeting of the Eastern Psychological Association, Baltimore.

Poulton, J. L., Paul, S. C., & Ostrow, E. (1982). *Personal competence: Conceptualization, measurement and preventive implications.* Paper presented at the annual meeting of the American Psychological Association, Washington, DC.

Rabkin, J. G., & Struening, E. C. (1976). Life events, stress and illness. *Science, 194,* 1013–1020.

Reifler, C. B., & Liptzin, M. B. (1969). Epidemiological studies of college mental health. *Archives of General Psychiatry, 20,* 327–333.

Sandler, I. N. (1979). *Development of the College Student Life Experience Scale.* Unpublished manuscript, Arizona State University.

Schaffer, K. F. (1980). *Sex-role issues in mental health.* Reading, MA: Addison-Wesley.

Schwab, J. J., Bell, R. A., Warheit, G. J., & Schwab, R. B. (1979). *Social order and mental health.* New York: Bruner/Mazel.

Segal, B. (1966). Epidemiology of emotional disturbance among college undergraduates: A review and analysis. *Journal of Nervous and Mental Disease, 143,* 348–361.

Veroff, J., Douvan, E., & Kulka, R. A. (1981). *The inner American: A self-portrait from 1957–1976.* New York: Basic.

Wilcox, B. (1981). Social support, life stress and psychological adjustment: A test of the buffering hypothesis. *American Journal of Community Psychology, 9,* 371–386.

4

Social Network Interviews as Sources of Etic and Emic Data: A Study of Young Married Women

Catherine H. Stein and Julian Rappaport
University of Illinois at Urbana–Champaign

The concepts of social networks and social support have captured the attention of a growing number of researchers and practitioners. Studies suggest that social support has a role in buffering stress (Dean & Lin, 1977; Lin, Simeone, Ensel, & Kuo, 1979) mitigating the effects of physical illness and psychological distress (Gore, 1978; Brown, Brolchain, & Harris, 1975; Henderson, 1977) and influencing the use of professional helping services (McKinley, 1973; Croog, Lipson, & Levine, 1972). Authors cite the study of social networks as a means to understand complex person-environment interactions and inform community interventions (Mitchell & Trickett, 1980; Walker, McBride, & Vachon, 1977; Wellman, 1981; Mueller, 1980). While much of network research can be traced to ideas originating in sociology and anthropology (Gottlieb, 1981; Fischer, 1976), psychologists add their unique concern for the nature of dyadic network relationships and proceed to use a network approach to study the "psychological questions" of individual differences such as differential adaptation to stress and variations in psychological well-being (Hirsch, 1979; Tolsdorf, 1976; Pattison, DeFrancisco, Frazier, Wood, & Crowder, 1975; Wilcox, 1981). However, methodological problems within the area of social network research are many (Sokolovsky & Cohen, 1981; Gottlieb, 1981; Phillips, 1981) and conceptualizations are few (Hirsch, 1981; Marsella, & Snyder, 1981). There is no systematic psychological theory of social networks that permits a set of coherent predictions. Rather, much of the field is characterized by intuitively pleasing ideas about the nature of social networks and social support and a search for empirical relationships conducted in largely ad hoc fashion on a variety of populations. Network measures are often of uncertain construct validity and are largely accepted on the basis of face validity (Stein, 1984).

This state of affairs is not necessarily peculiar to network research, and is certainly not a reason to abandon the field. It is, however, a reason to consider the nature of data that it is acceptable to collect and report. Rather than to reflexively limit ourselves to the kind of data that is immediately quantifiable, it may be useful to report on our qualitative observations as well.

Psychologists have available to them, by training and convention, a set of highly sophisticated research techniques and procedures for data collection and analysis. Unfortunately, in new areas that lack well-formulated theory there is a temptation to allow the methodological tail to wag the conceptual dog. Social network

The names of the respondents in this chapter have been changed for confidentiality.

researchers, in the rush to gain acceptance of their domain as a legitimate area of psychological inquiry, run the risk of skipping an important step. The usefulness of engaging in a period of observation and description has been demonstrated throughout the history of science. During the early stages of inquiry in a new area, a broad, hypotheses generating approach to data collection is desirable. The recent trend toward exclusive use of questionnaires in network research (Procidano & Heller, 1983; Duncan-Jones, 1981), while convenient, may be less informative than methods such as detailed interviews. Such methods permit the accumulation of qualitative as well as quantitative data. The need for a more open-ended methodology stems not only from the newness of the field, but also from the nature of the phenomena viewed from a *psychological* perspective.

Given the psychological complexity and richness of social relationships, it is appropriate for those who conduct psychological research to include methods that permit respondents to provide their own responses. While the structure and content of social networks as they relate to well-developed, quantifiable constructs may ultimately be of interest, it is premature to limit our research to the collection of specific and immediately quantifiable responses. The use of a semistructured interview format that allows time for the establishment of rapport and opportunities for collaboration between the researcher and the interviewee is particularly appropriate. Such a methodology can provide a rich source of information and permit the researcher to come a step closer to understanding the respondent's view of his or her social environment.

THE VALUE OF EMIC DATA ON SOCIAL NETWORKS

In his book on social networks and social support, Gottlieb (1981) contends that researchers from a variety of disciplines seek to understand "the manner in which human attachments are structured as systems of support and the resources that are exchanged among the members of these systems" (p. 1). Hence, researchers examine the networks of many different "kinds of people" (e.g., former mental patients, widows, housewives, or those experiencing physical illness) in order to better understand their daily interpersonal experiences.

Understanding, however, is a complicated task, and often researchers assume too much. Psychologists tend to use research designs and methods of measurement that are powerful in drawing statistically based nomothetic conclusions, but weak in description of individual experience. The lives of people, often referred to as "subjects," tend to be obscured in tables, graphs, and statistical tests. Anthropologists often have the reverse problem. The careful description of naturalistic observation and interview data used by anthropologists is difficult to quantify, but creates powerful human images.

The strength of a network methodology comes from its capacity to provide *both* qualitative and quantitative information. Social network methods, in the form of broad-based interviews, lend themselves to a potentially richer, more complex set of observations than those methods limited to a series of preset questions and forced choice responses. A social network interview can provide insights into the thought process, decisions, and experiences that moderate and influence the use of one's social network. To use the language of anthropology, etic and emic data can be conveniently accumulated simultaneously.

Emic analysis uses data accumulated through careful and detailed descriptions that are only later translated into variables. It lends itself to the discovery of how the subjects of an inquiry view their own behavior. " . . . Emic units . . . must be determined during analysis; they must be discovered, not predicted . . . They give tentative results, tentative units" (Pike, 1967, pp. 37-38). *Etic* analysis is based on previously obtained information and imposes preset categories on the new data. It tests hypotheses (Pike, 1967; Bloom, 1974; Rappaport, Seidman, & Davidson, 1979). Applying both sorts of analyses allows researchers to progress from hypothesis testing to hypothesis generation to new hypothesis testing research in longitudinal fashion.

Unfortunately, much current network research suffers from self-imposed limitations on methodology. Often, subjects are presented as interchangeable members of a class and our research task is limited to recording their responses to predetermined questions. In reporting results, the sources of the data are viewed impersonally. While multivariate data analyses help to refine our descriptions, the information obtained using such procedures to understand the individual people from whom we collect the data quickly reaches an upper limit. Data analytic procedures such as partial correlations can help to explain moderator variables, and data may be refined by comparison between groups through a variety of techniques such as discriminant function analysis. However, confined to narrow predetermined etic analysis, psychologists are far removed from the actual experience of their respondents. The skeleton of relationships among variables needs to be filled in with the human facts of life obtainable through the use of emic analysis, if we are to understand the people rather than the subjects we study.

The suggestion here is that if we are willing to pay attention to what people actually say—their words, their examples, their style of communication and thought processes, as well as to how they answer specific predetermined quantifiable questions, we will increase our understanding and be more likely to develop meaningful theory. Such research requires that we collect our data in appropriate ways.

In her recent study of women's psychological development, Carol Gilligan reports that when she interviewed women their "voices sounded distinct" from men's (Gilligan, 1982, p. 1). She suggests "that the way people talk about their lives is of significance, that the language they use and the connections they make reveal the world they see and in which they act" (p. 2). While some network researchers acknowledge the importance of qualitative data (Tolsdorf, 1976; Ingersoll, 1982), the recent trend toward use of questionnaires as the primary source of network and social support information (McFarlane, Neale, Norman, Roy, & Streiner, 1981; Zautra, 1983) seems to suggest that many have lost sight of the need for the kind of data of which Gilligan speaks.

The remainder of this chapter describes a study that applied both etic and emic analyses. The study addressed two different kinds of issues. The first set of questions concerned the relative contribution of existing social network variables in accounting for variations in psychological well-being for a sample of young married women. The second set of issues concerned an attempt to discover what the respondents themselves would consider important variables, even though the variables had not yet been identified by researchers.

SELECTION OF MEASURES FOR A STUDY
OF YOUNG MARRIED WOMEN

In this study we were interested in understanding the availability of social network relationships in the lives of young married women and the nature of those relationships as sources of both support and stress. The focus of our inquiry was a group of students' wives—women who are not themselves students, who may or may not work, but who view themselves, at least for the present, as primarily filling the role of "student's wife."

We chose to study this sample of young married women because they tend to be undergoing a difficult transitional period. In addition to the daily rewards and stresses of marriage and family, these women are usually some geographic distance from their extended families and their home community. Often they have limited financial resources and husbands who are absorbed in the responsibilities and pressures of their academic work. We hypothesized that to some extent the quality of their lives and their sense of psychological well-being would depend on their perceptions of the social network as a source of stress and/or support.

In trying to decide on an assessment strategy, we discovered that there is little agreement on the method of measurement or the relative importance of any number of possible variables that make up what is called a network. Indeed, the lack of a coherent theory and a wide variety of independently developed measurement indices make choices among network variables difficult. The same problems exist in choosing among measures of well-being used in social support and network studies.

Network variables in the psychological literature have been classified according to their primary concern with network structure, the characteristics or content of network ties, or the function of network relationships (Mitchell & Trickett, 1980; Tolsdorf, 1976; Marsella & Snyder, 1981). While these three conceptual categories are not completely independent of one another (e.g., some aspects of overall network structure can be influenced by the content of relationships and vice versa), such a classification scheme does provide for a means of understanding the current status of network research. A brief description of the three categories and the kinds of variables found in the literature that are representative of each, is presented below:*

I. Structural characteristics: describes the morphological characteristics of the network (Tolsdorf, 1976).
   A. Size: the number of individuals with whom the focal person has contact.
   B. Role relationships: e.g., kin, friends, work associates, neighbors.
   C. Total density: the extent to which members of the focal person's network contact each other independently of the focal person (Mitchell, 1969). Computed as the number of actual ties among network members divided by the total number of possible ties.
   D. Boundary density: the extent of connections between kin and nonkin sectors of the focal person's network. Computed as the number of actual connections between kin and nonkin sectors divided by the possible number of kin-nonkin connections.

*Modified from Mitchell & Trickett, 1980.

E. Frequency of contact: the frequency with which the focal person makes contact with network members. Contact can include phone and letters as well as face-to-face contact.

F. Regularity of contact: the constancy of contact of focal person with network members.

II. Content of network ties: refers to the properties of the dyadic relationships (linkages) between focal person and network members. Sometimes discussed as "characteristics of component linkages" (Mitchell & Trickett, 1980) or "qualitative dimensions" (Marsella & Snyder, 1981).

A. Multidimensionality (or multiplexity): the number of roles served by the relationship.

B. Reciprocity: the degree to which affective and instrumental support aid is both given and received by the focal person.

C. Satisfaction: the degree to which the focal person is content or satisfied with existing network relationships.

III. Functional characteristics: describes linkages in which one individual serves some function for the focal individual (Tolsdorf, 1976). The most frequent function assessed in the literature is social support or informal helping.

A. Support, advice, feedback (Tolsdorf, 1976).

B. Cognitive guidance, social reinforcement, tangible assistance, socializing, emotional support (Hirsch, 1980).

C. Emotionally-sustaining behaviors, problem-solving behaviors, indirect personal influence, environmental action (Gottlieb & Todd, 1979).

As the above indicates, structural characteristics describe the morphological properties of social networks. Examples of such variables include size of the network, role relationships such as the percentage of kin, friends or work associates, and network density (the extent of connections between network members). Content characteristics of networks describe the nature of the linkages between the focal person and network members. Variables that tap these more "qualitative" aspects of dyadic relationships include multidimensionality (the number of roles served by the relationship), relationship reciprocity, and satisfaction. Functional aspects of networks describe linkages in which a given person serves some function for the focal individual. Social support or informal helping behaviors are the most frequent examples of what may be considered as functional characteristics of networks. A number of social support taxonomies have been proposed (see Wethington, 1982 for a review) with variables including advice, feedback, social reinforcement, emotional and instrumental support. Well-being variables accessed in network studies have included self-report mental health measures such as mood and symptomatology, life satisfaction, as well as interviewer ratings of psychosocial adjustment.

Researchers have used a variety of populations to study the relationship between social networks and individual well-being. Populations studied have included college students, psychiatric patients, high-risk adolescents, individuals undergoing divorce and other major life changes and the elderly (Hirsch, 1979; Tolsdorf, 1976; Cauce, Felner, & Primivera, 1982; Sokolovsky, Cohen, Berger, & Geiger, 1978; Lowenthal & Robinson, 1976).

Given the variety of network and well-being measures and the range of populations to which they have been applied, we found it necessary to begin our work in this area by conducting research of a methodological nature. We decided to conduct a methodological study of the relative utility of a variety of network measures to predict psychological well-being. Given the lack of a well-developed theory, this necessitated the use of a variety of network measures and well-being measures followed by principal components analysis to reduce the total number of variables to a manageable subset. We were aware that entry into the field forced us to use an initial set of measures that had been developed on populations other than the one in which we had an interest. Given our belief in the value of emic and qualitative analysis, particularly at a time when the categories to be studied were largely those that have originated in the heads of researchers, we decided to collect our data in such a way as to provide both quantifiable assessments of commonly used variables and qualitative information provided by the women whose lives we wished to understand. The logical choice was to use a semistructured interview that would yield data on both previously identified and and yet unknown categories of concern to the women. We will first outline the procedures we used in interviewing the respondents. We will discuss the quantitative network information obtained from the interviews and the strategies used for statistical analysis of the data. We will then summarize the qualitative findings and contrast those results with the quantitative information we obtained.

STUDY OF STUDENTS' WIVES

The research discussed here was designed to assess the relationship between a variety of social network variables, psychological well-being, and marital adjustment measures among a "normal" (nonpsychiatric, nonstressed) sample of 40 women who were married to students, but not students themselves.

The subjects were 40 women living in married student housing at the University of Illinois. They ranged in age from 22-34 years (mean age = 25, SD = 3.06). The women were chosen at random from a list of housing residents of American descent and were contacted by telephone to solicit their participation. In order to increase the likelihood that respondents would have had the opportunity to establish local social networks, only women who had been living in town for at least one year and were not currently enrolled at the University or any other college were asked to participate.

Interviews were conducted in a 2 month period. Women were interviewed in their homes in two sessions, each interview averaging 60 minutes in length with a range from 45-90 minutes. The second interview was conducted within a week of the first session for all 40 respondents.

In the first session, each respondent was asked to provide some basic demographic information such as age, length of time married, income, and employment status. The respondent then delineated the members of her social network on an "intimacy" dimension by listing the first name of the people in her life into one of three groups: 1) those people in her life whom she "knows the best and feels the closest to;" 2) important people in her life "people that you know well and feel close to, but who did not make the first group;" and 3) "any other people that need to be included on a list of people in your life." Each woman was then asked to rank those listed within each group in order of how close she felt toward them. The final product was a list of people in each woman's life, ordered on a dimension of perceived closeness or intimacy. This network delineation served as the basis for subsequent inquiry about the respondent's social network. Measures of total network size, and percentage of intimates (people listed in the first group relative to the total network) were calculated. Relationship, frequency of inter-action, and geographic location information for each network member was obtained. Respondents were then asked to cluster the people in their network as they commonly thought of them and to provide labels for each network cluster. In a task to be completed between sessions, respondents were asked to provide ratings of mutuality, satisfaction, multidimensionality, and problem-solving orientation for each network member.

In the second session, each interviewee was asked to think of the last time she had had a problem in each of five life domains 1) marriage; 2) finances; 3) physical health; 4) emotional well-being; 5) children (if applicable). The nature of each problem was recorded along with time of occurrence. The respondent was then asked to list any one that she went to for help or advice when experiencing that problem. The total number of people listed across life domains was considered to be her informal helping network. A mean number of helpers across all domains for each respondent was calculated.

The respondent indicated, on a 5-point scale, the perceived helpfulness of each member of her network after the last time she sought advice or assistance. She then indicated as many helping behaviors as applied to the last time she went to each helper for assistance from a list of seven helping behaviors taken from work on formal and informal help-seeking (Colten & Kulka, 1979). In addition, the respondent was asked to discuss any costs or disadvantages in seeking assistance from each member of the helping network. The percentage of the total helping network who performed each helping behavior as well as the percentage of helpers for whom the respondent indicated disadvantages in seeking help was calculated. Each woman completed the following six self-report measures of psychological well-being: the Profile of Mood States (POMS) (McNair, Loor, & Droppleman, 1971); the Hopkins Symptom Checklist (HSCL) (DeRogatis, Lipman, Rickels, Uhlenhuth, & Covi, 1974); the Life Events Survey (LES) (Sarason, Johnson, & Siegel, 1978); the Center for Epidemiologic Studies Depression Scale (CES-D) (Radloff, 1977); the Texas Social Behavior Inventory (TSBI) (Helmreich & Stapp, 1974); and the Locke-Wallace Scale of Marital Adjustment (Locke-Wallace) (Burgess, Locke, & Thomas, 1971).

The POMS is a list of 65 adjectives that describe moods or feelings experienced in the past 7-day period. The HSCL is a 58-item checklist that represents symptom configurations commonly observed among outpatients. The CES-D Scale is a 20-item self-report scale designed to measure depressive symptomatology in the general population. The TSBI is a 16-item self-report inventory assessing self-esteem. The LES is a 57-item self-report measure assessing the frequency and impact of life events experienced in the past one year period. The Locke-Wallace is a 16-item self-report measure of marital adjustment.

For data reduction purposes, the well-being measures were submitted to a principal components analysis. The number of components were chosen according to Kaiser normalization criterion, then subject to a varimax rotation. A three component solution, accounting for 83% of the total variance, emerged when the six well-being measures were submitted to principal components analysis. The three orthoginal well-being components represent *traditional psychiatric measures of well-being* (POMS, HSCL, CES-D, LES): *marital adjustment* (Locke-Wallace) and *self-esteem* (TSBI) and account for 47%, 21%, and 16% of the total variance respectively.

The interview was designed to yield a variety of quantifiable indices of each woman's social network. The network variables were selected to represent the structural, functional, and relationship categories currently found in the literature. The network variables representing each of the three conceptual categories were subjected to separate principal components analyses in order to empirically reduce the total number of variables by combining those which were highly correlated. This procedure yielded four structural components (accounting for 64% of the total variance), three relationship content components (accounting for 75% of the total variance), and three functional components (accounting for 71% of the total variance). These network variables that load on each component are presented in Table 1.

These structural, content, and functional components of social networks were then entered into three stepwise multiple regression analyses using each well-being component as a criterion variable. The use of stepwise multiple regression analysis allowed us to obtain a set of prediction equations designed to account for the largest share of the variance in each of the well-being components using the smallest number of network components.

In addition to permitting the quantification of network characteristics, the

Table 1 Principal components solutions for structural, content, functional, and well-being variables

Components	Item and factor loadings
Structural (64% of total variance)	
Density (23%)	Total density (.88)
	Boundary density (.76)
	Total size (− .57)
Nonlocal kin relations (17%)	% Kin (.61)
	% Hometown (.70)
	% Irregular contact (.66)
	Face-to-face contact (− .66)
Indirect contact (13%)	Mean phone contact (.81)
	Mean letter contact (.66)
	Number of clusters (− .56)
Intimates (11%)	% Intimates delineated (.84)
	Number of best friends (.43)
Relationship content (75% of total variance)	
Problem sharing orientation (37%)	Mean self problem sharing (.96)
	Mean other problem sharing (.90)
Multidimensionality (22%)	% Multidimensional relationships (− .89)
	Mutuality (.65)
Reciprocity (16%)	Mean relationship satisfaction ratings (− .70)
	Mean difference rating for problem sharing (.82)
Functional (71% of total variance)	
Expression (16%)	% Helpers who listen (.73)
	% Helpers with disadvantages (− .73)
Informational helping (24%)	% Helpers who refer (.82)
	% Helpers who give advice (.81)
Instrumental helping (18%)	% Helpers who helped take action (.71)
	% Helpers who offered insight (.78)
	% Helpers who cheered or comforted (.59)
Validation (13%)	% Helpers who shared a similar experience (.88)

nature of the interview allowed each woman to reflect on the meaning of her responses and freely interpret them to the interviewer. Women were given the opportunity to express their feelings, think out loud, and elaborate on their experiences. In turn, the interviewer was free to ask questions, request clarifications and otherwise explore interesting but unanticipated tangents, so as to provide a protocol filled with qualitative observations and detailed descriptions of the participants' lives. We made a conscious effort to understand what each woman was saying about herself and those closest to her. While it would have been more convenient for us to obtain the quantitative network information without attending to the women's own reflections or pursuing additional information, we decided to pursue a more open-ended strategy in order to permit emic analysis.

RESULTS OF THE ETIC ANALYSIS

The social network components selected to answer the first set of questions were entered as predictors into a set of stepwise regression equations in order to assess their predictive power vis-à-vis each of the three well-being components.

Results of this portion of the study are reported in detail elsewhere (Stein, 1984). In summary, we found network measures to have significant and differential predictive power in accounting for variation in reported psychological well-being. Network components were found to significantly predict variations in traditional psychiatric measures of well-being and self-esteem. No significant relationship was found between network components and a measure of marital adjustment. The results of the regression analyses for the self-esteem and psychiatric measures of well-being are presented in Table 2.

Social Network Characteristics and Traditional Psychiatric Measures of Well-Being

The data suggest that a helping network that respondents view as providing an opportunity for expression is conducive to positive mental health as defined by traditional psychiatric measures. Two factors also relating to positive mental health were having a loosely knit social network with whom indirect contact is maintained and reporting a small percentage of intimates relative to total network size. The women who reported the fewest mental health problems also reported having contact with a diverse network, while having a few intimates who they feel can be counted on to listen to their problems without fear of negative consequences.

The results of the regression analysis underscore the relative importance of structural components in accounting for psychiatic well-being scores in the current sample. The regression equation predicting psychiatric well-being scores included three out of the four structural components, only one functional component, and none of the content components.

In one respect, the primary role of structural components in accounting for psychological well-being scores can be taken as empirical validation of the utility of a network methodology. If replicated, such findings suggest that studies assessing only functional aspects of social support in relation to psychological well-being could benefit from the inclusion of simple structural indices of social networks.

Table 2   Multiple regression analysis using structural, content, and functional components
to predict psychological well-being components

Criterion	Predictors	Class of variables	r	Multiple R	R^2 Change	F
Traditional	Expression	Functional	.46***	.461	.231**	10.30
Psychiatric	Intimates	Structural	.32**	.539	.078**	7.61
Measures	Density	Structural	.26*	.606	.076***	6.98
(POMS, HSCL,	Indirect contact	Structural	.34*	.696	.116***	8.22
CES-D, LES)	Problem sharing	Content	.02	.703	.010	6.67
	Reciprocity	Content	.03	.709	.008	5.58
	Validation	Functional	.13	.712	.004	4.72
	Informational helping	Functional	.04	.713	.0007	4.01
	Instrumental helping	Functional	.13	.714	.0001	3.43
Self-esteem	Nonlocal kin relations	Structural	.32**	.328	.108*	4.60
(TSBI)	Expression	Functional	.12	.420	.068*	3.46
	Multidimensionality	Content	.30*	.472	.046	2.44
	Indirect contact	Structural	.06	.508	.036*	3.05
	Informational helping	Functional	.22	.551	.045*	2.97
	Density	Structural	.11	.557	.029*	2.75
	Instrumental helping	Functional	.12	.595	.020	2.31
	Validation	Functional	.20	.609	.016	2.28
	Reciprocity	Content	.12	.616	.008	2.04
	Intimacy	Structural	.07	.617	.001	1.78

*p < .05.
**p < .01.
***p < .001.

Social Network Characteristics and Self-Esteem

All three classes of measures account for a significant percentage of variation in self-esteem scores. Results indicate that the structural components of nonlocal kin relations, indirect contact with network members, the functional component of expression and the content component concerned with multidimensionality are all positively correlated with self-esteem. The functional component of informational helping is negatively related to self-esteem scores. The pattern of these findings in relation to self-esteem suggests that among women with high self-esteem, who are in the role of student's wife, kin, and nonlocal relations constitute a major part of their social networks. Frequent contact with network members is made by phone and letter. Such women have network members with whom they feel free to express their needs when having problems, and do not feel that they receive informational help such as advice or referral when they do seek assistance.

These findings suggest that different mechanisms may be important in understanding self-esteem and psychiatric concepts of well-being. Components accounting for the variance in self-esteem scores are more evenly distributed across the three conceptual categories compared with network predictors of psychiatric measures. The pattern of the data for self-esteem emphasizes quality and maintenance of particular kinds of network relations rather than the overall structural composition of the network.

Social Network Characteristics and Marital Adjustment

Network measures, while predictive of psychiatric symptomatology and self-esteem did not predict marital adjustment. The lack of a relationship between network components and marital adjustment may be interpreted as evidence for discriminant validity. It is reasonable to assume that marital adjustment is primarily concerned with the dyadic relationship and as such would not be best tapped by a broad social network assessment. A lack of relationship between network measures and marital adjustment scores suggests that the self-reported well-being criteria are tapping more than a self-report style that ignores content.

HYPOTHESES AND VARIABLES GENERATED BY EMIC ANALYSIS

At this point in the research, had we chosen to use a more limited assessment procedure, the results of the study would have given us an interesting and useful analysis of group data relevant to the predictive utility of network components, but little information about how the women themselves understand and experience their social networks. However, given our exploratory interview we were able to proceed with an emic analysis. The nature of emic analysis is quite distinct from the nature of etic analysis. While emic data might initially appear less startling and more "obvious," we contend that such data is fundamental to a deeper understanding of etic categories.

During the course of the interviews we were struck by the diversity of attitudes and resources among these young married women, despite the similarity of their problems and circumstances. Most of the women complained of problems of living on a very tight budget, in modest surroundings, with a husband whom they saw infrequently due to his academic commitments in a town that did not feel like home. What differentiated these women from one another was not their present circumstances, but the way they spent their days, the people they considered important, the relationships they felt they could count on and their feelings about themselves, and their life.

Work, Children and Self-Esteem

An interesting aspect of interviewing was learning how a variety of women living in similar circumstances spent their time. Of the 40 women interviewed, 35% were employed full time, 30% were homemakers, 15% were employed part time in the home and 20% worked part time outside of the home. It was particularly interesting to learn how women who were not working a full-time job structured their days.

Talking with these women provided insights into their struggle to balance the demands of working and motherhood. Most of the women working part time used other members of the housing complex either as resources in securing employment in the home or in securing the child care needed to maintain outside employment. It was also striking to note the relationship between employment status and reports of self-esteem and marital satisfaction. Below we describe the activities and general attitudes of those women who worked part time either in or out of the home. We then compare ratings of self-esteem and marital adjustment among these two groups and to those who consider themselves homemakers. It is important to keep in mind that our observations are based on a small number of women and our descriptions are offered as examples of how a more qualitative emic analysis enriches predetermined quantitative analysis.

All of the women employed in the home had children. The most frequent job done at home was babysitting or childcare. While all of the respondents mentioned that childcare was a way to supplement their income, these women also discussed feelings of satisfaction that their work enabled other mothers to gain outside employment or to continue with school. It was typical for these women to be responsible for anywhere from three to six children (including their own) in their small two bedroom apartment. These respondents spent about 6-8 hours each day tending to the needs of infants and toddlers; making meals, changing diapers, synchronizing naptime schedules, and supervising playground rituals.

Joan, a 28-year-old mother of three, explains: "I don't really mind babysitting at all. I have to tend my own [children] anyway. . . . And besides, it gives Nancy [my employer] a chance to finish school. She [Nancy] could never do it without me."

It is also interesting to note that some of these respondents not only included the mothers of those children for whom they provide daycare as members of their social network but also the children themselves. Take the case of Sue, a 22-year-old mother of a 1½-year-old girl. Sue babysits for three children, five days a week, for 6-8 hours a day. These three children were included in Sue's network along with their mothers, Amy, Laurie, and Peggy. Sue also included the names of five of her daughter's playmates (ages two through five) as important people in her life. This example reflects a more general sense of the importance of children and the family in these women's lives. The challenges and rewards of motherhood occupy most of their days and network relationships and attitudes about children and family are consistent with the way these respondents spend their time.

Despite the complexity of the tasks they perform and the responsibility involved in tending children, those respondents who remain at home score low on a self-report measure of self-esteem, relative to other women with children in the sample. In fact, several of the women with the most demanding child care jobs (women with the largest numbers of children to care for) reported the lowest self-esteem scores. To understand more about how these women viewed themselves, we examined the content of the specific items they endorsed on the self-esteem scale. It appears that women who work part time in the home do not have difficulty endorsing statements regarding self-confidence (e.g., "I would describe myself as self-confident." "I would describe myself as one who attempts to master situations.") but do have difficulty with statements tapping assertion or social competence (e.g., "When I am in disagreement with other people, my opinion usually prevails." "Other people look up to me." "I have no doubts about my social competence.") While it is impossible to determine cause and effect, it is not surprising that these women would structure their days primarily in the home where they could initiate contact with others as they wished.

Seven of the eight women who worked part time outside of the home also had children. These women had a variety of jobs which included substitute teaching, medical technician, and clerk-typist positions. Their reasons for seeking employment included the need to supplement family income, the chance to use their education, the need to have friends outside of the home and a basic desire to "get out of the house." While two of the women reported their husbands as the primary resource for daycare, most of them used mothers in the housing complex as babysitters while they were at work. Several of these women mentioned the availability of childcare and other children as the most positive aspects of their living environment.

Joyce, a part time school teacher and mother of two children describes her living environment: "I love the grassy areas [around the complex] and having all of these kids around for my kids to play with ... having someone who I can leave my kids with if I get called [to work] is a real life saver too. . . . It's just that these apartments are just too small for more than two people."

Sandy, a violin teacher with a 9-month-old son describes her feelings about living in married student housing. She states: "We like our apartment real well, but then we have a real nice view out of our window, nicer than most. The greenness of the area and all the kids around is really great . . . "

It appears that these women appreciate an environment that provides an opportunity for both their children and themselves to interact with others. The importance of relationships outside of the home is often reflected in these women's reports of their social networks. These respondents include children in their networks less frequently and often report co-workers as friends.

The majority of these women report high self-esteem relative to other respondents with children. In contrast to women employed in the home, these workers have no trouble endorsing statements that reflect high self-confidence, assertiveness, and social competence. They also provide a contrast to the mixed self-esteem scores given by the homemakers in the sample.

It is interesting to note that the diversity of activities enjoyed by these women is not necessarily associated with higher reports of marital satisfaction. In fact, the majority of women who work part time outside of the home report low marital adjustment as measured by the Locke-Wallace relative to other respondents with children. Of the three groups of women, homemakers most frequently report high levels of marital adjustment as measured by the Locke-Wallace. Those women employed in the home were split in their ratings of marital satisfaction, and women employed outside of the home were lowest in marital adjustment.

Feelings of Obligation

In the planning phases of the study we had considered assessing the role of "obligation toward kin" as an important factor in shaping women's social networks. While psychology focuses on the primacy of early parental relations in personality development, it has relatively little to say about how kin relations influence our lives throughout the life cycle. However, there is much sociological evidence demonstrating the important role of women in maintaining family ties throughout adulthood. Such research suggests that women know more kin and consider them to be more important in their lives than do men (Adams, 1968); and that women are more likely than men to represent the nuclear family in kin contacts and functions involving family members (Leichter & Mitchell, 1967). Sociologists also find that daughters express closer affection to both parents than do sons (Komarovsky, 1964) and that married adults are more likely to be in more frequent contact with the wife's family than with the husband's (Reiss, 1962). The degree of felt obligation toward kin may be an important influence on the configuration of network relations and the use of informal help for young married women. Consequently, early in planning our research we sought to obtain some psychological understanding of the process of obligation.

A review of the psychological and sociological literature on obligation in kinship revealed few empirical studies. The studies found failed to define the concept of obligation or consider problems arising from direct methods of measurement (Reiss, 1962; Bahr & Nye, 1974; Muir & Weinstein, 1962; Shulman, 1975). Yet we felt that obligation in kinship was an important and often subtle influence in women's lives. We assumed that since a sense of felt obligation was influenced by societal norms and expectations that the construct might be highly sensitive to "social desirability" factors in its measurement. It also occurred to us that women might not be able to identify or articulate feelings of obligation in a direct fashion. For these reasons, the construct of obligation could not be satisfactorily operationalized as a rating on a scale. It was the complexity of the phenomena and the lack of previous empirical research on obligation in kinship that convinced us not to assess the construct quantitatively, but to be alert for instances in the interview process that could provide clues to a relationship between obligation, social networks, and psychological well-being.

This strategy proved wise in two respects as it allowed us to obtain a qualitative sense of the importance of felt obligation in these women's lives and provided us with information about the "manifestations" of felt obligation in the quantitative data. In the course of interviews, we found that women spontaneously talked about their relationships with kin and about the conflicts and responsibilities they assumed as a "natural" part of their roles as wives and mothers. This increased our belief that felt obligation toward family of origin had an impact on social network configuration, use of helping resources, and psychological well-being. The quantitative data collected seemed to "make sense" in light of differences in these women's experience of obligation toward kin relations.

In an effort to concretize our observances on felt obligation in kinship, we will first summarize the differences we observed for women with differing home responsibilities and experiencing different levels of self-reported psychological well-being. We will provide examples using the respondents own words to support our descriptions and link these descriptions to differences in the quantitative data. For the purposes of these analyses, the women are first divided into four subgroups based on their psychosocial adjustment scores and on the presence or absence of children.

For women with children who report lower distress scores, kin ties were often seen as providing continuity and stability to one's life. There was often little distinction made between their own family of origin and their in-laws in terms of expressing affection or asking advice. Several women commented on the geographical distance between their kin and themselves, stating how distance hindered the children "getting to know" grandparents, aunts, and uncles. Women often cited the life experience of other family members as a prime reason for their seeking help from them. Expression of feelings about their kin relations were frequently voiced when discussing problems and sources of help or advice.

Cindy is a 22-year-old homemaker and mother of one. She relies heavily on her family and her husband's parents for help and advice. Cindy explains:

My family and one other friend are all the people I really need when I have problems. . . . I go to my mother because she understands and cares, I respect her judgment and I know she won't lead me in the wrong direction. . . . And Mike's father [my father-in-law] Joe, he's great. . . . He offered to give us financial help and he's able to give it, so we took him up on it for now. . . . I know my older sister, Jenny, is always there . . . and I'm already in the habit of going to her [for help] . . . . The only thing I regret is that Jenny is so far away—my nephew Peter is growing up so fast and she hasn't even seen [my baby] Jason yet.

Marsha, age 23, mother of a 9-month-old son, is grateful that she can draw on her parents' experience. She states:

"I'd be silly not to use my family for help. . . . My mom thinks like I do about a lot of things. She and Dad have had a lot of experiences with the same sorts of problems that [my husband] Jack and I now face."

Not all women with low distress scores and children expressed close relationships with their family of origin. There were a few women who spoke of neutral or strained relationships with kin, particularly parents. However, these women seemed to have church affiliations which served as significant sources of continuity and stability in their lives. For them, their sense of obligation appears to have been transferred to an "adopted" church family.

For example, 28-year-old Ellen is a mother of three children ranging in ages from 2-5 years. She also provides child care in her home for a 3-year-old girl. Of the nine people she goes to for help six are friends from church. Church friends were seen as "people who come from the same circumstances and share a perspective for living. They are not critical, have good ideas, and help me find the right solution." While Ellen is in contact with her parents by letter, she does not include them in her everyday life. She explains, "My life is here now, and my church friends keep me grounded in a Christian perspective. They help add direction to my life."

Robin is a 22-year-old mother of one who works part time in the home as a typist. Robin reports strained relations with her family of origin as they "often try to impose their beliefs on me and influence my relationship with my husband." Robin chose not to include some important church people on her social network list because of her husband's disapproval of her church friendships. During the course of the interview, Robin reported being quite active in church functions and considers her church relationships as an important factor in "my being able to settle in town." Robin explains: "Although I write to my family regularly, I feel more attached to the people here [in my church] who share my beliefs. While my family are Christians, the people here act on their faith more the way I think is good. I feel comfortable with them."

None of the women who expressed a positive sense of family obligations were among the high-distress women. However, those who experience their obligations negatively, were found in both the high and low distress groups. Mothers who report high levels of distress tend to view kin relations less benevolently. Kin ties often represent responsibilities that must be attended to despite the often unpleasant consequences of interacting with family members. They are not free of the felt sense of obligation, but rather, experience it negatively.

Connie, age 25, is in touch with her mother by phone about once a week. She feels that it is important to keep in touch even though they often "don't get along." Connie explains "my mother likes to feel needed and part of my life. The problem is that when I talk to her about my marriage, she gives me bad advice. Her solutions are dishonest and my problems turn into a discussion of her problems. She gets very emotional and takes any criticism as a personal attack."

When describing reasons for choosing her mother-in-law as a helper, 27-year-old Maryann explains "I have no choice!" I mention something and she asks ten thousand questions about it. I have an obligation to be in touch. . . . The woman is smothering. She puts me on the defensive whenever I mention [my husband] Brad. But I've got to be nice to her. She's family."

It is also interesting to note that four of the six mothers reporting the highest distress scores also report "adopting" nonkin relations into kin roles. What seems to occur among the women with children who have a negative experience in their sense of family obligation is that they look to others for sources of support. However, at least in this sample, the "others" were not always able to compensate for the strain of family obligations.

Elizabeth, a 32-year-old mother of one and director of a child development center reports a somewhat strained relationship with her mother. Elizabeth describes her neighbor and helper Betty as "an older woman, a kind of mother figure." Betty is the godmother to Elizabeth's 18-month-old daughter, Mary, and Elizabeth is able to "rely on her for advice and help in raising Mary."

Kathleen is a neighbor to whom 25-year-old Elaine goes for help or advice about her two-year-old child. Elaine describes Kathleen as "an older woman, around age 32, who is very matronly. She is like a second mother. She is someone I talk to when I have questions about [my son] Aaron . . . but I don't share other aspects of my personal life."

The expression of obligation and family ties appears somewhat different for women without children. Respondents with low distress scores tend to view kin relations as a base of security to be used in time of need. These women frequently report having close relationships with kin, but tend to emphasize the importance of relationships with their husband and friends. The use of kin for help is much less frequent than for women with children and usually revolves around obtaining financial assistance from parents, when needed.

Sarah, age 27, has a social network characterized by friends. Her father-in-law, John, is the only family member listed in her helping network. Two months previous to the interview, the couple approached John for a loan. Sarah explains, "I was against it but [my husband] Jack worries to death about money. I figure that we could wait and use his dad if we absolutely needed it, but Jack asked him, since his dad can afford to give us a loan."

Helen, 25 years old, relied on her parents for financial assistance, although the majority of her helping network consisted of friends. When discussing the disadvantages in going to her father for help, Helen stated, "As far as finances go, I feel reluctant to go to him as I feel a need for independence . . . I'm married and I feel I shouldn't mooch. He understands my financial need though, and I know he'll help out if I really need it."

Women without children who report higher levels of distress more often emphasize the "shoulds" involved in interacting with kin. These women are often very conscious of normative expectations regarding responsibility to kin. Feelings regarding societal expectations about kin are often expressed when they are asked to delineate their network on a intimacy dimension. When asked to list those people toward whom respondents feel the closest and know the best, several women spontaneously noted "Oh, here's the place I should list my family." It appears that these women listed extended family members more from an expectation that family members should be considered intimate, than from an "accurate" reflection of those network members who fill the need for closeness.

Margie is a 24-year-old secretary who has been married for 2 years. Of the 51 people Margie lists as members of her social network, the first 30 are relatives. These include extended family such as cousins and in-laws Margie sees infrequently. Margie explains simply, "I think family should come first in my life."

Karen is a 21-year-old bookkeeper. Of the 26 network members listed, she indicated her husband and 12 family members as those "people I feel the closest to and know the best." Five of her in-laws were included in the remaining 14 relationships listed. Karen discussed the financial problems involved with buying family members Christmas presents. "I feel like I should give everyone in the family a gift just because they are my family. . . . But I guess I'll have to make each person something because the money is so tight."

Our observations seem to indicate that feelings of obligation toward kin play a different role for women at different stages in the life cycle. It appears that women with children think differently about kin relations than those without children and that differences in self-reported psychological well-being can also be used to characterize attitudes regarding kin. The emic data indicates that women with low distress scores tend to see kin as a source of continuity and security. Mothers frequently use kin as informal helpers and report few negative consequences in so doing. Women without children report a sense of security in being able to call on their kindred in time of need.

In contrast, women with high distress scores seem to experience obligation toward kin negatively. Mothers report a pressure to use kin as informal helpers despite the negative consequences in so doing. Women without children feel an obligation to list kin as intimates despite the actual closeness associated with their relationships.

COMBINING ETIC AND EMIC DATA
TO GENERATE NEW HYPOTHESES

Qualitative and emic analyses not only allows for description useful in operationalizing the concept of felt obligation, but can also provide a context in which to understand the quantitative findings and suggest future hypotheses. For example, we found a significant negative correlation between percentage of intimates listed in the respondent's network and psychological well-being, that is, those who report a large percentage of people they "know the best and feel closest to" also report higher psychological distress scores. A number of plausible hypotheses may be generated to explain this finding. For example, it may be that the relationship between intimacy and well-being is a U-shaped function: that reporting either large or small numbers of intimates might be problematic for women.

Seeing the percentage of intimates listed as an operationalization of felt obligation places the finding in an entirely different context. Given our qualitative analyses, thoughts about the meaning of the correlation can no longer be confined to the construct of intimacy. It is quite possible that those women with a high degree of felt obligation feel pressure to list all of their family members among those who they "know the best and feel the closest to." This operationalization of intimacy, based on face validity, is now called into question. Qualitative information regarding the perceptions of the respondents about their networks and kin relations allow the researcher to check the meaning of network variables.

Of course, the descriptive data used to support the concept of felt obligation in this example is also open to alternative explanations. One possibility is that differences in expression of felt obligation are a function of psychological adjustment. It is conceivable that women reporting high levels of distress see all relationships more negatively and therefore report more problems with kin relations than do women with lower distress scores. If so, differences in reported responsibilities to kin may be a function of an overall negative response style found among distressed women.

However, other indices used in the study suggest that high distress women do not have an overall negative response style. For example, there were no significant correlations between mean ratings of satisfaction or mutuality of network members and psychological adjustment. It is reasonable to assume that these indices of relationship content would also be affected if responses were merely a function of response style. At any rate, researchers now have a set of hypotheses generated through the application of emic analysis, which lends itself to future hypothesis testing. The observational information generated from the present study may help quantify the construct of felt obligation. Systematic investigations of the characteristics of felt obligation as an aspect of support and/or stress now should be conducted. Our point here is that sensitivity to both etic and emic data can elucidate present findings and inform future investigations in unpredictable ways.

CONCLUSION

Researchers in the area of social support are acknowledging the importance of viewing social relationships as sources of both support and stress. Many authors point to a network methodology as a means for understanding the process of informal helping and resource exchange in people's lives (Gottlieb, 1981; Wellman, 1981). We feel strongly that the potential of a network methodology comes from its capacity to generate both etic and emic data. The complex nature of human relationships requires us to use both the quantitative and clinical expertise that we have as psychologists. We must allow ourselves discovery by both detailed observation as well as quantitative analysis if the potential of a social network methodology is to be fully realized.

REFERENCES

• Adams, B. N. (1968). *Kinship in an urban setting.* Chicago: Markham.
Bahr, H. M., & Nye, F. E. (1974). The kinship role in contemporary community: Perceptions of obligations and sanctions. *Journal of Contemporary Family Studies, 5,* 17–25.
Bloom, L. (1974). Commentary. *Monographs of the Society for Research in Child Development, 39,* 82–88.
Brown, G. W. Bhrolchain, M. N., & Harris, T. (1975). Social class and psychiatric disturbance among women in an urban population. *Sociology, 9,* 225–254.
Burgess, E. W., Locke, H. J., & Thomas, M. M. (1971). *The family.* New York: Van Nostrand.

Cauce, A. M., Felner, R. D., & Primavera, J. (1982). Social support in high-risk adolescents: Structural components and adaptive impact. *American Journal of Community Psychology, 10,* 185-205.

Colten, M. E., & Kulka, R. (1979). *The nature and perceived helpfulness of formal and informal support.* Paper presented at the annual meeting of the American Psychological Association, September.

Croog, S. M., Lipson, A., & Levine, S. (1972). Help patterns in severe illness: The role of kin network, non-family resources and institutions. *Journal of Marriage and the Family, 34,* 32-41.

Dean, A., & Lin, N. (1977). The stress buffering role of social support. *Journal of Nervous and Mental disease, 166,* 7-15.

DeRogatis, L., Lipman, R., Rickels, K., Uhlenhuth, E., & Covi, L. (1974). The Hopkins symptom checklist (HSCL): A self-report symptom inventory. *Behavioral Science, 19,* 1-15.

Duncan-Jones, P. (1981). The structure of social relationships: Analyses of a survey instrument. *Social Psychiatry, 16,* 55-61.

Fischer, C. S. (1976). *The urban experience.* New York: Harcourt, Brace, Janovich.

Gilligan, C. (1982). *In a different voice: Psychology theory and women's development.* Cambridge, MA: Harvard University Press.

Gore, S. (1978). The effect of social support in moderation on the health consequences of unemployment. *Journal of Health and Social Behavior, 19,* 157-165.

Gottlieb, B. H., & Todd, D. M. (1979). Characterizing and promoting social support in natural settings. In R. F. Munoz, L. R. Snowden, & J. G. Kelly (Eds.), *Social and psychological research in community settings.* San Francisco, CA: Jossey-Bass.

Gottlieb, B. H. (1981). Social networks and social support in community mental health. In B. H. Gottlieb (Ed.), *Social networks and social support.* London: Sage.

Helmreich, R., & Stapp, J. (1974). Short forms of the Texas social behavior inventory: An objective measure of self-esteem. *Bulletin of the Psychonomic Society, 4,* 473-475.

Henderson, S. (1977). The social network, support and neurosis. *British Journal of Psychiatry, 131,* 185-191.

Hirsch, B. J. (1979). Psychological dimensions of social networks: A multimethod analysis. *American Journal of Community Psychology, 7,* 263-277.

Hirsch, B. J. (1980). Natural support systems and coping with major life changes. *American Journal of Community Psychology, 8,* 159-172.

Hirsch, B. J. (1981). Coping and adaptation in high-risk populations: Toward an integrative model. *Schizophrenia Bulletin, 7,* 164-171.

Ingersoll, B. (1982). *Combining methodological approaches in social support research.* Paper presented at the annual meeting of the American Psychological Association, August.

Komarovsky, M. (1964). *Blue-collar marriage.* New York: Random House.

Leichter, H. J., & Mitchell, W. E. (1967). *Kinship and casework.* New York: Russell Sage Foundation.

Lin, N., Simeone, R. S., Ensel, W. M., & Kuo, W. (1979). Social support, stressful life events and illness: A model and an empirical test. *Journal of Health and Social Behavior, 20,* 108-119.

Lowenthal, M., & Robinson, B. (1976). Social networks and isolation. In R. Benstock & E. Shanans (Eds.), *Handbook of aging and the social sciences.* New York: Van Nostrand.

Marsella, A. J., & Snyder, K. K. (1981). Stress, social supports and schizophrenic disorders: Toward an interactional model. *Schizophrenia Bulletin, 7,* 152-163.

McFarlane, A. H., Neale, K. A., Norman, G. R., Roy, R. G., & Streiner, D. L. (1981). Methodological issues in developing a scale to measure social support. *Schizophrenia Bulletin, 7,* 90-100.

McKinley, J. B. (1973). Social networks, lay consultation and help-seeking behavior. *Social Forces, 51,* 275-292.

McNair, D. M., Loor, M., & Droppleman, L. (1971). *Manual for the profile of mood states.* San Diego: Educational Industrial Testing Service.

Mitchell, J. C. (Ed.). (1969). *Social networks in urban situations.* Manchester, England: Manchester University Press.

Mitchell, R. E., & Trickett, E. J. (1980). An analysis of the effects and determinants of social networks. *Community Mental Health Journal, 16,* 27-44.

Mueller, D. (1980). Social networks: A promising direction for research on the relationship of the social environment to psychiatric disorder. *Social Science and Medicine, 14,* 147-161.

Muir, D. E., & Weinstein, E. A. (1962). The social debt: An investigation of lower-class and middle-class norms of social obligation. *American Sociological Review, 27*, 532–539.

Pattison, E. M., DeFrancisco, D., Frazier, H., Wood, P. E., & Crowder, J. (1975). A psychosocial kinship model for family therapy. *American Journal of Psychiatry, 132*, 1246–1251.

Phillips, S. L. (1981). Network characteristics related to the well-being of normals: A comparative base. *Schizophrenia Bulletin, 7*, 117–124.

Pike, K. L. (1967). *Language in relation to a unified theory of the structure of human behavior*. The Hague: Mouton.

Procidano, M. E. & Heller, K. (1983). Measures of perceived social support from friends and from family: Three validation studies. *American Journal of Community Psychology, 11*, 1–24.

Radloff, L. (1977). The CES-D scale: A self-report depression scale for research in the general population. *Applied Psychological Measurement, 1*, 385–401.

Rappaport, J., Seidman, E., & Davidson, W. S. (1979). Demonstration research and manifest versus true adoption: The natural history of a research project to divert adolescents from the legal system. In R. F. Munoz, L. R. Snowden, J. G. Kelly (Eds.). *Social and psychological research and community settings*. San Francisco: Jossey-Bass.

Reiss, P. T. (1962). The extended kinship system: Correlates of and attitudes on frequency of interaction. *Marriage and Family Living, 24*, 333–339.

Sarason, J. G., Johnson, J. H., & Siegel, J. M. (1978). Assessing the impact of life changes: Development of the life experiences survey. *Journal of Consulting and Clinical Psychology, 46*, 932–946.

Shulman, N. (1975). Life-cycle variations in patterns of close relationships. *Journal of Marriage and the Family, 37*, 813–821.

Sokolvsky, J., & Cohen, C. (1981). Toward a resolution of methodological dilemmas in network mapping. *Schizophrenia Bulletin, 7*, 109–116.

Stein, C. H. (1984). *The social networks of young married women: A methodological inquiry*. Unpublished master's thesis, University of Illinois at Urbana-Champaign.

Tolsdorf, G. (1976). Social networks, support and coping: An exploratory study. *Family Process, 15*, 407–417.

Walker, K., MacBride, A., & Vachon, M. L. (1977). Social support networks and the crisis of bereavement. *Social Science and Medicine, 11*, 35–41.

Wellman, B. (1981). Applying network analyses to the study of support. In B. H. Gottlieb (Ed.), *Social networks and social support*. London: Sage.

Wethington, E. (1982). *Can social support functions be differentiated: A multivariate model*. Paper presented at the annual meeting of the American Psychological Association, August.

Wilcox, B. (1981). Social support in adjusting to marital disruption: A network analysis. In B. H. Gottlieb (Ed.), *Social networks and social support*. London: Sage.

Zautra, A. J. (1983). Social resources and the quality of life. *American Journal of Community Psychology, 11*, 275–290.

II

CAREER, MARRIAGE, AND FAMILY STRESSORS

5

Sex Differences in Depression: The Role of Spouse Support

Beth E. Vanfossen
State University of New York, Brockport

A number of different studies have established that smaller proportions of married women than married men experience emotional well-being. Unlike never-married women, who are reported to be generally better off emotionally than never-married men, married women are more likely than men to be depressed, to be unhappy with their marriages, and to have a negative image of themselves (Gove, 1972; Campbell, 1975; Silverman, 1968; Pearlin, 1975; Radloff, 1976; Gurin, Veroff, & Feld, 1960; McKee & Sherriffs, 1959). The research reported here is concerned with the question: In what ways do patterns of social interaction within the institution of marriage contribute to sex differences in emotional well-being?

Bernard (1971) has argued that women are disadvantaged in marriage because they are less likely than husbands to receive the social supports they need from their spouses. She states that the provision of social support has been socially defined as the dominant function of women in marriage, which they fulfill by alternatively raising the status of others in their families, giving help, rewarding, agreeing, concurring, complying, understanding, and passively accepting. The difficulty for women emerges not because they are involved in providing such support, but rather because they are in turn deprived of such nurturant support from intimate others within the family circle.

Two social science perspectives have suggested explanations of why women might receive less social support than men within the family. One, emerging from functionalist theory (Parsons, 1949; Zelditch, 1955), suggests that the patterned division of labor within the family, based on reproductive roles, delegates to women the tasks of providing nurturance and emotional sustenance (the "expressive function"), while men are delegated the tasks of achievement and accomplishment in the external environment (the "instrumental function").

The other hypothesis, emerging from conflict theory, suggests that women's lesser social support is a product of the institutionalized male dominance prevalent in industrial society. For example, the "devaluation of femininity," a dominant idea in the cultural socialization of young children, is a natural outcome of such male dominance, and may lead to the lessened respect with which wives are sometimes treated by their spouses and children.

While there has been considerable social science interest recently in the relationship of social support to mental health, few reports have examined sex differences in receiving such support (two exceptions are Belle, 1982, and Warren, 1976). Rather, the research has by and large emphasized one of two ways in which social support may be related to emotional well-being: (1) social support networks may intervene between stressful life events and psychological distress (Myers, Lindenthal, & Pepper, 1975; Rabkin & Streuning, 1976; Dean & Lin, 1977; Gore, 1978; Nuckolls, Cassel, & Kaplan, 1972); and (2) social support may have an independent beneficial effect on emotional makeup (Williams, Ware, & Donald, 1981; Lerner, 1973; Kaplan, Wilson, & Leighton, 1976; Henderson, 1977). In this paper, I explore these two possibilities within the framework of a focus upon sex differences in social support.

GENERAL FRAMEWORK

To pursue the question of how sex differences in social support mechanisms may contribute to sex differences in emotional well-being, I first postulate a perspective on the linkages between the mental health of individuals and their relationships to the social institutions in which they operate. The perspective assumes that three conditions precede and affect emotional disposition: (1) the quality of the individual's interface with major social institutions; (2) how well the individual is able to carry out major role expectations and performance; and (3) how prevalent and how helpful are the social supports provided by intimate others.

It is useful at this point to clarify conceptually these three conditions. *Social institutions* are stable patterns of behavior, values, and role expectations that have developed around the basic activities each society must undertake in order to survive, such as creating and distributing goods, and reproducing the species. Individual well-being is greatly affected by the individual's particular relationship to those institutions. An unemployed man is maladjusted to the economic institution as is a poor, divorced mother. Disadvantaged groups, such as the poor and minorities, are systematically allocated less favorable connections to major institutions by the patterns established by dominant groups. Harmful experiences with the major social institutions can result from any one of three conditions: deficits in the individual resources needed for institutional interface (such as job skills); institutional coercion as exists for those roles low in power and high in onerous duties; and low reward levels as when work is unpraised or pay levels do not provide a living wage.

One major way individuals interface with institutions is by occupying statuses within the institutions such as employee or mother. *Roles* are the behaviors expected of the occupants of statuses. Difficulty in role performance is often experienced by the individual when roles contain internal strains, such as work overload demands or contradictory requirements, or when two major roles expected of the individual are in conflict. Roles that are not easy to perform may have deleterious mental health consequences for the individual.

The third condition affecting emotional well-being is *social support*. Much of our internal orientation to our lives, our assessment of who we are and where we are going, grows out of the significant contacts and ties we have with a few other persons—members of our families, work colleagues, or friends, for example. Their treatment of and attitudes toward us affects our view of ourselves, our senses of mastery, and our conceptions of where we belong in the social order. We constantly try to protect our sometimes fragile view of ourselves from self-deprecation and shame, and we may be helped in this endeavor by those who are close to us. Calamities can be softened by the sympathetic assessments offered by the significant others in our lives.

In order to examine the connection among these conditions, I developed a structural equation model of the effects of institutional interface, role strains, and spouse supports on depression, self-esteem, and mastery. This model subsequently was used to examine data on mental health collected through interviews with a representative sample taken in Chicago in 1974. In the model, the background control variables (age and education) appear first, under the assumption that they are causally prior to the remaining variables. They are followed by a block of variables measuring stresses arising either from role strains and conflicts experienced in the day-to-day routines, or from defects in the individual's interfacing with major institutions (occupational, economic, and familial). Entered next into the equation are measures of spouse support, which may act as buffers between stress and emotional response. These measures are of primary interest in this study. The dependent variables, entered last as the final causal outcomes, are self-esteem, mastery, and emotional depression. The time-sequence of the ordering of the variables in the model is supported by evidence presented in prior reports that changes in institutional stresses precede changes in self-concept and sense of mastery (Pearlin, Menaghan, Lieberman, & Mullan, 1981), and that deficits in spouse interactions precede depression (Vanfossen, 1981).

The model is applied to several groups that are expected to be differentially affected by their relationship to institutions: employed husbands, unemployed husbands, employed wives, unemployed wives, and employed and unemployed fathers and mothers. These groups are distinguished because they differ both in institutional interface and in major role expectations. The central foci of the analysis are two: how spouse supportiveness intervenes between institutional stressors and psychological well-being, and how the identified mechanisms may vary by sex.

The data used for this analysis are part of a larger investigation into the social origins of stress conducted by Pearlin (1975; also see Pearlin & Johnson, 1977; Pearlin & Schooler, 1978; Pearlin et al., 1981). The sample consisted of 2,300 adults between the ages of 18 and 65, and was representative of the U.S. census-defined urbanized area of Chicago, which includes suburban areas as well as Chicago proper. The subsample employed in the present research consists of 624 employed husbands, 94 unemployed husbands, 256 employed wives, and 579 unemployed wives. The data were collected through interviews that explored the conflicts and frustrations people experience as they engage in their social roles as parents, marriage partners, workers, and breadwinners.

The interview schedule, which was devised over a 2-year period, asked about the coping repertoires people employ in dealing with the strains they experience in these roles, and about the extent to which they experience symptoms of various states of psychological disturbance. The development of the interview schedule was based on the identification of recurrent themes in open-ended interviews with 100 respondents about the problems associated with their daily lives.

Measurement of Stressors

For evidence of the quality of the ties of the individual to major institutions, I have chosen to focus the analysis on stresses of work, financial affairs, and parenting. Items measuring problems in these areas were submitted to factor analysis, and internally consistent scales were constructed.

The concept of occupational stressors is measured by a scale of six items denoting personal relations on the job and feelings of job security. The Likert-type items called for respondents to indicate how often people acted toward them as if they were persons without real feelings, people treated them in an unfriendly way, and they were treated unfairly by another person. They were also asked whether they agreed with the following statements: "I can count on a steady income," "My work has good fringe benefits such as sick pay and retirement," and "There is always a chance I may be out of a job." These items thus measure the quality of social relations at work as well as the adequacy of the job rewards. The alpha coefficient for the occupational stress scale is .93.

The work of homemakers is measured by a scale of seven items concerning the meaning and consequences of housework. Homemakers were asked how often they had free time for themselves, used their talents and abilities in doing housework, really enjoyed the work, were lonely for the company of adults during the day, were tired out from doing housework, were uninterested or bored with doing housework chores, and were not appreciated for their work in the house.

The financial stressor is measured by a scale of four items concerning the difficulty the respondent has in meeting financial obligations. Respondents were asked if they were able to afford furniture or household equipment that needs to be replaced, if they could afford the kind of car they needed, how much difficulty they had in meeting the monthly payments on their family's bills, and how much money they had left over at the end of the month. The alpha coefficient for the financial difficulty scale is 0.70.

Parenting stress is measured by a scale of four items asked of parents whose children were between the ages of 5 and 21 and were residing in the household. Parents were queried on how often they were disobeyed by their children, treated without proper respect, their advice and guidance were ignored, and how often they had to give some attention to the correction of misbehavior in the house. The alpha coefficient for the parenting stressors scale is .95.

Measurement of Spouse Support

Supportiveness was conceptualized as consisting of four different kinds of support that one person may offer another: affirmation, affection, reciprocity, and helpfulness. Respondents were asked a number of questions that indicate the degree to which they feel they are the recipients of spouse support.

Affirmation is the kind of support a person can give to another by helping the other become the kind of person she or he wants to be, and by appreciating what she or he already is. Three items in the schedule are related to the concept of affirmation. Respondents were asked whether they agreed or disagreed with the following statements: "My (husband/wife) seems to bring out the best qualities in me," "My (husband/wife) is someone who appreciates me just as I am," and "My marriage doesn't give me enough opportunity to become the sort of person I'd like to be." The alpha reliability coefficient is 0.74.

Intimacy is suggested by three items concerning affection and closeness. Respondents were asked how strongly they agreed or disagreed with the following statements: "My (husband/wife) is someone I can really talk with about things that are important to me," "My (husband/wife) is someone who is a good sexual partner," and "My (husband/wife) is someone who is affectionate toward me." The alpha reliability coefficient for this scale is .78.

Reciprocity in marriage is indicated by three items measuring perceived inequity. Respondents were asked how strongly they agreed or disagreed with the following statements about their relationships with their spouses: "Generally I give in more to my (husband's/wife's) wishes than (he/she) gives in to mine," "My (husband/wife) usually expects more from me than (he/she) is willing to give back," and "My (husband/wife) insists on having (his/her) own way." The alpha coefficient is .75.

Helpfulness is measured by degree of agreement with one item: "I can rely on my (husband/wife) to help me with most of the problems that have to be taken care of in the family." While the other three support measures tap the expressive and emotional supports given by the spouse, this item asks more about instrumental, concrete actions of responsibility and helpfulness.

Measurement of Self-Concept

Self-concept can be conceptualized as consisting of two related, but separate, components: mastery and self-esteem. Mastery indicates the degree to which people feel they have control over the forces that affect their lives. It is measured by five items that ask respondents to agree or disagree with the following statements: "There is really no way I can solve some of the problems I have," "Sometimes I feel that I'm being pushed around in life," "I have little control over the things that happen to me," "I often feel helpless in dealing with the problems of life," and "There is little I can do to change many of the important things in my life." The alpha coefficient of reliability is .78.

Self-esteem is measured by the widely-used Rosenberg scale (Rosenberg, 1965) that consists of 10 items asking the respondent's agreement with statements about his/her worth, self-satisfaction, and self-respect. Typical items are "I feel that I'm a person of worth," "I feel I do not have much to be proud of," and "I wish I could have more respect for myself." The alpha coefficient of reliability is .85.

Measurement of Depression

The interview included a large number of questions commonly employed in surveys as indicators of emotional well-being (Pearlin, 1975). The scale used in this study is a 6-item scale of depression condensed through factor analysis from an 11-item scale developed by Lipman, Rickles, Covi, Derogatis, and Uhlenhuth (1969) and Derogatis, Lipman, Covi, and Rickles (1971). Respondents were asked how frequently in the preceding week they had experienced each of the following symptoms: lack of enthusiasm for doing anything; a poor appetite; felt lonely; felt bored or had little interest in doing things; had trouble getting to sleep or staying asleep; and felt downhearted or blue. To form the scale, the scores on all six items were added together so that high scores indicate high levels of depression. The alpha coefficient for the depression scale is .76.

Measurement of Background Characteristics

Age and education of respondent have been included in the analysis as control variables to ensure that the correlations of the exogenous variables with depression are not due to other, more powerful, influences in the social environment. These social and demographic variables have been mentioned in the literature as being important.

SEX DIFFERENCES IN DEPRESSION
BY MARITAL STATUS

Recall that a central question in this analysis concerns the social sources of the sex differences in emotional well-being. As noted by Klerman and Weissman (1980), an important piece of evidence that the vulnerability of women to depression is related to the social context in which they exist is the data suggesting that marriage is protective for males but detrimental for females. Let us examine our data to see if the prior findings are confirmed.

Table 1 portrays the percentage of men and women who are very depressed by marital status. The figures reveal that depression rates of men and women are similar for the never married, the separated, and the widowed. Only among the married and the divorced do women show significantly higher rates of depression, twice that of men among the divorced, and 2-½ times that of men among the married. Pearlin and Johnson (1977) have shown that the higher rates of depression of divorced women are due to the greater problems faced by women in parenting, financial survival, and social connection. Table 1 further suggests that while married women are less likely than unmarried women to be depressed, marriage is not nearly as protective a state for them as for men. Klerman and Weissman's argument stands. Now let us turn to the question of how institutional, role, and support variables might illuminate the nature of the sex difference in the protective influence of marriage.

SEX DIFFERENCES IN SOCIAL SUPPORT
AND STRESS

Social Support

A comparison of the responses of husbands and wives concerning the amount of support they receive from their spouses shows that there are statistically significant differences between the sexes, but also that these differences are small. (For a comparison of the means, see Vanfossen, 1981.) On the average, consistently about 8–9% more men than women indicate that they receive affirmation, reciprocity, and help with family problems from their spouses. (The correlations of sex with those supports is − .09, − .10, and − .11, respectively, all statistically significant at the .01 level.) The differences between husbands and wives in their

Table 1 Marital status and depression

Marital status	Depressed men (%)	N	Depressed women (%)	N	Difference (%)
Never married	35.3	150	40.5	138	5.2*
Married	14.6	720	35.7	869	21.1***
Separated	55.6	18	57.1	84	1.5
Divorced	23.5	34	47.6	107	24.1**
Widowed	41.4	29	44.1	143	2.7

*p < .05; **p < .02; ***p < .01.

responses to the item relating to shared intimacy are even smaller, around 5% ($r = -.05$, $p > 0.01$). Overall, these differences are not great, and provide only marginal support for the idea that wives are more supportive than are husbands.

Institutional Stress

The sex differences with regard to the stressful situations examined in the study are moderate. Wives are more likely to experience two of the three stressors measured. That is, in comparison to husbands, wives are considerably more likely to experience stress concerning parenting problems ($r = .19$, $p < .01$), slightly more likely to experience stress concerning financial problems ($r = 0.07$, $p < .01$), but equally likely to experience stress concerning occupational problems ($r = 0.03$, $p < .21$).

For most of the measured variables, the employment status of the husband or wife does not seem to affect the levels of support they receive, with several exceptions. Employed wives receive less affirmation from their spouses than do unemployed wives; employed wives have higher levels of self-esteem than do unemployed wives; and employed wives report greater financial problems than do unemployed wives. Unemployed husbands have lower self-esteem and sense of mastery, are more depressed, and have more financial problems than do employed husbands.

SEX AND EMPLOYMENT DIFFERENCES IN STRESSOR EFFECTS ON EMOTIONAL WELL-BEING

Financial Stressors

At this point I explored the results of regression analyses using the financial problems scale as the first stressor input. Details are presented in Table 2, which gives the results separately for the three dependent variables—depression, self-esteem, and mastery, and for the four employment-sex groups. In each case, a regression of the dependent variable on only the background controls and the stressor was first calculated. Then, a second set of calculations were performed, in which the four support variables were simultaneously entered into the equation. The results show not only how important each support variable is in itself, but also what happens to the effect of the stressor on the outcome variable when the effects of the spouse supports are considered.

The coefficients in the table represent the degree to which the independent variable is related to the dependent variable when the influences of the other variables in the equation are simultaneously taken into account. By convention, when statistically significant coefficients rise above .10, we begin to attribute to them substantive significance. The R^2s recorded under the calculations for each dependent variable indicate the percentage of the variance in the dependent variable which is "accounted for" by the variance in the independent variables included in the equation. Thus, for example, age, education, and financial stress account for 5% of the variance in the depression of employed husbands, while these variables plus the four spouse support variables account for 21% of the variance.

Table 2 Standardized multiple regression coefficients for the regressions of depression, self-esteem, and mastery of financial stress and support variables

Depression

	Husbands		Wives	
	Employed	Unemployed	Employed	Unemployed
Age	-.12***	.09	-.11*	-.02
Education	.01	.12	.01	.01
Financial stress	.14***	.30***	.08	.11***
Intimacy	-.23***	-.57***	.02	.05
Affirmation	-.22***	-.39***	-.23***	-.35***
Reciprocity	-.00	-.09	-.11*	-.02
Helpfulness	-.01	-.11	-.12	.03
R^2	.21	.32	.17	.17

Self-Esteem

	Husbands		Wives	
	Employed	Unemployed	Employed	Unemployed
Age	.07*	-.01	.16***	.11***
Education	.12***	.07	.17***	.16**
Financial stress	-.15***	-.39***	.01	-.24***
Intimacy	.14	.10	.09	.00
Affirmation	.25***	-.07	.29***	.32***
Reciprocity	-.05	.17	.10	.02
Helpfulness	.06	.06	-.06	.01
R^2	.20	.15	.19	.22

Mastery

	Husbands		Wives	
	Employed	Unemployed	Employed	Unemployed
Age	-.02	.02	-.11**	-.10**
Education	.15***	.22**	.18***	.14***
Financial stress	-.19***	-.28***	-.23***	-.22***
Intimacy	.08*	.28***	.04	.09***
Affirmation	.20***	.06	.14*	.27***
Reciprocity	.05	.04	.19***	.11***
Helpfulness	.06	.08	.04	.02
R^2	.19	.28	.28	.24

Table 2 suggests that when families are unable to pay their bills, to afford goods such as furniture, or to save, then their relationship to the economic system is an emotionally problematic one. Husbands and wives are strongly affected by financial difficulty, which has strong deleterious effects upon self-esteem and mastery. This is particularly true for the unemployed males (but not at all true for the self-esteem of employed wives, the single exception). Finally, for all four groups, financial difficulty is associated with depression. Unemployed husbands are particularly likely to be depressed by financial difficulties.

Occupational Stressors

In Table 3, the mental health effects of the conditions of employment for employed husbands and wives, and the conditions of housework for unemployed wives are revealed. Problems of work affect employed husbands more strongly than employed wives. Homemakers, however, are as highly affected by deleterious work conditions as are employed husbands. All groups experience lowered self-esteem and mastery when work stress is high, and are more inclined than the less stressed to become depressed.

Parenting Stressors

The sample size of unemployed fathers was too small for meaningful analysis, so they were dropped from the examination of parenting stressors. For the remaining groups, the results vary from the previous findings. Having disobedient and disrespectful children is only slightly related to lower self-esteem, and even less to mastery. However, its presence does strongly relate to the probability of emotional depression. Both fathers and mothers have higher levels of emotional depression when their children are disobedient and disrespectful. Employed mothers with parenting problems are the most likely of the three groups to become depressed.

ROLE OF SPOUSE SUPPORT IN BUFFERING EFFECTS OF STRESSORS

As shown in Tables 2-4, in almost all cases, when spouse supports are entered into the structural equations, the sizes of the stressor coefficients drop significantly, suggesting that the presence of a supportive spouse does indeed attenuate the deleterious impact of stressful conditions. For example, for employed husbands, the coefficient for the relationship between occupational problems and depression drops from .27 to .19 when spouse supports are included in the analysis. For employed wives, the coefficient for the relationship between parental problems and depression drops from .40 to .30. These findings indicate that having a supportive spouse lowers the probability that a person will become depressed by occupational stress, or financial problems.

Of the 30 different statistical analyses, only 8 do not show a decline of more that .03 points in the coefficients for the stressors as spouse supports are introduced into the equation. While in only one case does the introduction of spouse supports reduce the stressor coefficient to zero, the evidence is consistent with the idea that spouse supports help reduce the deleterious psychological consequences of the stresses of institutional and role deficits. Exceptions occur in the case of unemployed husbands, for whom a supportive spouse does not cure the depression and lowered self-esteem related to financial problems, and in

Table 3 Standardized multiple regression coefficients for the regressions of depression, self-esteem, and mastery on occupational/homemaker stress and supports

	Depression				Self-Esteem				Mastery			
	Husbands		Wives		Husbands		Wives		Husbands		Wives	
	Employed	Unemployed	Employed	Unemployed	Employed	Unemployed	Employed	Unemployed	Employed	Unemployed	Employed	Unemployed
Age	−.09**	.12**	−.11*	.01	.04	.07*	.15**	.14**	−.02	−.01	−.10	−.15***
Education	.02	.01	−.03	.05	.15***	.15***	.12**	.16***	.20***	.19***	.22***	.20***
Occupational or homemaker stress	.27***	.19***	.11*	.35***	−.27***	−.20***	−.19***	−.24***	−.23***	−.17***	−.14*	−.33***
Intimacy		−.22***	.01			.13***	.08		.08*	.08*	.05	.12**
Affirmation		−.20***	−.23***			.23***	.27**		.19***	.19***	.15*	.22***
Reciprocity		−.01	−.12*			−.05	.09		.05	.05	.22***	.11**
Helpfulness		.01	−.13*			.06	−.05		.06	.06	.05	.01
R²	.09	.23	.18	.12	.10	.21	.23	.11	.19	.19	.24	.25

on parental stress and support variables

	Depression							
	Husbands				Wives			
	Employed		Unemployed		Employed		Unemployed	
Age	—.04	—.06			—.02	—.08	—.06	—.02
Education	.01	.00			—.10	—.08	.02	.01
Parenting stress	.23***	.21***			.40***	.30***	.15***	.14***
Intimacy		—.20***				.06		.02
Affirmation		—.19***				—.21***		—.41***
Reciprocity		.05				—.08		—.01
Helpfulness		.00				—.19*		—.01
R^2	.05	.16			.17	.29	.03	.19
	Self-Esteem							
Age	.04	.06			.05	.00	.03	.00
Education	.18***	.19***			.17**	.16**	.23***	.22***
Parenting stress	—.12**	—.10*			—.15*	—.07	—.09*	—.09*
Intimacy		.14**				.11		.07
Affirmation		.29***				.32***		.39***
Reciprocity		.09*				.08		.07
Helpfulness		—.05				.15		.03
R^2	.04	.18			.05	.18	.05	.23
	Mastery							
Age	—.04	—.03			—.17**	—.12*	—.09*	—.12**
Education	.17***	.16***			.28***	.25***	.08	.06
Parenting stress	—.14***	—.12**			—.07	.03	—.03	—.03
Intimacy		.06				.05		.14**
Affirmation		.24***				.11		.32**
Reciprocity		.08				.18**		.09
Helpfulness		.05				.14		.04
R^2	.05	.16			.10	.24	.02	.25

*$p < .10$; **$p < .05$; ***$p < .01$.

the case of employed husbands and unemployed wives, whose senses of self-esteem and mastery do not seem to be particularly tied up with their parenting problems, consequently, their self-esteem and mastery are not elevated much by having a supportive spouse when the children are disobedient.

Comparisons of Kinds of Spouse Support

Which type of spouse support is the most effective in promoting mental well-being varies for husbands and wives, and for the employed and the unemployed. Most of the literature and prior research on social support has focused heavily on the value of having a confidant, a sympathetic listener. While the results of this study do point up the positive benefits of such intimacy, particularly for males, having the presence of an affirming spouse consistently is revealed to be of greater importance. Recall that the affirmation scale is composed of three items concerning how much the spouse appreciates the respondent, brings out his/her best qualities, and how much the marriage helps respondent become the person she/he would like to be. For all groups, affirmation is a very important support. If the spouse appreciates the respondent, and helps the respondent become the person she or he would like to be, then low self-esteem and mastery, and high depression are much less likely.

By contrast, reciprocity is important as a buffering spouse support mainly for the employed wives, and for them, most strongly in its effect upon sense of mastery. Further, whether or not the spouse can be counted on to help with family matters does not have a buffering effect except in the case of employed wives, for whom the impact of all three stressor conditions is lessened by a helpful spouse. The importance of having a helpful spouse may be particularly salient for employed wives because they are frequently faced with a condition of role overload as they attempt to juggle simultaneously the demands of job and homemaking (Vanfossen, 1981).

Independent Effects of Spouse Supports

Perhaps the most impressive relationships revealed in the results are the strong, independent effects of spouse supports on the emotional well-being measures. This is equally true for husbands as for wives. Having someone who is a confidant and who will appreciate that one is important, not only softens the effects of deleterious institutional interfaces, but also contributes in a direct and independent way to emotional well-being. In almost all cases, the amount of variance in mastery, self-esteem, and depression explained by the predictor variables is far greater when spouse supports are included in the equations, than when only the stressors and background characteristics are included. For example, the percentage of the variance in depressive symptoms of the unemployed husbands that is associated with the variance in their financial difficulties is 9, while that associated with variance in financial difficulties *plus* spouse supports is 32, an increase of 21%. This does not deny the impacts of the stressors, which are quite strong, but rather points up the underlying importance of the independent effects of the quality of the marital relationship.

DISCUSSION

There are three important findings emerging from the analysis. The first is that there is only a modicum of substantiation for the implications of both functionalist and conflict theory that suggest that wives are more likely than husbands to provide social support. According to the reports of spouses, slightly more wives than husbands express appreciation, are helpful with family problems, and submerge their own wishes. The differences are not great in magnitude, and it would be erroneous to attempt to predict the supportiveness of a spouse on the basis of his or her sex.

Second, while the interactional qualities of the marital relationship do indeed appear to buffer somewhat the stressful effects of economic deprivation and of imperfect role relationships at work and in parenting, spouse supports are important primarily because of their powerful, independent impact upon emotional well-being. Thus, in those families not characterized by high stresses such as economic deprivation, parenting problems, or occupational maladaptation, mental health nevertheless is crucially affected by the quality of the interpersonal relationship between the spouses.

Third, the types of social support offered by the spouses vary in their impact upon emotional well-being. One kind of support, affirmation of the spouse, is revealed to be very important to emotional well-being for all sex and employment groups, and particularly so for wives. By contrast, and contrary to general expectations, listening and providing affection turn out to be less important than affirmation to the well-being of wives, although these supports clearly are quite important to the husbands. Why there might be these sex differences is intriguing. The items measuring affirmation, you may recall, dealt with the degree to which the spouse appreciated the respondent, the spouse brought out the best qualities in the respondent, and the marriage gave the respondent the opportunity to become the kind of person she or he would like to be. These are items depicting the degree to which the person's view of self is enhanced by the spouse's orientations. (It is perhaps significant, in this regard, that in Tables 2–4 affirmation is revealed to have a greater impact upon self-esteem than upon mastery.) Perhaps the *content* of spouse interaction (respect, high evaluation) is more crucial than the form (listening, loving.).

Reciprocity and equity are particularly important to the employed wives, whose senses of mastery decline and depression increase when they experience demanding husbands. In an earlier paper dealing with the same data set (Vanfossen, 1981), reciprocity was found to be intertwined with the "role overload" employed wives are likely to experience because of their dual roles as employee and housekeeper. Wives who felt overwhelmed by their duties, who believed their husbands to be demanding and unwilling to help in matters in the home, and who had conflict with their husbands over these conditions, were particularly likely to be depressed women. The current study finds in addition that the level of reciprocity in marriage affects wives' feelings of mastery as well as their levels of depression.

The findings support both the functionalist and conflict views of gender roles. The functionalist view, focusing on the efficiency of the traditional division of labor within the family into expressive and instrumental roles is somewhat supported by two findings: (1) wives are slightly more likely than husbands to provide expressive support; and (2) impairments to the successful functioning of traditional gender roles are more disturbing to the respondents than impairments to the functioning of nontraditional gender roles. Thus, employed husbands are more depressed by stressful occupational conditions than are employed wives; unemployed husbands are more upset when their financial situation is poor than are unemployed wives; and employed wives are more upset by parenting problems than are employed husbands (but note here that unemployed wives are not depressed by parenting problems, which constitutes an exception to the generalization being enunciated).

Conflict theory, which illuminates dominance relations, likewise receives a modicum of support from two findings. One is that more wives than husbands report low levels of spouse reciprocity (for example 36% of the wives and 28% of the husbands agree that they give in to their spouses' wishes more than vice versa). Additionally, employed wives are more likely to express appreciation of their husbands than vice versa (according to their spouses' reports), which can be interpreted as evidence of status differentials. Nevertheless, neither functionalist theory nor conflict theory receives overwhelming substantiation from the data, which suggests that the complexity of marital realities are not fully illuminated by the theories.

IMPLICATIONS FOR INTERVENTION

The implications of these findings for the clinician treating depressed women are several. One is that to understand depression, it is quite important to look at the institutional and role context surrounding the troubled individual. Strategies oriented toward improving the job situation, reducing role overload, or solving financial difficulties may help create a context within which emotional despair can lift.

In addition, it is clear that for many depressed women the development of a more supportive relationship with the spouse would provide a firm foundation for emotional well-being. Thus, family therapy, in which husbands become involved in the clinical process, seems justified. These results have shown that women are particularly vulnerable to depression when their spouses do not appreciate them, and further that men's social training may be less likely than that of women's to include praise of another as a legitimate and desirable technique of living. Through family therapy, husbands could become sensitized to the need for sympathetic responsiveness to spouse. Thus, the therapist may find it effective to teach the spouse of the depressed client how to bestow praise, and also that it is acceptable to do so.

However, a potential problem that may need to be considered by the therapist is that the husband's evaluation of his wife may reflect society's evaluation of women. The *content* of the interaction is important here, not just the form. While it is one thing to instruct a husband in how to listen sympathetically, it is another to get him to value who and what his wife is. The insights of conflict theory are relevant: in societies still tainted by male dominance, as all industrial societies are, femininity, womanhood, and women's roles represent qualities that are less respected. There is nothing inherently unimportant, for example, about raising children to be good citizens, and yet the homemaker feels herself compelled to apologize for what is assumed to be a low-skill, low-importance set of tasks. The employed wife may be doing double-duty by working a 40-hour week and also maintaining a home, and yet her contribution is often considered to be secondary to that of the "head of the household." So long as economic and political resources rest primarily in the hands of men, male activities will be more highly valued than female activities. Thus, the deeply-rooted bases of the devaluation of femininity may pose additional barriers to therapeutic intervention.

The problem the interventionist faces, then, is in part the problem of how to counteract the societal devaluation of femininity. Final solutions are likely to come only after the gender inequities in the economic system, such as occupational sex segregation and wage differentials, are attenuated. Prior to that time, a partial solution might result from alterations in the cultural patterns that reinforce gender inequality. For example, educational programs in schools could emphasize the historical contributions of women to art, literature, and politics. Perhaps television executives could be convinced that it would be to their economic advantage to create television stories and commercials that portray women, as well as men, as being capable of taking action, being forceful, and as being worthy of respect and esteem.

In the less macroscopic arena, therapeutic interventionists could help remedy the situation by organizing and catalyzing support groups among wives aimed at helping them find sources of self-esteem and mastery independent of their roles as wives. In addition, family therapy could include exercises designed to bring to consciousness the supportive and nonsupportive interpersonal dynamics underpining the spousal relationship, exercises such as reverse role playing by husband and wife. Finally, through counseling and discussion, the clients could be made aware of the importance of interpersonal support in forestalling the negative mental health effects of occupational, parental, or financial conditions.

REFERENCES

Belle, D. (Ed.). (1982). *Lives in Stress: Women and Depression.* Beverly Hills, Calif.: Sage Publications.

Bernard, J. (1971). *Women and the public interest: An essay on policy and protest.* Chicago: Aldine.

Campbell, A. (1975). The American way of mating: Marriage si, children only maybe. *Psychology Today, 3,* 37–42.

Dean, A., & Lin, N. (1977). The stress-buffering role of social support. *Journal of Nervous and Mental Disease, 165,* 403–417.

Derogatis, L., Lipman, R., Covi, L., & Rickles, K. (1971). Neurotic symptom dimensions. *Archives of General Psychiatry, 24,* 454–464.

Gore, S. (1978). The effect of social support in moderating the health consequences of unemployment. *Journal of Health and Social Behavior, 19,* 157–165.

Gove, W. (1972). The relationship between sex roles, marital status, and mental illness. *Social Forces, 51,* 34–44.

Gurin, G., Veroff, J., & Feld, S. (1960). *Americans view their mental health.* New York: Basic.

Henderson, S. (1977). The social network, support and neurosis. The function of attachment in adult life. *British Journal of Psychiatry, 131,* 185–191.

Kaplan, B., Wilson, R., & Leighton, A. (Eds.). (1976). *Further explorations in social psychiatry.* New York: Basic.

Klerman, G., & Weissman, M. (1980). Depressions among women: Their nature and causes. In M. Guttentag, S. Salasin, & D. Belle, (Eds.), *The mental health of women.* New York: Academic.

Lerner, M. (1973). Conceptualization of health and social well-being. *Health Services Research, 8,* 6–12.

Lipman, R., Rickles, K., Covi, L., Derogatis, L., & Uhlenhuth, E. (1969). Factors of symptom distress. *Archives of General Psychiatry, 21,* 328–338.

McKee, J., & Sheriffs, A. (1959). Men's and women's beliefs, ideals and self-concepts. *American Journal of Sociology, 64,* 356–363.

Myers, J., Lindenthal, J., & Pepper, M. (1975). Life events, social integration and psychiatric symptomatology. *Journal of Health and Social Behavior, 16,* 421–427.

Nuckolls, D., Cassel, J., & Kaplan, B. (1972). Psychosocial assets, life crisis and the prognosis of pregnancy. *American Journal of Epidemiology, 95,* 431–441.

Parsons, T. (1949). An analytical approach to the theory of social stratification. In T. Parsons, *Essays in sociological theory.* Glencoe, IL: Free Press.

Pearlin, L. (1975). Sex roles and depression. In N. Datan (Ed.), *Life-span developmental psychology.* New York: Academic.

Pearlin, L., & Johnson, J. (1977). Marital status, life-strains and depression. *American Sociological Review, 42,* 704–715.

Pearlin, L., & Schooler, C. (1978). The structure of coping. *Journal of Health and Social Behavior, 19,* 2–21.

Pearlin, L., Menaghan, E., Lieberman, M., & Mullan, J. (1981). The stress process. *Journal of Health and Social Behavior, 22,* 337–356.

Rabkin, J., & Struening, E. (1976). Life events, stress, and illness. *Science, 194,* 1013–1020.

Radloff, L. (1976). Sex differences in depression: The effects of occupation and marital status. *Sex Roles, 1,* 249–265.

Rosenberg, M. (1965). *Society and the adolescent self-image.* Princeton: Princeton University Press.

Silverman, C. (1968). *The epidemiology of depression.* Baltimore: Johns Hopkins University Press.

Vanfossen, B. (1981). Sex differences in the mental health effects of spouse support and equity. *Journal of Health and Social Behavior, 22,* 130–143.

Warren, R. (1976). Stress, primary support systems, and the blue collar woman. In D. McGuigan (Ed.), *New Research on women and sex roles.* Ann Arbor, Mich.: Center for Continuing Education for Women.

Williams, A., Ware, J., & Donald, C. (1981). A model of mental health, life events, and social supports applicable to general populations. *Journal of Health and Social Behavior, 22,* 324–336.

Zelditch, M. (1955). Role differentiation in the nuclear family: A comparative study. In T. Parsons & R. Bales (Eds.), *Family socialization and interaction process.* New York: Free Press.

6

Three Mile Island: Social Support and Affective Disorders among Mothers

Zahava Solomon
Tel Aviv University

INTRODUCTION

There is some evidence that mothers of young children have elevated rates of depression (Weissman & Klerman, 1977; Brown, Bhrolchain & Harris, 1975). Clearly, not all mothers of young children however, actually develop emotional disorder, either in everyday life or even when facing adversity. This has led researchers and clinicians to search for stress mediators to explain why some women are more likely than others to develop psychiatric disorder following a stressful experience. In this chapter the Three Mile Island (TMI) nuclear disaster is employed as a "natural experiment" enabling us to put the stress moderating role of one potential stress mediator, social support, to empirical test.

The incident at the Three Mile Island (Eastern Pennsylvania, U.S.A.) nuclear facility began on March 28, 1979. It entailed radiation leaks that lasted several days. In subsequent days, it was seen as a potentially life-threatening event for many thousands of people. Although the TMI incident has been labeled a "disaster," the situation was different from previous natural or man-made disasters in many respects. Unlike other disasters, no lives were lost, no property was damaged and, although 60% of the population was evacuated, no one was subsequently relocated. Moreover, exacerbation of the initial stress continued through the study period. The "disaster" was in no small part a result of nonstop media coverage and of new reports about continuous radiation leaks and problems of decontaminating the plant.

PSYCHIATRIC DISORDER IN MOTHERS OF YOUNG CHILDREN

Mothers of young children at Three Mile Island were focused upon due to the frequent observation in epidemiological studies that women tend to have higher rates of affective disorder than men (Weissman & Klerman, 1977), and thus constitute a high-risk group. Rates of mental disorder are higher for women than men at every stage of their life cycle. Among women, the young and married were

This research was supported in part by NIMH Contract No. 278-79-0048 (SM). I wish to thank Evelyn Bromet, Ph.D. for the use of the data.

noted to exhibit the highest rates of psychopathology (Strole, Langner, Michael, Opler, & Rennie, 1962; Alarcon & Covi, 1972).

Brown et al. (1975), reported that 27% of the women they sampled with at least one child under 6 years of age had an affective disorder compared to 13% among other women. Moss and Plewis (1977), in assessing the level of mental distress (symptoms of anxiety and depression) among women with a child under 5 years of age, found that 52% had a moderate or severe distress problem in the 12-month period prior to the interview. Others found 30% of the mothers of 3-year-old children to have a depressive disorder during the year prior to interview (Richman, 1977). These studies imply that the stresses associated with caring for young children combined with other environmental stressors impinging on young women precipitated the onset of disorder.

Stresses of motherhood are related to a relatively isolated existence, little opportunity for relaxation outside the home, and the responsibility of caring for young children (Gavon, 1966). Depressed mothers reported extensive confinement to the home, resulting in drastic curtailment of outside social activities (Le Masters, 1976). The role of deficient social ties among depressed women was also suggested by Weissman and Paykel (1974). Women may have a greater requirement for social relationships and particularly for affectional ties than men and when these needs are not met the risk of affective disorder rises (Henderson, Byrne, & Duncan-Jones, 1981).

STRESS–ILLNESS RELATIONSHIP

One traditional approach in the study of the stress-illness relationship is the assessment of health effects of catastrophic events. Evidence indicating that increased morbidity follows excessive stress in concentration camps has been reported (Eitinger, 1964, 1973; Bethleheim, 1958). Following a severe tornado as many as 90% of interviewed survivors suffered from some form of acute emotional or psychosomatic effect (Fritz & Marks, 1954). However not everyone exposed to adversity subsequently exhibits disturbance. In fact, individuals vary considerably in their reaction to similar massive stressful experiences. Some individuals react to stress maladaptively or develop illness while others appear to be unaffected. The critical issue raised by this study is the need to explain why some women are more likely than others to develop psychiatric disorders when facing such massive threats as these.

SOCIAL SUPPORT AS A MODERATOR
OF STRESS

Several theorists have suggested that the noxious effects of stress may be modified or attenuated by social support (e.g., Antonovsky, 1979; Cassel, 1976). Women who do not have an intimate confidant exhibit greater psychological distress than those possessing even one intimate other (Brown et al., 1975; Miller & Ingham, 1976; Roy, 1978). Thus while mothers of young children are at high risk for psychological and physical problems, this is less so for those mothers possessing intimate ties.

The notion that under conditions of adversity most individuals find that the presence of others is not only comforting, but also promotes adaptive behavior, prevails in the literature on disasters. A number of studies of survivors of the Nazi Holocaust reported that their fantasizing about loved ones promoted coping (e.g., Eitinger, 1964). Similarly, survivors of a naval disaster reported that such fantasizing and the presence of peers enabled them to endure in their struggle for survival (Henderson & Bostock, 1977). Others, however, suggested that when disaster strikes it often involves entire social networks leaving few people to give to others (Hobfoll, 1985).

AIMS OF PRESENT STUDY

The primary aims of the study were to investigate (1) the relationship between disaster-related stress and affective disorder among mothers of young children; and (2) the role of social support as a mediator of disaster-related stress in relation to affective disorder in this group. The present nonconcurrent prospective study is part of a multicohort project that was conducted by the Psychiatric Epidemiology Training Program at the University of Pittsburgh. Women exposed to the TMI incident were studied along with a control group composed of women who resided in the Beaver County area in western Pennsylvania. Beaver County was chosen as a comparison site because nuclear reactors are located there, and the population characteristics are reasonably comparable to those of the TMI area. The reactions of these two groups of women one year after the TMI incident are focused upon in this chapter.

SAMPLE CHARACTERISTICS

While the entire population in the TMI area was exposed to the incident, mothers of preschool children were believed to constitute a particularly "high-risk" group. They were subjected to more warning than any other group, and having young children they had concerns about radiation damage to their children. Mothers of preschool children were ordered to evacuate if they resided within a 5-mile radius of the plant.

The study group was composed of 327 recent mothers who resided in the TMI area. A control group of 134 comparable recent mothers were recruited from Beaver County. The sample was selected in the following manner: all birth announcements appearing in the Dauphin, York, and Lancaster County newspapers (TMI sample) and Beaver County newspapers (comparison site) between January 1, 1978 and March 28, 1979 were examined. Lists of women living within 5-10 miles of the nuclear plants were compiled in each of the two areas. Distance from the plants was determined by checking addresses against detailed maps. These potential addresses were verified using the 1978 telephone directories. The complete lists were randomized. Letters were sent to 524 women in the TMI area, among whom 396 were contacted by telephone and found to be eligible. Of these, 327 (83%) were interviewed in the first round of interviews. Letters were sent to 251 mothers in Beaver County of whom 190 were contacted by telephone and found to be eligible. Of these, 134 (71%) were interviewed in the first round of interviews. The difference in the response rates between the two sites was surprising. In fact, a higher refusal rate was anticipated among the TMI mothers because many of them had been interviewed on one or more occasions in the past.

For the second interview, one year later, 15 women (9.4%) were lost to follow-up in the TMI group and 10 women (7.7%) were lost to follow-up in the Beaver County Group. Data analyzed in this study pertain to 436 women who were interviewed the second time: 124 women in Beaver County and 312 women in the TMI area.

The background characteristics of the mothers in the sample demonstrate that the 327 mothers in the TMI group and the 124 mothers in Beaver County were rather similar. Remarkable similarity is observed in both groups in regard to: ethnic background (96% white), age distribution (median age of 28 and over two-thirds of the mothers were under 30 years old), and family status (most mothers were married and had one or two children). Both groups were typified by stable residency in their communities. The two groups were also comparable in terms of major physical illness and past emotional problems.

Protestants were more prominent in the TMI area, whereas in Beaver County Catholics and Protestants were equally represented. TMI area mothers attained higher education levels, and more women in this group were employed outside the home. However, total reported family income was lower among the TMI mothers.

MEASUREMENTS

Sociodemographic and background information, social support, and psychiatric status were assessed.

Sociodemographic Characteristics

The background characteristics of the subjects were assessed via the Sociodemographic Questionnaire. This questionnaire was designed to collect standard social background information on age, sex, race, education, occupation, income, family size, age of children, and length of time at present residence.

Social Network

Social network variables were assessed by employing the Social Network Interview that was developed by Mueller and staff of the Psychiatric Epidemiology Program at the University of Pittsburgh.* This interview provides detailed information about an individual's social network.

The interview schedule first asked the participant to list the members of her primary social network (i.e., those persons with whom the subject has had an ongoing personal relationship during the past year). The respondent was then asked questions about each of the listed network members, and several characteristics of network structure were measured: proportion of kin and nonkin relationships, homogeneity in terms of age and sex, geographic dispersion, duration of relationship, and frequency of contact. TMI respondents were also asked whether network members were evacuated during the incident and whether the incident changed any social relationship. The individual was next asked to indicate her closest intimate

*Copies of the Social Network Interview and information about its psychometric properties may be obtained from Dr. Evelyn Bromet, Department of Psychiatry, Western Psychiatric Institute and Clinic, 3811 O'Hara Street, Pittsburgh, PA 15261.

network members and was asked questions concerning recent network changes and general satisfaction with social support that is derived from these intimate ties. In the present analysis three indices of social support were calculated:

(1) instrumental support (e.g., help in the form of running errands, loaning money, and generally doing things for the other person);
(2) expressive support (e.g., sharing intimate feelings, giving advice); and
(3) having a confiding relationship with one's spouse. The decision to employ this somewhat limited measure of confiding relationship was based on earlier reports (Brown et al., 1975; Roy, 1978) that have demonstrated the unique significance of this relationship for women.

Mental Health Status

The evaluation of mental health status entailed the measurement of both psychiatric symptomatology as well as diagnosable disorder. Psychiatric symptomatology was assessed using the Self-Report Symptom Inventory (SCL-90). The SCL-90 is composed of 90 self-report items rated on a 5-point distress scale. The scale has been factor analyzed and nine symptom dimensions have been identified, among them anxiety and depression. The SCL-90 has been well validated (Derogatis, Rickels, & Rock, 1976; Goldberg, Rickels, Downing, & Hesbacker 1976). Anxiety and depression symptoms were defined as scores above the median normative score.

A modified version of the life-time version of the Schedule for Affective Disorders and Schizophrenia (SADS-L) was used for making mental health diagnostic evaluation. The SADS is a structured interview that provides systematic and reliable data for classifying psychiatric disorders according to the Research Diagnostic Criteria (RDC) of Spitzer, Endicott, and Robins (1978). The SADS-L was selected for the present investigation because it offers a comprehensive assessment of a subject's clinical symptomatology and functioning, has been widely used in clinical investigations, and has proven reliability (Spitzer et al., 1978). Definite major depression indicates severe, prolonged depressive mood. Minor depression indicates some feelings of depression. Probable depression suggests either less severity or briefer duration of depression than definite major depression. One score was used for generalized anxiety.

INTERVIEWERS

The entire interview took 1½ hours on the average. Interviews were conducted by 37 interviewers, 26 in the TMI area and 11 in Beaver County. Interviewers were clinically experienced and highly trained individuals with a minimum of 4 years of clinical experience and a master's degree or doctorate in a relevant field. Screening also entailed an assessment of the applicant's attitudes toward nuclear power in order to eliminate candidates with strong biases for or against nuclear energy.

DATA ANALYSIS

The research question pertained to the stress social support-disorder model. This is an antagonistic model of interaction. It postulates that social support decreases the pathogenic effect of stress while in itself has no separate effect on the dependent variable. In statistical terms the model predicts second-order interaction. The relationship of three sets of variables—stress, social support, and affective disorder—was examined. Using the log-linear modeling, each possible association of the three variables was assessed in terms of its contribution to the total variance. The most parsimonious model was the most acceptable. The log-linear analysis was selected because it permits choosing among models of interaction to determine the model that best fits the data. Furthermore, it enables assessment of the contribution of a parameter to the total variance by adding that parameter to an existing model and determining whether the new model formed by adding the new parameter fits the data significantly better than the original model (Everitt, 1977). All women, TMI and Beaver County groups, are included in the following analysis.

FINDINGS

In the present study the relationship between stress, social support, and affective disorder were assessed. Specifically, the research addressed itself to two questions:

(1) Is the TMI stress related to elevated rates of affective disorder in mothers of young children?
(2) Does social support mitigate the noxious effect of the TMI stress on psychiatric status?

Effects of the TMI Disaster on Psychiatric Disorders

The one year prevalence rates of affective disorders (SADS-L) in the TMI mothers (high stress) and the low stress comparison group are displayed in Table 1. TMI women were higher than control in definite major depression, probable depression, minor depression, and general anxiety. Symptoms of anxiety were determined again by using the anxiety subscale of the SCL-90. The data on symptoms of anxiety were similar in the TMI and the Beaver County groups as the

Table 1 Distribution of depression and anxiety by site and time of onset

Outcome	TMI N	TMI (%)	Beaver County N	Beaver County (%)
Major depression				
Definite major depression with onset after TMI	22	7.05	4	3.22
Probable major depression with onset after TMI	7	2.24	2	1.61
Major depression (probable and definite) with onset before TMI	97	31.09	36	29.03
Minor depression				
Minor depression with onset after TMI	4	1.3	0	0.0
Minor depression with onset before TMI	16	5.1	10	8.0
Generalized anxiety				
Anxiety with onset after TMI	14	4.5	1	0.8
Anxiety with onset before TMI	16	5.2	2	1.6

TMI mothers reported only slightly higher rates of anxiety (45.8% vs. 41.1% Beaver County). No differences were found for symptoms of depression which were similar to levels of symptoms of anxiety. The results clearly indicate that rates of psychiatric disorder (SADS-L) of mothers were consistently higher in the TMI group than in the Beaver County group, but the rates themselves were low. This and the lack of anxious and depressive symptomatology as measured by the SCL-90 suggests that both groups were relatively healthy.

Furthermore, the rates that were observed in the present study are somewhat lower than rates reported in other community studies (Brown et al., 1975; Paykel, 1978) where subjects were not exposed to any drastic event. So, while the findings indicate that there were mental health consequences of the incident, they were not overwhelmingly drastic and negative. Mothers of preschool children who experienced the event appeared to have overcome the trauma by the first anniversary of the TMI incident. This suggests that only a small portion of the variability in the psychiatric status of the sample can be attributed to the TMI incident at this time.

Stress and Psychiatric Disorder as Moderated by Social Support

As to the second research question the causative model of stress-illness was expanded to include social support. Here the aim was to investigate the role of social support as a moderator of stress in relation to (a) depression and (b) anxiety. Three types of social support were assessed: (1) instrumental support, (2) expressive support, and (3) a confiding relationship with one's spouse. The relationship between these variables was assessed via the log-linear statistics. Fifteen log-linear analyses were computed as each measure of social support was considered separately. The relationship of the outcome measure in question, with stress and each measure of social support are depicted in Tables 2–4.

In the first five analyses, instrumental support (see Table 2) was employed as a measure of social support. Results indicated that instrumental support was not significantly linked with psychiatric disorder. This was true across all measures of depression and anxiety. Furthermore, no second-order interaction, which is a necessary condition for the mediating effect of instrumental support, was observed.

A second set of analyses was carried out using expressive support as a measure of social support (see Table 3). With regard to definite major depression and symptoms of depression no significant link between these measures and expressive support was observed. Moreover, expressive support did not appear to be operating as a moderator of stress.

Results for expressive support do, however, endorse a significant association between expressive support and major depression (definite and probable combined), generalized anxiety, and symptoms of anxiety. In all these instances this relationship was independent of stress as no second-order interaction between stress, expressive support, and affective disorder was observed. Hence, the role of expressive support as a mediator of stress was not substantiated by our data.

The third set of analyses examined the role of a confiding relationship with one's husband in attenuating the noxious effects of stress. The results depicted in Table 4 show that no first- or second-order interaction that reaches significance was noted with regard to definite major depression, definite and probable major

Table 2 Log-linear analysis of the relationship between instrumental support (A), stress (B), and affective disorder (C)

Type of support	Psychiatric outcome	AB	BC	AC	ABC	Model of best fit
Instrumental	Definite major depression	1.07	2.91	0.05	1.92	A B C
	Definite and probable major depression	1.18	3.13	0.62	2.62	A B C
	Generalized anxiety	0.72	4.68*	1.78	0.98	BC
	Symptoms of depression	1.35	7.26*	1.16	0.07	BC
	Symptoms of anxiety	1.15	0.93	0.73	1.98	A B C

Note. All χ^2 with one degree of freedom.
*$p < 0.05$.

depression, generalized anxiety, and symptoms of depression. Not having a confiding relationship with one's husband was, however, associated with elevated risk for symptoms of anxiety. Contrary to prediction, the results show that in no instance does the second-order interaction make a significant contribution. In other words, the data do not support the hypothesis that confiding relationships attenuate the pathogenic effect of stress.

On the whole, a differential effect for the different measures of social support was noted. Specifically, instrumental support appeared to be unrelated to any of the outcome measures, whereas expressive support was associated with major depression, generalized anxiety, and symptoms of anxiety. Having a confiding relationship with one's husband was linked with symptoms of anxiety only. In none of these cases, however, did social support interact with stress level to attenuate resultant disorder.

Importance of the Quality of Support

An explanation that may shed light on the differential effect of instrumental and emotional support (including a confiding relationship) is offered by Andrews, Tennant, Hewson, & Vaillant (1978). They postulate that the quality of a supportive emotional relationship rather than the quantity of the help available is the principle determinant of well-being. Thus, it may be argued that sharing

Table 3 Log-linear analysis of the relationship between expressive support (A), stress (B), and affective disorder (C)

Type of support	Psychiatric outcome	AB	BC	AC	ABC	Model of best fit
Expressive	Definite major depression	0.01	2.86	0.94	2.14	A B C
	Definite and probable major depression	0.00	2.95	4.71*	0.84	AC
	Generalized anxiety	0.11	5.01*	4.26*	0.61	AC, BC
	Symptoms of depression	0.00	6.95*	1.23	0.06	BC
	Symptoms of anxiety	0.00	0.83	3.90*	0.09	AC

Note. All χ^2 with one degree of freedom.
*$p < 0.05$.

Table 4   Log-linear analysis of the relationship between confiding relationship (A), stress (B), and affective disorder (C)

Type of support	Psychiatric outcome	AB	BC	AC	ABC	Model of best fit
Nonconfiding relationship with husband	Definite major depression	1.70	2.47	1.76	0.20	A B C
	Definite and probable major depression	1.62	2.68	0.90	0.64	A B C
	Generalized anxiety	0.02	2.78	0.83	0.21	A B C
	Symptoms of depression	0.02	5.90*	0.39	2.61	BC
	Symptoms of anxiety	0.06	0.22	4.68*	1.42	AC

Note. All χ^2 with one degree of freedom.
*$p < 0.05$.

feelings about a stressful experience and every day hassles mitigates detrimental impact. At the same time, while instrumental support makes life more comfortable, it is not related to mental health.

Lack of emotional support may also have an effect somewhat similar to that of the separate effect of stress. If Henderson & Bostock's (1977) position is adopted it appears that individuals require a minimal level of emotional support to maintain well-being. When the social environment does not meet these "attachment needs," it not only fails to facilitate coping skills, but also contributes to psychopathology. Furthermore, individuals who exhibit emotional disorders may have a "negative network orientation." This phrase, coined by Tolsdorf (1976), describes a situation where individuals are unwilling to utilize network resources in time of need. Their coping styles are inefficient and self-defeating.

Finally, the association between emotional support and psychiatric disorder may be related to the fact that these two variables are often confounded. In this regard two situations are frequently described: (1) Depressed individuals may have a negative perspective of their social world and thus falsely underestimate the extent of support available to them; and (2) The relationship between social support may be a long-term consequence of mental illness. Specifically, a deterioration of social ties may be a result of a gradual disease process. Since data in earlier studies as well as in the present investigation are cross-sectional, the interpretation of the direction of this association is difficult.

Does Social Support Moderate the Effects of Stress?

In the present study, contrary to what was hypothesized, no second-order interaction was observed between social support, stress, and psychiatric outcome. The findings suggest that emotional support exerts a deleterious effect independent of the extent of stress, but the role of social support as a moderator of stress was not substantiated.

Reviewing the literature, it appears that two trends are reported. The first body of research (e.g., Nuckols, Cassell, & Kaplan, 1972; Medalie & Goldbrout, 1976) provides evidence in support of the stress-buffering effect of social support. On the other hand, several recent studies (Andrews et al., 1978; Liem & Liem, 1976; Miller & Ingham, 1976) as well as the present study found no evidence of the mediating action of social support. Hence the second group of investigators concluded that the social support-psychopathology relationship is independent of stress. What can account for these incongruent findings? A number of explanations are offered. First, it is conceivable that conceptual and methodological differences may account for the lack of confirmation of the earlier findings. In this regard, there has been wide variability in conceptual definitions as well as in measures of social support across the various studies, as pointed out by Thoits (1982). Most investigators have not attempted to formulate a clear conceptual definition of social support, and few have attempted to develop valid and reliable measures of the construct. For example, Brown et al. (1975) and Lowenthal and Haven (1968) extracted items from available data (e.g., presence of a confidant, living alone or with others), termed these items social support, and then proceeded with analysis. Furthermore, there is some evidence that not all types and sources of social support are equally effective in reducing distress (Dean, Lin, & Ensel, 1980; Eaton, 1978). Hence, it is plausible that the particular dimensions of social ties that were addressed in this study do not interact with stress to limit strain.

Part of the problem in resolving this issue also may be related to the measures of stress typically used. In all the above-mentioned studies where social support allegedly moderates stress, stressful life events checklists were employed as a measure of stress. However, stressful life events and social support appear to be highly confounded. That is, many of the events queried in these studies involved change in one's personal network (Mueller, 1982). An example of this is provided by Hammer, Barrow, & Gutwirth (1978), who illustrate how the death of a "significant other" may mean the loss of an intimate and confiding relationship. In contrast, the measure of stress employed in the present study did not result in loss of social ties.

Choice of outcome criteria is another relevant factor. Andrews et al. (1978), reviewing studies that confirm the stress buffering effect of social support, noted that studies that had obtained a strong interaction effect (confirming the stress-mediating role) used physical illness as their outcome measure. They posit that the relationship between stress and support is different in physical and psychiatric illnesses. Hence, it may be postulated that social support and stress are related to some disease entities, but are not related to others.

A final explanation concerns the differences between studies in terms of distance in time from the event. In the current study, one year had already passed. It is conceivable that a stress-buffering effect was apparent during the immediate period following the event. One year later, the women involved seemed to have returned to reasonably normal functioning, so little residual stress may have been left to buffer (Hobfoll & Walfisch, 1984). Even if still distressed, supporters might expect women to "stand on their own two feet" and function independently by this time.

IMPLICATIONS FOR CLINICAL CARE

This study set out to investigate the role of social support in affective disorder among mothers of preschool children. The stress-mediating effect of social support was not substantiated here. At the same time, our results clearly point at a link between lack of supportive close ties and risk of affective disorders in mothers. This was most salient in regard to the more intimate social ties a woman has. This finding is consistent with an earlier observation regarding the necessity of close social ties of women for the maintenance of their well-being (Henderson, et al., 1981).

Other findings, not presented here, suggest a moderate link between symptoms and impairment of social functioning among depressed/anxious mothers.* The social functioning of women, especially when their children are young, is of considerable importance. Not only does depression cause suffering in the afflicted mothers, but it also poses a serious problem for their children. Specifically, mothers' social functioning is believed to have a crucial effect on their children's well-being. Hence, a mother who suffers from depression is less likely to engage in the much-needed affectionate and supportive relationship with her child. In light of the seriousness as well as the high prevalence of affective disorder in mothers of preschoolers, it is suggested that therapeutic intervention should be of a preventive nature and aim at:

(1) strengthening and improving the mothers' capacity to engage and maintain long-term meaningful intimate relationships;

(2) involving "significant others" in the depressed mother's social network in her treatment and mobilizing "significant others" to provide the depressed mothers with their much-needed support; and

(3) developing informal community support systems in the form of self-help groups from which participating mothers will derive support.

RESEARCH IMPLICATIONS

The stress-buffering role of social support was not confirmed by our data. However, it seems that conceptually this model remains attractive in explaining the differential effect of stress. Furthermore, since social support appears to be more amenable to change through intervention, it appears to be a fruitful field of future research. More research is needed on the model that:

(1) uses refined multidimensional measures of social support;
(2) uses truly independent sets of measures;
(3) uses a prospective design, and
(4) tests the model in relation to a variety of disease entities.

*Data is available from the author upon request.

REFERENCES

Alarcon, R. O., & Covi, L. (1972). The precipitating event in depression; Some methodological considerations. *Journal of Nervous and Mental Disease, 155,* 379–391.

Andrews, G., Tennant, C., Hewson, D. M., & Vaillant, G. (1978). Life event stress, social support, coping style and risk of psychological impairment. *Journal of Nervous and Mental Disease, 166,* 307–316.

Antonovsky, A. (1979). *Health, stress and coping.* San Francisco: Jossey-Bass.

Brown, G. W., Bhrolchain, M. N., & Harris, T. (1975). Social class and disturbances among women in an urban population. *Sociology, 9,* 225–254.

Brown, G. W., Davidson, S., Hartis, T., Maclean, U., Pollack, S., & Prudo, R. (1977). Psychiatric disorder in London and North Ulster. *Social Science and Medicine, 11,* 367–377.

Cassel, J. (1976). The contribution of social environment to host resistance. *American Journal of Epidemiology, 104,* 107–123.

Dean, A., Lin, N., & Ensel, W. M. (1980). The epidemiological significance of social support systems in depression. In R. G. Simmons (Ed.), *Research in community and mental health,* Vol. 2. Greenwich, CT: JAI Press.

Derogatis, L. R. (1977). *The SCL-90 manual F: Scoring, administration and procedures for the SCL-90.* Baltimore: Johns Hopkins University.

Derogatis, L. R., Rickels, K., Rock, A. F. (1976). The SCL-90 and the MMPI: A step in the validation of the new self-report scale. *British Journal of Psychiatry, 128,* 280–289.

Dohrenwend, B. P., Dohrenwend, B. S., Kasal, S. U., & Warheit, G. J. (1979). *Report on the task group on behavioral effects to the president's commission on the accident at Three Mile Island.* Washington, DC.

Eaton, W. W. (1978). Life events, social supports and psychiatric symptoms: A re-analysis of the New Haven data. *Journal of Health and Social Behavior, 19,* 230–234.

Eitinger, L. (1964). *Concentration camp survivors in Norway and Israel.* London: Allen & Unwin.

Eitinger, L. (1973). A follow-up of the Norwegian concentration camp survivors' mortality. *Israel Annals of Psychiatry, 11,* 199–209.

Endicott, J., & Spitzer, R. (1978). A diagnostic interview: The schedule for affective disorders and schizophrenia. *Archives of General Psychiatry, 35,* 837–853.

Everitt, B. (1977). *The analysis of contingency tables.* London: Chapman & Hall.

Fritz, C. E., & Marks, E. S. (1954). The NORC studies of human behavior in disaster. *Journal of Social Issues, 10,* 26–41.

Gavon, H. (1966). *The captive wife: Conflicts of housebound mothers.* London: Routledge & Kegan Paul.

Goldberg, D. P., Rickels, K., Downing, R., Hesbacher, P. (1976). A comparison of two psychiatric screening tests. *British Journal of Psychiatry, 129,* 61–67.

Hammer, M., Barrow, S. M., & Gutwirth, L. (1978). Social networks and schizophrenia. *Schizophrenia Bulletin, 4,* 522–545.

Henderson, S., & Bostock, T. (1977). Coping behavior after shipwreck. *British Journal of Psychiatry, 131,* 15–20.

Henderson, S., Byrne, G. O., & Duncan-Jones, P. (1981). *Neurosis and social environment.* Australia: Academic.

Hobfoll, S. E. (1985). The limitations of social support in the stress process. In S. G. Sarason & B. R. Sarason (Eds.). *Social Support Theory, research and applications.* (pp. 391–414). The Hague: Martinus Nijhoff.

Hobfoll, S. E., & Walfisch, S. (1984). Coping with a threat to life: A longitudinal study of self concept, social support and psychological distress. *American Journal of Community Psychology, 12,* 87–100.

Le Masters, E. E. (1976). Parenthood as Crisis. In: Parad, H. (Ed.), *Crisis Intervention: Selected Readings.* Family Service Association.

Liem, J. H., & Liem, R. (1976). *Life events, social supports and physical and psychological well-being.* Paper presented at the Annual Meeting of the American Psychological Association, Washington, D.C.

Lowenthal, M. F., & Haven, C. (1968). Interaction and adaptation: Intimacy as a critical variable. *American Sociological Review, 33,* 20–30.

Medalie, J. H., & Goldbrout, U. (1976). Angina pectoris among 10,000 men: I: Psychological and other risk factors as evidenced by a multitude analysis of five-year incidence study. *American Journal of Medicine, 60,* 910–921.

Miller, P. M., & Ingham, J. G. (1976). Friends, confidants and symptoms. *Social Psychiatry, 11,* 51–58.

Moss, P., & Plewis, L. (1977). Mental distress in mothers of pre-school children in inner London. *Psychological Medicine, 1,* 641–652.

Mueller, D. (1982). Social networks: A promising direction for research on the relationship of the social environment to psychiatric disorder. *Social Science and Medicine, 14,* 147–161.

Nuckolls, K. B., Cassel, J., & Kaplan, B. H. (1972). Psychosocial assets, life crisis and prognosis of pregnancy. *American Journal of Epidemiology, 95,* 431–441.

Paykel, E. S. (1978). Casual relationship between clinical depression and life events. Paper presented at the American Psychological Association, Washington, DC.

Richman, N. (1977). Depression in mothers of preschool children. *Journal of Child Psychology and Psychiatry, 17,* 75-78.

Roy, A. (1978). Vulnerability factors and depression in women. *British Journal of Psychiatry, 133,* 106-110.

Spitzer, R., Endicott, J., & Robins, E. (1978). Research diagnostic criteria: Rationale and reliability. *Archives of General Psychiatry, 35,* 773-782.

Strole, L., Langner, T. S., Michael, S. T., Opler, M. K., & Rennie, T. A. C. (1962). *Mental health in the metropolis: The midtown Manhattan study.* New York: McGraw-Hill.

Thoits, P. A. (1982). Conceptual, methodological and theoretical problems in studying social support as a buffer against life stress. *Journal of Health and Social Behavior, 23,* 145-159.

Tolsdorf, C. C. (1976). Social networks, support and coping: An exploratory study. *Family Process, 15,* 407-417.

Weissman, M. M., & Paykel, E. (1974). *The depressed woman: A study of social relationship.* Chicago: University of Chicago Press.

Weissman, M. M., & Klerman, G. (1977). Sex differences and the epidemiology of depression. *Archives of General Psychiatry, 34,* 98-111.

7

Marital and Employment Role-Strain, Social Support, and Depression among Adult Women

Carol S. Aneshensel
University of California at Los Angeles

The origins of depression among women are of considerable concern because of the greater prevalence of depression among women than men, and because depression is the most common diagnosis of mental disorder in the general population. Weissman and Myers (1978), for example, report current point prevalence rates of 6% for major and minor depressive disorders. Epidemiologic surveys using depressive symptom scales such as the Center for Epidemiologic Studies Depression (CES-D) scale used in this study have generally reported considerably higher prevalence rates (e.g., Comstock & Helsing, 1976; Frerichs, Aneshensel, & Clark, 1981). Although estimates of the sex differential in depression also vary according to the criteria used to define a case, there is abundant evidence of an overall female excess. Weissman and Klerman, in their exhaustive 1977 review, report female to male ratios of depression ranging from 1.6:1 through 2:1 for community and patient populations in the United States between 1945 and 1970. For the general community population studied in this investigation, the initial prevalence estimates yielded a sex ratio of 1.8:1 (Frerichs et al., 1981). The factors related to the occurrence of depression among these women after a period of one year are examined here with particular focus on the interplay of those factors that have been the central focus of attempts to explain the sex differential—strains surrounding occupational and familial roles.

Social explanations of the origins of depression among women and of the excess of symptomatology among women have focused on the sex-role theory explicated by Gove and others (Gove, 1972, 1979; Gove & Tudor, 1973; Gove & Geerken, 1977). This conceptualization utilizes the markedly different occupational and familial roles of men and women to explain sex differences in mental disorder in general, and in depression in particular. According to Gove (1972), it is the roles occupied by women, rather than some characteristic of women's generalized sex role, that makes women more susceptible to mental disorder.

Marital status figures prominently in this theoretical orientation. The sex differential is seen as deriving from the higher rates of disorder among married

This research was supported by grant 1-R01-MH32267 from the Center for Epidemiologic Studies, National Institute of Mental Health. The author wishes to thank Virginia A. Clark for her valuable comments and Virginia Hansen for editorial support.

women than married men, even though the married of both sexes tend to have lower rates than the unmarried (Gove, 1972, 1979; Gove & Tudor, 1973). These rates are seen as a function of the social roles typically occupied by men and women, with the roles of the married differing more than those of the unmarried. Extensive familial role demands constitute the key explanatory element, placing greater stress on married women than on married men, or on the unmarried of either sex. Empirical support for the effect of being married on the sex differential in depression has been mixed (cf. Cleary & Mechanic, 1983; Fox, 1980; Radloff, 1975).

The results of an earlier analysis of the cross-sectional data constituting the initial phase of this investigation yielded partial support for the social-role theory (Aneshensel, Frerichs, & Clark, 1981). The sex differential in depression was found to be related to the roles occupied by men and women, increasing as these roles diverge. While the sex differential tended to be larger among those with more extensive family role obligations, these groups, in general, tended to have relatively low depression levels. There was little sex difference among those with low family role obligations, but both sexes tended to have high levels of depression.

Central to the social-role theory of depression among women is the stress attendant upon various occupational and familial role constellations. Most investigations, however, particularly those directed at explaining the sex differential in depression, have treated stress as an implicit concomitant of certain roles and have focused primarily on the occupancy of those roles, rather than on the actual stressors occurring within them. Several exceptions to this generalization are instructive. Pearlin and Lieberman (1979), for example, report that women are more vulnerable than men to problems persisting within their marriages. These persistent strains are in turn related to symptoms of depression and anxiety. Key problems that persist within intact marriages are even more likely to produce distress than disruptions of the marriage. Pearlin and Johnson (1977) also report that the unmarried are both more exposed to, and more vulnerable to, persistent life strains than the married. Specifically, the unmarried are more likely than the married to experience economic strains and social isolation, and such hardships are more likely to result in depression among the unmarried. Although parental responsibilities are less concentrated among the unmarried, where they do exist they have a greater negative impact on the unmarried.

Marriage thus appears to benefit the psychological health of women, but marital stress appears to result in psychological distress. Do marital problems outweigh the advantage associated with being married? We examine this question first. Then the joint impact of strains originating in both employment and marital roles is examined, as is the possible exacerbating condition of having children in the household, and the potential ameliorating effect of social support. Before examining these relationships, a brief description of the study that forms the basis for these analyses is presented.

STUDY BACKGROUND

The Los Angeles depression study is a longitudinal survey of the antecedents and consequences of depression in the general population. The first phase consisted of a one-year panel survey which forms the basis for this chapter. A recently completed second phase extends the panel study to 4 years. In 1979,

1,003 Los Angeles County adults—a representative sample of the county—were interviewed in the first wave of the one-year panel study. A detailed description of the sampling procedures and the characteristics of the sample is reported elsewhere (Frerichs et al., 1981); the response rate of the first interview was 66%. A total of four interviews were conducted at 4-month intervals, but data are presented here for only the initial and final interviews (which span the entire study year) because the variables of central interest—marital and employment role-strain and social support—were not assessed at the two middle interviews. Of the 590 women interviewed at time one, 490 (83%) were reinterviewed in person at time four. All fieldwork for the study was conducted by professional interviewers from the UCLA Institute for Social Science Research.

The dependent measure used in this study was the Center for Epidemiologic-Studies Depression (CES-D) scale. This 20-item scale measures the current level of depressive symptomatology in the general population with the emphasis on the affective component, depressed mood. Content, criterion-oriented and construct validities, as well as test-retest and internal-consistency reliabilities, are reported in detail elsewhere (Radloff, 1977; Weissman, Sholomskas, Pottenger, Prusoff, & Locke, 1977). Respondents were asked the frequency with which they experienced each of the symptoms during the previous week, with response categories ranging from 0 for less than one day through 3 for 5 to 7 days. A cutpoint score of 16 or greater on the summated composite scale is typically used to designate individuals as depressed.

Statistical analyses were performed using the log-linear program (P4F) of the BMDP statistical software package (Dixon, 1981).* The current level of depression at time four is treated as the dependent variable in all of these analyses which statistically control for the initial level of depression at time one.

---

*This method is advantageous not only because it permits the multivariate analysis of categorical variables, but also because effects are assessed for each individual category of the variables included in the model. The adequacy of a hypothesized model is assessed by comparing the extent to which the expected cell frequencies deviate from the observed frequencies: a large likelihood ratio chi-square (LR χ^2) value relative to the degrees of freedom indicates a lack of fit, or that necessary effects have been omitted from the model. When two alternate models are nested—the parameters in one are a subset of those in the other—the likelihood ratio chi-square difference in fit tests the statistical significance of the effects not included in the more parsimonious model (with degrees of freedom equal to the difference in the number of parameters estimated in the two models). The multivariate effects of all explanatory variables on depression at time four are assessed in this manner.

Depression at time four is treated as the dependent variable in all of the models presented here. This is a special case of the general log-linear model, which does not treat any of the variables as dependent, referred to as a logit model. The explanatory variables are treated as fixed through the inclusion of the term specifying all possible interactions among the independent variables (Swafford, 1980). In this case, second-order effects involving the dependent variable are analogous main effects in analysis of variance, and third-order effects are analogous to two-way interactions; first-order effects represent unequal marginal distributions. These effects, however, are quantified here as multiplicative effects on the expected odds of being depressed. Odds are simply the frequency depressed divided by the frequency not depressed, that is, the ratio of depressed to not depressed. Effects of 1.00 indicate no effect, since they leave the product unchanged. Effects greater than 1.00 indicate increased odds, while effects less than 1.00 indicate decreased odds. The substantive interpretation of these effects is enhanced by treating one category of the independent variable as a reference category by setting its effect equal to 1.00 (no effect on the odds) and scaling the remaining effects (dividing by the value of the coefficient set to one).

Several previous reports on this study have examined some of the issues addressed here including the impact of marital and employment roles on depression among women and men (Aneshensel et al., 1981), and the effects of stress and social support on depression (Aneshensel & Frerichs, 1982; Aneshensel & Huba, 1984; Aneshensel & Stone, 1982).

MARITAL ROLE–STRAIN AND DEPRESSION

The first issue to be examined is the risk of depression associated with strain in a woman's relationship to her husband, relative to the risk associated with being unmarried. If it is marriage per se that is beneficial to a woman's psychological well-being, then even women with stressful marriages should be less likely to be depressed than the unmarried. Alternately, marital strain may offset any advantage relative to being unmarried.

Marital strain was measured with a 6-item Likert-type scale encompassing non-acceptance by spouse (e.g., I cannot be completely myself around him), and nonreciprocity (e.g., he insists on having his own way).* Using the median as a cutpoint, respondents were classified into one of the following three categories: not married, married with low strain, and married with high strain. To examine both concurrent and across-time effects, the four-way contingency table created by the cross-classification of the time one and time four measures of both marital role-strain and depression was analyzed.**

Current marital role-strain was significantly related to the outcome measure of depression ($p = .03$) while controlling for initial role-strain and depression. When current role-strain is controlled, however, initial marital role-strain was not significantly related to depression ($p = .15$), although initial depression was highly related to subsequent depression ($p < .0001$).

The magnitude of the impact of current marital role-strain on depression is given in Table 1. A review of the zero-order association indicates that married women with low strain have the lowest odds of being depressed, but that married women with high strain have greater odds than unmarried women, differences that are statistically significant [LR χ^2 (2) = 8.77, $p < .05$]. Multiplicative effects on the odds of being depressed can be quantified by use of the odds ratio, which is the odds in one category divided by the odds in a reference category. Compared to married women with low strain, those with high strain are almost three times more likely to be depressed, whereas the unmarried are approximately twice as likely to be depressed.

A somewhat different pattern is observed when the effects of previous marital role-strain and depression are controlled for in the multivariate analysis. In this case, being married with low strain is still related to decreased odds of being depressed, while being unmarried or married with high strain is related to increased

*Items for this scale were adapted from a larger pool of items constituting scales developed by Pearlin and Schooler (1978).
**Treating depression at time four as the dependent variable, the first log-linear model tested contained the third-order interaction of the independent variables, and the second-order effects pairing each of the independent variables—initial marital role-strain, current marital role-strain, and initial depression—with the dependent variable. This baseline model provided an excellent fit to the data [LR χ^2 (12) = 12.26, $p = .43$]. The effects on depression are assessed by nested model comparisons with this model.

Table 1 Effects of marital role-strain on the odds of being depressed (CES–D ⩾ 16) at time four

Marital role-strain	N	Odds^a	Odds ratio^b	Multiplicative effects on the odds, controlling for time one role-strain and depression	
				Logit coefficient^c	Dummy coefficient^d
Not married	241	.22	1.81	1.44	2.64
Low strain	146	.12	1.00	.55	1.00
High strain	103	.34	2.74	1.27	2.33

$^a N$ depressed divided by N not depressed.
^{b}Odds depressed divided by odds depressed for low strain.
^{c}From the baseline model incorporating the third-order interaction of the independent variables (current role-strain, initial role-strain, initial depression) and the second-order effects of the independent variables on the dependent variable of depression at time four.
^{d}Effect relative to low strain calculated as the logit coefficient divided by the logit coefficient for low strain.

odds. The unmarried, however, have slightly greater odds than married women of experiencing high strain. Treating low strain as the reference, it can be seen that being either unmarried or married with high strain substantially multiplies the odds of being depressed.

All of this indicates that it is not being married in and of itself that is beneficial to a woman's psychological well-being, but having a satisfactory relationship with her husband. Those who do not have an adequate relationship with their husbands have a risk of being depressed that approximates that of the unmarried. These results are consistent with those of Gove, Hughes, and Style (1983) who recently reported that unhappily married persons are in poorer mental health than the unmarried, and who concluded that while marital status is more important for males, the affective quality of marriage is more important for females.

EMPLOYMENT ROLE–STRAIN AND DEPRESSION

The second key element in the social role theory of depression among women centers on the impact of family roles on employment roles. Family obligations decrease the probability of working for women and may lead to role conflict or overload, whereas increased family role commitments, if anything, increase the probability of working for men and justify rather than conflict with extensive occupational involvement. Whereas married men typically have two potential sources of gratification—the family and work—housewives are largely restricted to one major area of gratification—the family (Gove & Tudor, 1973). Frustrated in one role, men can presumably turn to the other, but nonworking wives lack a major alternative to the family. Although employed wives and mothers have the same two potential sources of gratification available to comparable men, they presumably experience more psychological distress resulting from role overload and conflict (Gove & Tudor, 1973; Gove & Geerken, 1977).

Conflict and stress inherently surround occupational and familial roles for women. There is no simple choice to opt for one role or the other or for dual roles. Rather, the social atmosphere conspires to make the housewife role a continuing alternative to pursuing a career, and family obligations routinely necessitate compromises in career advancement. This socially structured role conflict constitutes a unique source of stress for women.

Again, attention in this area has been focused more on the occupancy of roles than on attendant strains associated with them. Thus, Haw (1982) notes that although the past 30 years have witnessed a dramatic increase in the participation of women in the work place and a qualitative change in the type of jobs that women occupy, little attention has been focused on the physical and psychological outcomes associated with work-related stress among women. Haw concludes that many of the studies on women concern employment or occupational status or workload, with the implications being that employment per se is stressful for women. Pearlin and Lieberman (1979), however, report that women are more likely to be caught up in both the loss and acquisition of jobs and to experience occupational reward deprivations while men are more often exposed to overloads and depersonalizing experiences at work.

To address these issues, we consider now the relative impact of not working and work-related strain on depression. Occupational strain was measured with a 7-item scale comprising overload (e.g., I have more work than I can handle), depersonalization (e.g., people act as if I am a person without real feelings), and inadequacy of rewards (e.g., I can count on a steady income). With the median as a cutpoint, respondents were classified as follows: not employed, employed with low strain, and employed with high strain.*

An analysis parallel to the one reported for marital role-strain was conducted to ascertain the effects of employment role-strain on depression; similar results were obtained.** The effect on depression of current employment role-strain was highly significant ($p = .008$), while the effect of initial role-strain was not significant ($p = .21$). Thus, controlling for previous depression and role-strain, employment role-strain was found to be related to the concurrent odds of being depressed.

As shown in Table 2, the zero-order effect of employment role-strain on depression is similar to that reported for marital role-strain. The odds of being depressed are least among employed women with low strain, somewhat greater among those employed with high strain, and greatest among women who are not employed, differences that are statistically significant (LR χ^2 (2) = 9.95, $p < .01$). The odds ratios demonstrate that not being employed increases the odds of depression relative to being employed in a low-strain job to a greater extent than does experiencing a high level of strain at work. The logit coefficients indicate that, controlling for previous depression and role-strain, being employed reduces the odds of being depressed, whereas not being employed increases the odds. Employed women experiencing high strain are somewhat more likely to be depressed than those with low strain, but women who are not working are three times more likely to be depressed.

In general, then, women have lower odds of being depressed if they are working irrespective of the level of strain at work than if they are not working. Work-related

---

*Items for this scale were adapted from a larger pool of items constituting scales developed by Pearlin and Schooler (1978).

**The comparable baseline model again provided an excellent fit to the data [LR χ^2 (12) = 9.08, $p = .70$]. The statistical significance of effects on depression was assessed by nested comparisons with the baseline model.

Table 2   Effects of employment role-strain on the odds of being depressed
(CES–D ⩾ 16) at time four

Employment role-strain	N	Odds[a]	Odds ratio[b]	Multiplicative effects on the odds, controlling for time one role-strain and depression	
				Logit coefficient[c]	Dummy coefficient[d]
Not employed	194	.31	2.40	1.85	3.01
Low strain	183	.13	1.00	.61	1.00
High strain	113	.20	1.56	.88	1.44

[a]N depressed divided by N not depressed.
[b]Odds depressed divided by odds depressed for low strain.
[c]From the baseline model incorporating the third-order interaction of the independent variables (current role-strain, initial role-strain, initial depression) and the second-order effects of the independent variables on the dependent variable of depression at time four.
[d]Effect relative to low strain calculated as the logit coefficient divided by the logit coefficient for low strain.

strain increases the odds of being depressed but not to the extent of not working. This result contrasts with the results reported for marital role-strain, where the odds of being depressed for married women with high strain were roughly comparable to those of being unmarried.

MARITAL AND EMPLOYMENT ROLE–STRAINS AND DEPRESSION

For both marriage and employment, then, women who occupy these roles and experience relatively low levels of strain have the lowest odds of being depressed. Women who occupy these roles and experience high levels of strain, and women who do not occupy these roles have relatively higher odds of being depressed. What, then, is the joint impact of marital and employment roles and strain? Do problems at work exacerbate the impact of problems with one's husband? Does having a relatively problem-free marriage reduce the impact of high levels of strain at work? Do marital problems have a greater impact among working than nonworking wives?

Previous comparisons have largely focused on the married and have contrasted women and men. Gove and Geerken (1977), for example, report that among the married, unemployed wives experience higher levels of frustration that seem attributable to familial role demands than do employed husbands or wives. These include incessant demands, a desire to be alone, and loneliness, frustrations which in turn help to explain the higher level of psychiatric symptomatology among unemployed wives. Other studies suggest that marital strain may have a different impact among wives who are working than among wives who are not working. Thus, Cleary and Mechanic (1983) find that marital satisfaction is less important in its effect on depression among working wives than among working men or housewives, and that job satisfaction is more important for men. Vanfossen (1981) reports that not receiving affirmation from one's husband is more associated with depression of nonemployed wives than is intimacy, whereas intimacy is more important for husbands, suggesting that marital roles impact more on identity for women than for men. For employed wives, affirmation and equity were found to be important determinants of depression, whereas intimacy was not related to depression. Furthermore, expressive support from husbands did not provide a buffer against depression associated with poor work relations. Role overload coupled with a lack of support from their husbands was associated with extremely high levels of depression.

The joint impact of family and employment roles was examined in an earlier analysis of some of the data presented here (Aneshensel et al., 1981). Among women, having a family, being married, or being employed was associated with lower levels of depression, but having both a work and a family role did not seem to provide the additional diminishing effect on depression that it had for men.

Work and family roles appear to have a similar impact on physical health status. Verbrugge (1983) notes that there is widespread concern that women's increasing involvement in multiple roles may harm their physical health due to increased stressors and decreased time to spend on health problems. She finds, however, that employed married parents tend to have the best health profile, while those with none of these roles tend to have the worst health profile. Thus, women with both job and family roles enjoyed health benefits from each role and incurred no special health disadvantage or benefit from having multiple roles. This finding is important in that physical illnesses and its restriction of normal activities acts as a stressor in elevating symptoms of depression (Aneshensel & Huba, 1984).

The joint impact of current marital and employment role-strains on depression at time four was assessed by testing a series of nested log-linear models.* Controlling for initial depression and other type of role-strain, the effects on depression of employment role-strain ($p = .04$) and marital role-strain ($p = .03$) remained statistically significant.

Conceptually, the interaction term of the two types of role-strain and depression can be interpreted as meaning that the impact of employment role-strain or marital role-strain on depression is contingent upon the other type of role-strain. This term, however, was not statistically necessary to the fit of the model to the data [LR χ^2 difference (4) = 1.84, $p = .77$]. This means that the impact of each type of role-strain on depression is relatively independent of the occupancy of the other role, or the level of strain in that role. That is, being unmarried or having high marital strain have approximately the same impact on depression among women who are not employed, women who have low strain at work, and women who have high strain at work. Similarly, not being employed or having high strain at work appear to have the same impact on depression irrespective of marital status or marital strain.

Marital and employment role-strain do not significantly interact in their impact on depression, but they do combine to produce joint effects. In the absence of an interaction effect, the combined effect on the odds depressed is the product of the individual effects for the specific categories of each of the two variables. Table 3 presents these effects for each of the nine possible combinations of marital and

---

*The baseline model containing the effects of each of these variables on depression provided an excellent fit to the data [LR χ^2 (12) = 9.18, $p = .69$]. Effects on depression and the interaction of the types of role-strain on depression were assessed by nested comparisons with this baseline model.

Table 3 Multiplicative effects on the odds of being depressed (CES–D ≥ 16) at time four relative to low marital and employment role-strain

Marital role-strain	Employment role-strain			Total
	Not employed	Low strain	High strain	
Not married	3.41	1.64	2.25	1.64
Low strain	2.08	1.00	1.37	1.00
High strain	5.47	2.63	3.60	2.63
Total	2.08	1.00	1.37	

Note. These dummy-coded multiplicative effects were obtained from the logit coefficients from the baseline model incorporating the third-order interaction of the independent variables (current marital and employment role-strains, and initial depression) and the second-order effects of the independent variables on the dependent variable of depression at time four.

employment role-strains, using those who are low on strain as the reference category.

This comparison reveals that the odds of being depressed are at least two times as great for all but two combinations of role and strain levels as they are for married employed women who are low on both types of strain. The greatest difference is for those women experiencing high strain in their marriage who are not working. These women have substantially greater odds of being depressed than women who experience high strain at work in addition to high strain in their marriages. Similarly, they have substantially greater odds of being depressed than women who are not married and who experience high strain at work. The contrast with women who are low on both types of strain is also particularly marked for women who are high on both types of strain and for women who are both unmarried and not employed.

Women who experience strain both at work and at home thus have a substantial risk of being depressed as compared to women who experience little strain in either or both roles. While there does not appear to be a synergistic relationship between these strains, they do have a cumulative, negative impact on women's psychological well-being. Having a dual role in and of itself does not appear to have this effect, but rather experiencing strain in each role is the deciding factor. In fact, dual-role women with little strain in either role appear to have the lowest risk of being depressed. Furthermore, women with marital problems who work, even in a stressful job, appear to have somewhat lower risk of being depressed than similar women who do not work. Thus, with respect to the risk of being depressed, women with marital problems appear to be better off if they are working, while women with work problems appear to be better off married only if they have satisfactory marriages.

IMPACT OF PARENTAL ROLES

We should consider, at least briefly, one further aspect of familial roles that may impact on the relationship between depression and marital or employment role-strain for women—being a mother. As with marriage and employment, being a parent is a potential source of both fulfillment and frustration. Furthermore, the presence of children may confound the impact of other sources of stress. For example, having children in the household may exacerbate the impact of work-related stress by placing additional, potentially conflicting, demands on the working mother, or may ameliorate such stress by providing an alternate source of gratification. Cleary and Mechanic (1983), for example, find that the impact on depression of being a parent, parental satisfaction, and number of minors in the household is greatest for working wives, and conclude that the combination of being a parent and working contributes to depression among women but that this combination of roles is not as stressful for men. To address such issues, separate log-linear models of depression at time four were assessed for both marital and employment role-strain, and cross-classified by parental role status: does not have children, has children living in the household, or has children not living in the household.

The results for both types of role-strain were similar. In both models tested, the effect of role-strain on depression remained statistically significant, but the effect of parental role on depression was nonsignificant, as was the interaction of parental role and role-strain on depression. The effect, then, of both employment and marital role-strain on depression was similar among women who were nonparents and mothers irrespective of whether or not their children lived with them.

This lack of a relationship may result from a difference in the meaning of parenting across the wide age range of women studied. A finer measure of strain experienced within the parenting role is needed before any definite conclusions can be drawn with respect to the effect on depression of being a mother, or the interaction of this role with other sources of strain.

IMPACT OF SOCIAL SUPPORT

Thus far, we have been concerned with the impact on depression of occupying familial and employment roles and strain in these roles. Clearly, however, stress does not always lead to psychological distress. Some who are exposed to high levels of stress remain relatively symptom-free, whereas others, with comparatively low levels of stress, experience substantial levels of depression. For example, while it may seem intuitively easy to see why women with stressful marriages and jobs tend to be depressed, many of these women do not evidence symptoms of depression. Attempts to explain why stress produces negative outcomes among only some individuals have focused in large part on the potential stress-buffering effects of supportive social ties. The critical point of the stress-buffering model is that effective social support modifies the effect of stress; specifically, the effect of stress on psychological impairment is greatest among those with limited as opposed to adequate sources of social support. In statistical terms, this amounts to specifying the presence of an interaction effect between stress and social support on depression. While most previous studies have found both stress and social support to be related to psychiatric symptoms, interaction effects have been found in only some of these studies (e.g., Brown & Harris, 1978; Eaton, 1978; LaRocco, House, & French, 1980; Warheit, 1979); others show no such effects (e.g., Andrews, Tennant, Hewson, & Vaillant, 1978; Aneshensel & Stone, 1982; Lin, Simeone, Ensel, & Kuo, 1979). These divergent results appear to be related in part to methodological issues, including the measurement of the domains and analytic strategies for assessing buffering effects (Thoits, 1982).

The major alternative to the buffering model is that support has direct, positive effects on psychological well-being by fulfilling a person's needs for affiliation, belonging, respect, social recognition, affection, and nurturance (Kaplan, Cassel, & Gore, 1977). By implication, the frustration of these needs (lack of support) may itself constitute a source of stress (Rabkin & Struening, 1976). Other analyses of the data from this study have shown that social support is related to decreases in depression (Aneshensel & Frerichs, 1982; Aneshensel & Huba, 1984), but have not supported the buffering model (Aneshensel & Stone, 1982). These results suggest that social support, instead of merely protecting an individual against the negative impact of stress, may itself be important in ameliorating depressive symptoms.

We turn now to the question of whether social support—perceived social support in this case—reduces the impact of being unmarried or not employed or of high strain associated with being married or employed. To assess perceived social support at time four, respondents were asked how often during the past 2 months there was someone who provided them with socioemotional support (e.g., was thoughtful when you were tired) and instrumental assistance (e.g., helped you with your problems).* Responses to this 6-item scale were trichotomized into categories of low, moderate, and high support.

Separate log-linear models were assessed in which the effects of either employment role-strain or marital role-strain on depression were assessed within the context of varying levels of social support.** For both types of role-strain, the effect of social support on depression was highly significant, with women who are low on support having the highest odds of being depressed.

When controlling for support and prior depression, the effect of employment role-strain on depression remained statistically significant ($p = .03$), but the interaction of role-strain and support on depression was nonsignificant ($p = .99$). Such a finding means that employment role-strain has approximately the same impact on depression among women of differing levels of perceived social support. The joint impact of role-strain and support is shown in Table 4. The effects on the odds of being depressed are expressed here in reference to those who are low on employment strain or high on perceived social support. Thus, for the joint effects the reference category is employed women of low strain who are high on social support. All other combinations of these two dimensions yield higher relative odds for being depressed. Thus, all women who perceive that they have inadequate social support have substantially higher odds of being depressed than employed women with low strain and high support, with the difference being greatest for such women who are not employed.

The results for marital role-strain are different and more complex. When controlling for support and prior depression, the effect of marital role-strain on depression becomes nonsignificant ($p = .17$), and its interaction with support on

*Items for this scale were selected from the Sense of Support Scale developed by D. M. Panagis and L. M. Adler (Unpublished manuscript, 1977).

**In each case, a baseline model was tested comprising the effects on the dependent variable of depression of each of the independent variables—initial depression, perceived social support, and either marital role-strain or employment role-strain. The baseline model provided a good fit to the data for both marital role-strain [LR χ^2 (12) = 15.67, $p = .21$], and employment role-strain [LR χ^2 (12) = 12.38, $p = .42$]. The significance of the third-order interaction of role-strain, support, and depression was assessed as the incremental fit achieved by adding the term to the appropriate baseline model. This term assesses the stress-buffering function of social support.

Table 4   Multiplicative effects on the odds of being depressed
(CES–D ≥ 16) at time four relative to low marital or
employment role-strain and high perceived social support

	Perceived social support			
	Low	Moderate	High	Total
Employment role-strain[a]				
Not employed	6.16	3.02	2.04	2.04
Low strain	3.02	1.48	1.00	1.00
High strain	3.78	1.85	1.25	1.25
Total	3.02	1.48	1.00	
Marital role-strain[b]				
Not married	5.14	.93	1.66	1.26
Low strain	1.66	2.41	1.00	1.00
High strain	4.48	4.86	2.32	2.33
Total	2.14	1.42	1.00	

[a]Dummy-coded multiplicative effects obtained from the baseline model incorporating the third-order interaction of the independent variables (current employment role-strain, perceived
social support, and initial depression) and the second-order effects
of the independent variables on the dependent variable of depression at time four.
[b]Dummy-coded multiplicative effects obtained from the model
incorporating the third-order interaction of the independent
variables (current marital role-strain, perceived social support, and
initial depression), the second-order effects of the independent
variables on the dependent variable of depression at time four, and
the third-order interaction of marital role-strain, perceived social
support, and depression.

depression is marginally nonsignificant ($p = .06$). These results appear to derive
at least in part from the significant association between support and role-strain,
with the unmarried and women with high marital strain being more likely to
perceive low levels of support than married women with low strain who are most
likely to perceive high levels of social support. (This type of association was not
found for employment role-strain and social support.) Compared to a model
containing both effects, however, the omission of the main effect on depression
of marital role-strain and its interaction with social support significantly decreases
the fit of the model to the data ($p < .05$). The differential effects on the odds of
being depressed by marital role-strain and support (including the interaction effect)
are presented in Table 4, but should be viewed with caution due to their marginal
statistical significance.

Compared to married women with low strain and high support, only one group,
unmarried women with moderate support, has slightly lower odds of being
depressed. Unmarried women with low support and married women with high
strain and low to moderate support have substantially greater odds of being
depressed. For the unmarried, the risk of depression appears in large part to be a
consequence of a perceived lack of support. Low support is not only associated
with higher odds of being depressed; the unmarried are also more likely to perceive
that they receive inadequate support. Similarly, high marital strain increases the

odds of depression when coupled with low to moderate support, and is also associated with a perception of low support.

ROLE–STRAIN AND SOCIAL SUPPORT

Certainly marriage and employment are rewarding experiences for many women and have a positive impact on their psychological well-being, but this is clearly not always the case. The results of this study suggest that slippage between the normatively prescribed constellation of adult social roles and women's actual experiences in enacting these roles may account, at least in part, for this impact on depression. Marriage and, to an increasing extent, employment, are the socially sanctioned roles for adult women. Occupancy of these roles serves to integrate the individual into the social system providing a structured means of directing behavior, maintaining identity, and achieving important life goals. The type of strain that has been examined here taps in large part a woman's sense that her expectations concerning these roles have been violated in some way. That is, in occupying these roles, she has conformed to societal expectations, but finds that her experience in these roles does not conform to the social definition of the appropriate rights, duties and patterns of behavior that adhere to the role. Women categorized as having high marital strain report that their husbands are nonaccepting of their behavior and of the type of person that they are or would like to become and also feel that the relationship is nonreciprocal. Similarly, women with high occupational strain feel depersonalized at work, perceiving that they receive inadequate rewards for their work and that their job demands are excessive. In both instances, the women apparently feel that others are not meeting their expectations and tend to perceive that they are not living up to the expectations of others. These circumstances may well lead to feelings of self-estrangement and estrangement from others that may be conducive to the development of depressive symptomatology.

The centrality of marriage and employment to adult social life highlights the importance of strain in these roles. These roles are not undertaken lightly, nor are they easily changed. The high degree of commitment to these roles magnifies the impact of problems when they occur. This is particularly true for marriage. Employment roles are not easily changed, either, without incurring potentially large negative consequences, particularly in light of the current occupational opportunity structure. With restricted alternatives, then, women with unsatisfactory marriages or jobs may feel powerless to alter the source of their strain, which may in turn be a major source of psychological distress. Similarly, transitioning from being unmarried or not working is a major role change that is largely contingent upon others. Dissatisfactions then may be seen as long-term problems that lack easily obtained alternatives. Both women who do not occupy these roles and those who experience high strain within them may therefore be vulnerable to psychological distress because they lack realistic alternatives, and perceive that the problems they are encountering will persist for long periods of time and be difficult to resolve because solutions may involve altering situations or individuals over which they have little control or which extract a high price in terms of emotional pain.

That social integration is a critical dimension linking marital roles and strains to depression is supported by the results pertaining to social support. A perception of having rewarding sustaining ties to others is related to being married, but even more so to having an accepting, reciprocal relationship with one's husband. The differences in depression among the married and unmarried appear to be strongly related to whether or not there are supportive ties to others. Unmarried women tend to perceive that they have inadequate ties to others, but those who do have such ties have decreased odds of being depressed. Married women with high strain also tend to perceive that they have inadequate support and consequently are at substantial risk of being depressed. In one sense, married women appear to have a greater potential risk than unmarried women. Their sense of social support appears to be strongly dependent upon their relationship with their husband. Indeed, a perceived lack of support may be a critical component of marital strain, or a cause of such strain. Marital problems thus pose a double threat by imposing strain and by jeopardizing intimacy.

Social support appears to have a major direct effect on women's psychological well-being. Irrespective of the level of strain in marital and employment roles, or the absence of such roles, the perception of adequate support is beneficial in and of itself, and its absence is a source of distress. Thus, close interpersonal relationships are not merely coping resources brought into play to combat persistent problems encountered in marital and employment roles. Instead, they play a major role in the maintenance of psychological well-being.

While this study has concentrated on depression as an outcome of marital and employment role-strain, it is also possible that depression impacts on these roles as well. For example, depression may be a factor contributing to not working or being unmarried, as would be predicted by a social selection model. Alternately, among the married and the working, depression may contribute to strain by impeding role performance and thereby eliciting negative reactions from others. In addition, depression may enhance the perception of strain in either of these roles, and may additionally decrease the perception of support from interpersonal relationships. Nonetheless, it is clear that role-strain, social support, and depression interact in a rather complex fashion.

The results of this study indicate that in considering the sources of depression among women it is important to examine the constellation of the social roles that they occupy, and also, the level of strain experienced in each of these roles. It is not marriage per se or employment per se that impacts on a woman's psychological state, but the quality of her experience within those roles—the extent to which these roles provide her with a sense that she is valued and accepted by others, that she is satisfactorily meeting the expectations of others, and that they are meeting her expectations. In considering marital and employment role-strains, it is clear that the total impact on the psychological state of the woman is a function of both sets of roles, and of her perceived ties to significant others.

Women experiencing strain in their marriages and in their jobs are particularly at risk, as are women who are neither employed nor married. Women who are not working and experiencing problems with their husbands are also at risk, in part because of a perceived lack of support. Conversely, women who are both working in a situation that produces little strain and who have an accepting and reciprocal relationship with their husbands have the best odds of psychological well-being.

REFERENCES

Andrews, G., Tennant, C., Hewson, D. M., & Vaillant, G. E. (1978). Life event stress, social support, coping style, and risk of psychological impairment. *Journal of Nervous and Mental Disease, 166*, 307–316.

Aneshensel, C. S., Frerichs, R. R., & Clark, V. A. (1981). Family roles and sex differences in depression. *Journal of Health and Social Behavior, 22,* 379-393.

Aneshensel, C. S., & Frerichs, R. R. (1982). Stress, support, and depression: A longitudinal causal model. *Journal of Community Psychology, 10,* 363-376.

Aneshensel, C. S., & Stone, J. D. (1982). Stress and depression: A test of the buffering model of social support. *Archives of General Psychiatry, 39,* 1392-1396.

Aneshensel, C. S., & Huba, G. J. (1984). An integrative causal model of the antecedents and consequences of depression over one year. In J. R. Greenley (Ed.), *Research in community and mental health,* (Vol. 4). Greenwich, CT: JAI Press.

Brown, G. W., & Harris, T. (1978). Social origins of depression: A study of psychiatric disorder in women. London: Macmillan.

Cleary, P. D., & Mechanic, D. (1983). Sex differences in psychological distress among married people. *Journal of Health and Social Behavior, 24,* 111-121.

Comstock, G. W., & Helsing, K. J. (1976). Symptoms of depression in two communities. *Psychological Medicine, 6,* 551-563.

Dixon, W. J. (Ed.). (1981). *BMDP Statistical Software 1981,* Berkeley: University of California Press.

Eaton, W. W. (1978). Life events, social supports, and psychiatric symptoms: A re-analysis of the New Haven data. *Journal of Health and Social Behavior, 19,* 230-234.

Fox, J. W. (1980). Gove's specific sex-role theory of mental illness: A research note. *Journal of Health and Social Behavior, 21,* 260-267.

Frerichs, R. R., Aneshensel, C. S., & Clark, V. A. (1981). Prevalence of depression in Los Angeles County. *American Journal of Epidemiology, 113,* 691-699.

Gove, W. R. (1972). The relationship between sex roles, marital status, and mental illness. *Social Forces, 51,* 34-44.

Gove, W. R. (1979). Sex differences in the epidemiology of mental disorder: Evidence and explanations. In E. S. Gomberg & V. Franks (Eds.), *Gender and disordered behavior: Sex differences in psychopathology.* New York: Brunner/Mazel.

Gove, W. R., & Geerken, M. R. (1977). The effect of children and employment on the mental health of married men and women. *Social Forces, 56,* 66-76.

Gove, W. R., Hughes, M., & Style, C. B. (1983). Does marriage have positive effects on the psychological well-being of the individual? *Journal of Health and Social Behavior, 24,* 122-131.

Gove, W. R., & Tudor, J. F. (1973). Adult sex roles and mental illness. *American Journal of Sociology, 78,* 812-835.

Haw, M. A. (1982). Women, work and stress: A review and agenda for the future. *Journal of Health and Social Behavior, 23,* 132-144.

Kaplan, B. H., Cassel, J. C., & Gore, S. (1977). Social support and health. *Medical Care, 15,* 47-58.

LaRocco, J. M., House, J. S., & French, J. R. P., Jr. (1980). Social support, occupational stress, and health. *Journal of Health and Social Behavior, 21,* 202-218.

Lin, N., Simeone, R. S., Ensel, W. M., & Kuo, W. (1979). Social support, stressful life events, and illness: A model and an empirical test. *Journal of Health and Social Behavior, 20,* 108-119.

Pearlin, L. I., & Johnson, J. S. (1977). Marital status, life-strains and depression. *American Sociological Review, 42,* 704-715.

Pearlin, L. I., & Lieberman, M. A. (1979). Social sources of emotional distress. In R. G. Simmons (Ed.), *Research in community and mental health,* (Vol. 1). Greenwich, CT: JAI Press.

Pearlin, L. I., & Schooler, C. (1978). The structure of coping. *Journal of Health and Social Behavior, 19,* 2-21.

Rabkin, J. G., & Struening, E. L. (1976). Life events, stress, and illness. *Science, 194,* 1013-1020.

Radloff, L. S. (1975). Sex differences in depression: The effects of occupation and marital status. *Sex Roles, 1,* 249-265.

Radloff, L. S. (1977). The CES-D scale: A self-report depression scale for research in the general population. *Applied Psychological Measurement, 1,* 385-401.

Swafford, M. (1980). Three parametric techniques for contingency table analysis: A nontechnical commentary. *American Sociological Review, 45,* 664-690.

Thoits, P. A. (1982). Conceptual, methodological, and theoretical problems in studying social support as a buffer against life stress. *Journal of Health and Social Behavior, 23,* 145-158.

Vanfossen, B. E. (1981). Sex differences in the mental health effects of spouse support and equity. *Journal of Health and Social Behavior, 22,* 130-143.

Verbugge, L. M. (1983). Multiple roles and physical health of women and men. *Journal of Health and Social Behavior, 24,* 16-30.

Warheit, G. J. (1979). Life events, coping, stress, and depressive symptomatology. *American Journal of Psychiatry, 136,* 502-507.

Weissman, M. M., & Klerman, G. L. (1977). Sex differences and the epidemiology of depression. *Archives of General Psychiatry, 34,* 98-111.

Weissman, M. M., & Myers, J. K. (1978). Affective disorders in a US urban community. *Archives of General Psychiatry, 35,* 1304-1311.

Weissman, M. M., Sholomskas, D., Pottenger, M., Prusoff, B. A., & Locke, B. Z. (1977). Assessing depressive symptoms in five psychiatric populations: A validation study. *American Journal of Epidemiology, 106,* 203-214.

8

Stress, Coping, and the Social Milieu of Divorced Women

Brian L. Wilcox
University of Virginia

Marital disruption is widely recognized as a significant disruptive force in the lives of those who experience it. This fact is particularly troubling in light of the current incidence of marital separation and divorce. While sources differ in their estimates of the numbers of persons currently experiencing marital disruption and their prognostications for the future, all sources agree that a substantial proportion of the population has been or will be affected in some way by a disrupted marriage. The total number of divorces has risen from .4 million in 1960 to approximately 1.1 million in 1979, and the total number of persons directly affected by these divorces (spouses and children) is now around 3.3 million per year (Glick, 1979).

The consequences of marital disruption have been examined from a wide variety of perspectives. Epidemiologists, for example, have documented a consistently strong relationship between marital status and utilization of health and mental health services (Bachrach, 1976; Verbrugge, 1979). Psychologists have directed their attention largely to the emotional and developmental consequences of the aftermath of divorce, focusing on both the spouses and their children (Hetherington, Cox, & Cox, 1978). Sociologists have attended primarily to the social and economic consequences of marital disruption (Brandwein, Brown, & Fox, 1974; Espenshade, 1979). The picture that emerges from these diverse lines of inquiry portrays marital disruption as a uniformly negative social stressor.

One interesting finding that emerges from a careful review of both the clinical and empirical literature on divorce is that the experience of divorce is hardly uniform. One is struck by the diversity of reactions to divorce and the variability in the nature of the process of marital disruption itself. Some individuals appear to undergo intense and sustained emotional turmoil following the termination of a marital relationship, while others appear to experience little more than a sense of relief that an oppressive relationship is ended. The process of marital disruption runs from smooth and simple to stormy and complex. As the nature of divorcing in the United States changes, it will be interesting to observe whether procedural innovations (such as no-fault divorce and divorce mediation) and changing norms and attitudes will alter the nature of the reactions to divorce.

The research reported in this paper was supported by a grant from the University of Virginia Research Policy Council.

My gratitude is expressed to Linda Johns, Kim Campbell, Diane Kaseman, and Mary Hudson, who contributed to the data collection process.

In any event, the diversity of reactions to marital disruption, and the variability in the nature of the experience of divorce, is sometimes masked by a tendency among researchers to portray divorce as a "stressful life event," as an independent variable with a unitary stimulus value. This type of misconception is reinforced by the appearance of divorce on most (if not all) life event checklists. The association of a single "readjustment weight" with divorce on many checklists further augments this misconception. The intent of this chapter is to dispel this notion by reviewing evidence that portrays marital disruption as a complex stressor sequence experienced in different ways by different individuals. In developing this theme, I will devote particular attention to the effect of the divorcing person's social milieu on the divorce process and the effect of the divorce process on the divorcing person's social milieu. Furthermore, the results of a recently completed longitudinal study of the stress and coping process following marital disruption will be described. In keeping with the overall theme of this volume, the research reported here will focus on stress, coping, and the social milieu of a sample of divorced women.

DIVORCE AS A COMPLEX STRESSOR SEQUENCE

In an excellent article, Bohannan (1970) sets out some of the major life domains that might be affected by marital disruption:

> I have called these six overlapping experiences (1) the emotional divorce, which centers around the problem of the deteriorating marriage; (2) the legal divorce, based on grounds; (3) the economic divorce, which deals with money and property; (4) the coparental divorce, which deals with custody, single parent homes, and visitation; (5) the community divorce, surrounding the changes of friends and community that every divorcee experiences; and (6) the psychic divorce, with the problems of regaining individual autonomy (p. 34).

These categories, while largely conceptually derived, fit nicely with the empirical literature describing the process of divorce.

Numerous studies have noted that the earliest focal stressor for divorcing individuals is the emotional trauma associated with the recognition that the marital relationship is in danger of ending (Bloom & Caldwell, 1981; Goode, 1956; Weiss, 1976). Emotional trauma seems to be near its peak for women just prior to actual separation; men, on the other hand, experience their highest levels of emotional and behavioral symptomatology after the separation has commenced (Bloom & Caldwell, 1981). This should not be taken to imply, however, that the emotional reactions to marital disruption are speedily resolved. Chiriboga & Cutler (1977) note that a sizable proportion of the subjects in their study continued to experience various forms of emotional trauma well after the finalization of the divorce.

Later emotional turmoil seems to be centered less around the disruption of the marital relatioship and more around the strains created as a consequence of the divorce. The legal proceedings surrounding divorce are viewed by many as a significant source of stress. This assumption has undergirded the efforts by lawmakers to move away from the once predominant adversarial approach to divorce proceedings. Research on this issue has been inconclusive; while data suggest that encounters with the legal system are clearly burdensome, these encounters do not appear to affect social and psychological adjustment (Spanier & Anderson, 1979; Spanier & Castro, 1979). Economic concerns appear to be a major source of postdivorce stress, particularly for women (Brandwein et al., 1974; Espenshade, 1979; Weitzman, 1981) and especially for women supporting young children (Hetherington, Cox, & Cox, 1979a; Ross & Sawhill, 1975). Strains appear to result from a lack of knowledge about financial matters and money management (although divorced women appear to actually manage their money better than their former spouses; see Hampton, 1975), the depletion of financial assets, the failure of the former spouse to provide child support, and the lingering effects of financial discrimination with respect to insurance, credit, mortgages, etc.

A central source of stress, particularly for women, is the parenting role. Hetherington and her colleagues (1979; Hetherington et al. 1978; 1979a; 1979b) detail the types of changes in parent-child relationships brought about by divorce. Divorced mothers tend to rely heavily on negative behaviors such as the use of negative sanctions and commands, especially with their sons. The parent-child relationship, being as highly valued as it is as a source of satisfaction for most parents, is particularly stressful for divorced parents, as what was once a rewarding relationship becomes a source of concern. Fortunately, this situation appears to resolve itself in a relatively brief period of time. Hetherington et al. (1979a), report that the first year after divorce is the most problematic time period, and that by 2 years after divorce the parenting practices and mother-child relationships have substantially improved.

Another considerable source of stress that is central to the theme of this volume is the effect marital disruption has on interpersonal relationships. It must also be noted now, however, that the divorced person's interpersonal relationships serve as a source of support and strength as well as a source of stress. I will first examine the issue of divorce as a disruptive force in interpersonal relationships, and then will consider the supportive roles that these relationships play.

The process of marital disruption alters virtually every major role fulfilled by an individual. Inasmuch as this is the case, these role changes have reverberating effects throughout the interpersonal network. Nearly all of the divorcee's relationships change to some degree; some relationships are strengthened in the process, some seem to wither. The variety of changes that occur have been described by Weiss (1975, 1979). In the short run, many divorced women perceive their social relationships as taking a change for the worse. In a recent study, Wilcox (1981) reports that most women experience considerable "turnover" in their network of supportive others following a divorce. The average turnover in these networks was 58.5%; the average network also decreased in size by about three members. The changes appear to have been particularly acute for those women whose predivorce friendships were somehow dependent on the link between husband and wife. In quite a number of cases the predivorce friendships of the wives were with the spouses of their husband's friends and business associates. These types of friendships often cooled or vanished altogether following the separation. The women in this study also reported feeling initially estranged from their old friends as well, although this appeared to be due as much to the divorcing women's own uncertainties about how to deal with some old friends who were part of the "couple" world, and these feelings of estrangement were generally short-lived. Relationships with family members can also be strained by the occurrence of a divorce. As Weiss (1975) points out, "parents, especially, assume the right to comment on the separation, to criticize it, to disapprove or approve of it, perhaps going on until the separated individual is driven to exasperation" (p. 132). Again, Wilcox (1981) reports that his sample of divorced women found their family members to be sources of considerable stress as well as support.

In addition to being potential sources of stress, the social relationships of divorcing persons are important sources of emotional support and instrumental assistance. In an early study of single-parent families, Bernard (1964) noted that those divorced women who were a part of a caring, supportive network of friends and family members seemed to adapt more easily to the demands of single parenthood than women who were more isolated from potential sources of support. This observation has been confirmed by a variety of investigators. Colletta (1979) reports a significant relationship between the amount of support received (and satisfaction with that support) and the child-rearing practices of a sample of divorced mothers. Those mothers receiving what they viewed as adequate support interacted with their children in a more positive, open fashion than did those mothers who reported support deficits. In a second study (Raschke, 1977), postdivorce adjustment was found to be significantly associated with the respondent's level of social participation and perceived level of support. This relationship held even when statistical controls for age and sex were utilized.

Two studies have examined the patterns of help-seeking following divorce. Chiriboga, Coho, Stein, and Roberts (1979) found that friends, relatives, and counselors were the sources of support most frequently turned to. These researchers found a significant positive relationship between the degree of stress experienced and the degree of utilization of support resources. A recent study by Wilcox and Birkel (1983) paints a somewhat more complex picture of the help-seeking process following divorce. They report that the source of support chosen is dependent in part on the nature of the stressor as well as on the structure of the help-seeker's support network. For example, women with loose knit (low density) networks were most likely to rely on their own resources or turn to friends when coping with a major disagreement with a family member; women with tight knit (high density) networks tended to rely largely on themselves but also on professional helpers.

The relationship between characteristics of one's social support network and adjustment has been the subject of two recent studies. Wilcox (1981) found a significant relationship between network density (the ratio of actual to possible social relationships between network members) and adjustment of women after one year of divorce. Women who showed various signs of successfully adjusting to divorce had significantly less dense postdivorce networks than did those women exhibiting moderate to high levels of distress. These results, which parallel Hirsch's (1980) findings in a study of recent widows suggest that low density networks may be predictive of more effective coping by divorcees. While this is literally the case, the full picture is somewhat more complex. Low density networks may be more adaptive than high density networks in situations that result in considerable disruption of one's major social roles for a variety of reasons. Hirsch (1979) suggests that low density networks contain a greater diversity of role-partners who can facilitate coping with new role demands, and that the probability of finding another person whose needs and interests are congruent with one's own is greater in a low density network. Furthermore, high density networks are frequently (but not always) dominated by family members who, while frequently supportive, are viewed as inappropriate sources of help for certain kinds of problems, such as sexual matters, and sources of stress in many instances (Wilcox, 1981). These correlational results are complicated by the fact that measures of density are actually rather crude indices of network structure, and fail to reflect the inherent structural variability of networks of similar or identical densities. Close examination of most low density networks reveals that they are composed of several segments, frequently differentiated on the basis of relationship type (e.g., family, friends, co-workers, neighbors, etc.). These segments vary considerably in density, although, on the average, they are relatively loose knit. Nevertheless, most of these low density networks contain segments that themselves are high density. Few of the high density networks, however, seem to contain low density segments. It may be, then, that low density networks are more strongly associated with positive coping and adjustment than high density networks because they offer the advantages of both structural arrangements (see Wilcox & Birkel, 1983).

Finally, the relationships between network structure, support, and psychological well-being are described by McLanahan, Wedemeyer, & Adelberg (1981). These researchers report a relationship between network type ("family of origin," extended, and conjugal networks) and the availability of different types of social support. Furthermore, they note that the relationship between network structure and well-being was contingent upon the role orientation of the women in their sample; women desiring to establish a new identity found more support for that orientation in low density networks; women attempting to reaffirm their existing identities found high density networks most facilitative of that goal. Additionally, McLanahan et al. found that many of the divorcees in their sample changed both their role orientations and their dominant network structures over time.

STRESS AND THE SOCIAL MILIEU OF DIVORCE: A LONGITUDINAL STUDY

The preceding review, which is in no sense exhaustive, does illustrate some of the problems an investigator must confront when studying stress and coping in relationship to marital disruption. First, marital disruption is an extremely complex stressor sequence. As previously mentioned, the reactions to and the process of marital disruption are impressive in their variability. Some individuals adapt with seeming ease while others show signs of distress years later. Likewise, for some individuals the adaptations required are relatively minor while for others they are extensive. Studies of the stress and coping process following marital disruption have only recently begun to reflect these complexities in the research designs used. Second, the relationship between marital disruption and the individual's social milieu is equally complex. The majority of studies have focused solely on the potential positive aspects of social relationships, although, as indicated in the foregoing review, one of the more stressful consequences of a divorce seems to stem from the changes that occur in one's social milieu. Researchers must view the social milieu as a potential source of stress as well as a potential source of support.

The present study sought to contribute to the knowledge base of stress and coping following marital disruption by viewing both divorce and the social milieu in a somewhat more differentiated fashion than is usual. A sample of recently divorced women were studied intensively for the first 2 years following their divorces. Particular attention was devoted to detecting changes in the nature of the adaptational demands placed on these women over time. Another central theme guiding the study was the relationship between the changing adaptational demands and the role played by the social milieu in either facilitating coping or exacerbating distress.

METHODOLOGY

Sample

Data for this study were derived from a series of interviews conducted with and journals kept by 100 recently divorced women, as well as from a sample of 100 stably married women matched with the divorced sample on age, age at first marriage, and number of children. The divorced women were identified and contacted through court records in Charlottesville and Albemarle county in central Virginia. The sample of married women was recruited from a variety of neighborhood organizations. Only women who were divorcing for the first time were included in the divorced sample; women in the comparison group were all in their first marriages.

In recruiting the divorced sample, 121 women were contacted by a research assistant before the desired sample size of 100 was achieved, resulting in a response rate of 81%. During the first 3 months of the study 9 of the original 100 women moved from the area of the study and were replaced. Another seven of the women in the divorced group left the area subsequent to this initial period and were not replaced. Additionally, three women decided to withdraw from the study after participating for nearly a year and, thus, were not replaced. Those women completing the study ($n = 90$) were compared with those who completed only a portion of the study ($n = 10$) with respect to age, number of children, length of separation prior to divorce, and initial level of psychological and somatic distress. None of these variables significantly discriminated between the two groups.

In order to arrive at a comparison sample of 100 stably married women (76%), 132 women were contacted. Of that group six women failed to complete the final stages of the study. Additionally, two of the women in the comparison group separated from their spouses during the course of the investigation and were therefore excluded from all analyses. A demographic profile of the total sample is provided in Table 1.

Table 1 Demographic characteristics of study samples (mean values)

Demographic variable	Divorced sample ($n = 90$)	Comparison sample ($n = 91$)
Age	36.2	35.1
Age at 1st marriage	20.4	21.0
Education (grade level)	13.6	14.0
Number of children	1.4	1.7

Note. None of the means differ significantly.

Procedure

The data collection procedure was conducted over a 23-month period for each subject. The measures used in the study were derived from interviews, structured journals kept by the participants, and self-report questionnaires.

Interviews

All of the women were first interviewed approximately one month after their divorce was finalized. This initial 3-hour interview accomplished several tasks. During the interview, respondents completed a thorough demographic history, a series of psychological measures assessing perceived social competence (Helmreich & Stapp, 1974), self-esteem (Rosenberg, 1965), mood (McNair, Lorr, & Droppleman, 1971), depression (Radloff, 1977), a measure of psychophysiological distress based on Langner's (1962) symptom checklist, and a measure of general life satisfaction, the Index of Well-Being (Campbell, Converse, & Rodgers, 1976). An additional three measures were developed specifically for the present study and administered during the initial interview. The Domains Satisfaction Scale was based on the work of Campbell et al. (1976), and assessed the respondents' satisfaction with some specific life domains. These included family life, health, neighborhood, friendships, housework, employment, leisure activities, standard of living, and savings and income. Satisfaction with each of these life domains was measured along a 7-point scale ranging from completely satisfied (7) to completely dissatisfied (1). An additional domain question concerning satisfaction with marriage was asked of the comparison group subjects. Respondents also completed an extensive social network assessment questionnaire (Wilcox, 1981). During the network assessment, data were collected on several structural characteristics of networks (size, density, multiplexity, boundary density) as well as the frequency of interaction with network members, and the spatial dispersion and durability of the relationships. Finally, a scale to measure perceptions of social support availability, the Index of Perceived Support, was administered to all subjects. This scale taps four support dimensions: emotional, appraisal, informational, and tangible support. Respondents were also asked to indicate the likely sources of each type of support. Additionally, respondents were asked to evaluate each of the supporters mentioned as a potential source of conflict and strain as well as support. Ratings on the Conflict-Strain Scale varied from 1 (not a source of conflict or strain) to 5 (a source of considerable conflict or strain).

Additional interviews were conducted at 12 and 24 months postdivorce. These interviews were identical with the one month interview with the single exception that the demographic history was excluded.

Questionnaires

At 6, 12, 18, and 24 months postdivorce, each subject received and completed the Hassles and Uplifts Scales (Kanner, Coyne, Schaefer, & Lazarus, 1981). These scales were designed to assess the relatively minor negative and positive events experienced by persons on a daily basis. Respondents were asked to report the experience of hassles and uplifts over the prior month.

Journals

During weeks 8, 16, 24, 60, 68, and 76 of the study, respondents were asked to keep journals over the next 7-day period detailing any problems they confronted and how they dealt with those problems. A detailed form for reporting coping strategies was developed based on the Ways of Coping Checklist created by the Berkeley Stress and Coping Project (Folkman & Lazarus, 1980). Particular emphasis was placed on the help-seeking activities of the respondents. The respondents were requested to complete a coping strategies checklist for each problem mentioned during the 7-day period.

RESULTS AND DISCUSSION

The absolute quantity of data precludes a full reporting of all analyses relevant to the nature of the stress and coping process and the particular role played by the social milieu of the divorced women in that process. An attempt will be made to highlight those analyses which, first, contrast the experiences of divorced versus nondivorced women and, second, explicate the relationship between the social milieu and processes of adaptation and adjustment.

Problem Domains

The nature of the stressors differentially confronted by the divorced and nondivorced respondents was examined in several ways. First, separate multivariate analyses of variance were conducted for the three administrations (at 1, 12, and 24 months postdivorce) of the Domains Satisfaction Scale. The mean values for each subscale at each of the three administrations appear in Table 2. All three of the overall MANOVA F tests were significant ($p < .05$). Univariate ANOVAs were conducted to provide a more fine-grained picture of these results. At the time of the first administration, the divorced respondents scored significantly lower than the nondivorced sample on every domain subscale. By 12 months postdivorce, the divorced respondents reported significantly lower levels of satisfaction with the

Table 2 Mean values for the domain satisfaction scales at each administration

Scale	Divorced sample ($n = 90$)			Comparison sample ($n = 91$)		
	1 mo.	12 mo.	24 mo.	1 mo.	12 mo.	24 mo.
Family life	3.13*	4.29*	4.54*	5.84	6.01	6.22
Health	4.44*	5.28	5.43	5.76	5.65	5.86
Neighborhood	4.53*	5.38	5.67	5.92	6.13	6.04
Friendships	4.92*	6.15	6.10	6.42	6.36	6.51
Housework	3.67*	3.99*	4.24*	5.78	5.62	5.60
Employment	4.16*	4.71*	5.06	5.43	5.40	5.57
Leisure activities	3.04*	4.43*	5.62	5.95	6.20	6.14
Standard of living	2.79*	3.16*	3.92*	5.26	5.40	5.40
Savings and income	2.64*	2.77*	2.98*	4.55	4.47	4.53

Note. Statistical comparison between groups were made only at corresponding time intervals (1 mo. with 1 mo., etc.).
*$p < .05$.

Table 3 Mean values for hassles and uplift scales at each administration

	Divorced sample		Comparison sample	
Administration	Hassles	Uplifts	Hassles	Uplifts
6 months	33.7*	21.5*	20.2	26.4
12 months	28.1*	19.3*	22.4	25.7
18 months	23.2	19.6*	18.9	24.8
24 months	21.8	24.0*	19.6	28.1

*$p < .05$.

following domains: family life, housework, employment, leisure activities, standard of living, and savings and income. Following the third administration (24 months) the divorced women reported significantly lower levels of satisfaction on only four of the nine subscales: family life, housework, standard of living, and savings and income. Additionally, the divorced women reported being significantly more satisfied with their friendships.

A second set of analyses focused on the differential experience of hassles and uplifts across four different time periods (6, 12, 18, and 24 months postdivorce). Again, separate MANOVAs were calculated for each of the time periods. The mean values for the hassles and uplifts subscales are presented in Table 3. The hassles-uplifts MANOVA at 24 months failed to reach statistical significance; the other three analyses were significant. Univariate ANOVAs were again conducted. At 6 and 12 months, the divorced respondents reported significantly more hassles and significantly fewer uplifts. At 18 months postdivorce, the two groups still differed significantly with respect to the frequency of reported uplifts but not with respect to hassles. Again, at 24 months the two groups differed significantly with respect to the frequency of reported uplifts, although the difference was modest and, due to the sizable correlation between the hassles and uplifts scales, the MANOVA was not significant.

Finally, the two groups were compared with respect to the types and numbers of problems indicated in their journals. The divorced respondents reported significantly more problems for five of the six journal periods, the lone exception being week 60. The mean number of problems reported per week is presented in Table 4. A close examination of the journal responses revealed some interesting

Table 4 Mean number of problems reported in journals at each administration

Administration	Divorced sample	Comparison sample
Week 8	9.2	4.4
Week 16	8.6	5.1
Week 24	7.7	3.7
Week 60	5.4	5.5
Week 68	7.6	5.3
Week 76	6.9	4.8

Note. All comparisons are significantly different, $p < .05$, except week 60, which is nonsignificant.

differences paralleling the findings from the Hassles and Uplifts scales. The divorced respondents, for example, frequently reported that their problems stemmed from the absence of positive events rather than a particularly high incidence of negative events. One woman summarized her situation in the following words: "It's not so much that I'm overwhelmed by problems like taking care of my child or paying the rent or fighting with my ex-husband or my family. I've learned to deal with those things. What really bothers me is a feeling I have that my life should be more than it is, that nothing much good is happening." This trend toward reporting fewer positive experiences did, however, decrease with time. The one type of problem that seemed to persist centered around continued concerns about child-rearing issues. The divorced mothers frequently mentioned problems concerning their children's behavior at home. Many of these mothers expressed considerable feelings of guilt about not spending enough time with their children. This finding is interesting in light of another set of results indicating that the two groups of mothers did not differ with regard to the amount of time spent interacting with their children.

These three sets of results indicate that those women comprising the divorced sample do indeed seem to be exposed to greater numbers of problems in a variety of life domains than the comparison sample. Shortly after the divorce, these women reported significantly higher rates of daily hassles and general problems, significantly lower rates of uplifts, and significantly greater dissatisfaction with the entire range of life domains. By the end of the 2 year period following divorce, the differences between the two groups were still apparent but not nearly as striking. Significant differences still existed with respect to general problems, uplifts, and four of the domain satisfaction scales. The continuing areas of stress seem to center around family life and child-rearing concerns, economic worries, and the absence of positive events.

Psychological Well-Being

Several different measures were used in an attempt to capture the range of adjustment reactions experienced by the divorced women. These measures ranged from an instrument designed to assess one's general sense of life satisfaction to measures of depression and psychophysiological distress. Because of the different nature of each of these indicators, each measure was analyzed separately using a repeated measures analysis of variance. The two groups differed significantly on all three measures. The divorced sample scored significantly lower than the comparison group on all three administrations of the Index of Well-being (Campbell et al., 1976). The mean scores for the two groups were 6.62, 9.84, and 9.77 for the divorced sample; 11.49, 11.21, and 12.12 for the comparison sample. The two groups also differed significantly across all three administrations of the measure of depression (CES-D; Radloff, 1977), with the divorced group scoring significantly higher. The mean CES-D scores were 22.23, 18.44, and 14.92 for the divorced sample and 8.84, 8.09, and 8.35 for the comparison sample. Another way to examine the scores on the CES-D is to look at the percentage of persons scoring above certain cutoff points thought to be associated with a high probability of being identified as a "case." The application of the traditional cutoff point, 16, results in 12% of the comparison sample and 29% of the divorced sample being identified as "cases" at 24 months postdivorce. It should be noted, however, that the use of such cutoff scores typically results in a high false positive rate (Myers & Weissman, 1980). Finally, the two groups differed significantly on the first two administrations of the measure of psychophysiological distress, with the divorced women showing initially higher levels of distress. The mean scores for the two samples were 2.93, 2.42, and 1.98 for the divorced sample; 2.01, 1.83, and 1.95 for the comparison sample.

The results from these measures of psychological well-being suggest that the period following divorce is a stressful time in these women's lives, and that this interval of adaptation may last longer than commonly believed. Even at the end of the 2 year follow-up period the divorced group continued to score markedly higher on the measure of depression and substantially lower on the measure of life satisfaction. Over twice as many of the divorced women scored at or above the CES-D cutoff score of 16 than was the case for the comparison sample. Nevertheless, it should be kept in mind that even at the assessment occurring one month following the divorce, over 50% of the divorced women scored within the "normal" range on the CES-D, and that by the end of the study over 70% fell below the cutoff point. Even those women who fell above the cutoff point tended to show a decrease in self-reported symptomatology over time. Clearly, the divorced sample, while continuing to experience considerable stress, exhibit marked positive adaptation as well.

Adaptation and the Social Milieu

As was mentioned earlier, considerable attention has been devoted recently to the role of close relationships in attenuating reactions to stressful life events. A number of investigators have argued that the support provided by significant others plays a crucial role in postdivorce adaptation. Results from the present study are intended to shed additional light on the relationship between characteristics of the divorced individuals' social milieu and their adjustment. Because of the sheer number of analyses conducted, the results will necessarily be presented in summary form. Additionally, the focus here will be on the divorced women themselves rather than on the comparison between the divorced and nondivorced samples.

Descriptive Characteristics of Networks

The structural characteristics of the divorced respondents were markedly different than those of their married counterparts, particularly during the early stages of the research. At the point of the first network assessment (one month postdivorce), the two groups differed significantly with respect to network size ($\bar{X} = 8.3$ vs. 16.4 for the divorced and comparison groups, respectively) and network density ($\bar{X} = .41$ vs. .25). The density coefficient can be interpreted as the proportion of network members who interact with one another independent of their interactions with the respondent, or as the probability that any randomly selected network member has a relationship with any other randomly selected network member. Thus, the divorced women reported significantly smaller and more dense networks than the comparison subjects, a finding in line with the research reviewed earlier. The primary difference between the two groups with respect to the makeup of the networks is found in the relative proportions of family members versus friends and acquaintances. Consistent with the results of previous studies, the networks of the divorced women had a much higher percentage of family members than did those of the comparison sample (52% vs. 28%, respectively).

An attempt was made to determine whether the two groups might have differed with respect to network size and density prior to the occurrence of marital disruption for the divorced subjects. During the initial interview all of the divorced subjects were asked to describe, in a retrospective fashion, the nature of their social networks 6 months prior to separation. The preseparation networks differed neither in size nor density from those of the women in the comparison group. Data gleaned from the interviews also suggests that these considerable differences in network structure probably did not exist prior to the divorce. During the interviews the divorced women frequently mentioned the changes occurring in the structure of their networks as one of the more stressful aspects of their adaptation to the event. Most of the women suggested that their friends seemed uncomfortable in dealing with them as "single" women. A substantial minority of the divorced women felt themselves partly to blame for the deterioration in their friendship network. Many of these women, for example, felt that they had become a drain on their friends' time and emotional resources or that their friends had justifiably grown bored of hearing about their problems. Other women felt that most of their friends simply didn't understand what they were experiencing, and these respondents reported that they withdrew from their old friends. The overall impression, however, is that the size and density differences do not point to a preexisting difference between the social milieus of the groups but, rather, reflect adaptations occurring in response to the marital disruption.

With time, these differences diminished but did not disappear altogether. At 12 months postdivorce, the groups still differed on both structural indices. Mean values for the network size and density variables, respectively, were 12.4 and .36 for the divorced sample, and 17.0 and .21 for the comparison sample. At 24 months the groups no longer differed significantly with respect to network size ($\bar{X} = 15.7$ for the divorced sample versus 16.4 for the comparison sample), but still differed with respect to the density or interconnectedness of their networks ($\bar{X} = .33$ and .22, respectively). Thus, even 2 years following the termination of their marriages, the divorced women exhibited structural differences in the composition of their social networks. Interestingly, the density difference at 24 months was only partially attributable to family membership in the network. The other major contributor to density difference stems from the involvement on the part of a number of the women in single parent groups. The increases in network size occurring over time appear to be due to the entrance of new social contacts, many of whom are drawn from groups such as Parents Without Partners (PWP), rather than the reestablishment of old friendships. New friends made within the context of formal organizations such as PWP tend to interact with one another to a relatively high degree, thus contributing to the higher density coefficients found for the divorced women.

The two groups were also compared with respect to two interactional (or nonstructural) network characteristics: frequency of interaction and durability of relationships. At the time of the first interview the divorced sample reported a much higher level of interaction with their networks than did the comparison sample. The divorced women reported seeing each member of their network an average of 2.4 times during the past week (excluding persons residing with the respondent); the corresponding figure for the women in the comparison sample was .83. This difference decreased but remained statistically significant over the 2-year period. At 24 months the mean number of interactions per network member for the divorced and comparison samples, respectively, was 1.33 versus .77. Interestingly, if those contacts established through formal organizations such as PWP are excluded from the analysis, the divorced sample actually shows a lower (nonsignificant) frequency of interaction with their network members. This squares with data derived from the interviews in which many of the divorced women complain of relative social isolation aside from the weekly group meetings.

With respect to the durability (mean duration) of the network relationships, the two groups differed significantly at the time of the first and third interview, although the direction of the difference was reversed at the two points in time. The divorced women reported that they had known their network members significantly longer than the women in the comparison group during the first interview. At the time of the second interview the difference was no longer significant, yet during the third interview the divorced women reported knowing their network members for a shorter mean duration than the women in the comparison group. This reversal can be easily understood by noting the changes in the composition of the divorced women's networks over time. As noted earlier, shortly after divorce, the networks of the divorced women were composed largely of family members. With time this state of affairs changed. New friends acquired through a variety of contexts (single parents groups, work) resulted in a substantial drop in the mean duration of the relationships in the network.

Social Support, Social Interaction, and Adaptation

Several interesting results emerged when the measures of social support, social network, and help-seeking were examined in relationship to measures of psychological adaptation to divorce. For the sake of brevity, only those analyses concerning depression and life satisfaction will be presented. The first analysis, presented in Table 5, examined the intercorrelations between the various measures of social milieu at the 12-month data collection point. Most of the intercorrelations are easily interpreted and do not bear comment. An exception, however, is the

Table 5 Intercorrelation matrix of social milieu indices

				Value of r					
Scale	1	2	3	4	5	6	7	8	9
1. Total support	–	.73	.69	.54	.61	−.28	.26	.11	−.12
2. Emotional support		–	.82	.63	.49	−.41	.25	.22	−.17
3. Appraisal support			–	.61	.57	−.30	.28	.13	−.23
4. Informational support				–	.70	−.06	.34	−.28	−.09
5. Tangible support					–	−.15	.39	−.10	.19
6. Conflict-strain						–	−.20	.29	.39
7. Network size							–	.59	−.24
8. Network density								–	.39
9. Help-seeking (frequency)									–

Note. All r values above .27 are statistically significant, $p < .01$.

relationship between help-seeking frequency and the other measures of social milieu characteristics. Help-seeking frequency is significantly (positively) correlated with both network density and the index of conflict-strain. Additionally, although not reaching statistical significance, it is of note that help-seeking frequency is negatively correlated with four of the five indices of perceived social support. Persons high in emotional, appraisal, informational, and total support tended to seek help less frequently in response to self-identified problems than did persons with lower scores on those perceived support scales. Persons with high density networks also sought help significantly more frequently than did those with less dense networks. This relationship is best understood as reflecting the fact that high network density is itself significantly associated with the index of conflict and strain. Note also the significant association between this measure of conflict and strain and the frequency of help-seeking. The emerging picture suggests that persons with high density networks seek help frequently from sources that, in addition to providing various types of support, also seem to act as a source of conflict and strain. This relationship makes some sense when one considers the fact that high density networks are often kin dominated. Previous research has shown that divorced individuals often perceive family members as sources of considerable stress as well as support (Weiss, 1975; Wilcox, 1981). The interview transcripts confirm this interpretation; divorced women who were reliant to a large extent on their families for support complained that their parents often made them make outright requests for assistance, and that their parents exacted a "toll" in repayment for offers of help. These "tolls" often took the form of a perception of increased freedom to intrude into the personal affairs of the divorced women and offers of unwanted advice.

The second set of analyses examined the correlations between the social milieu indices and the measures of psychological adjustment. Depression scores are significantly correlated with emotional support ($r = -.29$), appraisal support ($r = -.35$), conflict strain ($r = .34$), network density ($r = .31$), and help-seeking ($r = -.41$). The negative association between help-seeking is particularly interesting in that it replicates a finding reported by Pearlin and Schooler (1978). In a later statement (Pearlin & Schooler, 1979), these authors noted two possible interpretations of this finding: 1) there may be an important distinction between help-seeking and help-getting, with those persons who receive the most effective help being so thoroughly enmeshed in a network of supportive others "that they neither have to solicit help in order to receive it nor are necessarily aware of having been a recipient" (p. 204); and 2) seeking help may result in, rather than result from, high levels of psychological distress (c.f. Gore, 1979). The longitudinal nature of the present study allows for the testing of these two propositions. The results of this analysis suggest that high levels of help-seeking actually results in increased levels of depression, although this effect is not particularly large. The extensive literature on recipient reactions to aid suggest several possible explanations for this finding. Under certain circumstances the provision of help can backfire and actually leave the person worse off than she was before being "helped." An extensive literature now exists suggesting that helpers may at times do more harm than good (see Coates, Renzaglia, & Embree, 1983; Fisher, DePaulo, & Nadler, 1981 for reviews). Additionally, the act of seeking help can have important self-threatening implications for the help-seeker (Fisher, Nadler, & Witcher-Alagna, 1982). Again, data from the interviews suggest that both of these mechanisms might be in operation here. A number of the women complained about the nature of the "help" sometimes offered in response to requests for aid. One woman commented that her requests for empathy and understanding were frequently met with suggestions that she "forget about" her problems and "get back in the swing of things." Another woman noted that her requests for companionship were often dealt with by "fixing me up with a date I didn't want." Numerous women complained about having to ask friends and family members for help, referring to such instances as "degrading," "difficult," and "depressing."

Scores on the index of life satisfaction are significantly correlated with emotional support $(r = .45)$, appraisal support $(r = .37)$, conflict-strain $(r = -.32)$, and help-seeking $(r = -.43)$. The interpretations of these associations seem relatively straightforward, with reasons similar to those discussed above underlying the negative correlation between help-seeking frequency and life satisfaction.

An intuitively appealing means of examining the relationship between character-istics of the social milieu and psychological adjustment involves the contrasting of those divorced women scoring high versus low on the measures of adjustment using discriminant function analysis. Social milieu measures collected at 12 months postdivorce were used in an attempt to discriminate between persons identified as depressed or nondepressed at the final data collection point. With respect to depression, two groups, depressed versus nondepressed, were created by using a score of 14 and above as the index of the presence of depression. It should be noted that the scale used here might be interpreted more accurately as assessing depressed mood rather than instances of diagnosable clinical disorder. Additionally, a cutoff score of 14, rather than the usual 16, was employed in order to maintain approximately equal sized groups. A direct discriminant function analysis was conducted using all of the indices of social milieu characteristics as predictors of group membership, with the sole exception of the help-seeking variable, which was shown earlier to be related to the depression score in a complex fashion. A single, statistically significant, discriminant function was calculated. The loading matrix of correlations between predictor variables and the discriminant function suggests that appraisal support is the most powerful variable in distinguishing between the two groups. The depressed women have substantially lower scores on the appraisal support scale than do the nondepressed women. Two other variables contribute to the discriminant function, conflict-strain and network density, with the depressed group having significantly higher mean values for both the conflict-strain scale and the network density variable. These three variables remained significant even after adjusting for Type I error rate and adjusting for the overlap between the predictor variables. Using a jackknife classification procedure to assess the performance of the discriminating predictors, 63 of the 90 women (70%) were classified correctly.

A similar analysis was conducted with respect to the measure of life satisfaction, the Index of Well-Being. Two groups, high and low life satisfaction, were created by splitting the sample at the median value of the scale (10) at the 24 month data collection point. The same set of predictor variables were utilized. Again, a single statistically significant discriminant function was derived from the analysis. The loading matrix between the predictor variables and the discriminant function suggests that emotional support is the most powerful single discriminating variable. Women in the high life satisfaction group report a significantly higher mean value on the emotional support scale than do those with lower scores on the Index of

Well-Being. One other variable, appraisal support, contributed to the discriminant function. However, only emotional support discriminates between the high and low life satisfaction groups after adjusting for the correlations between the predictor variables and making adjustments to keep the Type I error rate at or below .05. Again, a jackknife procedure led to 55 of the 90 women (61.1%) being correctly classified.

This set of results suggests that characteristics of the divorced woman's social milieu may contribute significantly to her psychological adjustment. The variables predictive of adjustment vary, however, with the particular measure of adjustment. Higher levels of depression are best predicted by low levels of appraisal support, high levels of conflict-strain within the network, and high network density. The importance of appraisal support is in keeping with the results of a study by Cohen and Hoberman (1983) in which an index of appraisal support was the sole significant correlate (from amongst the indices of support) of psychological adjustment. An abundance of evidence from other sources also suggests that appraisal support (feedback about one's self, social comparison, etc.) should bear strongly on psychological adjustment (see Cohen & McKay, in press; Wills, 1983). One would expect, also, that high levels of conflict or strain emanating from network members would contribute to feelings of depressed mood. The results seem to suggest that this is the case. Finally, the relationship between density and psychological adjustment replicates findings from an earlier study (Wilcox, 1981). Hirsch (1979), Wilcox (1981), and Wilcox and Birkel (1983) discuss the possible reasons for the relationship between high network density and high psychological distress elsewhere.

CONCLUSION

The present study was undertaken with the hope of explicating some of the relationships between life stress, social milieu factors, and psychological adjustment for women coping with a significant life transition, divorce. The strength of the study lies in the longitudinal design employed. Such a design allows for a glimpse of the stress and coping process that is not able to be viewed when using cross-sectional designs.

The demands associated with adaptation to the many role changes associated with divorce are discernable from the results of the analyses of the problem domains of most concern to the divorced and comparison groups. The picture that emerges from these analyses suggests that the period immediately following divorce is an intensely stressful one. The divorced sample rated each of the nine life domains as less satisfying than did the women in the comparison group. These differences declined with time. At the conclusion of the 2 year follow-up period the divorced women were still significantly less satisfied with four of the life domains. Two of these domains reflect continued economic concerns; the other two reflect insecurities about their abilities to raise their families and their feelings of being overwhelmed by the task of home care and maintenance. These findings are mirrored, to a considerable extent, in the analyses of experienced hassles and uplifts. The divorced women report significantly higher levels of hassles at 6 and 12 months postdivorce, and significantly lower levels of uplifts over the entire 2-year period. These data, along with the results from the journals and the interviews, suggests that it is the absence of positive events, rather than the presence of negative events, that is perceived as particularly problematic for these women once they have established a certain degree of equilibrium following the divorce.

The experience of divorce is, as was mentioned earlier, a complex stressor sequence that places considerable demands on the adaptational capabilities of the individual. The picture that emerges from the analyses of the measures of psychological adjustment provides cause for both concern and optimism. The moderately high scores on the index of depression and the low scores on the life satisfaction measure for the divorced women are causes for concern. Even 24 months after divorce, over twice as many women in the divorced sample have depression scores above the "case" cutoff point. The cause for optimism resides in the fact that the divorced women's scores on these two measures show a nearly linear improvement with time. The present results do, however, attest to the fact that adaptation to marital disruption is clearly a long term process.

Finally, those analyses examining the relationships between characteristics of the social milieu and psychological adjustment bolster the findings of previous research pointing to the importance of these factors. The present results suggest that different aspects of psychological adjustment may be differentially affected by different components of supportive milieu. Results from the discriminant function analyses suggest that depression is most strongly moderated by appraisal support while life satisfaction is best predicted by emotional support. This finding lends, in a limited sense, credibility to the emerging theoretical perspective in the social support literature that proposes that specific linkages may exist between types of stressors, types of support, and types of adjustment (Cohen & McKay, in press; Wilcox & Vernberg, 1985). Additionally, these analyses replicate previous findings suggesting a link between low density and more positive forms of adjustment. An additional finding of considerable interest is the important role played by network conflict and strain. Analyses not presented here suggest that the conflictual processes within networks may often undercut and overwhelm the supportive processes. Finally, the interesting set of relationships between help-seeking and adjustment should caution us against presuming network support is a panacea of any sort. Many experts in the field of social support have argued that the principle mechanism through which support has its protective and ameliorative effects is through the process of cognitive secondary appraisal. It is the perception that one is supported, rather than the actual provision of support or help, that leads to beneficial effects. The present results lend credence to Pearlin and Schooler's (1978, 1979) claim that persons who are well supported may simply never need to make requests for help and may be unaware of the fact that a "helping" transaction has occurred. This is clearly an issue that bears additional attention on both a theoretical and empirical level.

Clearly, many important questions concerning the relationships between social milieu factors and adjustment to divorce remain to be explored. Comparative studies between the adjustment of men and women would be particularly interesting in light of the oft reported sex differences in perceptions of support and actual levels of help-seeking and social interaction. The present study was limited largely by the relatively small sample size. Compared to many studies of adaptation following divorce, the sample was actually rather large. The requirements of many of the more powerful data analytic methods, however, require larger samples. Even with these limitations, studies such as this one, bearing as they do on the uncovering of risk factors associated with coping with marital disruption, have important theoretical and practical implications.

REFERENCES

Bachrach, L. L. (1976). *Marital status and mental disorder: An analytical review* (DHEW Publication No. ADM75-127). Rockville, MD: National Institute of Mental Health.

Bernard, S. (1964). Fatherless families: Their economic and social adjustment. *Papers in Social Welfare*, (7). Waltham, MA: Florence Heller Graduate School for Advanced Studies in Social Welfare.

Bloom, B. L., & Caldwell, R. A. (1981). Sex differences in adjustment during the process of marital separation. *Journal of Marriage and the Family. 43*, 693-701.

Bohannan, P. (1970). The six stages of divorce. In P. Bohannan (Ed.), *Divorce and after* (pp. 33-59). Garden City, NY: Doubleday.

Brandwein, R. A., Brown, C. A., & Fox, E. M. (1974). Women and children last: The social situation of divorced mothers and their families. *Journal of Marriage and the Family, 36*, 498-514.

Campbell, A., Converse, P. E., & Rodgers, W. L. (1976). *The quality of American life.* New York: Sage.

Chiriboga, D. A., Coho, A., Stein, J. A., & Roberts, J. (1979). Divorce, stress, and social supports: A study in help-seeking behavior. *Journal of Divorce, 3,* 121-135.

Chiriboga, D. A., & Cutler, L. (1977). Stress responses among divorcing men and women. *Journal of Divorce, 1,* 95-106.

Coates, D., Renzaglia, G. J., & Embree, M. C. (1983). When helping backfires: Help and helplessness. In J. D. Fisher, A. Nadler, & B. M. DePaulo (Eds.), *New directions in helping: Vol. 1. Recipient reactions to aid* (pp. 251-279). New York: Academic.

Cohen, S., & Hoberman, H. M. (1983). Positive events and social supports as buffers of life change stress. *Journal of Applied Social Psychology, 13,* 99-125.

Cohen, S., & McKay, G. (in press). Social support, stress, and the buffering hypothesis: A theoretical analysis. In A. Baum, J. E. Singer, & S. E. Taylor (Eds.), *Handbook of psychology and health: Vol. IV.* Hillsdale, NJ: Erlbaum.

Colletta, N. D. (1979). Support systems after divorce: Incidence and impact. *Journal of Marriage and the Family, 41,* 837-846.

Espenshade, T. J. (1979). The economic consequences of divorce. *Journal of Marriage and the Family, 42,* 615-626.

Fisher, J. D., DePaulo, B. M., & Nadler, A. (1981). Extending altruism beyond the altruistic act: The mixed effects of aid on the help recipient. In J. P. Rushton & R. M. Sorrentino (Eds.), *Altruism and helping behavior* (pp. 367-422). Hillsdale, NJ: Erlbaum.

Fisher, J. D., Nadler, A., & Witcher-Alagna, S. (1982). Recipient reactions to aid. *Psychological Bulletin, 91,* 27-54.

Folkman, S., & Lazarus, R. S. (1980). An analysis of coping in a middle-aged community sample. *Journal of Health and Social Behavior, 21,* 219-239.

Glick, P. C. (1979). Children of divorced parents in demographic perspective. *Journal of Social Issues, 35,* 112-125.

Goode, W. J. (1956). *After divorce.* New York: Free Press.

Gore, S. (1979). Does help-seeking increase psychological distress? *Journal of Health and Social Behavior, 20,* 201-202.

Hampton, R. (1975). Marital disruption: Some social and economic consequences. In G. Duncan & J. N. Morgan (Eds.), *Five thousand American families—Patterns of economic progress: Vol. 3.* (pp. 163-186). Ann Arbor: Institute for Social Research.

Helmreich, R., & Stapp, J. (1974). Short forms of the Texas Social Behavior Inventory (TSBI), an objective measure of self-esteem. *Bulletin of the Psychonomic Society, 4,* 473-475.

Hetherington, E. M., Cox, M., & Cox, R. (1978). The aftermath of divorce. In J. H. Stevens & M. Matthews (Eds.), *Mother-child, father-child relations* (pp. 56-78). Washington, DC: National Association for the Education of Young Children.

Hetherington, E. M. (1979). Divorce: A child's perspective. *American Psychologist, 34,* 851-858.

Hetherington, E. M., Cox, M., & Cox, R. (1979a). Stress and coping in divorce: A focus on women. In J. E. Gullahorn (Ed.), *Psychology and Women: In transition* (pp. 95-128). Washington, DC: Winston & Sons.

Hetherington, E. M., Cox, M., & Cox, R. (1979b). Play and social interaction in children follow-
ing divorce. *Journal of Social Issues, 35,* 26–49.
Hirsch, B. J. (1979). Psychological dimensions of social networks: A multimethod analysis.
American Journal of Community Psychology, 7, 263–277.
Hirsch, B. J. (1980). Natural support systems and coping with major life changes. *American
Journal of Community Psychology, 8,* 159–172.
Kanner, A. D., Coyne, J. C., Schaeffer, C., & Lazarus, R. S. (1981). Comparison of two modes
of stress measurement: Daily hassles and uplifts versus major life events. *Journal of
Behavioral Medicine, 4,* 1–39.
Langner, T. S. (1962). A twenty-two item screening score of psychiatric symptoms indicating
impairment. *Journal of Health and Social Behavior, 3,* 269–276.
McLanahan, S. S., Wedemeyer, N. V., & Adelberg, T. (1981). Network structure, social support,
and psychological well-being in a single-parent family. *Journal of Marriage and the Family,
43,* 601–612.
McNair, D. M., Lorr, M., & Droppleman, L. F. (1971). *Profile of Mood States (POMS).* San
Diego: Educational and Industrial Testing Service.
Myers, J. K., & Weissman, M. M. (1980). Use of a self-report symptom scale to detect
depression in a community sample. *American Journal of Psychiatry, 137,* 1081–1084.
Pearlin, L., & Schooler, C. (1978). The structure of coping. *Journal of Health and Social
Behavior, 19,* 2–21.
Pearlin, L., & Schooler, C. (1979). Some extensions on "The structure of coping." *Journal of
Health and Social Behavior, 20,* 202–205.
Radloff, L. (1977). The CES-D scale: A self-report depression scale for research in the general
population. *Applied Psychological Measurement, 1,* 385–405.
Raschke, H. J. (1977). The role of social participation in postseparation and postdivorce adjust-
ment. *Journal of Divorce, 1,* 129–140.
Rosenberg, M. (1965). *Society and the adolescent self image.* Princeton: Princeton University
Press.
Ross, H., & Sawhill, I. (1975). *Time of transition: The growth of families headed by women.*
Washington, DC: The Urban Institute.
Spanier, G. B., & Anderson, E. A. (1979). The impact of the legal system on adjustment to
marital separation. *Journal of Marriage and the Family, 41,* 605–613.
Spanier, G. B., & Castro, R. (1979). Adjustment to separation and divorce: An analysis of 50
case studies. *Journal of Divorce, 2,* 241–253.
Verbrugge, L. M. (1979). Marital status and health. *Journal of Marriage and the Family, 41,*
267–285.
Weiss, R. S. (1975). *Marital separation.* New York: Basic.
Weiss, R. S. (1976). The emotional impact of marital separation. *Journal of Social Issues, 32,*
135–145.
Weiss, R. S. (1979). *Going it alone.* New York: Basic.
Weitzman, L. J. (1981). The economics of divorce: Social and economic consequences of
property, alimony, and child support awards. *UCLA Law Review, 28,* 1181–1268.
Wilcox, B. L. (1981). Social support in adjusting to marital disruption: A network analysis.
In B. H. Gottlieb (Ed.), *Social networks and social support* (pp. 97–115). Beverly Hills:
Sage.
Wilcox, B. L., & Birkel, R. C. (1983). Social networks and the help-seeking process: A
structural perspective. In A. Nadler, J. D. Fisher, & B. M. DePaulo (Eds.), *New directions in
helping, Vol. 3: Applied perspectives in help-seeking and -receiving* (pp. 235–253). New
York: Academic.
Wilcox, B. L., & Vernberg, E. (1985). Conceptual and theoretical dilemmas facing social
support research. In I. G. Sarason & B. R. Sarason (Eds.), *Social support: Theory, research,
and application* (pp. 3–20). The Hague: Martinus Nijhof.
Wills, T. A. (1983). Social comparison in coping and help-seeking. In B. M. DePaulo, A. Nadler,
& J. D. Fisher (Eds.), *New directions in helping: Vol. 2, Help-seeking* (pp. 109–141). New
York: Academic.

III

VIOLENCE TOWARD
WOMEN

9

The Victim of Rape and the Role of Life Change, Coping, and Social Support during the Rape Trauma Syndrome

Libby O. Ruch
University of Hawaii at Manoa

Joseph J. Leon
California State Polytechnic University, Pomona

Recent research has established that rape and other forms of sexual assault have a highly traumatic and enduring effect on the victim (e.g., Burgess & Holmstrom, 1979; Frank & Stewart, 1983; Kilpatrick, Resick, & Veronen, 1981; Kilpatrick, Veronen, & Resick, 1979; McCahill, Meyer, & Fischman, 1979; Ruch & Chandler, 1982, 1983; Ruch & Leon, 1983; Williams & Holmes, 1981). Burgess and Holmstrom (1979) reported that rape victims characteristically experience a similar pattern of symptoms, which they term the *rape trauma syndrome* (RTS). The RTS has two phases—the *acute* phase, where the primary response is fear for personal safety, followed by the *reorganization* phase, characterized by diverse symptoms such as phobias, insomnia, sexual dysfunctions, and major changes in life style. In a longitudinal study of psychological distress among rape victims and a comparison group of nonvictims, Kilpatrick and colleagues found that victims suffer an acute and generalized response during the early stages of the RTS and that symptoms of fear and anxiety continue for at least one year postassault (Kilpatrick et al., 1979, 1981).

Thus, the research findings indicate that rape and other forms of sexual assault are life crises of major proportions for the victim. Such research is important on a basic level, to further understanding of processes by which women as a category are victimized in society, and on a therapeutic level, to provide an empirical basis for designing effective and sensitive mental health interventions for rape victims. Since sexual assault is a stressful life event, data on how victims cope in the aftermath of a rape and factors that affect recovery are relevant also to the medical sociology, community psychology, and psychiatric literature dealing with issues such as life stress and social support systems (see, for example, the entire issues of *Journal of Health and Social Behavior,* June, 1979; March, 1982).

The authors wish to acknowledge the helpful criticisms and suggestions made by John W. Gartrell, Peggy A. Thoits, and Stevan E. Hobfoll on the preliminary version of this chapter.

NEED FOR THEORY IN RAPE RESEARCH

A basic criticism that can be raised about research on sexual assault trauma concerns the general lack of theoretical activity.* Although an atheoretical approach is often characteristic of relatively new fields, it contributes to several of the methodological weaknesses discussed by Katz and Mazur (1979) and others. For example, a major result is the proliferation of different measures of trauma used in various studies that in turn generate conflicting results.

In this chapter, a theoretical model of longitudinal rape trauma with specification variables will be proposed and selected hypotheses derived from it. The model will build on the earlier rape literature and literature from other relevant areas, such as social support and life change, to elicit a more in-depth understanding of the complex interaction of social-psychological and assault variables over time.

EXPLORATORY MODEL OF ADJUSTMENT DURING THE RAPE TRAUMA SYNDROME

Concept of Sexual Assault Trauma

Sexual assault trauma refers to the effects of the assault on the victim's life. The victim's concerns may be focused on physiological aspects, such as physical injury, venereal disease, and pregnancy, or on social-psychological problems, such as interpersonal and sexual relationships. The concept of sexual assault trauma may include both the acute, or relatively immediate reaction to the assault, and also the long-range effects of the assault on the victim. Sexual assault trauma is conceptualized here as having two theoretically distinct dimensions: The *type* of sexual assault trauma refers to the particular emotional concern or problem the victim experiences, and the *level* of sexual assault trauma is defined as the degree to which the victim is affected by the sexual assault.

Overview of the Model

The RTS Adjustment Model is proposed to guide research on longitudinal rape impact and the role of preassault and postassault factors and their interrelationships in the recovery process. Due to the complexity of the phenomenon and the exploratory nature of the model, our purpose is to examine the major relationships between these variables and trauma.

Bassuk (1980), following Sifneos (1960, 1967) proposed that the severity of the impact of a sexual assault, as with other life crises, can be explained by three primary factors: (1) past history of the victim that increases her vulnerability; (2) nature of the event precipitating the crisis; and (3) attempts made by the victim to cope with the crisis. Our model, which elaborates upon this perspective (see Figure 1), has five major components, that contain an array of more specific independent variables.** To understand how much more devastating a sexual

---

*Exceptions include Kilpatrick et al. (1981) who have begun to approach sexual assault trauma within the context of social learning theory and the Ruch and Chandler (1983) exploratory theoretical model of rape trauma as a function of preassault and assault variables.

**For a more detailed treatment of the independent variables within the clusters and a factor analysis of the model, see Ruch and Chandler (1983) and Ruch and Hennessy (1982).

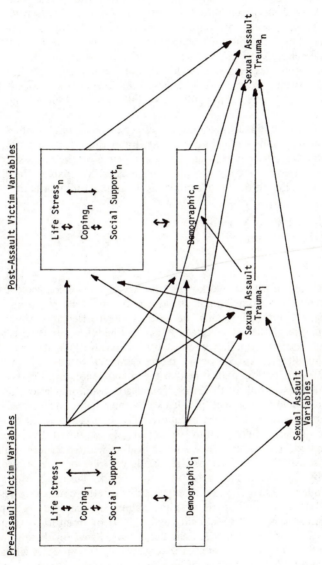

FIGURE 1   The RTS Adjustment Model.

139

assault can be for some victims and not others, relevant aspects of the victim's history are hypothesized to include both her *demographic characteristics* (e.g., age, ethnicity, marital status) and *life stresses prior to assault* (e.g., prior life change, mental health or substance abuse problems, and sexual victimization). The nature of the event precipitating the crisis refers to the *sexual assault* variables, such as the relation to assailant, use of weapons and other forms of force, victim resistance, and physical injury. Attempts made by the victim to cope with the assault include *coping mechanisms,* such as relying on family and friends, devising rape avoidance strategies, and minimizing the horror of the attack through social comparisons. Bassuk's perspective is enlarged to include the concept of *social support,* which we argue, will significantly influence the course and outcome of the RTS.

The model in Figure 1 distinguishes the effect of preassault variables and their effect on relatively immediate trauma (Time$_1$) and the effect of both preassault and postassault variables on subsequent trauma (Time$_n$). The discussion will deal first with hypothesized relationships between preassault variables and immediate trauma, before turning to the more complex issue of longitudinal trauma.

Effect of Preassault Variables on Short-Term Trauma

Sexual Assault

Our prediction in earlier work was that assaults involving violence, injury, forced entry into the home, unknown assailants, and multiple assailants evoke the most severe emotional trauma, because of the particularly brutal and life-endangering nature of the sexual attack (Ruch & Chandler, 1983). This prediction was consistent with the findings of most others (see Katz & Mazur, 1979, for a review of this literature). However, recent empirical studies have failed to substantiate this prediction, indicating that the phenomenon may be more complex than anticipated. McCahill et al. (1979) found a curvilinear relationship between assault variables and adjustment problems. Assaults with known assailants and minimal or no physical injury were as emotionally devastating as the more stereotypical "bad" rapes, where victims were violently assaulted by strangers and physically injured. Two multivariate studies dealing with short-term trauma have failed to elicit significant effects of the assault variables on the level of trauma experienced by the victim soon after the rape (Frank, Turner, & Stewart, 1980; Ruch & Chandler, 1983). A possible explanation for the conflicting results that have emerged in this literature is whether trauma is measured by type (as by Burgess & Holmstrom, 1979; McCahill et al., 1979) or intensity of response (as by Frank et al., 1980 and Ruch & Chandler, 1983). Based on these findings, our hypothesis will be modified to predict that sexual assault variables will affect the nature of the problem experienced by the victim (trauma type) but not the intensity of the response (trauma level).

Preexisting Life Stresses on the Victim

The next set of variables pertain to the level of stress on the victim at the time of the assault, stemming from preexisting mental health or substance abuse problems, prior sexual victimization, and recent life change.* Our prediction, as consistent with most previous research, is that trauma will be greater when the assault compounds a prior sexual victimization (Burgess & Holmstrom, 1979; Frank, Turner, & Stewart, 1980).** Women with mental health or substance abuse problems at the time of the assault are also at particularly high risk for a severe and prolonged reaction during the RTS. This prediction is consistent with studies on relatively short-term trauma (Frank & Stewart, 1983; Ruch & Chandler, 1983). Whether such effects of prior mental health are sustained over time is less clear from the literature and is an important area for future research. Burgess and Holmstrom (1979) found that prior mental health problems were associated with delayed recovery, but Kilpatrick, Veronen, and Best (unpublished manuscript) reported that neither a history of previous psychological difficulties nor treatment distinguished distress levels among victims 3 months after the rape.

The relationship between life change and the onset and severity of physical and mental health problems has been reported in a wide variety of studies (Dohrenwend & Dohrenwend, 1974; Gunderson & Rahe, 1974; Thoits, forthcoming). A life change event is defined as an occurrence that induces or is indicative of a modification in the individual's accustomed way of life (Holmes & Masuda, 1974). Various issues in this research tradition, such as whether change per se or undesirable change is important, have been subject to considerable debate (Thoits, forthcoming).

Although it seems logical to view rape as a stressful life event in the context of other stressful events, surprisingly little work has been done on the effect of prior life change on rape victims, and the available research findings are inconsistent. Burgess and Holmstrom (1979) found no relationship between recent life change (within 6 months) and length of recovery time, but that a major family loss at least 2 years before actually facilitated recovery. In contrast, Ruch, Chandler, and Harter (1980) found a curvilinear relationship between life change and sexual assault trauma measured immediately and 2 weeks postassault. Victims experiencing moderate life change during the year before the assault were less traumatized than victims with severe changes or no life changes. Evidence of a more sustained effect of life change on trauma is provided by Kilpatrick et al. (unpublished manuscript). Victims with low distress levels 3 months postrape tended to have fewer life changes during the previous year than highly distressed victims. The low-distress victim was less likely to have lost a close family member (other than spouse) to death and was more likely to have had loving intimate relationships with men during this time.

Although several differences between these studies, such as dependent variables and assessment procedures, may account for these contrasting findings, it is quite

---

*Other variables not dealt with here but conceptually relevant to this category include chronic role strains or stresses (Pearlin, Lieberman, Menaghan & Mullan, 1981), other forms of sexual victimization than rape (e.g., spouse abuse, sexual harassment), and nonsexual criminal victimization (e.g., being a victim of an attempted murder or robbery).

**There is some evidence, however, that prior sexual victimization has a delayed effect. Ruch and Chandler (1983) found, contrary to prediction, that previously raped victims were significantly *less* traumatized than first-time victims when assessed within hours of assault. In a follow-up study about 2 weeks later (Ruch & Leon, 1983), prior rape victims had become more traumatized than first-rape victims (in fact the prior rape variable was the strongest predictor of the *degree of change* from intake to follow-up).

possible that Burgess and Holmstrom's (1979) results may be attributable (1) to insufficient variation on the life change measure, since no victim had experienced major events within 6 months preassault, and (2) to the fact that even the effect of a severe life crisis, such as a family loss, may have been resolved when sufficient time has elapsed (in this study 2 years or more). Thus, our prediction is that *recent* life change occurring within one year of the rape will affect sexual assault trauma.

Social Support and Coping

Social support is defined as the degree to which a person's basic social needs are gratified through interaction with others (Kaplan, Cassel, & Gore, 1977). Such needs may be met by either the provision of instrumental or socioemotional aid (Thoits, 1982). Although relatively little systematic study of social support and sexual assault trauma has been conducted, the concept of social support has recently become an area of intense activity in medical sociology, community psychology, and psychiatry. According to Turner, Frankel, and Levin (1983), the quantity and range of available evidence leaves little doubt that social support is importantly related to diverse forms of psychological distress and disorder.

A number of issues are the subject of continued discussion, including the meaning of the concept and its measurement (for reviews of this literature, see Thoits, 1982; and Turner et al., 1983). A particularly relevant issue to our topic is whether social support influences mental health directly or modifies the effect of life change (e.g., Lin, Simeone, Ensel, & Kuo, 1979; Pearlin, Lieberman, Menaghan, & Mullan, 1981; Thoits, 1982; Turner et al., 1983). Further, if the role of support is to modify the potential stress-illness relationship, does it do so by acting as an antecedent factor reducing the likelihood of life change, particularly undesirable events, or as a buffering factor, following the occurrence of life change that affects the interpretive meanings of the event and emotional response to it. According to Thoits (1982, 1983), one of the difficulties in assessing the findings on social support is the possible confounding of the direct effects of life events on social support and the interactive (buffering) effects of life events with social support, biasing the results in favor of the buffering hypothesis. The problem, especially when life events are measured before social support, is that many life events either are indicators of change in social support (e.g., death of spouse, divorce) or evoke change in support systems (e.g., loss of job, moving). Longitudinal designs with repeated measures of life events, social support, and psychological distress are necessary to avoid this problem.

Coping is hypothesized to be another important aspect influencing the course and outcome of the RTS. According to Menaghan (1982), coping, like stress, is a popular but increasingly ambiguous concept with empirical knowledge and conceptualization lagging considerably behind the popular interest. What is meant by coping has not been agreed upon (see Menaghan, 1982). We view coping in terms of the typical or usual preferences or ways of approaching problems. Such coping attempts can be on an individual level, where the victim relies primarily on her own strengths and resources; on an interpersonal level, where she deals with problems by turning to personal networks, such as family and friends, for help and support; or on an institutional level, where the victim contacts a treatment center, criminal justice agency, or church.

Two recent studies (Turner & Noh, 1983; Pearlin et al., 1981) are especially relevant here as their analyses include both life change and social support variables.

In a study designed to add to the understanding of the well-known relationship between social class position and psychological distress, Turner and Noh examine the effects of social class, life change, social support, and personal control on psychological distress for 312 women who have recently given birth. Using a stepwise regression analysis, Turner and Noh find that social support, life change, and personal control are significant and social class approaches significance. When regressions are done partitioning for class, social support and life change are significant predictors for upper-class women; social support, life change, and personal control for middle-class women, and only life change for lower-class women. These findings demonstrate that social support is a powerful factor with the upper and middle classes, but not so for the lower-class women when life change is in the equation.

With respect to whether social support and personal control have main or interactive effects, the findings are both "conditional and complex" (Turner & Noh, 1983). Social support appears to have a main effect on middle-class women but matters only for those lower-class women experiencing high levels of life change. The effects of personal control are largely limited to middle-class women, buffering the potential influence of high and medium life change on psychological distress.

Some caution is advisable, before generalizing from these results to rape victims, due to the cross-sectional design of the research and the considerable decrease in sample size as controls are introduced. On a more theoretical level, rape and childbirth can both be viewed as life changes of considerable magnitude but obviously they vary as to social desirability which may impact on the role of life change, social support, and sense of personal control.

The work by Pearlin et al. (1981) is especially relevant as their model of the stress process integrates the concepts of life change, coping, and social support. Life change events are viewed as sources of stress, creating or exacerbating already existing chronic role strains, that erode the individual's positive sense of self-esteem and mastery. Social support and coping are potential mediators of stress, either altering the stressful circumstances or mediating their impact. Results from their longitudinal study of 1,106 adults indicate that life change, as measured by job disruption, influences depression directly and indirectly by affecting enduring role strains (particularly economic ones), that in turn are associated with a diminished sense of mastery and self-esteem. Depression is not significantly related either to coping or social support, indicating that these variables have no direct effect on depression. However, when job disruption occurs, social support and coping appear to affect depression indirectly by helping individuals to maintain their self-image and sense of worth.*

Thus, the literature clearly implies that social support and coping are critical areas for study among rape victims to determine: (1) if social support and coping affect the probability of sexual victimization, (2) whether and how support and coping influence sexual assault trauma, and (3) whether the effect of support and coping on sexual assault trauma is similar or dissimilar to the effects of these

---

*The complexity of this phenomenon is indicated by the Pearlin et al. (1981) data. While social support may reduce the negative effects of life changes, such as job disturbance, on self-esteem and so indirectly affect depression, some life events (such as death of child) are associated with depression, but not with loss of self-esteem and mastery, raising the issue of whether coping and social support function similarly with different kinds of life changes.

variables on other kinds of life crises and other forms of psychological distress. Such data will have important implications for developing mental health interventions for victims. More specific research questions include: (1) do social support and coping efforts buffer the effects of rape on the victim (that is, given one is raped, will the victim with positive social support and coping withstand the assault better than those without); and (2) do social support and coping buffer the effect of *other* life changes the victim was experiencing before the assault (that is, will the rape victims with severe life change events be less emotionally traumatized when they have positive coping and support than when they do not)? Related issues include the relative impact of different kinds of social support groups and coping styles in the course of the RTS.

Turning to the rape literature, several works have suggested that a victim's ability to deal with a sexual assault reflects her own coping skills and social support systems (Burgess & Holmstrom, 1979; Burgess, Groth, Holmstrom, & Sgroi, 1978; Frank & Stewart, 1983). With respect to coping, Burgess and Holmstrom found that positive mechanisms used by rape victims are both actions, such as moving, travel, or visiting relatives, and employment of cognitive defenses. The latter include explanation (why they were raped), minimization (their rape was not as bad as others), suppression (trying to forget the attack), and dramatization (frequently talking about the rape with friends). However, some responses, such as substance abuse and suicidal acts, were not positive. Of the 92 victims in their sample, 1 woman committed suicide and 2 died from the medical complications of alcoholism.

The theoretical model includes three different ways of coping with problems: Reliance on family and friends (personal networks), reliance on helping professionals, and reliance on one's self. Such coping styles are hypothesized to be beneficial for the victim. Data on coping presently being analyzed indicate that when victims are asked how they usually cope with problems, 56% report that they rely on family and friends, 44% rely on themselves, and 26% rely on helping professionals (the victims can name more than one coping style). Analysis of bivariate correlations between the different coping styles shows that victims who usually cope through reliance on family and friends are significantly less apt to rely on self and professionals. The relationship between relying on self and professionals is not significant, indicating that some victims who rely on themselves also seek professional help and others do not. A preliminary analysis of the data indicates that when trauma scores are regressed on the coping style variables, coping style of victim is not a significant predictor of trauma at intake but becomes important at the follow-up assessment. Then, as predicted, victims who rely on themselves or on their family and friends have significantly lower trauma levels than those who do not use these coping styles.

Frank and Stewart (1983) call attention to the crucial role of social support in the RTS by pointing out that "the victim reacts first to the assault and then to the response of her social network to the knowledge of the assault." Following Pearlin et al. (1981), we view sexual assault as a severe life crisis, generating fear, anxiety, and other stress reactions. The rape constitutes an assault on the victim's entire "self," eroding her positive sense of self-esteem and mastery. Thus, social support from personal networks or from treatment center personnel should be especially critical for rape victims to buffer the stress.

As suggested by Hobfoll (in press) and Pearlin et al. (1981), it is overly simplistic to assume that social networks are necessarily available or effective modifiers of the stress process. This is an especially important issue in the case of rape, which has been traditionally stigmatizing to the victim and significant others. Thus, when dealing with social support for the rape victim, it is important to investigate both (1) whether the victim has a social group or network readily available to call upon, as indicated by measures such as living with others and marital status; and (2) whether the victim's social relationships actually function as a source of social support, providing instrumental aid and especially intimacy, warmth, understanding, and emotional support. Moreover, it is necessary not only to ascertain how supportive such relationships are "in general" to the victim but also the specific response of the social group to the rape as these may be quite different.

The theoretical model includes three kinds of potential support groups: family, friends, and church. Victims are predicted to be more vulnerable if they lack an available support group or if potentially supportive persons available to them are in fact unsupportive. The living situation of the victim may also influence her capacity to deal with a sexual assault. It is hypothesized that, because they may have less available social support, victims living alone at the time of the assault will be highly traumatized. Another high-risk victim is the woman living with her husband, whom McCahill et al. (1979) suggest may have to cope not only with her own feelings but also with the nonsupportive reaction of her spouse.

Turning to the available data on social support and sexual assault trauma, the evidence suggests that victims *perceive* that social support is a crucial resource during the RTS. Williams and Holmes (1981) investigated the perceived need for social support by directly asking the victims what they had wanted or needed soon after the assault. Forty-four percent said that they wanted a generalized "someone" for support and understanding; another 22% specified a certain person. Ethnic group was a factor as black and Caucasian women most often mentioned a more generalized source of support, Mexican Americans, a specific person. To investigate which support groups were perceived by the victims as effective, Williams and Holmes asked the victims directly, using a forced-choice format, which persons were most helpful. Significant others perceived most helpful in descending order were boyfriend or fiancé, then husband, other family member, close friends, mother, and father. At the institutional level, most helpful were rape crisis workers, followed by medical staff, police, professional counselors, and clergy. Thus, the Williams and Holmes results indicate that victims perceive that social support facilitates their recovery and that some social and institutional networks are more helpful than others.

The important issue of whether or not social support actually does reduce trauma is not resolved however. Burgess and Holmstrom (1979) stress the positive function of social support. Most of the victims in their sample did have social relationships, such as family, friends, and work associates, meeting their psychological needs. The minority of victims lacking stable sources of social support were forced to depend solely on their own devices, prolonging recovery. Conditions contributing to the lack of social support for these victims included living alone, unemployment, geographical isolation from family, and a lack of communication with family.

McCahill et al. (1979) studied the living situations of victims and found that victims living with their husbands had more adjustment problems than those living with parents or siblings. These findings imply that the availability of social support, in terms of living with others, is not the only dimension in recovery. Instead, some social living situations are more beneficial than others, with proximity to the family of orientation (parents or siblings) facilitating recovery. Note, however, that the victims studied by Williams and Holmes (1981) perceived their spouses or boyfriends were *more* helpful than their parents so more research is needed to clarify these important questions.

To further complicate the issue, two recent empirical studies have largely failed to demonstrate the importance of social support groups in the recovery process. Williams and Holmes (1981) found no significant relationship between crisis scores and either personal or institutional support systems. Potential problems with generalizing from this study have been previously noted. Ruch and Chandler (1983) investigated the effect of social support on relatively immediate sexual assault trauma by asking the victims with whom they lived, as an indication of whether or not support systems were readily available to the victim, and whether the support stance of their social networks was positive or negative. Although caution is necessary in interpreting these results because the victims were interviewed soon after the assault and before the full import of the reaction of significant others could be felt, the data reveal interesting facets of the social support systems for victims of sexual assault that deserve more thorough investigation. Approximately three-fourths (77%) of the victims were living with others, such as parents, husbands, roommates, at the time of assault; 23% lived alone. With respect to the perceived support stance of their social networks, 72% of the victims at intake reported that their families (parents or husbands) were supportive; 87% had supportive friendships. Only 10% of the sample mentioned their church as a source of support. The bivariate correlations between the different support groups show that there is a significantly negative relation between supportive friendships and supportive families, suggesting that victims tend to either have supportive families or supportive friendships but not both.

The living situation of the victim is important in affecting whether the victim's family or friends are her source of social support. Women living with their parents were significantly more apt to view their family (in this case presumably parents) as more supportive, whereas women living alone or with spouses tended to view their friendships as more supportive. Are friends as equally supportive to married and unmarried women? When marital status and supportive friendships are correlated, single women are significantly more apt than married women to view their friendships as supportive. Apparently, the married woman facing the initial impact of a sexual assault is less apt to perceive her social relationships as supportive than are single women, who are more likely to have supportive families when living at home or supportive friendships when they have left home and are living elsewhere.

Regressions of trauma scores on the social support variables indicate that only one of the social support variables in the model, victim's living situation, is a significant predictor of initial trauma level. Victims living with parents were less traumatized than victims living alone or with a spouse. Whether the support stance of the victim's social groups (family, friends, church) was perceived as positive or negative did not add a significant increment to the variance explained. Preliminary analysis of the effects of social support variables on trauma level at the follow-up assessment indicates that none of the social support variables distinguish trauma level. Thus, these data imply that with the possible exception of the victim's living situation, social support appears not to have as significant an impact on relatively immediate rape trauma as expected, but does not preclude the importance of social support during subsequent stages in the RTS.

Because of its relevance to this chapter, additional analyses were conducted on the one social support variable, living situation, which was significantly related to trauma at intake. As might be expected certain demographic variables correlate significantly with living situation. Age is highly related to living situation, with older victims tending to live with spouses or alone and younger victims with their parents. The results of the regression analysis using a hierarchical model show that living situation continues to add a significant increment when age is controlled, whereas age does not when living situation is controlled. Thus, whom the victim lives with is an important variable at intake irrespective of the age of the victim. There is also a significant relationship between marital status and living situation as might be expected since most married women are living with their spouse at the time of the assault. However, single women may be living either alone *or* with their parents, so regressing sexual assault trauma on living situation controlling for marital status enables us to compare trauma levels of single victims living alone versus those living with their parents. The difference is significant with the more traumatized victims living alone. Thus, in summary, the data indicate that married women are more emotionally traumatized than single women, but living situation is important for single women who are at more risk when living alone than with parents or other relatives.

Victim's Demographic Variables

Consistent with previous studies, the response to victimization is expected to reflect the demographic variables of the victim, such as age, socioeconomic status, religion, and ethnicity (e.g., Burgess & Holmstrom, 1979; Burgess et al., 1978; Ruch & Chandler, 1979, 1982, 1983). In a study on short-term trauma, Ruch and Chandler (1983) tested the effects of the demographic variables in the theoretical model. Ethnicity and marital status of the victims were the most significant predictors of initial trauma level, with married, non-Caucasian women the most traumatized. Data on longer-term effects are now being analyzed but indicate that by the follow-up assessment employment status affects trauma, with employment facilitating recovery.

ADDITIONAL THEORETICAL CONSIDERATIONS: DIRECT OR INDIRECT EFFECTS OF PREASSAULT VARIABLES ON SHORT-TERM TRAUMA

Having delineated clusters of preassault variables and specific hypotheses linking them to trauma, it is possible that the effect of these variables on the RTS is *direct* (indicated by lines connecting the independent variable and $trauma_1$) or *indirect* (indicated by lines connecting different independent variables). For example, a stressful life change (LC), such as a recent divorce or separation, may affect trauma (T) relatively directly by increasing the woman's emotional vulnerability and rendering her less able to deal with the rape (LC → T). However, if the divorce results in a loss of social support (SS) for the victim, then the effect of life change is indirect through social support (LC → SS → T). (For a more detailed discussion of the effect of life change on the probability of receiving social support, see Thoits, 1982).

Similar and potentially reciprocal relations exist between the other preassault variables. For instance, social support and mental health (MH) may affect trauma directly or through each other. More specifically, the woman lacking socially supportive relationships is likely to have mental health or adjustment problems and so experience higher trauma when assaulted (SS → MH → T); likewise, a victim with mental health or adjustment problems may have already alienated her family before the assault and so lack social support that might otherwise facilitate her recovery (MH → SS → T).

Demographic variables of the victim may also affect trauma directly *or* indirectly by affecting the victim's life stresses, coping, and support systems. For example, if married women are more traumatized than single women, is this effect due to the reaction of the support systems (as suggested by McCahill et al., 1979) or to the higher incidence of mental health problems among married women (see Gove & Tudor, 1973, on the adverse association of marriage and mental health of women)? Ruch and Chandler (1983) explored this issue particularly with respect to marital status and ethnicity, which were found to be significant predictors of initial trauma level. Victim's ethnicity, however, did not correlate significantly with the other independent variables influencing initial trauma, suggesting that the effect of ethnicity during the early phase of the RTS is direct and not via the social support or mental health variables.

Marital status is significantly related both to living situation and to the support stance of friends. The strong association between marital status and living situation can be readily explained because married women will very likely be living with spouses, not alone or with their parents. However, the association of marital status and supportive friendships is interesting because the elevated trauma levels of the married women may reflect the lack of social support from friends. The regression analysis indicates that when supportiveness of friends is controlled, the effect of marital status remains significant, but having supportive friends does not add a significant increment when marital status is controlled. In other words, being married adversely affects the nature of the victim's friendships, but married women are more vulnerable even when the fact that they tend to lack supportive friends is held constant. More generally, the effect of the demographic variables, ethnicity and marital status, appear to be mainly direct in the most immediate phase of the RTS, but longer-term relationships need investigation.

LONGER-TERM TRAUMA AS A FUNCTION OF PREASSAULT AND POSTASSAULT VARIABLES

Although the assumption can be made that the relatively immediate effects of rape reflect primarily the nature of the sexual assault and the characteristics of the victim prior to assault, the process becomes more complex as time passes and where both pre- and postassault factors come into play.

The preassault characteristics of the victim may continue to affect her response later in the RTS ($Trauma_n$). We expect that prior mental health problems and major life crises (such as death or major illness in the family) may be particularly important here as these phenomena generally take time to resolve even without a rape aggravating the situation. The available evidence concerning the long-term effects of prior life stresses and adjustment problems is contradictory. Supportive evidence is provided by the McCahill et al. (1979) study, which found that increased adjustment problems one year postrape were associated with prior adjustment problems, such as a history of truancy or trouble with police. In contrast, Kilpatrick et al. (unpublished manuscript) reported that all items regarding psychiatric history and treatment were not significantly related to psychological distress when victims were assessed 3 months after the assault.

The demographic variables of the victim are also predicted to have longer-term consequences, but again this issue is unresolved in the available literature. Kilpatrick et al. (unpublished manuscript) did not find that demographic variables such as age, ethnicity, education, marital status, and religious preference, predicted level of distress 3 months following assault, whereas McCahill et al. (1979) reported that the victim's age was associated with adjustment problems at the one-year assessment.

The variables relating to the assault can also have a sustained effect on the victim. McCahill et al. (1979) found that brutal rapes had a greater effect than other types at the one-year assessment period compared to soon after the assault. They speculate that life-threatening assaults shatter the victim's basic sense of trust and security in herself and her physical and social environment. The victim's awareness of her own vulnerability develops with time but is a relatively direct, although delayed, effect of the rape.

Longer-term trauma ($Trauma_n$) will also reflect in part the victim's initial response to the assault ($Trauma_1$). Ruch and Leon (1983) found that the adjustment during the first weeks of the RTS reflected the initial level of trauma (e.g., initially highly traumatized women tend to remain elevated). Similarly, Kilpatrick et al. (unpublished manuscript) reported that distress level measured 6–21 days postassault best predicted psychological distress at the 3-month assessment. It is reasonable to assume, especially if other positive interventions do not occur, that such trends will continue over a more extended time.

Lastly, variables such as social support and coping are not necessarily static phenomena. How a victim copes ($Coping_n$) or her social support ($Support_n$) may be altered with time. Conversations with rape crisis counselors suggest that such changes can be positive or negative. For example, in some cases the rape has the effect of drawing the family together and improving communication, presumably facilitating recovery. In others, relationships with significant others become strained and unsupportive, exacerbating the rape trauma. Which situation is more difficult for the victim of rape—facing the long-term implications of a sexual assault with a social environment that is already negative and unsupportive, or facing an environment that has been generally supportive in the past but withdraws support following the rape?

An additional assumption made in the model is that certain assault and pre-assault variables will affect postrape social support and coping and so have an indirect effect on long-term trauma. Findings by Frank, Turner, and Stewart (1980) are suggestive of such indirect effects. They found that prior sexual victimization, although not affecting measures of depression, anxiety, or fear, was associated with significant disruption in social functioning in the victim's immediate household within a month of the rape. In other words, the preassault characteristics of the victim (in this case prior rape) were negatively affecting the personal support system of the victim. In this situation, we would expect a delayed recovery because of the negative effects of prior rape on social support.

The assault may also have indirect effects as suggested by Frank, Turner, and Stewart (1980), who found that social adjustment within the immediate family was better when the assailant used a weapon to intimidate the victim. These results imply that certain rape situations are more easily perceived as legitimate rapes and so the support stance of the family is more positive. The central issue here is that the rape itself and related factors may cause changes in the social support and coping variables, which in turn impact on long-term trauma facilitating or impeding recovery.

IMPLICATIONS

Implications for treatment services are clear. The cumulative research on the RTS provides unequivocable evidence of the urgent need for rape treatment centers to provide both crisis intervention and longer-term counseling and support services for victims. Interview protocols in rape centers should include questions on coping styles, social support, and life stresses the victim had *prior* to assault and *changes* that occur subsequent to the assault to evaluate the present and potential effect of the sexual assault on the victim during the RTS. The available data indicate that while sexual assault is virtually always traumatizing to the victim, several types of high-risk victims emerge: the woman with preexisting life stresses from life change events, substance abuse, or mental health problems; the woman who faces the fearsome implications of a sexual assault without sufficient coping skills; and the woman with initially severe psychological distress soon after the assault. Such high-risk victims should be targeted for special attention in the delivery of both crisis intervention and follow-up services.

With respect to prevention, it is important to have public information programs about sexual assault. At present, some rape treatment centers attempt to provide educational services to debunk the myths traditionally surrounding sexual assault and to inform the community about the RTS and available treatment services. Given the insufficient resources of many centers, an alternative strategy is to include this information systematically into school curricula. Receiving such information would be helpful not only for those who may be victimized subsequently but also for potential social support groups. Education on the RTS also needs to be targeted toward personnel in rape-related organizations (police, prosecuting attorneys) and other organizations (clergy, community mental health professionals) where the victim may turn for assistance.

Lastly, the review of the literature indicates that despite an increase in our knowledge about the RTS, crucial questions remain to be answered about longitudinal rape trauma and factors affecting recovery. Systematic uniform assessments on victims over time are needed as well as an increased understanding of the complex interplay of the victim's prior stresses, coping strengths, and social support. With the development of rape treatment centers across the nation, it is possible to gather abundant empirical data on the treatment needs of victims and treatment strategies. Especially needed are data banks large enough for multivariate analysis and longitudinal assessments of victims with repeated measures of life change, coping, and social support.

REFERENCES

Bassuk, E. L. (1980). A crisis theory perspective on rape. In S. L. McCombie (Ed.), *The rape crisis intervention handbook: A guide for victim care.* New York: Plenum.

Burgess, A. W., Groth, A. N., Holmstrom, L. L., & Sgroi, S. (1978). *Sexual assault of children and adolescents.* Lexington, MA: Lexington.

Burgess, A. W., & Holmstrom, L. L. (1974). *Rape: Victims of crisis.* Bowie, MD: Brady.

Burgess, A. W., & Holmstrom, L. L. (1979). *Rape: Crisis and recovery.* Bowie, MD: Brady.

Dohrenwend, B. S., & Dohrenwend, B. P. (Eds.). (1974). *Stressful life events: Their nature and effects.* New York: Wiley.

Frank, E., & Stewart, B. D. (1983). Treatment of depressed rape victims: An approach to stress-induced symptomatology. In P. J. Clayton & J. E. Barrett (Eds.), *Treatment of depression: Old controversies and new approaches.* New York: Raven.

Frank, E., Turner, S. M., & Stewart, B. D. (1980). Initial responses to rape: The impact of factors within the rape situation. *Journal of Behavioral Assessment, 2*(1), 39–53.

Gove, W. R., & Tudor, J. F. (1973). Adult sex roles and mental illness. *American Journal of Sociology, 78,* 812–835.

Gunderson, E. K., & Rahe, R. (1974). *Life stress and illness.* Springfield, IL: Thomas.

Hobfoll, S. E. (1985). The limitations of social support in the stress process. In I. G. Sarason & B. R. Sarason. *Social support research, theory and application.* The Hague: Martinus Nijhof.

Holmes, T. H., & Masuda, M. (1974). Life change and illness susceptibility. In B. S. Dohrenwend & B. P. Dohrenwend (Eds.), *Stressful life events: Their nature and effects.* New York: Wiley.

Kaplan, B. H., Cassel, J. C., & Gore, S. (1977). Social support and health. *Medical Care, 15*(5), Supplement, 47–58.

Katz, S., & Mazur, M. A. (1979). *Understanding the rape victim: A synthesis of research findings.* New York: Wiley.

Kilpatrick, D. G., Resick, P. A., & Veronen, L. J. (1981). Effects of a rape experience: A longitudinal study. *Journal of Social Issues, 37*(4), 105–122.

Kilpatrick, D. G., Veronen, L. J., & Best, C. L. *Factors predicting psychological distress at three months postrape.* Unpublished manuscript.

Kilpatrick, D. G., Veronen, L. J., & Resick, P. A. (1979). The aftermath of rape: Recent empirical findings. *American Journal of Orthopsychiatry, 49*(4), 658–669.

Lin, N., Simeone, R. S., Ensel, W. M., & Kuo, W. (1979). Social support, stressful life events and illness: A model and empirical test. *Journal of Health and Social Behavior, 20*(2), 108–119.

McCahill, T. W., Meyer, L. C., & Fischman, A. M. (1979). *The aftermath of rape.* Lexington, MA: Lexington.

Menaghan, E. (1982). Measuring coping effectiveness: A panel analysis of marital problems and coping efforts. *Journal of Health and Social Behavior, 23*(3), 220–234.

Pearlin, L. I., Lieberman, M. A., Menaghan, E. G., & Mullan, J. T. (1981). The stress process. *Journal of Health and Social Behavior, 22*(4), 337–356.

Ruch, L. O., & Chandler, S. M. (1979). Ethnicity and rape impact: The response of women from different ethnic backgrounds to rape and rape crisis treatment services in Hawaii. *Social Process in Hawaii, 27,* 52–67.

Ruch, L. O., & Chandler, S. M. (1982). The crisis impact of sexual assault on three victim groups: Adult rape victims, child rape victims, and incest victims. *Journal of Social Service Review, 5*(1/2), 83–100.

Ruch, L. O., & Chandler, S. M. (1983). Sexual assault trauma during the acute phase: An exploratory model and multivariate analysis. *Journal of Health and Social Behavior, 24*(2), 174–185.

Ruch, L. O., Chandler, S. M., & Harter, R. A. (1980). Life change and rape impact. *Journal of Health and Social Behavior, 21*(3), 248–260.

Ruch, L. O., & Hennessy, M. (1982). Sexual assault: Victim and attack dimensions. *Victimology, 7*(1–4), 94–105.

Ruch, L. O., & Leon, J. J. (1983). Sexual assault trauma and trauma change. *Women and Health, 8*(4), 5–21.

Sifneos, P. (1960). A concept of emotional crisis. *Mental Hygiene, 44,* 169–180.

Sifneos, P. (1967). Two different kinds of psychotherapy of short duration. *American Journal of Psychiatry, 123,* 1069–1074.

Thoits, P. A. (1982). Conceptual, methodological, and theoretical problems in studying social support as a buffer against life stress. *Journal of Health and Social Behavior, 23*(2), 145–158.

Thoits, P. A. (1983). Main and interactive effects of social support: Response to LaRocco. *Journal of Health and Social Behavior, 24*(1), 92–95.

Thoits, P. A. (forthcoming). Dimensions of life events as influences upon the genesis of psychological distress and associated conditions: An evaluation and synthesis of the literature. In H. B. Kaplan (Ed.), *Psychosocial stress: Trends in theory and research.* New York: Academic.

Turner, R. J., Frankel, B. G., & Levin, D. (1983). Social support: Conceptualization, measurement and implications for mental health. In J. R. Greenley (Ed.), *Research in community and mental health, Vol. III.* Greenwich, CT: JAI Press.

Turner, R. J., & Noh, S. (1983). Class and psychological vulnerability among women: The significance of social support and personal control. *Journal of Health and Social Behavior, 24*(1), 2–15.

Williams, J. E., & Holmes, K. A. (1981). *The second assault: Rape and public attitudes.* Westport, CT: Greenwood.

10

Coping and Social Support among Battered Women: An Ecological Perspective

Roger E. Mitchell
Stanford University and Veterans Administration
Medical Center, Palo Alto, California

Christine A. Hodson
Alameda County Hall of Justice
Hayward, California

Social support and coping have become increasingly popular concepts that are seen as providing a new perspective on our understanding of psychological distress and on our options for intervention (e.g., Dohrenwend & Dohrenwend, 1981; Gottlieb, 1983). The belief that vulnerability to stress is influenced by both the coping responses that individuals use and the supportive (or nonsupportive) responses they receive has led to investigations of the health promotive and health protective effects of support and coping among such diverse groups as disaster victims, pregnant teenagers, divorced individuals, and abused women (Gottlieb, 1983; Hodson, 1982; Mitchell & Hodson, 1983; Walker, 1983). The result has been calls for more support-oriented preventive interventions that might increase individuals' capabilities to withstand and overcome stressful situations (e.g., Bloom, Hodges, & Caldwell, 1982).

An examination of the emerging social support and coping literature, however, reveals some potentially disturbing limitations in its focus. The preponderance of studies in this field have linked deficits in social support and coping to individual distress, but have not examined the broader social context out of which stress, coping, and support processes emerge. Although we are increasingly able to document the deleterious *effects* of deficits in individual coping and support (e.g., Mitchell, Billings, & Moos, 1982), there has been little study of the *determinants* of such patterns: What are the characteristics of environments and social systems

Preparation of this manuscript was supported in part by NIMH Grant MH08603. The authors wish to thank both the residents and staff members of the shelters who generously gave their time. In addition, we wish to thank Cathy Birtley Fenn, Gail Price, Valerie Simmons, and Forrest Tyler for providing comments on earlier drafts of this manuscript.

All correspondence should be directed to Roger E. Mitchell, who is currently Director, Psychological Consultation Center, University of Rhode Island Department of Psychology, Kingston, RI 02881.

that are likely to promote effective coping or enhance the development of supportive social ties? What are the personal and environmental contexts that characterize individuals who are effective in establishing a wide repertoire of coping responses and a supportive social system? The failure to examine the broader social context of coping and support processes is a serious omission, since our research agendas strongly shape how we define both problems and the range of possible solutions (Caplan & Nelson, 1973). If we fail to ask how social support and coping processes are influenced by broader social system characteristics (e.g., how police responses to domestic violence calls influence women's subsequent coping efforts), we are not likely to view intervention into such systems as a possible alternative.

This chapter is concerned with examining how personal and contextual factors shape the patterns of social ties and coping responses likely to be displayed by battered women. First, we briefly review literature linking social support and coping to psychological functioning among battered women, and discuss the complexities involved in applying these concepts to the area of domestic violence. Second, we argue that an ecological perspective can enrich our understanding of the circumstances under which "effective" support and coping patterns emerge. Support and coping responses do not arise out of a vacuum, but occur as a function of the woman's life context. Thus, we present a theoretical framework that portrays several personal and contextual factors (e.g., childhood exposure to violence, attitudes towards women's roles, institutional responsiveness) that are likely to shape women's coping and support patterns. Wherever possible, we try to illustrate these more general points with data from our own research.

SOCIAL SUPPORT AND PSYCHOLOGICAL WELL-BEING

As initially formulated by such individuals as Cassel (1974), the "buffering hypothesis" implies that individuals with high levels of social support are less likely to show psychological maladjustment in the face of stress than are individuals with low levels of social support (see Mitchell & Trickett, 1980; Gottlieb, 1981). Supportive social systems are presumed to provide tangible assistance, promote more active coping, and help individuals maintain their sense of self-esteem in the face of difficulty (Heller & Swindle, 1983). Since battered women are often isolated from family and friends because of their partners' efforts to keep them dependent (Hilberman & Munson, 1977-1978), the experience of dealing with a violent husband is likely to become even more frightening and stressful because of the lack of supportive resources.

How should one go about trying to understand the role that social support plays in the domestic violence process? First, it seems important to conceptualize social support as involving several simultaneous and related aspects: (a) *perceived support* (i.e., ratings of the degree to which one feels that support is available or adequate); (b) *supportive transactions* (i.e., the degree to which supportive or help-giving behaviors actually occur); and (c) *the structure of the social network* (i.e., the patterning of the individual's social ties, such as the connectedness in family or work domains). Although levels of stress and functioning may be most strongly related to measures of perceived support, information about other aspects of the support process may highlight when and how perceived support is influenced. For example, women in the process of divorce were less likely to gain support from friendships that were developed and maintained primarily through the husband (Wilcox, 1981).

Second, one also needs to consider how the stressor at hand shapes the pattern of supportive responses that emerge. Although family and friends may quickly rally around an individual to provide support in response to stressful, but expected, life transitions (e.g., birth of a child, illness), they may be less sympathetic in response to stressful situations that arouse feelings of discomfort or disapproval, such as divorce or terminal illness (e.g., Kitson, Moir, & Mason, 1982; Wortman & Dunkel-Schetter, 1979). A battered woman may have a wide variety of social contacts, but may find that friends are uncomfortable when she tries to raise the issue of her violent relationship. Thus, it may be important to examine helping transactions around specific stressful events, as well as more global perceptions of support.

In some previous work (Mitchell & Hodson, 1983), we sought to examine the kinds of support women received for dealing with *the battering situation specifically.* Women who reported experiencing fewer avoidance responses and more empathic responses from friends also reported higher levels of mastery and self-esteem. Why do some women receive more supportive responses from friends than others? The results suggested a possible link between the structure of women's social ties and their supportiveness (i.e., the more that women's social ties overlap with those of their husband's, the more difficulty women may have in obtaining support in dealing with the battering situation). For example, women who had met a larger proportion of their friends through their partners, and who had fewer social contacts unaccompanied by their husbands, were more likely to encounter friends who responded to their help-seeking efforts by avoiding the issue or minimizing its seriousness. This may be because individuals who are friends of the man as well as the woman may be reluctant to involve themselves in "taking sides" in a marital dispute. Thus, battered women can find themselves lacking in social support for dealing with the battering situation even though they are not "socially isolated" in the more general sense.

COPING RESPONSES AND PSYCHOLOGICAL WELL-BEING

"People are rarely passive in the face of what happens to them; they seek to change the things they can, and when they cannot they use cognitive modes of coping by which they may change the meaning of the situation" (Lazarus & DeLongis, 1983, p. 248). Thus, researchers have increasingly examined coping responses as a way of understanding individual variability in response to stress. How individuals appraise problems, whether they initiate problem-focused strategies, and how they deal with the adverse emotional consequences of a stressful situation influences psychological well-being (Folkman & Lazarus, 1980; Lazarus, 1981; Pearlin & Schooler, 1978).

How are women likely to cope with a battering incident, and what are the likely consequences of such responses? Claerhout, Elder, and Janes (1982) compared a small group of battered women with a sociodemographically similar group of nonbattered women in their responses to hypothetical, battering-related, problem situations (e.g., "Your husband saw you downtown talking to a male friend and got very loud and angry"). Battered women generated fewer effective problem-solving alternatives and a greater number of avoidant and dependent strategies. Similarly, Walker and her colleagues (Walker, 1979) found that a large number of battered women reported using "avoidant" coping strategies in response to an episode of violence, (e.g., withdrawal; hiding the incident from others; not seeking outside help). Such strategies may be used as a means of "placating" the batterer and seeking to avoid his being "provoked" into further acts of violence. In our own research, women who used more active coping responses (e.g., "considered several alternatives for handling the problem" or "talked with a friend about the situation"), and fewer avoidant responses (e.g., "kept my feelings to myself") reported less depression and a greater sense of mastery (Mitchell & Hodson, 1983).

As Menaghan (1983) points out, though, specifying the particular coping behaviors that are likely to be most adaptive in helping the individual deal with specific stressors is a complex task. The effectiveness of particular coping strategies can vary as a function of several factors: (a) problem area or stressor, (b) time frame, (c) outcome criteria, and (d) patterns of responses.

Problem Area or Stressor

Some types of problems may be more amenable to coping efforts than others. Pearlin & Schooler (1978), for example, found that several coping strategies that were helpful in dealing with marital problems were much less effective in dealing with the strain associated with stressful financial and occupational situations. It becomes important to recognize the limits as well as the potential benefits of coping responses. In dealing with a battering relationship, active coping responses may help a woman to maintain her self-esteem, to avoid becoming isolated from friends and family, and to be better prepared to leave the relationship. It may be unrealistic to expect that coping responses in and of themselves may stop the pattern of battering.

Time Frame

Coping responses may have different effects depending upon whether one examines the short or the long-term consequences. For example, denial-like forms of cognitive coping may result in less stress *during* a crisis period (e.g., the terminal illness of one's child), but the failure to do such "anticipatory grieving" may result in higher levels of stress when the crisis period has passed (Lazarus, 1981). Similarly, avoidance or denial responses may delay a battered woman's having to deal fully with the emotional impact of the incident, and allow her to continue her usual social and occupational routines. To the extent that avoidance responses prevent her from taking active steps to provide for her own safety or to be prepared to leave the relationship, there are likely to be negative psychological consequences in the long run.

Outcome Criteria

Similarly, a coping response may vary in its effectiveness in reducing the individual's experience of distress, as opposed to its impact on the initial source of stress. Menaghan (1982), for example, found that the use of the coping strategy of negotiation had minimal effects on experienced distress, although it had a positive effect in reducing the subsequent occurrence of marital problems.

Patterns of Responses

Investigators have tended to examine the effects of coping responses individually. However, a particular coping response may have different effects depending upon the broader constellation of coping responses within which it is used. For example, denial or avoidance responses may be adaptive if they allow the individual to maintain his/her emotional equilibrium so that problem-focused responses can also be initiated. In our own data, we found some modest evidence that the combination of coping responses used had an impact over and above the effects of individual coping variables. For example, the effect of avoidance coping on self-esteem varies as a function of the degree of active-cognitive coping used as well. Avoidance coping is strongly associated with low self-esteem for those women who use lower levels of active-cognitive coping. Such avoidant responses have less of a relationship with self-esteem for those women who also use high levels of active coping.* In summary, these results demonstrate the usefulness of social support and coping in understanding individual distress, however complicated these relationships may sometimes become.

SOCIAL SUPPORT, COPING, AND PERSON–CENTERED BIAS

As social support and coping are increasingly linked to physical and psychological health among a variety of at-risk populations (e.g., divorced, bereaved, chronically ill), these constructs are becoming the basis for the development of preventive and treatment interventions (e.g., Bloom, Hodges, & Caldwell, 1982; Gottlieb, 1983). Such strategies make good intuitive sense: increasing the coping skills and level of support available to individuals should decrease the likelihood of their experiencing psychological disorder in the face of stress. At another level, though, the literature reveals a potentially disturbing pattern of person-centered bias in its focus; the preponderance of studies in this field have examined the links between social support and coping and individual distress, but have not examined the broader social context out of which such stress, coping and support processes emerge. This omission is a serious one. To the extent that the predominant research focus is to link individual deficits in coping and social support with individual problem behavior (e.g., poor coping skills are more prominent among women who are battered), there is a tendency to attribute causal significance to these person-centered characteristics (e.g., women continue to be battered because of their poor coping skills), and to develop person-centered solutions (e.g., Claerhout et al.'s [1982] suggestion of problem-solving skills training for battered women). Although such strategies *do* make sense at the individual level, an unintended consequence can be the fostering of person-oriented change strategies *to the exclusion* of system-change solutions (Caplan & Nelson, 1973). Researchers have not dealt with a broader set of questions regarding the role of the broader social context in

---

*Complete tables of results are available from the authors for those analyses not described fully in the text because of space limitations.

contributing to coping and social support deficits (e.g., What institutional factors encourage or discourage police from responding to domestic violence calls in ways that increase women's sense of control over their situation and their likelihood of sustaining active coping efforts?)

ECOLOGICAL PERSPECTIVE

An ecological perspective suggests several themes that redirect the focus of research on social support and coping in useful ways. First, an interest in adaptation and change over time is emphasized, thereby directing attention to how support and coping repertoires are "expressed, elaborated, and sustained" over the life of both the individual and the organization (Kelly, 1977). Second, persons and environments are seen as interdependent resources that create varied conditions for the expression of social support and coping (Trickett, Kelly, & Vincent, 1985). The task becomes one of trying to understand how personal, environmental and situational factors operate together to influence the help-seeking/help-giving and coping strategies that are chosen by individuals, as well as the patterns of social support and coping strategies that emerge within groups or organizations.

The framework presented in Figure 1 embeds social support and coping within a broader social context by linking them to a number of factors that have been thought to play a role in the domestic violence process. Although childhood exposure to violence, nontraditional attitudes toward women's roles, personal resources, and institutional responsiveness have been related to the psychological distress among women dealing with conflictual or violent marital relationships (Felton, Brown, Lehman, & Liberatos, 1980; Gelles, 1976; Pagelow, 1981; Walker, 1979), there has been little study of how these personal and contextual factors may socialize women to adopt and maintain particular coping and help-seeking patterns. For example, do women with fewer personal resources and less traditional sex-role attitudes exercise more limited coping responses in the face of increasing violence? What factors tend to bolster women's receipt and use of supportive resources? In the remainder of this chapter, we will address some of these issues using data from our own research.

STUDY BACKGROUND

The sample, measures, and methodology we employed in studying coping and support processes among a group of battered women are described in detail elsewhere (Hodson, 1982; Mitchell & Hodson, 1983). In brief, the sample consisted of 60 battered women who had sought assistance from one of six shelters in the San Francisco Bay area. To be included in this study, a woman must have been physically assaulted at least twice by a man with whom she had an intimate relationship. All but five were living with the batterer before coming to the shelter. The women had been in a relationship with their partners for a mean of 5.4 years, and physical abuse had begun a mean of 1.7 years after the start of the relationship. The mean age of the women was 27.4 years. Forty-eight percent of the women were Caucasian, 44% were black, and 8% were of other ethnic backgrounds. At the time of the battering incident, a mean of 2.1 children lived in the homes of the women who had children, and six of the women had no children.

To assess the constructs displayed in the blocks in Figure 1, the following measures were utilized:

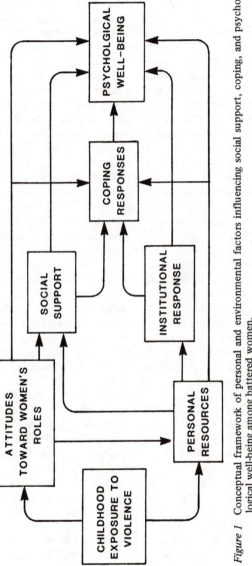

Figure 1 Conceptual framework of personal and environmental factors influencing social support, coping, and psychological well-being among battered women.

Childhood exposure to violence was assessed by asking women to rate the frequency with which they had been assaulted by their father, their mother, or had witnessed their father assaulting their mother. These individual scores were added to form a summary score.*

Attitudes toward women's roles. The degree to which women held traditional versus nontraditional views regarding women's rights and roles was assessed with the short form of the Attitudes toward Women Scale (AWS–short form; Spence, Helmreich, & Stapp, 1973). Respondents rated the degree to which they agreed with a variety of statements regarding vocational, educational, and intellectual roles, marital relations and obligations, etc. (e.g., "Husbands and wives should be equal partners in planning the family budget").**

Personal resources refers to a composite measure which included data about the woman's level of education, personal income (independent of the husband), occupational status of her current job, and occupational status of her "best" job. Each of these four scores was standardized and added together to form a composite index (Cronbach's Alpha = .73).

Institutional response. The response of social institutions to battered women's requests for assistance was assessed by asking respondents to complete scales describing whether police, lawyers, and therapists with whom they had contact had taken particular helpful or nonhelpful actions (e.g., "[the police] told me about other places to get help"; "[the police] never showed up at all"). A summary "average helpfulness" score was derived, based upon the number of institutions actually contacted.

Social support. In order to examine different aspects of the support process, five different measures of social support were constructed: (1) number of supporters; (2) visits with friends and relatives unaccompanied by one's partner; (3) visits with friends and relatives accompanied by one's partner; (4) empathic responses of friends to women's attempts to discuss the battering situation (e.g., "were sympathetic," "urged you to talk about how you felt"); and (5) avoidance responses of friends (e.g., "changed the topic," "pointed out the good parts of your relationship with your husband/boyfriend").

Coping. A measure developed by Billings and Moos (1981) to assess coping responses to stressful events was used to assess women's responses to battering incidents. Respondents checked whether they had used any of 17 different strategies for dealing with the battering incident which occurred prior to the incident which precipitated their coming to the shelter. Items were grouped into the following coping categories: (1) active cognitive coping (i.e., "attempts to manage the appraisal of the stressfulness of the event"); (2) active behavioral coping (i.e., "overt behavioral attempts to deal directly with the problem and its effects"); and (3) avoidance coping (i.e., strategies indicative of avoidance, denial, or tension reduction).

Psychological well-being was measured by several instruments: (1) the depression scale of the Brief Symptom Inventory (BSI), which is a shortened version of the

---

*In this sample, 22% of the women had witnessed their mother being "hit or beaten" by their father 11 or more times, and 32% of the women had been "hit or beaten (not just spanked)" during childhood by one or both of their parents 11 or more times.

**Due to an administrative error, one page of the AWS-Short Form was omitted, so that 15 items, rather than 25, were administered. The internal consistency of this scale (Cronbach's Alpha = .85) is comparable to that reported for the overall AWS-Short Form.

widely-used Hopkins Symptom Checklist (SCL-90) (Derogatis, 1975), (2) the 7-item mastery scale developed by Pearlin and Schooler (1978), and (3) the Rosenberg Self-Esteem scale (Rosenberg, 1979).

Levels of Violence. Although not displayed in the model in Figure 1, we also assessed the levels of violence in the woman's relationship with the batterer. The violence subscale of Straus' (1979) Conflict Tactics Scale (CTS) was used to measure the degree of violence directed by the man against the woman (e.g., "kicked, bit, or hit with a fist" and "threatened with a knife or a gun").

DETERMINANTS OF COPING RESPONSES AND SOCIAL SUPPORT

Social Context of Social Support

What factors shape whether women develop supportive social networks? In Table 1, social support variables are related to several of the variables displayed in the model in Figure 1: attitudes toward women's roles, personal resources, as well as level of violence in the current relationship. Women with greater personal resources and more nontraditional attitudes toward women's roles report greater numbers of supporters, more empathic responses from friends, and a larger proportion of friends that were met independently of the husband. In addition, greater personal resources are associated with fewer avoidance responses from friends, and greater socializing independent of one's partner. Thus, increased education, income and job skills may make it easier for women to gain access to nonmarital social roles that provide opportunities for developing friendships outside the marital context.

In contrast, increasing levels of battering are associated with greater isolation and decreased support. As the man becomes more abusive, he may also try to constrict the social life of his partner because of a fear that outside social contacts might encourage the woman to resist her husband's influence and control (Hilberman & Munson, 1977-1978). In addition, women may distance themselves from friends as they experience their own and their friends' discomfort in discussing the difficulties of responding to increased battering. Thus, women are likely to be at the greatest risk for seeing their social ties become constricted and less supportive at the very time that they may need social support the most.

The model in Figure 1 does not posit a direct link between violence in one's family of origin and the availability of social support in adulthood. Nonetheless, we did wonder whether such violence influenced women's attitudes about help-seeking. The respondents were asked to recall the first time they were battered by their spouse, and to rate the degree to which they had held a number of beliefs regarding the availability of help from friends and family. Women with high childhood exposure to violence waited longer before talking with anyone about their battering situation, and reported being more pessimistic about friends being *able* or *willing* to help. Growing up with violence in one's family may set expectations about the kinds of help one can expect from friends. In addition, there may be indirect effects of childhood violence upon subsequent support patterns. Women who had experienced or witnessed violence in their family of origin were more likely to hold traditional attitudes toward women's roles $(r = -.40)$. Having traditional attitudes toward women's roles was associated with having fewer

Table 1 Correlation of social support variables with attitudes toward women's roles, personal resources, and severity of violence[a,b]

	Number of supporters	Empathic responses of friends	Avoidance responses of friends	Social contacts (without partner)	Social contacts (with partner)	Number of friends met through partner
Attitudes toward women's roles[c]	.33**	.25*	—.16	.21	.22	—.26*
Personal resources (composite of income, education, and occupational status)	.38***	.45***	—.33*	.39**	.07	—.39**
Level of violence (conflict tactics scale)	—.30*	—.18	.35**	—.42***	—.07	.15

[a]Parts of this table were adapted from Mitchell and Hodson (1983).
[b]Ns vary due to missing data.
[c]Higher scores reflect more nontraditional attitudes.
*$p < .05$; **$p < .01$; ***$p < .001$.

personal resources and less extensive and supportive social networks. Thus, family violence may shape sex-role attitudes in ways that discourage women from taking a more independent stance in developing support networks and resources (e.g., job skills) for themselves.

Childhood Exposure to Violence, Sex-roles, and Coping

What factors influence a woman's use of more active rather than avoidant coping strategies in dealing with a battering situation? Walker (1979, 1983) argues that rigid sex-role socialization and exposure to violence during childhood are likely to increase one's susceptibility to becoming "trapped" in a battering relationship. Families that engage in high levels of violence are likely to model ineffective responses for either terminating or escaping violent relationships. Similarly, women who are socialized to hold rather traditional attitudes toward women's roles may see themselves as responsible for holding the family together, and find the threat of separation particularly stressful. In a study of marital conflict, for example, women with more traditional sex-role attitudes showed increasing psychological distress as marital stress became more severe; this was not the case for women holding more nontraditional attitudes (Felton, Lehman, Brown, & Liberatos, 1980). Thus, women with childhood exposure to violence and/or rigid sex-role socialization may find it particularly difficult to respond effectively to domestic violence.

To investigate these ideas, we examined some of the relationships among childhood exposure to violence, attitudes toward women's roles, current levels of violence in the relationship, and coping behaviors. Specifically, we wondered: Do women's coping responses to battering vary as a function of the degree to which they have experienced or witnessed violence in their family of origin? Similarly, do women's coping responses to battering differ depending upon the degree to which they hold traditional versus nontraditional attitudes toward women's roles? Regression analyses were constructed in which each type of coping response (active-cognitive, active-behavioral, avoidance) was predicted by severity of violence in the current relationship (i.e., Conflict Tactics Scale [CTS]), childhood exposure to violence, and an interaction term of severity of violence X childhood exposure. Analogous regression analyses predicted use of coping responses as a function of severity of violence in the current relationship, traditional versus nontraditional attitudes toward women's roles (i.e., Spence, Helmreich & Stapp's (1973) Attitudes toward Women scale [AWS]), and an interaction term of current violence (i.e., CTS) X attitudes toward women's roles (i.e., AWS).

The results were remarkably consistent. Women's coping responses to increasing levels of battering differed as a function of their childhood exposure to violence (i.e., there were significant severity of violence X childhood exposure to violence interaction terms). Women who had been exposed to violence in their family of origin were likely to use fewer active coping responses and more avoidant responses as the battering became more severe. Women who had not been exposed to violence in their family of origin were likely to use more active coping strategies in response to increasing violence; their use of avoidant coping responses was unrelated to severity of violence. These interaction terms contributed an average of 11% of explained variance to the prediction of coping behaviors.

Similar results emerged when attitudes toward women's roles was used as the moderator variable. For example, Table 2 presents the regression of active behavioral coping on severity of violence (i.e., CTS), attitudes toward women's roles (i.e., AWS), and a CTS × AWS interaction term. The significant interaction term indicates that the relationship between violence and active-behavioral coping varies according to the degree of nontraditional attitudes held. This interaction term is displayed graphically in Figure 2. For women who have more nontraditional attitudes toward women's roles (i.e., one standard deviation above the mean in this sample), increasing violence is associated with *greater* use of active-behavioral coping. For women who have more traditional attitudes toward women's roles (i.e., one standard deviation below the mean in this sample), increasing violence is associated with *less* use of active-behavioral strategies.*

Interestingly, no similar pattern of results was found when we examined how women dealt with nonbattering events. (Examples of nonbattering incidents included eviction, illness of a child, and difficulties with work supervisors).** We found no significant interaction effects predicting use of coping responses to nonbattering events, even though a variety of interaction terms were tried (i.e., CTS × childhood exposure to violence; CTS × AWS; severity of the nonbattering event × childhood exposure to violence; severity of the battering event × AWS). This suggests that the moderating effects of childhood exposure to violence and attitudes toward women's roles may be particularly salient when women are dealing with crises related to their partner or their role within the family.***

In summary, these results are consistent with Walker's (1983) notions that childhood exposure to violence can increase one's vulnerability to using more ineffective coping responses when faced with an abusive and violent relationship. These results also support the idea that nontraditional attitudes toward women's roles can

---

*The "crossover effect" in Figure 2 would seemingly indicate that for those at low levels of severity of violence (i.e., CTS), a lower score on AWS is associated with more active coping. This is misleading, since only 5% of the sample had a CTS score of less than 3. In fact, the dotted portion of the line indicates that there were no cases at all with CTS scores from 0–1.

**We recognize that distinctions between battering and nonbattering related events may be difficult to make. For example, trouble with work supervisors may stem from the woman's absenteeism after battering incidents, and a child's illness may be in part a psychological reaction to the degree of conflict within the family. Nonetheless, we think that crises involving violent interactions with one's spouse represent qualitatively different kinds of stressors.

***Complete tables of results are available from the authors for those analyses not described fully in the text because of space limitations.

Table 2 Regression of level of violence and attitudes toward women's roles on the use of active-behavioral coping

	B	β	Standard error of b	F
Violence (CTS)	− .008	− .009	0.105	0.006
Attitudes toward women's roles (AWS)[a]	.056	.266	0.025	5.032*
CTS × AWS	.038	.371	0.012	9.572**
Constant	3.780			

[a]Higher scores reflect more nontraditional attitudes.
*p < .05; **p < .01.

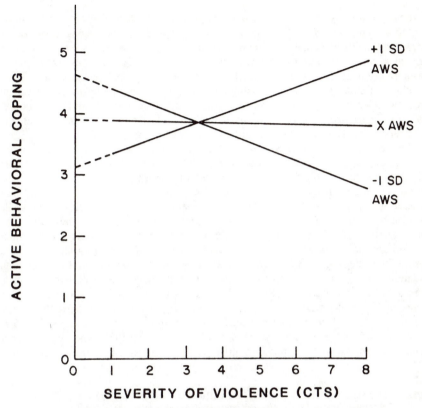

Figure 2 Regression of active behavioral coping on severity of violence (CTS) at three
levels of attitudes towards women's roles (AWS).

moderate the degree to which women may effectively deal with stress, especially in
a marital relationship (Felton et al., 1980).

Social Context of Coping

Although some theorists see coping styles as relatively stable personality traits,
such coping responses also occur within a broader psychosocial context. Friends,
families, and institutions can have a considerable impact on a number of aspects
of the coping process. For example, friends can help shape the individual's sense
of the nature and seriousness of the problem (e.g., do friends recommend that a
woman deal with her feelings of depression by "keeping busy to take her mind off
things" or by going to a professional to "really talk things through"?). Similarly,
institutions have social climates that promote or discourage the use of various types
of coping responses. To a large extent, though, studies of coping have focused on
intraindividual variables, rather than the broader psychosocial context out of
which such coping patterns emerge.

In this study, we were interested in exploring how coping responses of battered
women might be linked to interpersonal and institutional factors. We suspected
that women are most likely to take active steps to confront their situation directly

if they are in social contexts that encourage such behaviors. Some modest support for this hypothesis is presented in Table 3, where use of coping responses is correlated with personal resources, institutional responsiveness, social support variables, and attitudes toward women's roles. There is a greater likelihood of women using avoidance coping if they have fewer personal resources and fewer numbers of supporters. Active coping strategies were more likely to be used when women experienced positive responses from institutional sources, and when women did not experience avoidance responses from friends. Thus, how women deal with a battering situation is clearly linked to aspects of their social milieu.

An ecological perspective suggests that coping styles are not invariant across settings or situations. As the problems and resources which confront people change, so do individuals' efforts to adapt to and master their environment. Thus, we wondered about the generality of abused women's coping styles across problem situations. Do battered women display a general deficit in problem-solving skills, as Claerhout et al. (1982) suggest, or is there something specific about domestic violence that "pulls" for such responses? To investigate this, we asked the women in our sample to rate the degree to which they had used a variety of coping responses in dealing with a recent nonbattering stressful event as well as a battering incident. We found a significant difference in how women dealt with battering versus nonbattering events (Repeated measures MANOVA, Wilks Lambda = .71, approximate Multivariate $F = 6.91$, with 3,51 df, $p < .001$). In particular, these women responded to nonbattering events with more active-behavioral ($F = 5.77$ with 1,53 df, $p < .02$) and less df, $p < .001$). These results cannot be explained solely in terms of the possible greater stressfulness of battering incidents.

Table 3 Correlation of coping responses with attitudes toward women's roles, personal resources, institutional responsiveness, and social support variables[a,b]

	Active-cognitive coping	Active-behavioral coping	Avoidance coping
Attitudes toward women's roles[c]	−.01	.28*	−.12
Personal resources composite of income, education, and occupational status	.08	.20	−.48***
Institutional response composite of helpfulness of police, lawyers, and therapists	.31**	.25*	−.16
Social support variables			
Number of supporters	−.04	.06	−.32*
Empathic responses of friends to discussing battering	.16	.23	−.04
Avoidance responses of friends to discussing battering	−.37**	−.28*	.23

[a]Parts of this table were adapted from Mitchell and Hodson (1983).
[b]Ns vary due to missing data.
[c]Higher scores indicate more nontraditional attitudes.
*$p < .05$; **$p < .01$; ***$p < .001$.

Significant multivariate differences in coping persisted even after the severity of the nonbattering event was controlled statistically.* These results suggest that the pattern of ineffective coping women show in battering situations may not be representative of how they deal with problems in their lives more generally. Given that a more varied coping repertoire is available to some women, there is a need to explore what aspects of their personal and social context serve to elicit such coping patterns.

Limitations

As an initial research effort in a complex area, this study has described factors that we believe are important in influencing the psychological health of battered women. Nonetheless, we recognize several limitations of this work. First, alternative explanations of findings are possible, given the cross-sectional nature of the study. For example, although women's coping responses are likely to be shaped by the norms, values, and helping behaviors (or lack of them) provided by formal institutions and informal networks, it is also likely that women with more effective coping repertoires will be more adept at obtaining help. Second, there are likely to be a number of *reciprocal* processes that are not captured by the unidirectional model. For example, the structure of one's social network is likely to shape, and be shaped by, attitudes toward women's roles. Finally, we were unable to examine patterns of interaction between the couple (e.g., power dynamics), although we believe that the factors in the model are likely to be relevant.

CONCLUDING COMMENTS

We have been asked: How does one use expertise in examining and intervening in psychological processes at the individual and dyadic level without contributing to a process of "blaming the victim" and diverting energy from institutional change? We believe that an ecological perspective addresses this issue by redirecting the focus of research in useful ways. First, it suggests that both person-centered and system-centered views have validity in a complex world; the task is to understand how persons and environments operate interdependently to create varied conditions for the expression of effective social support and coping repertoires. It leads to such questions as: How do institutions and social systems promote the development of particular social network patterns, influence the availability of social support, and socialize individuals to adopt particular coping patterns? Conversely, how do personal characteristics influence the degree to which individuals utilize the social resources that are potentially available to them? Finally, what individual actions contribute toward making the institutions of which they are a part more likely to support adaptive behaviors? Such an ecological perspective attempts to understand how changes in both individuals and systems can contribute to adaptive behavior (Kelly, 1977).

Second, an ecological point of view suggests a focus on how individuals *actively* go about constructing coping and support patterns and *successfully* cope with

---

*Complete tables of results are available from the authors for those analyses not described fully in the text because of space limitations.

stressful situations. For example, are women who are able to successfully leave (or modify) relationships at the first display of violence distinctive in their patterns of coping responses, social support, and sex-role attitudes? What are the personal and contextual factors that characterize women who effectively deal with such situations? Given current levels of courtship violence among college students (Makepeace, 1983), studies of how young women deal with initial encounters of violence in relationships might help us to understand how to develop more effective individual and institutionally oriented interventions.

REFERENCES

Billings, A. G., & Moos, R. H. (1981). The role of coping responses and social resources in attenuating the stress of life events. *Journal of Behavioral Medicine, 4,* 139–157.
Bloom, B. L., Hodges, W. F., & Caldwell, R. A. (1982). A preventive intervention program for the newly separated: Initial evaluation. *American Journal of Community Psychology, 10,* 251–264.
Caplan, N., & Nelson, S. (1973). On being useful: The nature and consequences of psychological research on social problems. *American Psychologist, 28,* 199–211.
Cassel, J. (1974). Psychosocial processes and "stress": Theoretical formulations. *International Journal of Health Services, 4,* 471–482.
Claerhout, S., Elder, J., & Janes, C. (1982). Problem-solving skills of battered women. *American Journal of Community Psychology, 10,* 605–612.
Derogatis, L. R. (1975). *The brief symptom inventory.* Baltimore: Clinical Psychometrics Research.
Dohrenwend, B. S. & Dohrenwend, B. P. (Eds.). (1981). *Stressful life events and their contexts.* New York: Watson.
Felton, B. J., Brown, P., Lehman, S., & Liberatos, P. (1980). The coping function of sex-role attitudes during marital disruption. *Journal of Health and Social Behavior, 21,* 240–248.
Folkman, S., & Lazarus, R. S. (1980). An analysis of coping in a middle-aged community sample. *Journal of Health and Social Behavior, 21,* 219–239.
Gelles, R. J. (1976). Abused wives: Why do they stay? *Journal of Marriage and the Family, 38,* 659–668.
Gottlieb, B. H. (Ed.). (1981). *Social networks and social support.* Beverly Hills: Sage.
Gottlieb, B. H. (1983). *Social support strategies: Guidelines for mental health practice.* Beverly Hills: Sage.
Heller, K., and Swindle, R. W. (1983). Social networks, perceived social support, and coping with stress. In R. D. Felner, L. A. Jason, J. N. Moritsugu, and S. S. Farber (Eds.), *Preventive psychology: Theory, research and practice* (pp. 87–103). New York: Pergamon Press.
Hilberman, E., & Munson, L. (1977–1978). Sixty battered women. *Victimology, 2,* 460–470.
Hodson, C. A. (1982, August). *Length of stay in a battering relationship: Test of a model.* Paper presented at the meeting of the American Psychological Association, Washington, DC.
Kelly, J. G. (1977, August). *The ecology of social support systems: Footnotes to a theory.* Paper presented at the meeting of the American Psychological Association, San Francisco, CA.
Kitson, G. C., Moir, R. N., & Mason, P. R. (1982). Family social support in crises: The special case of divorce. *American Journal of Orthopsychiatry, 52,* 161–165.
Lazarus, R. S. (1981). The costs and benefits of denial. In B. S. Dohrenwend & B. P. Dohrenwend (Eds.), Stressful life events and their contexts (pp. 131–156). New York: Watson.
Lazarus, R. S., & DeLongis, A. (1983). Psychological stress and aging. *American Psychologist, 3,* 245–254.
Makepeace, J. M. (1983). Life events and courtship violence. *Family Relations, 32,* 101–109.
Menaghan, E. G. (1982). Measuring coping effectiveness: A panel study of marital problems and coping effectiveness. *Journal of Health and Social Behavior, 23,* 220–234.
Menaghan, E. G. (1983). Individual coping efforts and family studies: Conceptual and methodological issues. *Marriage and Family Review, 6,* 113–135.
Mitchell, R. E., Billings, A. G., & Moos, R. H. (1982). Social support and well-being: Implications for prevention programs. *Journal of Primary Prevention, 3,* 77–98.

Mitchell, R. E., & Hodson, C. A. (1983). Coping with domestic violence: Social support and psychological health among battered women. *American Journal of Consulting Psychology, 11,* 629–654.

Mitchell, R. E., & Trickett, E. J. (1980). Social networks as mediators of social support: An analysis of the effects and determinants of social networks. *Community Mental Health Journal, 16,* 27–44.

Pagelow, M. D. (1981). *Woman-battering: Victims and their experiences.* Beverly Hills: Sage.

Pearlin, L. I., & Schooler, C. (1978). The structure of coping. *Journal of Health and Social Behavior, 19,* 2–21.

Rosenberg, M. (1979). *Conceiving the self.* New York: Basic.

Spence, J. T., Helmreich, R. L., & Stapp, J. (1973). A short version of the Attitudes toward Women Scale (AWS). *Bulletin of the Psychonomic Society, 2,* 219–220.

Straus, M. A. (1979). Measuring intrafamily conflict and violence: The Conflict Tactics (CTS) Scale. *Journal of Marriage and the Family, 41,* 75–88.

Trickett, E. J., Kelly, J. G., & Vincent, T. A. (1985). The spirit of ecological inquiry in community research. In E. C. Susskind & D. C. Klein (Eds.), *Community research: Methods, paradigms, and applications* (pp. 283–333). New York: Praeger.

Walker, L. E. (1979). *The battered woman.* New York: Harper & Row.

Walker, L. E. (1983). The battered woman syndrome study. In D. Finkelhor, R. J. Gelles, G. T. Hotaling, & M. A. Straus (Eds.), *The dark side of families: Current family violence research* (pp. 31–48). Beverly Hills: Sage.

Wilcox, B. L. (1981). Social support in adjusting to marital disruption: A network analysis. In B. H. Gottlieb (Ed.), *Social networks and social support* (pp. 97–115). Beverly Hills: Sage.

Wortman, C. B., & Dunkel-Schetter, C. (1979). Interpersonal relationships and cancer: A theoretical analysis. *Journal of Social Issues, 35,* 120–155.

IV

WOMEN'S HEALTH

11

The Stress of Childbearing: Nurse-Midwives as a Source of Social Support

Cynthia S. Rand
Johns Hopkins University School of Medicine

Pregnancy and childbirth occupy unique positions among the common stressors in the lives of women. Like a serious illness, bearing a child involves dramatic physical changes, intimate and regular contact with medical personnel, and usually culminates in an experience of intense pain. Childbearing, much like an illness, commonly puts emotional and financial demands on a family. And yet unlike an illness, pregnancy is frequently eagerly planned and experienced with great pleasure and excitement. For most women, the pain of childbirth is integrally bound with the joyous anticipation of a new child. Pregnancy and childbirth are paradoxical experiences in which the pregnant woman can represent the epitome of bursting good health, and yet also be sharing many of the same stresses as a seriously ill woman. Even when pregnancy is a happy and planned experience in a woman's life, the physical and emotional changes that accompany the process clearly constitute major health and social stressors.

Childbearing has been scrutinized by researchers not only as a source of stress but also as a variable sensitive to life stress. Thus, pregnancy and childbirth must be viewed as both independent and dependent variables when stress relationships are considered. This chapter will review research which has considered childbearing from both perspectives. The particular focus of this chapter, however, will be those variables which have been found to mediate the stress of childbirth. One specific example of such a mediator, the nurse-midwife, will be considered, and a model of this form of social support will be discussed.

Cohen and McKay (1984) have proposed a specificity model of social support that suggests that stressors create specific needs, and that when social support meets those needs, that support will buffer the impact of the stressor. The demands and stresses of childbirth certainly create specific needs in the laboring woman. Nurse-midwives will be viewed in this model as situation-specific sources of support whose services are tailored to both the medical and emotional needs of women during uncomplicated childbirth. When a woman has a normal childbirth then her focus and that of the people with her can be on realizing a joyous, fulfilling birth experience. In this situation, nurse-midwives may well be ideally trained to support and encourage a fundamentally normal process. If, however, the health of the laboring woman or her unborn child should become imperiled, then the needs of the woman shift dramatically from wanting satisfying childbirth to wanting a safe childbirth, regardless of the technical and medical intervention required. In such a situation it would then be the physician who could provide the most specific and valuable support.

STRESS AND CHILDBEARING

Effects of Stress on Pregnancy and Childbirth

The impact of a pregnant woman's emotional experiences on the developing fetus has long been recognized in pregnancy folklore. In every known society there are rituals, taboos, and superstitions based on the belief that the behavior and attitudes of the pregnant woman can affect her health, her childbirth experience, and the health of her unborn child. With increasing scientific sophistication, the medical establishment in Western culture had largely dismissed these beliefs as old wives' tales by the beginning of the twentieth century (Ferreira, 1965).

In recent years, however, the growing research support for the impact of stress and emotions on human illnesses, such as hypertension and coronary heart disease has triggered a renewed interest in the role of maternal emotions and experiences on pregnancy and childbirth. Folk sayings, long ago dismissed, may be found to have a core of truth, built upon centuries of human observations and experience (Gruenberg, 1967).

Three broadly designed predictor variables have most often been used for examining the effects of stress on childbearing: life change, mental and emotional health, and anxiety. Several studies have found stressful life events and a negative attitude toward the pregnancy related to prolonged nausea and vomiting (Hetzel, Bruer & Poideven 1961; Heinstein, 1967) and to pre-eclamptic toxemia (Coppen, 1958; Pilowsky & Sharp, 1971). The work of Dodge (1972) has suggested a possible relationship between prenatal stress and infantile hypertrophic pyloric stenosis, a condition characterized by projectile vomiting that develops by the age of a few weeks. Morgan, Buchanan, and Abram (1976) found more reported prenatal life change using the SRE—Schedule of Recent Events (Holmes & Rahe, 1967), in the families of infants with hyaline membrane disease, a life-threatening respiratory problem. While intriguing, most of these studies were limited by their retrospective design.

Many researchers have argued that the predictive potential of stress variables would be increased if all pregnancy and childbirth complications were conceptualized as "derivatives of a single common process" (McDonald & Christakos, 1968). Rather than examining birth outcomes in terms of specific problems, such as hyaline membrane disease, the overall experience of pregnancy and/or childbirth is judged as normal or abnormal. The classification strategies differ from study to study, however, they usually include a heterogeneous variety of clinical complications drawn from obstetrical records, such as toxemia, subnormal Apgar ratings, stillbirth, and prolonged labor. An important factor in all such classifications, and a possible problem, is that both maternal and infant complications are combined into one rating.

One example of a study that employed this approach is the work of Nuckolls, Cassel, and Kaplan (1972). In examining the effects of life crisis and psychosocial assets on the prognosis of pregnancy they proposed that stress would have a variable consequence on a woman's pregnancy, depending on the psychological and social assets available to her. Women in their third trimester of pregnancy completed the SRE which measured life change during pregnancy and the 2 years preceding it. Analysis found no significant differences in the amount of life stress experienced by women with normal pregnancies and those with complications. They did find, however, that when life change had been great both before and during pregnancy, those women with greater psychosocial assets had only one-third as many complications as those women with few assets. This finding not only supports the relationship between life stress and childbirth complications, it also suggests that some women (in particular, women with few psychosocial assets) may be more vulnerable to this stress.

While many studies that have employed this approach have found increased prenatal life change and anxiety associated with a higher rate of complications (Davids & Devault, 1962; McDonald & Christakos, 1963: Gorusch & Key, 1974; Crandon, 1979) several methodological differences make these studies difficult to compare. The time frame for measuring stressors varies widely between studies, with one study using trait anxiety measured in the first month of pregnancy, another using ninth month stress and a third using repeated measures of state anxiety throughout pregnancy. A second problem is that the criterion for a complicated pregnancy or birth is unique to each study. A "normal" pregnancy in one study may be "abnormal" in another. In spite of these concerns, however, there appears to be support for the belief that increased levels of life change and anxiety can have a measurably negative effect on the natural course of childbearing.

Childbearing as a Stressor

One of the earliest research measures of life stress, the SRE—Schedule of Recent Events (Holmes & Rahe, 1967), classified pregnancy as a major life change, and as such, it was one of many stressors that could contribute to later physical (Dohrenwend & Dohrenwend, 1974) and psychiatric problems (Dekker & Webb, 1974). The stressful components of pregnancy are multiple including: physical changes and discomfort, fears about the unborn child's welfare, and concerns about the child's impact financially, maritally, and personally. While the entire process of childbearing can be conceptualized as a period of change, anxiety, and adaptation (Hanford, 1968; Levy & McGee, 1975; Leifer, 1977), it is the conclusion of pregnancy, childbirth, which usually creates the greatest stress. Perhaps more so than at any other time in her life, during childbirth a woman is not in control of her body or environment. She will be required to cope with the physical demands of birthing, as well as those stressors unique to a hospital environment. Medical personnel will direct what is done to her body and who she has contact with during childbirth. And underlying these experiences is a woman's inevitable anxiety about the well-being of her unborn child.

Of all the multiple stressors associated with childbirth, however, it is certainly the pain associated with labor and delivery that places the greatest demands on a woman's physical and mental resources. That this class of pain is generally viewed as completely normal, healthy, and largely inevitable distinguishes it from all other painful experiences. In addition, the end result of this pain is for most women the highly positive reinforcement of a new child (Kitzinger, 1978). Indeed, the pain of childbirth is unique, both in fact and in the way it is socially construed in different cultures. Despite a popular myth that "primitive" women have casual and painless childbirth, anthropological studies have not been able to make meaningful cultural distinctions in the amount of pain women experience during birth. Rather, it is the acceptability of expressing pain, modes of expression, attitudes toward birth, and ways of coping with childbirth pain that vary between cultures (Newton & Newton, 1979).

To deal with the demands of this stressful time, most American women have traditionally depended on their obstetrician, whose highest, and occasionally exclusive priority is the safety of mother and child (Oakley, 1980). While this technical skill and assistance certainly provides a necessary component of childbirth support, increasingly researchers have begun to consider other sources of support that appear to help women cope with the stress of childbirth. In addition, because of concern about both the immediate and long-term effects of obstetrical medication, the medical and behavioral sciences have begun to show interest in alternative ways of mediating childbirth pain (Arms, 1975).

MEDIATORS OF THE STRESS OF CHILDBIRTH

The two mediators of childbirth stress that have received the greatest research interest are childbirth preparation courses (a source of information) and the husband's presence during labor and delivery (a source of social support). The outcome variables designed to measure the efficacy of these interventions generally have included reported pain, amount of medication, satisfaction with the childbirth experience, and reduced maternal anxiety.

A study by Enkin, Smith, Dermer, and Emmett (1971) found that prepared women received less medication, reported more favorable birth experiences, and had less postpartum depression. Doering and Entwistle (1975) found a striking relationship between level of childbirth preparation and degree of awareness during birth. This awareness, in turn, was associated with a more positive birth experience. Few studies have found childbirth preparation classes to be related to reports of reduced pain or shorter labors, however, participation in a class has been repeatedly associated with less anxiety, less medication, and greater satisfaction (Davenport-Slack & Boylan, 1974; Klusman, 1975; Zax, Sameroff, & Farnum, 1975).

Frequently the effect of childbirth preparation has been examined in conjunction with the husband's presence during childbirth. Norr, Block, and Charles (1977) found that preparation and husband participation predicted less pain and more enjoyment during birth. Huttel, Mitchell, Fischer, and Meyer (1972) reported that prepared women who had their husbands with them received less medication and displayed fewer overt complaints or tensions.

Other birth companions besides a woman's husband have been shown to serve as powerful mediators of childbirth stress. Sosa, Kennell, Klaus, Robertson, and Urrutia (1980) found that Guatemalan women who had been accompanied by a supportive companion showed a lower rate of obstetrical complications, shorter labors, and were more responsive to their infants. They suggest that "there may be major perinatal benefits of constant human support during labor" (Sosa et al., 1980). Additional support for this suggestion is found in the work of Klein, Gist, Nicholson, and Standley (1981) who found that the simple physical presence of a supportive person (husband, friend, labor nurse) throughout the hours of labor was of more value in helping the laboring women cope than any specific care behaviors. Aside from physical presence, the next most valuable action of birth companions was touch. Women indicated postpartum that being touched during labor was an anxiety-reducing and positive experience.

Another source of support for some women today is the nurse-midwife, a professional caretaker whose proposed function combines both medical and emotional support. The role of the nurse-midwife during childbirth is not only to provide physical supervision and assistance, but also to provide support and encouragement for the laboring woman. Nurse-midwives are an increasingly popular alternative to traditional obstetrical care (Olsen, 1979). This option in obstetrical management is one component of a hot debate of both medical and consumer interest. At issue is the necessity and value of a traditional medical/disease orientation toward an essentially normal biological function: childbirth (Wertz & Wertz, 1977).

OPTIONS IN OBSTETRICAL CARE: RETURN OF THE NURSE-MIDWIFE

Pregnancy and childbirth have always occupied a unique place within established medicine, for here the physician's goal is not the prevention and elimination of an abnormal biological process, but rather, the support and encouragement of a normal biological process. Historically, the initial function of the physician in the childbearing process was limited to abnormal and medically complicated situations. Because of his training and experience in handling disease and biological deviance, the physician's role in childbirth was clearly delineated from that of the lay midwife. The midwife was considered the more appropriate attendant for the normal birth by reason of both her experience and sex (Rich, 1976). Gradually, however, this century witnessed the usurping of the lay midwives' traditional domain by the medical establishment. Strong arguments have been put forth in defense of this transition by the medical profession. Lay midwives were believed by physicians to be an uneducated group, with no understanding of the need for anti-sepsis, and a primitive dependence on folklore and superstition. Additionally, in the event of unexpected complications, the physician, unlike the midwife, had the skill and the medical training necessary for intervention. From the physician's perspective, midwifery had generally come to be associated with dirt and danger (Wertz & Wertz, 1977; Donnison, 1977). The modern woman seeking to avail herself of the best prenatal and childbirth care usually was counseled by the medical establishment that any obstetrical care outside the direct control of a physician was foolhardy, and very risky.

Increasingly, however, a rumble of discontent has been growing within the ranks of the obstetrical care consumer. The first waves of dissent came with the development of the natural childbirth movement (Litoff, 1978). Advocates of this approach, Grantly Dick-Read, Fredrick Lamaze, and others, encouraged women to believe that the childbirth experience was a joyous, important, and natural process that required only the proper relaxation and state of mind, rather than the oblivion provided by drugs. As more and more women came to experience and appreciate this orientation toward childbirth, they began to also question the technological and deviance orientation shared by most obstetricians (Arms, 1975). The concept that the pregnant woman is a consumer of obstetrical care, with a variety of safe options and choices has begun to challenge the sovereignity of traditional obstetrical medicine.

In the midst of this controversy, there has been a resurgence of interest in the role and value of midwifery in American obstetrical care. After over 40 years of disrepute, the profession is slowly starting to be viewed as a legitimate source of obstetrical care. Midwives are seen by many natural childbirth advocates as "protecting the completely healthy woman from unnecessary interference, impatience, overestimation of technology, and against human meddlesomeness" (Arms, 1975, p. 204).

Nurse-midwives are beginning to be accepted by obstetricians as a competent source of obstetrical care, thanks to their extensive medical training and the supervised nature of their practice. The fact that nurse-midwifery service has proved to be an inexpensive source of supplemental obstetrical care has also encouraged its acceptance. Other countries, particularly Great Britain and the Netherlands, have depended heavily for years on midwives to attend normal deliveries at home and in the hospital. Not only has their experience demonstrated the viability and safety of midwife care for normal deliveries, it has also suggested that the use of midwives may result in a lower rate of birth interventions, such as inductions and C-sections (Kitzinger & Davis, 1978). The question of whether the nurse-midwife can provide safe, professional medical care for the healthy pregnant woman no longer appears to be much in debate (Mann, 1981).

But if both a nurse-midwife and a physician are qualified medical providers for an uncomplicated pregnancy, then by what criterion should women choose their prenatal and delivery care? What, if any, are the objective and subjective differences and benefits of these two services? Among midwife advocates there appears to be a general belief that "physicians focus on the biological and technical aspects of disease (while) nurse-midwives, on the other hand, see themselves in terms of supporting role functions more consistent with the majority needs of the normal pregnant woman" (Coby, 1976). Despite its prevalence, however, the support for this belief is more anecdotal than scientific. Because of the relative recency of these obstetrical care options, very little research has examined the possible psychological or social consequences of the different types of care. In fact, research comparing physician's care to nurse-midwifery care has focused almost exclusively on physical and medical outcomes. One reason that such comparisons have been limited is that nurse-midwives usually see only those patients who have specifically opted for this type of care. As Olsen (1979) has reported, American nurse-midwifery attracts white, liberal, well-educated, upper-middle class women with a strong interest in their pregnancies. This self-selection factor has generally made comparative studies of physicians' care to nurse-midwife care unfeasible.

One study that did examine the relative support contributions made by physicians and nurse-midwives to the childbirth experience was conducted by this author at the Johns Hopkins Hospital. It was hypothesized that 1) In keeping with their different training and professional orientation, physicians would differ from nurse-midwives in their attitudes toward obstetrical care. Nurse-midwives would report a stronger belief in the importance of the obstetrical caretaker providing emotional support during childbirth, more interest in providing patient education, and less interest in the technical aspect of childbirth than physicians. And 2) since emotional support during childbirth is viewed as a critical mediating factor in coping with the stress of childbirth, this support is considered a key factor in a satisfying childbirth experience. Because of the hypothesized nurse-midwife emphasis on emotional support it was predicted that overall, nurse-midwife patients would be more satisfied with the support they received during labor and delivery than physicians' patients.

Nurse-Midwives as Agents of Social Support

This study was conducted through the Obstetrical Clinic of the Johns Hopkins Hospital in Baltimore, Maryland. Within 48 hours after childbirth 75 clinic patients were interviewed and administered a questionnaire designed to measure patient responses to obstetrical care during labor and delivery. In addition to measuring patient responses to care, the physicians and nurse-midwives providing obstetrical care were surveyed about their attitudes toward obstetrical care and toward their patients.

All interviewed patients were receiving medical assistance and had had healthy, uncomplicated pregnancies. Of the subjects 32% were delivered by nurse-midwives, 85% were black, the mean age was 22.1 years, mean education was 11.5 years, 85% had vaginal deliveries, 28% had taken childbirth preparation courses, and 47% had the baby's father with them during the delivery.

At the time of this study (1980–1981) low-risk adult patients in the obstetrical clinic were assigned to either the nurse-midwifery service or the physicians' service based on staff availability. While patients could request a change in their assignment, none did so during this study. Nurse-midwife care was provided by nine female student nurse-midwives and five female supervisory nurse-midwife faculty. The physician's care was generally provided by 22 first, second, and third year obstetrical residents (two of whom were women). Once a woman was assigned to either nurse-midwife or physician's care she remained with that service through delivery (barring complications). Both nurse-midwife and physician patients were seen by multiple caretakers throughout their prenatal care. All patients received their delivery care from the same service that had provided their prenatal care. Nurse-midwives however, did not manage complicated deliveries, or those deliveries that occured on weekends. During a patient's labor and delivery the nurse-midwives were required to follow essentially the same medical protocol used by the physician's service (i.e., IV's, fetal monitors, delivery in a delivery room).

T-test comparisons of nurse-midwife patients to physicians' patients for the variables of type of delivery, age, race, parity, number of abortions, number of prenatal visits, weight gain, husband's presence during delivery, and childbirth class attendance, found no significant differences. Women who were delivered by nurse-midwives tended to be slightly better educated (mean years of education = 12.0) than those delivered by physicians (mean years of education = 11.3, $p <$ .10).

A 14-item scale was developed to assess nurse-midwives' and physicians' attitudes toward obstetrical practices and obstetrical patients. This Likert-type measure had excellent inter-item reliability (Cronbach's Alpha = .78; Rosenthal, 1973). Overall responses on the Attitudes toward Obstetrical Care were strongly related to the type of caretaker completing the questionnaire ($r =$ .72, $p <$ .001). Correlations between type of caretaker and individual scale items found that nurse-midwives thought that their patients were less apathetic ($r = .38, p < .05$), and more reliable ($r = .66, p < .001$) than physicians believed of their patients. Nurse-midwives were also more positive and receptive to alternative forms of care during delivery ($r = .86, p < .001$), patient education ($r = .55, p < .001$), and to the importance of provid-emotional support during childbirth, than were physicians ($r = .47, p < .01$).*

Patient satisfaction with the social and emotional support they received during labor and delivery was assessed with a 7-item Likert-type scale (inter-item reliability Alpha = .67). The Support Scale questions measured patients' evaluations of the amount of personal attention, emotional support, and information they received from their caretakers during labor and delivery. Correlations between patient responses and type of caretaker found that nurse-midwife patients believed that they had received more personal attention during labor ($r = .28, p < .01$), more support ($r = .20, p < .05$), more careful explanations of procedures ($r = .30, p < .01$, and overall were more satisfied with their care ($r = .30, p < .001$) during labor and delivery than physicians' patients. Partial correlations controlling for education, age, and race found that these variables did not significantly influence these relationships. Multiple regression analysis with overall satisfaction with support as the dependent variable and type of delivery caretaker, age, race, education, and parity as independent variables found that only the contribution of delivery caretaker was significant ($F = 15.50$, $p < .001$, $df = 59$). For these subjects, 24% of the variance of the satisfaction with support assessment was attributable to the delivery caretakers.

Because some women who had received their prenatal care from nurse-midwives were delivered by physicians, it was possible that these women with last minute change of caretaker accounted for the lower assessment of support found among physicians' patients. Correlations computed on only those women whose prenatal caretaker matched their delivery caretaker revealed no such influence.

One question in the Support Scale asked women whether the labor nurses assisting at both physician and nurse-midwife deliveries were more helpful than their delivery attendant. It was this item that showed the strongest relationship with the type of delivery caretaker ($r = .51$, $p < .001$). It is frequently the case that labor nurses will stay with, and support the laboring patient when the delivery caretaker is unavailable. If nurse-midwives were with their patients more than physicians were with their patients, then this response might reflect the greater quantity of emotional support provided by the nurse-midwives, rather than the quality of support.

For many women, nurse-midwife support was in addition to their husband's companionship. Nearly 50% of the subjects had their husbands with them during childbirth (evenly divided between physician and midwife care), and all of these women reported this support to be positive and helpful. Surprisingly, women who had their husband's assistance and comfort were just as positive about their midwives' supportive value as were those women who lacked a family member's company. While the emotional support and encouragement provided by a nurse-midwife might have particular importance to a woman laboring without family help, it also appears that the support given by midwives to husband/wife team childbirth is notable and valued. Nurse-midwives, may, in fact, provide the optimal blend of skills and support necessary to help mediate the stressors of any normal

---

*Correlations indicate magnitude of relationships.

childbirth. Based upon this study's findings and drawing upon childbirth research already discussed a model of nurse-midwife support will next be considered.

MODEL OF SOCIAL SUPPORT
FOR NORMAL CHILDBIRTH

Childbearing has been discussed as an experience vulnerable to stress, as well as a powerful stressor itself. Those variables that appear to moderate the stress of childbirth have also been explored, with particular attention to the mediating contribution of nurse-midwives. It has been suggested that nurse-midwives are sources of social, as well as professional support, and that this support can positively influence a woman's birth experience.

Stress researchers have defined and measured social support in a variety of ways. However, the common defining element appears to be that the stressed individual is receiving and perceiving comfort, information, encouragement and/or practical assistance from others such as family, friends, professionals, or institutions. The ability of social support systems to both buffer stress responses and to increase an individual's ability to cope has received support in a variety of studies (Johnson & Sarason, 1979), including the already discussed work of Nuckolls et al. (1972). Cohen and McKay (1984) have suggested that different stressors will place different demands on an individual. Those forms of support that are most specific and appropriate to the stressed person's needs will be the most valuable, and will be most successful in mediating the effects of the stressor. This "specificity model" proposes, in essence, that not all support is of equal value in every stressful situation. Drawing upon this approach, it is suggested that the unique stresses of normal childbearing will be best mediated by the specific form of support provided by nurse-midwife care.

Based on the review of childbirth literature, it is suggested that the stress of normal childbirth can be mediated by three forms of support: 1) information, 2) emotional support, and 3) technical assistance.

Necessary information for the woman in labor would include details about hospital or medical procedures, updates on the progress of labor, status reports on the well being of the unborn child and techniques for breathing, pushing or other physical procedures. Emotional support would include encouragement, coaching, physical presence, touching and comforting a woman, as needed throughout the hours of labor and delivery. And finally, technical assistance would consist of those appropriate medical interventions that are judged on an individual basis to be necessary. Examples of this assistance include pelvic exams, measuring fetal heart rate, medication, and the delivery of the child. An important component of this technical assistance is the professional training, knowledge, and experience to deal with childbirth complications or emergencies, either personally, or by obtaining more qualified assistance.

These three forms of support can be provided by different individuals, however, typically, a woman depends on her physician for both information and technical assistance, while her husband (if present) functions as her primary source of emotional support. Husbands would rarely have the expertise necessary to provide either the technical information or assistance. And while some physicians attempt to provide emotional support to their patients, most do not have the time necessary to stay by a patient's side for hours. Additionally, the training and orientation of most physicians has been repeatedly cited for placing a low priority on the emotional needs of women in childbirth (Arms, 1975; Donnison, 1977). Nurse-midwives, however, are not only trained to consider and address the emotional needs of their patients, they also are fully qualified medical caretakers with the knowledge and skills necessary to provide any information or technical assistance required by normal childbirth. Because the nurse-midwife has the skills, orientation, and time necessary to provide the primary support requirements, it is suggested that this type of care will most specifically be able to mediate the stress of normal childbirth.

It is additionally suggested that the contributions of emotional support will be additive, such that a woman supported by both her husband and nurse-midwife will be better able to cope with childbirth than will a woman with only one source of emotional support. The contribution of a husband's support to childbirth has unique components, for his role is not only as coach and comforter, but also as the excited prospective father who has an intimate and lifelong stake in this experience. It may also be that beyond emotional support, the father's presence during childbirth will have far-reaching consequences for marital and family bonding. When a midwife and husband participate together in a birth, not only do they both support the laboring woman, it is often the case that the midwife will provide both information and emotional support to the father which in turn, allows him to function better in his support role. In sum, midwives and husbands serve different, but overlapping support roles for a woman in labor and delivery, with the optimal level of support provided when both are present.

DISCUSSION

One element of nurse-midwife care not discussed is the actual technical management of birth. Many would say that an additional valuable nurse-midwife contribution to the mediation of the stress of childbirth is this profession's general reluctance to medically interfere with the natural birth process. While midwives are trained to recognize birth problems and are equipped to personally address many of them, they are probably less likely to intervene prematurely than are physicians (Wertz & Wertz, 1977).

When a birth becomes complicated, however, the nurse-midwife will immediately defer to the care of a physician. Just as it has been suggested that the nurse-midwife is the caretaker best suited to mediate the stressors of normal childbirth, so it is the physician who can best address the most pressing stressors of a complicated birth. However, while the need for the technical expertise of the physician becomes paramount in a difficult birth, the need for emotional support and information is still present. When a nurse-midwife patient develops complications, such as an unexpected C-section, the usual midwife protocol is to place the medical management in the hands of a physician, but at the same time to continue providing support and information to the woman and her husband.

The support contribution of midwives has so far been exclusively considered in terms of childbirth. Because midwives place a high priority on patient education, as well as emotional support, they might play a role in mediating certain prenatal stressors that have been implicated in childbirth complications. First, prenatal midwife care, with its emphasis on emotional support, could contribute to a woman's social support system for coping with life stresses (family, financial, or emotional problems), and secondly, their concern with patient education might help ameliorate fears, misconceptions, and anxieties a woman might have about pregnancy and birth.

By what mechanism does the support of nurse-midwives mediate the stress of childbirth? One suggestion is that midwife support increases a woman's sense of personal mastery and competence in coping with the demands of birth. By actively reinforcing and supporting a woman through a difficult process, the midwife may encourage a woman to utilize her own internal resources for mediating stress. Additionally, as others have reported, social support may increase a woman's evaluation of her own self-worth, which in turn may increase her ability to cope (Hobfoll & Walfisch, 1984). The sex of nurse-midwives is also probably a key element in their effectiveness. From the beginning of recorded history women have been reported to turn to other women at their time of birth (Arms, 1975). As Oakley (1980, pp. 297–298) has suggested,

> Women are not necessarily more sympathetic attendants in childbirth, but they are probably so, and the traditional occupation of female nurse-midwifery has always placed a belief in nature—which amounts to a belief in women as their own deliverers—ahead of the contention that it is the pharmacological and mechanical technologies of medical science that are, in the twentieth century, the true deliverers of childbearing women.

It should not be inferred that physicians (typically male) are considered here to be inappropriate birth attendants. Physicians are highly trained professionals who are, in fact, the only appropriate caretakers for a childbirth requiring their expertise. Other countries have long recognized the efficiency and economy of using costly physicians where their skills are most needed, and using midwives for normal, uncomplicated births (Kitzinger & Davis, 1978). A physician would be the most appropriate attendant for a complex birth, but also for the care of any woman who strongly believed that the best obstetrical care was that care which was the most technical. The support value of nurse-midwife care would be nil if the patient were anxious or lacked confidence in her caretaker.

Successful mediation of the multiple stressors of childbirth has the obvious consequence of a more rewarding birth experience. Less obvious, are the possible effects of a positive birth experience on a new mother's self-confidence in interacting with her infant. A woman flushed with exhilaration and the pride of accomplishment that can accompany a satisfying birth may well have an advantage in developing her initial bond with her infant, as well as feeling confident in her own self-worth.

Whether social support is mediating the stress of a life crisis or of a life highpoint, the goal is still to increase an individual's ability to cope. In a life crisis social support can make a bad situation bearable, and in a life highpoint it can optimize pleasure and satisfaction. Both are areas worthy of future investigation and understanding.

REFERENCES

Arms, S. (1975). *Immaculate deception*. San Francisco: Houghton-Miffin.

Coby, J. (1976). *Evaluation of nurse-midwife care in a clinical setting*. Unpublished thesis, Yale University School of Nursing.

Cohen, S., & McKay, G. (1984). Social support, stress and the buffering hypothesis: An empirical review and theoretical analysis. In A. Baum, J. E. Singer, & S. E. Taylor (Eds.), *Handbook of psychology and health, Vol. 14.* Hillsdale, NJ: Erlbaum.

Coppen, S. A. (1958). Psychosomatic aspects of pre-eclamptic toxaemia. *Journal of Psychosomatic Research, 2,* 241-265.

Crandon, A. (1979). Maternal anxiety and obstetrical complications. *Journal of Psychosomatic Research, 23,* 109-111.

Davenport-Slack, B., & Boylan, C. (1974). Psychological correlates of childbirth pain. *Psychosomatic Medicine, 24,* 215-233.

Davids, A., & DeVault, S. (1962). Maternal anxiety during pregnancy and childbirth abnormalities. *Psychosomatic Medicine, 24,* 464-470.

Dekker, D. J., & Webb, J. T. (1974). Relationships of the social readjustment rating scale to psychiatric patient status, anxiety, and social desirability. *Journal of Psychosomatic Research, 18,* 125-130.

Dodge, J. (1972). Psychosomatic aspects of infantile pyloric stenosis. *Journal of Psychosomatic Research, 16,* 1-5.

Doering, S. G., & Entwisle, D. R. (1975). Preparation during pregnancy and ability to cope with labor and delivery. *American Journal of Orthopsychiatry, 45,* 825-837.

Dohrenwend, B. S., & Dohrenwend, B. P., (Eds.). (1974). *Stressful life events: Their nature and effects.* New York: Wiley.

Donnison, J. (1977). *Midwives and medicine men.* New York: Schocken.

Enkin, M., Smith, S. L., Dermer, S. W., & Emmet, J. O. (1971). An adequately controlled study of effectiveness of PPM training. In N. Morris (Ed.), *Psychosomatic medicine in obstetrics and synaecology,* (pp. 62-67). New York: S. Karger.

Ferreia, A. (1965). Emotional factors in prenatal environment. *Journal of Nervous and Mental Disorders, 141,* 108-117.

Gorsuch, R., & Key, M. (1974). Abnormalities of pregnancy as a function of anxiety and life stress. *Psychosomatic Medicine, 36,* 352-362.

Gruenberg, E. M. (1967). On the psychosomatics of the not-so-perfect fetal parasite. In S. Richards & A. Guttmacher (Eds.), *Childbearing–Its social and psychological aspects.* Baltimore: Williams & Wilkins.

Hanford, J. (1968). Pregnancy as a state of conflict. *Psychological Reports, 22,* 1313-1342.

Heinstein, M. (1967). Expressed attitudes and feelings of pregnant women and their relations to physical complaints of pregnancy. *Merrill-Palmer Quarterly, 13,* 217-235.

Hetzel, B., Bruer, B., & Poidevin, L. (1961). A survey of the relation between certain common antenatal complications in primiparae and stressful life situations during pregnancy. *Journal of Psychosomatic Research, 5,* 175-182.

Hobfoll, S. E., & Walfisch, S. (1984). Coping with a threat to life: A longitudinal study of self concept, social support and psychological distress. *American Journal of Community Psychology, 12,* 87-100.

Holmes, T. H., & Rahe, R. H. (1967). The Social Readjustment Rating Scale. *Journal of Psychosomatic Research, 11,* 213-218.

Huttel, F., Mitchell, I., Fischer, W., & Meyer, A. (1972). A quantitative evaluation of psychoprophylaxis in childbirth, *Journal of Psychosomatic Research, 16,* 81-92.

Johnson, J., & Sarason, I. (1979). Moderator variables in life stress research. In I. Sarason & C. Spielberger, (Eds.), *Stress and Anxiety: Vol. 6.* New York: Hemisphere.

Kitzinger, S., & Davis, J. (Eds.). (1978). *The place of birth.* Oxford: Oxford University Press.

Kitzinger, S. (1978). Pain in childbirth. *The Journal of Medical Ethics, 4,* 119-121.

Klein, R., Gist, N., Nicholson, J., & Standley, K. (1981). A study of father and nurse support during labor. *Birth and the Family Journal, 8,* 161-166.

Klusman, L. E. (1975). Reduction of pain in childbirth by the alleviation of anxiety during pregnancy. *Journal of Consulting Clinical Psychology, 43,* 162-165.

Leifer, M. (1977). Psychological changes accompanying pregnancy and motherhood. *Genetic Psychology Monographs, 95,* 55-95.

Levy, J. M., & McGee, R. K. (1975). Childbirth as crisis: A test of Janis's theory of communication and stress resolution. *Journal of Personality and Social Psychology, 31,* 171-179.

Litoff, B. (1978). *American midwives.* Westport, CT: Greenwood.

McDonald, R., & Christakos, A. (1963). Relationship of emotional adjustment during pregnancy to obstetric complications. *American Journal of Obstetrics and Gynecology, 86,* 341-348.

Mann, R. (1981). San Francisco General Hospital nurse-midwifery practice: The first thousand births. *American Journal of Obstetrics and Gynecology, 140,* 676–682.

Morgan, S., Buchanan, D., & Abram, H. (1976). Psychosocial aspects of hyaline membrane disease, *Psychosomatics, 17,* 147–150.

Norr, K. L., Block, C. R., & Charles, A. (1977). Explaining pain and enjoyment in childbirth. *Journal of Health and Social Behavior, 18,* 260–275.

Newton, N., & Newton, M. (1979). Childbirth in crosscultural perspective. In J. Williams (Ed.), *Psychology of women.* New York: Norton.

Nuckolls, K., Cassel, J., & Kaplan, B. (1972). Psychosocial assets, life crisis and the prognosis of pregnancy. *American Journal of Epidemiology, 95,* 431–441.

Oakley, A. (1980). *Women confined: Toward a sociology of childbirth.* New York: Schocken.

Olsen, L. (1979). Portrait of nurse-midwifery patients in a private practice. *Journal of Nurse-Midwifery, 24,* 10–17.

Pilowsky, I., & Sharp, J. (1971). Psychological aspects of preeclamptic toxaemia: A prospective study. *Journal of Psychosomatic Research, 15,* 193–197.

Rich, A. (1976). *Of women born: Motherhood as experience and institution.* New York: Norton.

Rosenthal, R. (1973). Estimating effective reliabilities in studies that employ judges ratings. *Journal of Clinical Psychology, 29,* 342–345.

Sosa, R., Kennell, J., Klaus, M. Robertson, S., & Urrutia, J. (1980). The effect of a supportive companion on prenatal problems, length of labor, and mother-infant interaction. *New England Journal of Medicine. 38,* 269–277.

Wertz, R. W., & Wertz, D. C. (1977). *Lying-in: A history of childbirth in America.* New York: Free Press.

Zax, M., Sameroff, A., & Farnum, J. (1975). Childbirth education, maternal attitudes, and delivery. *American Journal of Obstetrics and Gynecology, 123,* 185–190.

12

A Comparison of the Impact of Breast Cancer and Bereavement: Personality, Social Support, and Adaptation

M. L. S. Vachon
Clarke Institute of Psychiatry, Toronto, Canada

Throughout the course of a woman's life there are many life transitions that occur. Some of these transitions may have been chosen and anticipated, at least in part—e.g., educational and career choices, marriage, child bearing, and divorce. Other transitions in a woman's life may occur without her choice. These may include the development of a serious illness and the dissolution of a marriage through widowhood. Even in these unchosen and perhaps unanticipated life transitions a woman may respond in many different ways. She may experience no distress, she may be overwhelmed by distress, or she may initially have difficulty and then adapt. What factors cause women to respond differently?

Significant life events do not occur in a vacuum. A woman's response will be mediated by factors surrounding the particular life event including such variables as: 1) the severity of the illness or the nature of the death experience of the spouse; 2) the presence or absence of a social support system; 3) her personality characteristics; and 4) concurrent stressors in addition to this life event.

This chapter will compare the impact of two major life events—breast cancer and bereavement on the adaptation of women. The data are derived from two studies that were designed to be complementary. Each study followed a group of women from approximately one month after the diagnosis of cancer or husband's death until 2 years thereafter.* In addition further data on the death of women with breast cancer was obtained 8 years after their initial diagnosis.

*These studies were "The Importance of Psychosocial Milieu in the Treatment of Patients with Cancer" funded by the Ontario Cancer Treatment and Research Foundation Grant 298. Co-investigators were: W. A. L. Lyall, S. J. J. Freeman, A. Formo, J. Rogers, and J. Cochrane; and "A Preventive Intervention for the Newly Bereaved" funded by the Ontario Ministry of Health, Demonstration Model Grant DM158. Co-investigators were: W. A. L. Lyall, S. J. J. Freeman, J. Rogers, A. Formo, and K. Letofsky.

The author wishes to express her warm appreciation to J. Cochrane, S. Erle, W. Lancee, and H. Prince for their assistance in the preparation of this chapter.

THE EVENT

Breast cancer strikes 1 out of every 12 Canadian women. It is the major cause of cancer deaths among women and the leading cause of death in all women between the ages of 35-54. Because it tends to occur earlier than other major causes of death, such as cardio-vascular disease, it is the greatest cause of years of life lost by Canadian women (Canadian Cancer Society, 1982). The statistics throughout North America are very similar.

Widowhood is a major life event that affects even more women. The average woman is widowed at age 56 (Lopata, 1973) and will remain widowed for 20 years (Carter & Glick, 1970). In Canada 37% of widows are under age 65 and 4% are under age 45 (Statistics Canada, 1980).

Both breast cancer and bereavement require a major transition in the lives of a significant proportion of women and often require a radical change in women's sense of self. Breast cancer confronts the woman with an identity shift that involves acknowledging that she has (or has had) a potentially life-threatening illness and bereavement necessitates a major shift in identity as one adjusts to the new role of being an adult woman without a male partner. In both of these events one would expect that women would experience a considerable degree of distress. However, the impact of the stressors of breast cancer and bereavement may well differ. In the former, the woman experiences surgery, treatment for her cancer, and a prolonged period of uncertainty as she waits to see whether or not her disease will recur. Her anxiety may be further affected by taking adjuvant chemotherapy and/or being watched quite closely by her physician—both reminders that her disease may recur.

In bereavement a woman must confront the death of her spouse, experience a greater or lesser amount of grief in response to the meaning his death has for her and then begin to develop a new identity as an adult woman without a partner. It may be more likely that a widow will adapt to her new defined role whereas the woman with breast cancer may be unsure as to the impact this disease will have on her identity. Whereas a widow is a widow, a woman with breast cancer may be uncertain whether she is a woman who has breast cancer, a woman who has had the disease, or a woman who will again get the disease and may die from it.

MEDIATING VARIABLES

In attempting to determine the variables that may affect an individual's adaptation to a stressful life event social scientists have focused considerable attention on the interaction between social support and personality. Cobb (1976) defines social support as "information leading the subject to believe that he is cared for and loved, esteemed, and a member of a network of mutual obligations" (p. 300). He suggests that social support is a mediating variable that facilitates identity change by providing an individual with esteem support so that he feels he can go out and master a problem (cf. Rabkin & Struening, 1976; Dohrenwend & Dohrenwend, 1978; Dean & Lin, 1977). Numerous authors have attempted to measure the components of social support. One useful model by Gottlieb (1978) divides social support into four major categories: (a) emotionally sustaining behaviors; (b) problem solving behaviors, (c) indirect personal influence; and (d) environmental action.

One of the major debates in the life events literature at this point is the exact role that social support may play in mediating response to stressful life events. Some authors feel that social support primarily serves as a buffer against life's stressors. "Social support as a buffer is often described as if it were an invisible shield, like fluoride for teeth, except applied to those areas of the psyche and soma otherwise vulnerable to stress" (Schaefer, 1982, p. 98). Using this framework, social support has been found to buffer responses to such stressful life events as illness (Cobb, 1976; Croog, Lipson, & Levine, 1972; Finlayson, 1976; Vachon, Lyall, Rogers, Cochrane, & Freeman, 1981); stressful life transitions such as separation and bereavement (Glick, Weiss, & Parkes, 1974; Maddison & Walker, 1976; Weiss, 1976; Vachon, 1979; Vachon, Lyall, Rogers, Freedman, & Freeman, 1980; Vachon, Lancee, Sheldon, Lyall, & Freeman, 1982; Vachon, Sheldon et al., 1982); and stressful life events (Antonovsky, 1979; Brown, Bhrolchain, & Harris, 1975; D'Arcy & Schmitz, 1979; Gore, 1978; Henderson, 1977; Nuckolls, Cassell & Kaplan, 1972).

Other authors contend that social support has more than a buffering role in that it has pervasive effects on one's general sense of well-being, even without life's stressors. This corresponding sense of well-being, self-esteem, and social support may then increase one's ability to deal with life's stressors (Andrews, Tennant, Hewson, & Vaillant, 1978; Thoits, 1982; Turner, 1981; Williams, Ware, & Donald, 1981).

Two personality traits that have also been found to mediate one's response to stressful life events are self-esteem and mastery (Hobfoll & Walfisch, 1984; Pearlin & Schooler, 1978). With regard to the relevance of these variables in this study of adaptation to bereavement and breast cancer, it has been hypothesized by Brown et al. (1975) that individuals with a low sense of self-esteem may have more difficulty when confronted with situations involving loss than might women with a better sense of self-esteem. This vulnerability to loss situations is heightened if the woman experiencing loss is lacking a confidant from whom she can receive support.

Lacking a good sense of self-esteem, a woman confronted with a situation involving a major loss may experience this event as being still yet another blow to her feelings of self-regard. These authors contend that when a person is deprived of an important source of value which can be derived either from a person, a role, or an idea, then one can develop feelings of hopelessness. In response to this specific feeling of hopelessness which is related to the particular loss situation—in this case the threat to one's sense of femininity and possible threat to life implied by breast cancer or the loss of a husband through death—a more general feeling of profound hopelessness may develop which may lead to depression.

"We believe that what is crucial in determining whether the specific feelings of hopelessness develop into the three feelings that the world is meaningless, the self worthless, and the future hopeless, is a person's ongoing self-esteem, their sense of their ability to control their world and thus to repair damage, their confidence that in the end alternative sources of value will become available" (Brown et al., 1975, p. 14).

For a woman to have a feeling that she has an ability to control her world, repair the damages done, and develop a new sense of value it can be hypothesized that she will need to have both a strong social support system and a reasonably good sense of mastery and self-esteem. However, the direct relationship between these variables has not yet been clearly shown in the literature so the reader should be aware of some factors that complicate the interaction between these variables. For example, it has been noted that the social relationships in which we engage may not only provide social support, they may also prove to be a significant stressor (Levine & Scotch, 1973). In response to the crisis of bereavement or breast cancer for example a woman's significant others may draw closer to her in an attempt to provide support or they may withdraw out of fear or as a result of the impact of the crisis on their own lives. Simultaneously, the woman may also draw towards or away from her significant others as she attempts to assess the meaning this event will have in her life. It must also be acknowledged that not everyone seeks or needs equal amounts of social support in times of life stress. B. B. Brown (1978) studied people who did not seek help from their social system when confronted with a stressful life event and found they could be divided into two types. The "self-reliant" respondents had well integrated networks from which they could seek help if it was required, but they chose not to seek it, and the "reluctant nonseekers" who were dangerously handicapped and had the least effective coping repertoires, a comparatively unsupportive and unreliable informal network, and the lowest self-esteem of any group studied.

Finally, it should be noted that much of the literature on the effect of social support systems looks at the impact of an aggregate of recent life events whereas it will be seen that both breast cancer and bereavement may constitute individual chronic stressors both for the woman and her support system. This chapter will compare and contrast the variables that were found to mediate the impact of bereavement and breast cancer on two groups of women. It will be shown that there are demographic, psychological, and social support variables that are: (1) antecedent to the diagnosis of breast cancer or death of a spouse which affect adaptation to these events; (2) associated with high distress one month after diagnosis of cancer or the death of a spouse; (3) associated with the pattern of adaptation to the event; (4) predictive of and/or associated with high distress 2 years after the event; (5) correlated with later death from cancer; and (6) finally, it will be shown that it is possible to intervene to decrease the distress associated with both of these events.

BREAST CANCER SAMPLE

The breast cancer sample consisted of 168 women 65 years of age and under, who received radiotherapy treatment at Princess Margaret Hospital, in Toronto Canada for an initial diagnosis of breast cancer between June 1974 and July 1975. This antedated the widespread use of adjuvant chemotherapy.

Of the 202 consecutive patients admitted for breast cancer who were seen at the hospital during this period and who met the criteria of the study (e.g., 65 years of age or under, with an initial diagnosis of breast cancer to be treated by radiotherapy, and consent of their physicians), 88% agreed to participate in this 2-year longitudinal study. Of those women who did not participate 5% ($N = 11$) refused; 5% ($N = 11$) did not speak English and in 2% of the cases ($n = 4$) the physician withheld consent because of the patient's anxiety.

Of the 187 women who were actually eligible to participate, 168 women or 90% completed both the initial and the end-of-radiotherapy interviews and questionnaire. The women studied had a median age of 51 with a range from 28–65 years.

Almost three quarters of the women (73%) were married, 10% widowed, 9% separated or divorced, and 8% single. The sample was predominantly middle class on the Hollingshead Index of Socioeconomic Status (Hollingshead & Redlich, 1958). Thirty-eight percent came from Toronto while 62% were from other cities, towns, and villages across the province of Ontario. Among the women 72% were Protestant, 22% were Catholic, and 6% of other religious backgrounds. Most of the women (76%) had Stage Two breast cancer but 10% had Stage One disease and 14% had Stage Three breast cancer. Of these women, 63% had either a radical or modified radical mastectomy, 18% had a partial mastectomy or lumpectomy, 15% had a simple mastectomy, and 3% had no surgery.

BEREAVEMENT SAMPLE

The bereavement sample consisted of 162 widows who had been married to men who were aged 67 and under, had been Toronto residents, and who had died in 7 Toronto hospitals during a 17-month period in 1974-1975.

Of the women who were approached through the participating hospitals within a month of their husbands' death, 162 (88%) agreed to participate in this 2-year study of conjugal bereavement. Detailed descriptions of the sampling method have been provided elsewhere (Vachon et al., 1980; Vachon, Sheldon et al., 1982).

The bereavement sample was similar to the breast cancer sample in that the average age was 52 with a range from 22-69, and it was also predominantly middle class on the Hollingshead two-factor index. Religious affiliations for the sample were 75% Protestant, 15% Catholic, and 10% other. The widows were all Toronto residents, 68% had been born in Canada and 88% spoke English as their primary language. More than half (57%) lived with someone else, usually with their children. Twenty-nine percent were employed outside their homes and 71% were homemakers. Thirteen percent of the husbands had died suddenly, 45% died of cancer, 38% of chronic cardiovascular disease, and 4% of chronic alcoholism. The median length of final illness was about 6 months. Only 19% of the husbands had had a final illness of 2 weeks or less (Vachon & Lancee, et al., 1982).

PROCEDURES

Breast Cancer

At the time of completion of their initial radiotherapy treatment, usually 3–4 weeks following their initial diagnosis and surgery, patients were given a letter describing the project. Those who agreed to participate were given personal interviews and a self-administered questionnaire by the research assistant at the beginning and end of radiotherapy treatment, a 3-week process for most patients. Due to geographical distance follow-up was conducted by mailed questionnaires and telephone interviews at 6, 12, and 24 months following the date of the initial diagnosis. In addition data were obtained regarding the number of women who died by accessing their records in 1983 eight years after their initial diagnosis. At that time 49% of the women were dead, 21% having died during the first 2 years of the study.

Bereavement

Within 3 weeks after the husband's death, letters were sent to the widows on hospital letterhead and signed either by the attending physician or the hospital administrator. These letters requested the women's participation in a study designed to investigate the impact of bereavement and to assess the possibility of developing programs of intervention for the newly bereaved. Personal interviews including a self-administered questionnaire were conducted in the widow's home at 1, 6, and 24 months following bereavement. One-third of the sample were also interviewed at 3 months and two-thirds at 12 months but these results will not be described here.

MEASURES

The primary outcome measure in both studies was the self-administered 30-item Goldberg General Health Questionnaire (GHQ) developed by David Goldberg to screen for nonpsychotic psychiatric illness among patients coming to general medical practice (Goldberg, 1972). In recent studies, the GHQ has been used extensively in community samples and has been shown to correlate at least at the .70 level with intensity measures of psychological disturbance (Goldberg, 1979). Factor analysis suggests that GHQ questions tap four main dimensions: anxiety/insomnia, depression, anhedonia, anergia, and social dysfunction. Like other workers in the field, we have not put the label "likely to be psychiatrically ill" on those scoring above the cut-off point of 4 on the GHQ. Rather we have labeled those scoring 0–4 as low distress and those scoring 5 and above as high distress.

The author-constructed questionnaire and structured forced-choice interview also included the usual demographic information, as well as information pertaining to the particular life event. In the breast cancer study this included: information on the subject's history as a cancer patient including first symptom, time of delay in seeking treatment, doctor's response, and the way in which the woman learned her diagnosis. Social support variables including perceived helpfulness of family and friends, the number of people the woman felt she could count on to understand how she was currently feeling (versus needing to "keep up a front" instead of expressing feelings), and who specifically was of help in her adjustment. Further topics included changes in marital and sexual life; perceived helpfulness of professionals including family doctor, surgeon, and hospital staff; and ability to obtain information about the disease. The presence of concurrent stressors in addition to cancer, the perceived stressfulness of the disease, anticipated adjustment, and symptoms experienced during radiotherapy treatment were also investigated.

In the bereavement study questionnaire data included information regarding the circumstances surrounding the husband's final illness and death including: length and type of final illness, presence or absence of warning of impending death, whether each of the spouses knew death was coming, whether they communicated about this, and whether or not communication was perceived as making a difference. Social variables included questions similar to those asked of the breast cancer group regarding perceived helpfullness of family, friends, and professionals including physician, funeral director, and clergy, and changes in contact and relationships with family and friends.

At the 6-month interview both groups were also asked to complete the Cattell 16 Personality Factor Inventory (Cattell, Eber, & Tatsuoka, 1970). This is a widely used personality instrument that yields scores ranging from 1–10 on each of 16 different dimensions, identified by Cattell as personality "traits." This inventory was chosen because of its applicability across the many populations being studied by the author's colleagues in the Department of Social and Community Psychiatry at the Clarke Institute of Psychiatry.

RESPONSE RATE FOR FOLLOW–UP INTERVIEWS

Breast Cancer

The response rate for all subjects in the breast cancer study was 80% at 6 months; 67% at 12 months, and 57% at 24 months. However, as a percentage of those still alive at each of those time periods the response rate was 82%, (165 subjects living), 72% (156 subjects living) and 73% (131 subjects living).

The 2-year respose rate of 73% of living subjects is remarkable considering that one-quarter of the subjects living at 2 years had recurrent disease. Half the patients with recurrent disease responded to the 2-year interview. As might be expected, several of those who did not respond were too ill to do so.

Bereavement

The follow-up on the bereavement study resulted in contact with 108 widows at 6 months, 76 at 12 months (when only two-thirds of the subjects were to be inter-viewed), and 99 at 24 months. There was a low refusal rate of 7% initially, none at 6 months, 2% at 12 months, and 1% at 24 months, with the remainder of the subjects either having moved and left no forwarding address, being away for extended periods, or never home when phone calls were made during the day and evening. The rate of 61% being followed up at 24 months compares favorably with the literature.

SELECTED RESULTS

Antecedent Variables

In both studies antecedent variables that antedated the life crisis were investigated to discover whether in fact they influenced either long- or short-term adaptation to the life event. For example, it was thought that patient delay might influence the course of adaptation to breast cancer (Greer, 1974; Magarey, Todd, & Blizard, 1977; Patterson, 1975; Weisman & Worden, 1975) and that length of husband's final illness (Gerber, Rusalem, Hannon, Battin, & Arkin, 1975; Glick et al., 1974) and whether or not spouses talked about impending death might influence response to bereavement.

Breast Cancer

In the case of women with breast cancer 74% of the women discovered a lump themselves; 19% found a breast symptom other than a lump, and 7% had their lump discovered on a routine physical. The latter group had the lowest rate of recurrence and death (30%). Sixty-four percent of the women went to their physician within one month of diagnosis; 15% within 1–3 months, and 14% waited 3 months or more. Patient delay was not related to death.

In 85% of first presentations to a physician the woman was sent for a biopsy or mamogram but in 15% of the cases the women were either reassured that all was fine or were treated for nonmalignant breast disease. The death rate of those whose physicians delayed was significantly different, 68% of delayed cases died versus 46% of those whose physicians did not delay.

When these women were asked what happened to cause treatment delay several of them told of returning repeatedly to the doctor and being told everything was fine. If a woman is sent home with a lump that later proves to be malignant, apart from the potential dangers of such delay, the stage is set for a very stressful patient-physician relationship and distrust of doctors that may well exist throughout the course of the disease. Many of these women came to think of themselves as neurotic and were almost relieved to finally be diagnosed as having cancer. One woman said "I was so pleased to learn that I wasn't crazy; that there really was something there all the time." Needless to say that pleasure can be short-lived if the disease begins to progress quickly and the patient is haunted by thoughts of "if only."

Bereavement

Much of the literature on bereavement is concerned with whether age at the time of bereavement and the type of death (e.g., sudden or chronic illness) makes a difference. In this study, as will be seen below, younger widows (those under 55) and those whose husbands died after a short illness (defined as under 2 months duration) had more difficulty.

Given that this study was begun in the fairly early days of caregivers preaching openness regarding talking of impending death, we were interested to find whether or not dying patients and their spouses talked about impending death and more importantly whether this made a difference. Elsewhere we have reported the response of the widows whose husbands died from cancer (Vachon et al., 1977). Basically we found that even when women were told their husbands were going to die they often didn't believe the warning. Most couples didn't talk about impending death. Whether or not couples talked or didn't talk, however, the widow was usually satisfied with the approach they followed. In the 2-year follow-up we could find no evidence that whether or not a couple talked about impending death made any difference in long-term adaptation to bereavement. Most women seemed to feel that whatever decision they made at the time was the appropriate one. The decision as to whether or not to talk was probably in large manner a reflection of the couple's long-term relationship and their basic communication style.

VARIABLES ASSOCIATED WITH HIGH
DISTRESS AT INITIAL INTERVIEW

Using the Goldberg General Health Questionnaire (GHQ) as the major outcome measure in both studies it was found that the initial impact of bereavement was more traumatic than the initial impact of breast cancer. Initially 70% of the widows and 40% of the women with breast cancer reported experiencing high distress. The impact of the two events is of course quite different in that the death of a spouse is final and irrevocable while the diagnosis of breast cancer can be made somewhat more acceptable by the surgeon's comments "Well you had breast cancer, but I got it all." In the latter situation the woman is potentially left feeling that she has sacrificed a small part of her body to save her life. Quint (1966), suggested that while a woman might consider a mastectomy a major stress, at the same time she comes to view it as a symbol of cure as long as she is free of the disease. However, if there is a recurrence she may feel a sense of betrayal that even this mutilative surgery was not sufficient to spare her from further problems.

Table 1 shows a comparison of the factors associated with high distress in breast cancer and bereavement at the time of the initial interview. In both situations it can be seen that where there was less opportunity to anticipate the stressor (no previous family history of cancer or short final illness) there was the potential for a greater stress response.

The widows who rated themselves as having had a good marriage seemed to have more difficulty with bereavement than those who rated their marriages as being below average. However, the women with breast cancer who rated themselves as having a good marriage were more capable of adjusting to their crisis as a result of having received emotional support from their husbands. Initially 45% of the

Table 1 Factors associated with high distress on initial interview

Variable	Breast cancer	Bereavement
Sociodemographic	Higher social class	Ethnic background Younger age
Precrisis situation	No family history of cancer	Short final illness Poor health Good marriage Stressful final illness Previous psychiatric help
Social support	Need to keep up a front Less help than wanted from professionals Family doctor not very helpful	Not seeing old friends Multiple informal sources of help Low satisfaction with help
Current situation	Additional problems Had lumpectomy Current health average/poor Sex worse than usual Concern about personal appearance	Additional problems Religion not very helpful

married women reported that their relationship with their husband improved following their diagnosis and 89% of married women rated their husbands as having been helpful in their initial adjustment.

A lack of social support proved to be a major difficulty in both studies. Both at the time of the initial interview and with follow-up interviews the high-distress group of women were apt to perceive themselves as having difficulties with social support. In the breast cancer study this was reflected in needing to keep up a front instead if being able to express feelings openly, receiving less help than wanted from professionals, and finding that one's family doctor was not very helpful. In the bereavement study social support difficulties were expressed in seeing old friends less than usual and finding that one had help coming from many directions but feeling unsatisfied with this help.

The lack of satisfaction with help probably reflects a number of possible variables involving the woman's personality and her interaction with her social support system. It may be that the woman has a poor social system on which to draw as was already noted in the reference to B. B. Brown (1978), or it may reflect the withdrawal of others in a support system from someone in crisis (Vachon, 1979). So too, the woman's perception of the support being given her may have been distorted by her depression (Bloom, 1982; Peters-Golden, 1982).

Women who saw themselves as having health problems also had higher stress. Surprisingly 62% of women recently diagnosed as having breast cancer rated their health as being either good or very good in the month following diagnosis. The widows who had poor health prior to their husband's death and the woman with breast cancer whose health was average or poor following diagnosis had higher distress than healthier women. In both of these groups some of the women had significant physical problems (in addition to cancer) while other women seemed to have health problems primarily related to their distress.

In both groups women who had problems in addition to the crisis under study had more distress—these included family problems and illnesses, preexisting marital problems in the breast cancer group, and social problems. While this might be an obvious result, it suggests that problems cause additive stress, and contradicts the thinking of some that stress experiences have a "vaccinating" effect.

Surprisingly the women who had either a lumpectomy or partial mastectomy were the most distressed in the breast cancer group and this was generally true over the course of the study. This gives credence to the idea that it is the crisis of breast cancer, rather than simply the problems associated with the trauma of mastectomy, that poses the real problem for many women with this disease (Rosser, 1981). The women with lumpectomies were under more distress and were at least as likely as the other women to be both concerned about changes in their appearance following surgery and to be having sexual problems. Women with both of these latter characteristics were also noted to have higher GHQ levels. Despite the large number of reports in the literature regarding sexual problems following breast cancer (Jamieson, Wellisch, & Pasnau, 1978; Woods & Earp, 1978; Silberfarb, Maurer, & Crouthamel, 1980; Maguire, 1981; Wellisch, Jamieson, & Pasnau, 1978) only 11% of the women reported sexual problems on the initial interview and this figure changed very little over time.

PATTERNS OF ADAPTATION

Table 2 shows both the difference in the percentage of women having high distress in the two studies over the first 2 years of adaptation, and the patterns of distress followed by the women who completed the 2-year questionnaire. The patterns of distress were different between the two groups. The distress of the widows who initially started with a low GHQ stayed low in all but two instances (Vachon & Lancee et al., 1982) and the distress of the women with initially high GHQ either stayed high or gradually diminished. The pattern of the women with breast cancer was different in that some of the women who initially had low distress later had high distress often in response to a recurrence, low social support, or additional stressors. While 60% of the women with breast cancer experienced high distress at some point over the first 2 years of their disease, 40% never experienced any measurable distress even when they had a recurrence.

From Table 2 it can be seen that although a larger percentage of the widows initially had high distress, by the end of 2 years the percentage having high distress in both groups was approximately equal. Over time 70% of the widows and 60% of the women with breast cancer had high distress on at least one occasion. By comparison, in a general Australian community only 16% of women in the same age range had scores of 5 or higher (Finlay-Jones & Burvill, 1977).

VARIABLES ASSOCIATED WITH HIGH DISTRESS AT TWO YEARS

Table 3 compares the variables that were associated with high distress in each group at the end of 2 years. Those who had high initial distress, lower social class, and a lack of satisfaction with the help they received initially were significantly more apt to have high distress at the end of 2 years in both groups. As previously mentioned, the women with lumpectomies and those with no family history of cancer, and widows whose husbands died after a short illness, who had poor health and had previously had psychological help, were also more likely to have high distress later.

Table 2 Comparison of GHQ 5$^+$ and patterns of adaptation

Percentage of GHQ 5$^+$		
Interview	Breast cancer	Bereavement
Initial	41	69
6 months	26	46
12 months	29	38
24 months	25	28

Patterns of adaptation	
Breast cancer	Bereavement
High high 16%	High high 26%
High low 20%	High low 44%
Low low 53%	Low low 30%
Low high 10%	Low high 0%

Table 3 Factors associated with high distress at two years

	Breast cancer	Bereavement
Variables on initial interview	High initial GHQ Lower social class Less satisfied with help received initially Lumpectomy No cancer in family	High initial GHQ Lower social class Less satisfaction with help initially Short final illness Poor health Previous psychological help
Personality variables	High factor O-apprehensive	High factor O-apprehensive High factor Q-highly anxious Low factor C-emotionally less stable
Variables at 2-year interview	Less satisfied with help More apt to have recurrent disease Rate health as average or poor Additional stressors Rate disease as very stressful Had lumpectomy	Social support deficiencies Health problems Financial problems

Perhaps surprisingly only one personality variable was associated with high distress in both groups. This was Factor 0 on the 16 Personality Factor Inventory which Cattell describes as "apprehensive, self-reproaching, insecure, worrying, troubled" in contrast to its opposite which is described as "self-assured, placid, and secure." Factor 0 is comparable to sense of mastery or inversely to trait anxiety. The high stress group could be thought to be comparable to the group that George Brown and his colleagues (1975) described as being vulnerable to a sense of hopelessness and depression in response to a loss situation.

According to Brown, et al. (1975) the widows with high distress were seen to be "highly anxious" and "emotionally less stable, with lower ego strength" as opposed to "emotionally stable, higher ego strength" which may be most comparable to a sense of low versus high self-esteem, low self esteem being related to high trait anxiety.

While these findings must be viewed with caution given both the fact that the number of personality traits associated with distress was low and the response rate for the 16 personality factors was lower than for the other instruments they nonetheless provide some evidence in the expected direction.

At the end of 2 years both widows and women with breast cancer who perceived deficiencies in their social networks were apt to have high distress. For the women with breast cancer this was gleaned from the satisfaction with help index that measured whether the women were able to get as much information as they wanted about their disease, were satisfied with their family doctor and their surgeon, and were able to get as much help as they wanted from people in general. The high-distress women were less likely than the low distress to be getting the help they wanted.

The index for the widows suggested a deficit in social bonds that has been described in detail elsewhere (Vachon & Sheldon et al., 1982). It also included a deterioration in ties with one's own relatives, inlaws, and friends; having no one or only one person to count on to understand one's feelings; feeling no one cared; finding it difficult to carry on social activities alone; and not receiving as much help as wanted from family and friends. Some of these differences were apparent at the first interview, while other social support deficiencies developed over time.

FACTORS ASSOCIATED WITH DEATH IN WOMEN WITH BREAST CANCER

In addition to factors associated with high distress in the above two studies it also seemed worth looking at another poor outcome with breast cancer—that being death from the disease. There has been considerable interest in the literature regarding whether there are psychological factors that might serve as predictors of who will live and who will die with cancer (Derogatis, Abeloff, & Milesaratos, 1979; Weisman & Worden, 1975).

With regard to physical factors it was found that type of surgery and age were not significantly related to death at the 8 year follow-up. Fifty percent of the women with a mastectomy had died compared with 43% of those with a lumpectomy, 47% of those under age 55, and 54% of those over 56. With regard to stage of disease there was also no significant difference in death rate although the trend was in the direction that would be expected. At the time of the 8 year follow-up, 44% of women with Stage 1 disease, 47% with Stage 2, and 64% with Stage 3 disease were dead. This is a higher rate of death than might be expected for the Stage 1 group (Rosen, Saigo, Braun, Weathers, & DePalo, 1981).

The level of distress 2 years after diagnosis predicted the possibility of later death. Of the women who were experiencing high distress at 2 years only 42% were still alive at 8 years compared with 73% of those with low distress. This is perhaps not surprising since, as noted above, the high-distress group had a higher rate of recurrent disease than the low-distress group (35% vs. 13%).

Another finding of interest within the context of this chapter was that women who lived alone and widowed women were very likely to die of their disease. At the end of 8 years, 75% of widows and 70% of women who lived alone were dead. Of the women who were both widowed and living alone, 83% died compared with 67% of the widows who lived with someone. These figures are in marked contrast to the death rate of 45% for the women who were not widowed and were living with someone, usually a spouse and/or children. These figures are particularly alarming because they are not correlated with age. In an earlier study Bornstein, Clayton, Halikas et al. (1973) found that widows rated as being depressed 13 months after bereavement were significantly less likely to be living with their families than were nondepressed respondents. Whether depression in the widows we studied was related to their risk of dying presents an important question.

There were other factors that also were associated with later death. These included sexual problems and rating one's husband as anxious, both of which may reflect problems within the women's social support system.

Finally, the way in which a physician told a woman her initial diagnosis was also associated with the risk of later death. Some oncologists and surgeons have hypothesized that there is a connection between the physician's expectation of the patient's prognosis and the manner in which he or she relays a diagnosis to a patient. The women in this study reported learning their diagnosis is one of three ways: 1) they were told outright by their physicians, the information often accompanied by reassuring statements such as, "Well, it was cancer but it was just a small lump and I'm sure I got it all" (40%); or 2) they came to their own conclusions that they had cancer either when they found the lump or when they awoke from surgery (31%); or 3) they were helped by the doctor to come to their own conclusions (26%). This latter group had a disproportionate number of deaths (65% as compared to 40% of all others). It might be suggested that physicians had a clinical intuition that these women would not do as well and so held back rather than presenting an optimistic view. An alternative explanation might be that the women felt a level of pressimism in their physicians and in part almost as a self-fulfilling prophecy did not do as well as their cohorts.

INTERVENTION IN BEREAVEMENT AND BREAST CANCER

Both of the studies also had a controlled intervention as a part of the design. In the bereavement study the widows were randomly assigned to be contacted by a "widow contact," one of six women who had resolved their own bereavement reactions and had participated in a training course that examined the problems of bereavement, methods of supportive counselling, and the spectrum of community services that might be helpful to widows. The widow contacts offered unstructured one-to-one support including emotionally sustaining behavior, assistance with problem-solving behavior, indirect personal influence, and environmental action described by Gottlieb (1978). Primarily, however, they served as role models who showed that "I did it and you can too." Small group meetings were also held 6 months after bereavement. This program was found to accelerate the pathway of adaptation to bereavement in that by 6 months after bereavement the widows who were assigned to the program had increased intrapersonal adaptation and by 12 months, improved interpersonal adaptation when compared to the widows who were not assigned to the program. Two years after bereavement those widows in the experimental group who initially had high GHQ scores were significantly more likely to now have low GHQ scores than comparison controls with similar initial scores. In addition they were seen to have developed new relationships and new activities and were well on their way to developing a new sense of identity (Vachon, Lyall, Rogers, Freedman, & Freeman, 1980; Rogers, Vachon, Lyall, Sheldon, & Freeman, 1980).

The intervention with the breast cancer group involved a different model. Sixty-four women from outside Toronto who were undergoing radiotherapy at Princess Margaret Hospital and were staying at the Lodge (a residential facility for patients from outside of Toronto) were compared with 104 women living at home during radiotherapy treatment. Structured group meetings and unstructured cognitive and emotional support and encouragement to interact with other people with cancer formed the basis of this intervention which generally extended over a 3-week period. For those women whose GHQ score changed three points or more over the course of radiotherapy, residence in the Lodge was associated with a decreased risk of change for the worse and an increased probability of change for the better. Lodge patients were also more satisfied with the quantity, quality, and/or diversity of support offered to them than were women living at home (Vachon et al., 1981, 1982). Unfortunately this group support could not continue beyond the radiotherapy treatment because of the geographical differences involved. Follow-up did not show a long-term effect of the program probably because the women needed more ongoing help to deal with the problems involved in living with cancer.

DISCUSSION

Clearly there are implications of the above findings that might be explored. Of most importance is the clear evidence that social support systems have a crucial part to play at all stages in adaptation to each of these stressful life events and may even be related to whether people with cancer live or die.

These findings emerge from the time of the first interview in both studies with high distress being associated in both groups with a perceived lack of social support. Indeed 2 years after the crisis it can be seen that those who had deficits in their initial social support system were significantly more likely to remain under high distress. In addition those under high distress at the end of 2 years were likely to have deficiencies in their social support systems. These findings are similar to the studies of cancer patients by Weisman and Worden (Weisman & Worden, 1975, 1977; Mages, Castro, & Fobair, 1981; Bloom, 1982; Peters-Golden, 1982). With regard to bereavement they provide support for our earlier theoretical hypothesis (Walker, McBride, & Vachon, 1977) and substantiate the work of Maddison and Walker (1967), Maddison and Raphael (1976), Bornstein, et al. (1973), Lopata (1979), Raphael (1977), and Parkes (1980).

Perhaps most strikingly, studies indicate that living alone, especially if widowed, can predict death. Mages et al., (1981) also found that cancer patients who lived alone had more distress, although incidence of death was not reported. In addition problems within one's marital and sexual relationships, which may be associated with social support difficulties—either a lack of social support or problems within the support system—were also associated with risk of death. Funch and Marshall (1983) have also found social support and stressors to account for survival in women with breast cancer.

In both studies personality variables were predictive of later outcome in that subjects rated as being "apprehensive" had a poorer long-term outcome. While self-esteem and self-mastery were not directly studied on the 16 PF it was suggested that the one 16 PF variable found to be significant might be similar to them. This would tend to support the hypothesis that those with a low sense of self-esteem and mastery do worse. The fact that only one variable was significant with the women with breast cancer may be reflective of the fact that too general an instrument was chosen rather than a lack of relationship of distress to trait personality characteristics.

It was seen that the course of adaptation to bereavement seemed to result in high distress more frequently than in adaptation to cancer, although by the end of 2 years both groups were experiencing a similar level of distress. In both studies a large proportion of women experienced no measurable distress over the course of adaptation, while in contrast a substantial minority experienced little relief from distress. In both studies initial level of distress was correlated with later level of distress. For some women these events may not have been stressors, for others they were simply acute stressors, while for a third group they became chronic stressors.

It was found that in both groups of women it was possible to intervene to decrease the stress they experienced by providing them with a temporary community of others (Weiss, 1976) who were able to provide emotional support, cognitive road mapping, and practical help in adapting to this stressful life event and beginning the identity transformation it required. Future research might further consider the development and study of applied social support interventions.

REFERENCES

Andrews, G., Tennant, C., Hewson, D. M., & Vaillant, G. E. (1978). Life event stress, social support, coping style and risk of psychological impairment. *The Journal of Nervous and Mental Disease, 166,* 307-316.

Antonovsky, A. (1979). *Health, stress and coping.* San Francisco: Jossey-Bass.

Bieliauskas, L. S., & Garron, D. C. (1982). Psychological depression and cancer. *General Hospital Psychiatry, 4,* 187-195.

Bloom, J. (1982). Social support, accommodation to stress and adjustment to breast cancer. *Social Science and Medicine, 16,* 1329-1338.

Bornstein, P. E., Clayton, P. E., Halikas, J. A. et al. (1973). The depression of widowhood after thirteen months. *British Journal of Psychiatry, 122,* 561-566.

Brown, B. B. (1978). Social and psychological correlates of help-seeking behavior among urban adults. *American Journal of Community Psychology, 6,* 425-439.

Brown, G. W., Bhrolchain, M. M., & Harris, T. (1975). Social class and psychiatric disturbance among women in an urban population. *Sociology, 9,* 226-254.

Canadian Cancer Society. (1982). *Facts on breast cancer.* Toronto.

Carter, H., & Glick, P. (1970). *Marriage and divorce: A social and economic study.* Cambridge, MA: Harvard University Press.

Cattell, R. B., Eber, H. W., & Tatsuoka, M. M. (1970). *Handbook for the 16 personality factor questionnaire.* Champaign, IL: Institute for Personality and Ability Testing.

Cobb, S. (1976). Social support as a moderator of life stress. *Psychosomatic Medicine, 38,* 300-314.

Croog, S., Lipson, A., & Levine, S. (1972). Help patterns in severe illness: The roles of kin network, non-family resources and institutions. *Journal of Marriage and the Family,* 32-41.

D'Arcy, C., & Schmitz, J. A. (1979, June). *Some social parameters of disease in a provincial population.* Paper presented at the Canadian Anthropology and Sociology Association, Saskatoon, Saskatchewan.

Dean, A., & Lin, N. (1977). The stress-buffering role of social support. *The Journal of Nervous and Mental Disease, 165,* 403-417.

Derogatis, L. R., Abeloff, M. D., and Milesaratos, N. (1979). Psychological coping mechanisms and survival time in metastatic breast cancer. *Journal of the American Medical Association, 242,* 1504-1508.

Dohrenwend, B. S. & Dohrenwend, B. P. (1978). Some issues in research on stressful life events. *Journal of Nervous and Mental Disease, 166,* 7-15.

Finlay-Jones, R. A., & Burvill, P. W. (1977). The prevalence of minor psychiatric morbidity in the community. *Psychological Medicine, 7,* 475-489.

Finlayson, A. (1976). Social networks as coping resources: Lay help and consultation patterns used by women in husbands' post-infarction career. *Social Science and Medicine, 10,* 97-103.

Funch, D. P., & Marshall, J. (1983). The role of stress, social support and age in survival from breast cancer. *Journal of Psychosomatic Research, 27,* 77-83.

Gerber, I., Rusalem, R., Hannon, N., Battin, D., & Arkin, A. (1975). Anticipatory grief in aged widows and widowers. *Journal of Gerontology, 30,* 225-229.

Glick, I., Weiss, R., & Parkes, C. M. (1974). *The first year of bereavement.* New York: Wiley.

Goldberg, D. P. (1972). *The detection of psychiatric illness by questionnaire.* Maudsley Monograph No. 21. London: Oxford University Press.

Goldberg, D. P. (1979). *Manual of the general health questionnaire,* Windsor: NFER.

Gore, S. (1978). The effect of social support in moderating the health consequences of unemployment. *Journal of Health and Social Behavior 19,* 157-165.

Greer, S. (1974). Psychological aspects: Delay in the treatment of breast cancer. *Proceedings of the Royal Society of Medicine, 67,* 470-473.

Henderson, S. (1977). The social network, support, and neurosis–The function of attachment in adult life. *British Journal of Psychiatry, 131,* 185-191.

Hobfoll, S. E., & Walfisch, S. (1984). Coping with a threat to life: A longitudinal study of self-concept, social support and psychological distress. *American Journal of Community Psychology, 12,* 87-100.

Hollingshead, A., & Redlich, F. C. (1958). *Social class and mental illness: A community study.* New York: Wiley.

Jamieson, K. R., Wellisch, D. K., & Pasnau, R. O. (1978). Psychological aspects of mastectomy I: The woman's perspective. *American Journal of Psychiatry, 135,* 432-437.

Levine, S., & Scotch, N. A. (1973). *Social stress.* Chicago, IL: Aldine.

Lopata, H. (1973). *Widowhood in an American city,* Cambridge, MA: Schenkman.

Lopata, H. (1979). *Women as widows: Support systems.* New York: Elsevier.

Maddison, D., & Walker, W. (1967). Factors affecting the outcome of conjugal bereavement. *International Journal of Psychiatry, 113,* 1057-1069.

Maddison, D., & Raphael, B. (1976). Death of a spouse. In H. Gruenbaum & J. Christ (Eds.), *Marriage: Structure, dynamics and therapy.* Boston, MA: Little Brown.

Magarey, C. J., Todd, P. B., & Blizard, P. J. (1977). Psychosocial factors influencing delay and breast self-examination in women with symptoms of breast cancer. *Social Science and Medicine, 11,* 229-233.

Mages, N., Castro, J. R., & Fobair, P. (1981). Patterns of psychological response to cancer: Can effective adaptation be predicted? *International Journal of Radiation Oncology, Biology and Physics, 7,* 385-392.

Maguire, P. (1981). The repercussions of mastectomy on the family. *International Journal of Family Psychiatry, 1,* 485.

Nuckolls, K. B., Cassel, J., & Kaplan, B. H. (1972). Psychosocial assets, life crisis and the prognosis of pregnancy. *American Journal of Epidemiology, 95,* 431-441.

Parkes, C. M. (1980, July). Bereavement counselling: Does it work? *British Medical Journal, 5,* 3-6.

Patterson, R. (1975). Why do cancer patients delay? *Canadian Medical Association Journal, 73,* 931-940.

Pearlin, L. I., & Schooler, C. (1978). The structure of coping. *Journal of Health and Social Behavior, 19,* 2-21.

Peters-Golden, H. (1982). Breast cancer: Varied perceptions of social support in the illness experience. *Social Science and Medicine, 16,* 483-491.

Quint, J. C. (1966). Mastectomy–Symbol of cure or warning sign. In J. Folta and E. Deck (Eds.), *A Sociological Framework for Patient Care.* New York: Wiley.

Rabkin, J. G., & Struening, E. L. (1976). Life events, stress and illness. *Science, 194,* 1013-1020.

Raphael, B. (1977). Preventive intervention with the recently bereaved. *Archives of General Psychiatry, 34,* 1450-1454.

Rogers, J., Vachon, M. L. S., Lyall, W. A. L., Sheldon, A., & Freeman, S. J. J. (1980). A self-help program for widows as an independent community service. *Hospital and Community Psychiatry, 31,* 844-847.

Rosen, P. P., Saigo, P. E., Braun, D. W., Weathers, E., & DePalo, A. (1981). Predictors of recurrence in stage 1 (T$_1$ N$_0$ M$_0$) breast carcinoma. *Annals of Surgery, 193,* 15-25.

Russer, J. E. (1981). The interpretation of women's experience: A critical appraisal of the literature on breast cancer. *Social Science and Medicine, 15,* 257-265.

Sanger, C. K., & Reznikoff, M. (1981). A comparison of the psychological effects of breast-saving procedures with the modified radical mastectomy. *Cancer, 48,* 2341-2346.

Schaefer, C. (1982). Shoring Up the "Buffer" of Social Support. *Journal of Health and Social Behavior, 23,* 96-98.

Silberfarb, P. M., Maurer, L. H., & Crouthamel, C. S. (1980). Psychosocial aspects of neoplastic disease: I. Functional status of breast cancer patients during different treatment regimens. *American Journal of Psychiatry, 137,* 450-455.

Statistics Canada (1980). *Estimates of population by marital status, age, and sex for Canada.* Ottawa.

Thoits, P. A. (1982). Conceptual, methodological, and theoretical problems in studying social support as a buffer against life stress. *Journal of Health and Social Behavior, 23,* 145-159.

Turner, R. J. (1981). Social support as a contingency in psychological well-being. *Journal of Health and Social Behavior, 22,* 357-367.

Vachon, M. L. S. (1979). *Identity change over the first two years of bereavement: Social relationships and social support in widowhood.* Unpublished doctoral dissertation, Toronto, Canada: York University.

Vachon, M. L. S., Freedman, K., Formo, A., Rogers, J., Lyall, W. A. L., & Freeman, S. J. J. (1977). The final illness in cancer: The widow's perspective. *Canadian Medical Association Journal, 117,* 1151-1154.

Vachon, M. L. S., Lyall, W. A. L., Rogers, J., Freedman, K., & Freeman, S. J. J. (1980). A controlled study of self-help intervention for widows. *American Journal of Psychiatry, 137,* 1380-1384.

Vachon, M. L. S., Lyall, W. A. L., Rogers, J., Cochrane, J., & Freeman, S. J. J. (1981-1982). The effectiveness of psychosocial support during post-surgical treatment of breast cancer. *International Journal of Psychiatry in Medicine, 11,* 365-371.

Vachon, M. L. S., Lancee, W., Sheldon, R. A., Lyall, W. A. L., and Freeman, S. J. J. (1982). Predictors and correlates of high distress in adaptation to conjugal bereavement. *American Journal of Psychiatry, 139,* 998-1002.

Vachon, M. L. S., Sheldon, A. R., Lancee, W. J., Lyall, W. A. L., Rogers, J., & Freeman, S. J. J. (1982). Correlates of enduring distress patterns following bereavement: Social network, life situation and personality. *Psychological Medicine, 12,* 783-788.

Walker, K. N., MacBride, A., & Vachon, M. L. S. (1977). Social support networks and crisis of bereavement. *Social Science and Medicine, 11,* 35-41.

Weisman, A., & Worden, J. W. (1975). Psychosocial analysis of cancer death. *Omega, 6,* 6-79.

Weisman, A. D., & Worden, J. W. (1977). *Coping and vulnerability in cancer patients* (Research Report). Boston: Massachusetts General Hospital.

Weiss, R. S. (1976). Transition states and other stressful situations: Their nature and programs for their management. In G. Caplan & M. Killilea (Eds.), *Support systems and mutual help: Multidisciplinary explorations,* (pp. 213-232). New York: Grune & Stratton.

Wellisch, D. K., Jamieson, K. R., & Pasnau, R. O. (1978). Psychosocial aspects of mastectomy: II. The man's perspective. *American Journal of Psychiatry, 135,* 543-546.

Williams, A. W., Ware, J. E., & Donald, C. A. (1981). A model of mental health, life events, and social supports applicable to general populations. *Journal of Health and Social Behavior, 22,* 324-336.

Woods, N. F., & Earp, J. A. L. (1978). Women with cured breast cancer: A study of mastectomy patients in North Carolina. *Nursing Research, 27,* 279.

V

BEREAVEMENT
AND OLD AGE

13

Peer Support for Widows: Personal and Structural Characteristics Related to Its Provision

Elizabeth A. Bankoff
Northwestern University

Women undergoing the major life transition of widowhood are more apt to make a successful adjustment if they have strong supportive ties with others in similar life circumstances. This proposition gains support from a variety of theoretical perspectives including crisis theory (Caplan, 1964), reference-group theory (Hyman, 1942), theories of affiliation (Schacter, 1959), and social comparison processes (Gerard, 1963). As Gottlieb (1981) notes, these theories emphasize the key role played by persons in similar life circumstances for individuals experiencing the difficulties associated with major life transitions and crises. Such peers can best meet the need for sharing and comparing fears and uncertainties, reactions, problems, and problem-solving strategies. Moreover, as Walker, MacBride, & Vachon (1977), Lopata (1973, 1979), and Silverman (1972) have suggested, ties with peers in similar life circumstances can facilitate a widow's transition to being a single person again by introducing her to members of new networks supportive to her newly acquired needs as a single person, and by helping her learn the norms, standards, and expectations involved in performing her new role.

The most compelling evidence regarding the importance of peer support for women experiencing conjugal bereavement, however, is the consistently strong empirical link found between peer relations and morale among the widowed (Arling, 1976; Philblad & Adams, 1972; Lopata, 1973; Lowenthal & Haven, 1968; Walker et al., 1977; Silverman, 1967, 1970, 1972, 1981). Moreover, in the first step of an ongoing research endeavor to understand the role that social support plays in adaptation to widowhood, this author found that social support from widowed or otherwise single friends was the single most important support factor relating to the morale of relatively recent widows (Bankoff, 1983). That is, the support provided by peers in similar life circumstances was more strongly related to an enhanced sense of psychological well-being than was the support provided by any other subset of their informal social network (i.e., parents, inlaws, children, other close relatives, married friends, and neighbors).

The research reported in this chapter was supported with a grant from the National Institute of Mental Health, PH5#5, R01-MH30742. Morton A. Lieberman and Leonard D. Borman were the co-principal investigators.

Although identifying support factors that account for differential outcomes resulting from major changes experienced in adulthood is an important first step in any endeavor to understand and eventually, perhaps, augment successful adjustment to such changes (George, 1982), it is, nevertheless, only that—a first step. An important next step is to discover what factors influence the transmission and availability of these key supports (Mitchell & Trickett, 1980). As maintained by Eckenrode and Gore (1981), the study of social supports as stress-buffers is marred by the failure to identify factors that affect a network's ability to mobilize support. They argue for the need to look at the context and its constraints. Similarly, Cassel (1974) enjoins us both to find ways of identifying individuals at risk and to determine the forms of their social networks that should be strengthened in order to protect them from negative outcomes of stressful life experiences. This is the focus of this chapter. Broadly speaking, the ensuing discussion will be concerned with the identification of which widows in what context are apt to receive strong peer support. The corollary question is also of particular interest. That is, which widows in what context are not likely to receive this key support thereby being at risk of great emotional distress. To facilitate this discussion, a study that focused on these concerns will be examined in detail in this chapter.

In order to address this overarching issue, a determination of categories of factors potentially relevant to the provision of peer support is required. Since there is presently no general theory regarding the patterning of characteristics predictive of receiving strong support from peers, the selection of factors must necessarily be ad hoc, and to some extent opportunistic, drawing from relevant literature in the areas of support, social networks, friendship and peer relationships, and widowhood, per se.

There is evidence that two general sets of attributes have implications for the provision of social support: personal attributes of the individuals; and structural attributes of their social context, particularly of the social networks in which they are embedded.

PERSONAL CHARACTERISTICS AND PEER
SUPPORT PROVISION

Previous works suggest that certain personal attributes of the widow may influence her provision of peer support. Lopata (1973) found that the education and income levels of urban elderly widows distinguish between widows who are and are not friendless. The more educated and higher incomed widows are more apt to be involved with others in general and friends in particular. Moreover, a sharp drop in income level has been found to be related to a decrease in affiliation among the widowed (Harvey & Bahr, 1974). Others have found that as both health and finances deteriorate among older people, friendship relations tend to be adversely affected (Arth, 1962; Rose, 1965; Rosow, 1967). It should be noted, however, that Lopata (1973) did not find a relationship between the self-reported physical condition of elderly widows and their level of involvement in friendship relationships.

Blau's (1961) research indicates that the friendship relationships of younger women are more adversely affected by widowhood than those of older women. She explains this age difference in terms of social timing differences and the concomitant differences in the numbers of friends in similar life circumstances.

Lopata's (1973) research, however, indicates that old (and uneducated) widows tend to have little social interaction with others in general and have few friends in particular. Lopata (1973) has also found that widows who are not employed outside of the home tend to have fewer friends than do working widows.

Religious preference may also relate to the nature of social relationships. Laumann (1973) found in his study of friendship networks among urban males that Catholic men are more likely to be involved in interlocking and, therefore, intimate and affective friendship networks than are Protestant men. However, widowhood may alter this association as Lopata (1973) found that Catholic widows are apt to be less involved with friendship relationships than Protestant widows. Of course, it is also possible that the differences in these data may simply reflect sex differences.

Socioeconomic status may relate to widows' ability to make use of a support network (Walker et al., 1977). Lopata (1981) notes that socioeconomic status is related to the formation of friendships in the United States. She maintains that lower status adults frequently lack preconditions necessary for transforming acquaintances into friends. Williams (1959) has found that higher status women have more close friends than do women of lower status; they also have a wider community (e.g., community-based clubs and organizations) from which to draw friends. Moreover, adult friendship relationships among lower and working class women tend to be subordinated to kinship interactions (Adams, 1968; Brown, 1981; Gans, 1962; Komarovsky, 1964), whereas middle-class adults typically devote at least as much time to friends as they do to relatives (Axelrod, 1956). However, in comparison to its effects on the friendships of higher status women, widowhood may be less disruptive of the friendship ties that do exist among lower status women. Where middle-class adults tend to form couple-coordinated friendships, working-class couples typically maintain separate friendship relations that might, therefore, be less disrupted by the death of a woman's husband (Babchuck, 1965; Bott, 1957; Dotson, 1951; Gans, 1962; Hess, 1972; Komarovsky, 1964; Lopata, 1973).

Personological characteristics may also be relevant to peer support provision. Need for affiliation has been reported to distinguish between persons who have high versus low access to social support (Tolsdorf, 1976). It has also been found to be positively related to being enmeshed in an interlocking and, therefore, an intense, affective friendship network (Laumann, 1973).

Lopata's (1973) research suggests that such personal resources as self-confidence or self-esteem, and coping capabilities affect the widow's ability to utilize societal resources, including friends. Walker et al. (1977) similarly assert that a widow's coping capacity influences her ability to make use of a support network. Gottlieb (1981) argues from his research that particular personological variables such as coping styles and attitudes toward help-seeking can be used to identify prime candidates for interventions during stressful life transitions.

The extent to which widows were dependent upon their spouses for social inter-action may also affect the strength of their social ties with peers. Lopata's (1970) research indicates that the more multidimensional the involvement of the husband in the widow's life, the more disorganized her social life is apt to be following his death. Similarly, Bell (1981) suggests that widows who were highly dependent upon their husbands for social interaction may have less capacity for and willingness to enter into significant relationships with others upon being widowed.

Finally, there is indirect evidence that the neediness of the widows will also affect the level of peer support provided them. That is, as Bell (1981) has argued, equality or balance in exchange of support is implied in peer or friendship relationships. If the exchange becomes too one-sided, an inequality in the relationship would begin to exist, increasing the probability of a breakup in the relationship. That is, although friendships are expected to sustain themselves during short-term crises experienced by an individual, a question remains as to how well the relationship will endure if the crisis and, therefore, the neediness of one of the partners continues over a long period of time. If, after a year or longer, widows are still having severe adjustment problems, one might reasonably surmise that this will severely tax the friendship relationship due to the (apparent) inequality of exchange. As such, indicators of level of adjustment to the loss as well as to the new social role as a single rather than a married person appeared to be relevant characteristics to be examined in this study.

In sum, the relevant literature suggests that the following personal characteristics may be related to the provision of peer support for relatively recently widowed women: 1) Demographic attributes including age, education, socioeconomic status, work status, and religious preference; 2) Other life circumstances as potential stressors including health status, change in health status, financial status, and change in financial status; 3) Personological attributes including need for affiliation, self-esteem, coping mastery, and level of prior dependency on spouse for companionship and for arranging social interactions with others; and 4) Indicators of adjustment including single role-strain, level of preoccupation with spouse's death, frequency of visits to the grave, and length of time before the intense grief subsided. Therefore, the relationship between these personal characteristics and the provision of peer support was examined in the study under discussion.

NETWORK STRUCTURAL CHARACTERISTICS AND PEER SUPPORT PROVISION

As Gottlieb (1981), Walker et al. (1977), and Wellman (1981) among others have asserted, the structure of people's social environment affects their access to supportive resources relevant to adjustment to a major life transition. Several relevant categories of structural criteria can be delineated, including morphological characteristics of the friendship network, and interpersonal interaction characteristics of the friendship network, the kin network, and the large community network. Each of these categories includes characteristics that may be particularly relevant to the transmission of peer support for widows.

Morphological characteristics of the friendship network that have been identified as being most relevant to the network serving as a personal support system include: size, density (i.e., the extent to which friends of the focal individual also know each other), reachability (i.e., the ability to contact network associates), and homogeneity of marital status (i.e., the extent to which network associates share the same marital status as the focal individual) (Craven and Wellman, 1974; Hirsch, 1980; Laumann, 1973; Mitchell, 1969; Silverman, 1972; Walker et al., 1977; Wan, 1982). For example, Laumann (1973) found that men in dense or interlocking friendship networks were apt to form more intensive, intimate, affective friendship relationships than were men in radial or less dense networks. However, Hirsch

(1980) found a negative association between the density of young widows support networks and the quality of the support provided them.

The nature of interpersonal interaction was also considered to be important to examine in the context of this study. Frequency of contact with friends, while not necessarily implying high intensity in the relationships (Wan, 1982), certainly may affect access to peer support. Durability or the age of the friendship relationship may also be relevant. Laumann (1973) discovered that the longer the men in his study had known their closest friends the more likely they were to have formed an interlocking network and, therefore, the more likely they were to have intense, intimate relationships. The social condition of widowhood, however, may alter such an association. Lopata (1973) found that the widows in her study had much more frequent contact with new friends than with old friends.

The effect that strong kin involvement may have on the provision of peer support is unclear. It might be argued that when strong family support exists, there is less of a need for peer support. That is, if family and friends do meet the same interpersonal needs of individuals (Bell, 1981), then people with strong kin support may be less likely to need and, therefore, less likely to have strong peer support. However, Lopata (1973) and Arling (1976) found that elderly widows' integration into a friendship network was not related to frequency of contact with kin nor was it related to feelings of closeness with kin.

Participation in community-based organizations would seem to be related to the provision of peer support. That is, social, recreational, educational, or religious organizations can function as a medium for meeting people. The activities therein may provide a basis for the formation of social relationships (Kalish, 1982). Concomitantly, participation in self-help groups for the widowed may be particularly relevant. Not only will participating widows have an opportunity to meet new people, but as these groups comprise others in similar life circumstances, the opportunity to make friends with similar peers is obviously enhanced. In fact, participation in self-help groups for people experiencing a common life transition has been found to often result in peer relationships that endure beyond the structured group meetings (Barrett, 1978).

Finally, it might be argued that the more access one has to a range of helpers, including professional helpers, the less one would need and, consequently, have strong support from peers. However, Kalish (1982) maintains that professional helpers can only provide a limited relationship which, while appreciated, does not provide a substitute for the role of a friend or family member.

Overall, there appear to be a range of network structural characteristics that have promise as predictors of the mobilization of peer support for recently widowed women. The relationship between the amount of support provided relatively recently widowed women and the following structural characteristics was evaluated in the study being presented: 1) Morphological characteristics of the widows' friendship networks including size, homogeneity of marital status, density, and reachability; 2) Interpersonal interaction characteristics of the friendship network including frequency of contact with widowed or otherwise single friends, married friends, and neighbors, durability of the friendship relationships, and change in level of involvement with old friends (i.e., friends the widows had before they were widowed); 3) Interpersonal interaction characteristics of the kin network including frequency of contact with parents, inlaws, children, and other close relatives, and change in level of involvement with family members since the spouse's death; and 4) Interpersonal interaction characteristics of the community network including level of participation in community-based organizations both currently and prior to being widowed, level of involvement in self-help groups for the widowed, and use of professional service givers (e.g., clergy, psychiatrists).

PRACTICAL IMPLICATIONS OF RESEARCH

Such research has the potential to increase our theoretical understanding of the complex interplay between social support and adaptation to major changes experienced in adulthood. It also has the potential to provide strategic information for the planning of intervention strategies. As argued by Eckenrode and Gore (1981), a contextual study of support mobilization processes is "the most productive means to practical ends, because such analysis will provide an understanding of the conditions under which supports are available and can be mobilized to deal with life problems" (Eckenrode & Gore, 1981, p. 65).

Two sets of intervention guidelines can potentially be generated from this type of research. First, personal characteristics associated with receiving weak support from peers can be determined thereby allowing for the identification of the most vulnerable widows. Second, identification of network structures that act to constrain the transmission of adequate levels of peer support for widows can lead to the generation of guidelines for creating or redesigning deficient networks.

SAMPLE DESCRIPTION

These data were collected as part of a larger study of alternative help systems for the widowed conducted at the University of Chicago from 1979-1981 (see Lieberman & Borman, 1979 for study details). The present study's sample of widows comprises the subsample of Caucasian women ($n = 147$) who had been widowed between 19 and 35 months and reported that although they were beyond the first intense grieving phase of their bereavement, they were still experiencing grief as they struggled to adjust to this major life transition. Of these women 64% were employed at least part time, and 42% lived alone, although 93% were mothers. Forty-two percent were Catholic, 58% were Protestant, 22% had earned at least a bachelor's degree, while 10% had not completed high school. The mean age was 52 years—just slightly younger than the national average for widows of 56 years ("Aspects," 1981)—and the average number of years lived in their present community was 26.

This sample was previously selected for analyses of the relationship between social support and adaptation to widowhood (Bankoff, 1983, 1981). The results of these analyses indicated that peer support was a key social support factor relating to an enhanced sense of psychological well-being among these relatively recent widows. Peer support, therefore, was used as the independent or criterion variable for this further set of analyses.

ASSESSMENT OF PEER SUPPORT

Peer support was assessed in the following manner. Each respondent was asked to report how much of six different types of support they receive from their widowed or otherwise single friends. The six types of support included: contact, intimacy, assurance of emergency assistance, emotional support, guidance, and approval of a new lifestyle (i.e., sanction support). Each support item was answered on a 4-point scale (i.e., "not at all," "only a little," "somewhat," "very much"). In addition, the respondents were able to indicate inappropriate items by checking a fifth option: "not applicable." The peer support score was then derived by calculating the mean response across all six types of support provided by the respondents' widowed or otherwise single friends. The computed peer support grand mean was 2.87 ($SD = .63$).

Two groups of widows were then selected for further analyses. The Weak Peer Support group ($n = 28$) consisted of those widows whose peer support score fell at lease one standard deviation below the grand mean. The Strong Peer Support group ($n = 34$) consisted of those widows whose peer support score fell at least one standard deviation above the grand mean.

ASSESSMENT OF PERSONAL CHARACTERISTICS

The demographic characteristics considered in the analyses presented here were: age, years of formal education, socioeconomic status, work status immediately prior to spouse's death, current work status, and religious affiliation. Socioeconomic status was based on the occupational status scale developed by the National Opinion Research Center (1974).

Personological characteristics that were applied to these analyses included need for affiliation which was assessed by a four-item scale used by Laumann (1973) in his study of friendship networks of urban males. Other personological measures included self-esteem (Rosenberg, 1965), a coping measure of masterful orientation toward the environment (Pearlin & Schooler, 1978), and single item measures of prior dependency on spouse for both companionship and for arranging social get togethers with friends and family.

Measures of other life circumstances as possible liabilities for interpersonal interaction included two measures of health, the first a measure of health problems experienced, the second a measure of health changes experienced since the spouse's death. Questions about the respondents' current financial circumstances and financial changes experienced since the spouse's death were also included.

Indicators of adjustment to the loss included a measure of preoccupation with the spouse's death, a measure of the frequency of visits to the spouse's grave, and a measure of the length of time it took for the initial intense grief to subside. In addition, level of adjustment to the new single role was assessed by a single role-strain scale developed by Lieberman and Pearlin (1977) for a longitudinal study of adaptation in a normative population.

ASSESSMENT OF NETWORK STRUCTURAL CHARACTERISTICS

The morphological characteristics of the friendship network considered in these analyses were: size (i.e., the number of close friends; reachability (i.e., the count of unavailable friends); homogeneity of marital status (i.e., the percentage of widowed friends within the friendship network); and density (i.e., the extent to which the widows' closest friends also know each other).

Interpersonal interaction characteristics of the friendship network which were applied to these analyses included: indexes of frequency of contact with widowed or otherwise single friends, married friends, and neighbors; a measure of change in the frequency of contact with old friends since the spouse's death; and a measure of durability (i.e., how many of the respondents' close friends were made since being widowed). Interpersonal interaction characteristics of the kin network included: indexes of frequency of contact with parents, inlaws, children, and other close relatives; and a measure of change in frequency of contact with family members since being widowed.

Interpersonal interaction characteristics of the larger community network included a summary score of the current level of involvement in seven different types of community-based organizations (i.e., religious, educational, social, sports, recreational, community, and charity), and a summary score of the level of involvement in these organizations prior to being widowed. Other community network interaction characteristics included were a summary score of involvement in any of seven different self-help groups for the widowed, and two indexes of use of professionals for help with problems experienced since being widowed.

PERSONAL CHARACTERISTICS OF WIDOWS WHO RECEIVED STRONG VERSUS WEAK PEER SUPPORT

The results of the analyses of personal characteristics are reported in Table 1. Only one of the six demographic characteristics examined distinguished between widows who had strong versus weak support from peers. Compared to the strong peer support group, more of the widows who received weak peer support had been housewives before their spouse's death (66% vs. 30%). However, current work status did not distinguish between these two groups of widows, nor did age, education, or socioeconomic status. Similarly, although two-thirds of the widows who received strong peer support were Protestant and only a third were Catholic—a finding consistent with the results of previous research on friendship and religious preference among the widowed (cf., Lopata, 1973)—the religious preference of widows with weak peer support was evenly divided between these two religions. As such, religious affiliation also failed to be a distinguishing factor.

Although such personological characteristics as self-esteem and coping mastery (i.e., having a masterful orientation to one's environment) may, indeed, be important inner resources for women suffering conjugal bereavement, they apparently have little to do with obtaining the resource of peer support. These characteristics failed to differentiate widows with strong peer support from those with weak support from peers.

However, these two groups of widows did differ in terms of several of the personological characteristics examined. The widows with strong peer support had more need for affiliation than their counterparts with weak peer support. They also had been less dependent on their husbands for arranging social get togethers with family and friends. Finally, the widows with strong peer support also tended to have been less dependent on their husbands for companionship. Thus, it would appear that low need for affiliation and strong prior dependency needs vis-à-vis the husband are characteristics that act to constrain the process of peer support provision for relatively recent widows.

Table 1 Comparisons between widows with weak and strong peer support on personal characteristics

| Dimension of comparison | Groups | | Significance[a] |
	Weak peer support (*n* = 28)	Strong peer support (*n* = 34)	
Demographic characteristics			
Age	51.9	48.5	NS
Years of education	12.8	13.1	NS
Socioeconomic status	44.9	44.3	NS
Unemployed before spouse's death	66%	30%	.05[b]
Unemployed currently	36%	33%	NS[b]
Religious preference:			NS[b]
Catholic	50%	35%	
Protestant	50%	65%	
Personological characteristics			
Need for affiliation	2.1	2.7	.05
Self-esteem	4.6	4.9	NS
Coping mastery	4.1	4.7	NS
Dependency on spouse for:			
Companionship	3.4	3.0	.08
Arranging social get togethers	2.4	1.9	.05
Other life circumstances			
Health problems	3.9	4.1	NS
Health change (deterioration)	2.4	1.9	.009
Financial problems	2.0	1.8	NS
Financial change (deterioration)	3.5	3.2	.04
Adjustment indicators			
Single role strain	2.6	2.1	.000
Preoccupation with spouse's death	2.7	2.8	.07
Frequency visit grave	3.1	2.8	.05
Length of intense grief	2.6	2.2	.03

[a]All statistical analyses were calculated using t-tests between group means, unless otherwise indicated.
[b]Fisher's Exact Test.

The results of the analyses of other life circumstances indicate that these two groups of widows were not facing significantly different levels of health or financial problems. However, the amount of change that had been experienced in these two life domains did differ. The widows with weak peer support had experienced more change (i.e., deterioration) in their health as well as their financial circumstances since being widowed than had the strong peer support group. Taken together, this set of findings suggests that relative deprivation is a pertinent concept for the issue at hand. That is, while the absolute level of financial or health difficulties do not appear to constrain the process of peer support provision, the experience of a recent drop in the status of one or both of these important life domains does appear to have an inhibiting effect on the peer support process.

These data also indicate that the widows with weak peer support were having more adjustment difficulties than their counterparts with strong support from peers. That is, the widows with weak peer support were experiencing more strain in their new role as a single person. They were also less well-adjusted to the loss of their husbands, per se, as indicated by their more frequent visits to the grave, by the significantly longer time taken for their intense grief to subside, and by their tendency to be more preoccupied with their spouses' death. These data, then, lend some support to the notion that friendship relationships require a balance of exchange in order to remain vital. If one of the partners experiences severe personal difficulties for a relatively long period of time, the exchange can become too one-sided, thereby weakening the relationship and reducing the amount of support provided. However, it is also possible that the lack of strong peer support itself may have been impeding the recovery evidenced among women receiving strong peer support.

NETWORK STRUCTURAL CHARACTERISTICS OF WIDOWS WHO RECEIVED STRONG VERSUS WEAK PEER SUPPORT

The results of the analyses of the structural characteristics are reported in Table 2. Homogeneity of marital status was the only morphological characteristic of the friendship network that distinguished between widows with strong versus weak peer support. A higher proportion of the close friends of the widows with strong peer support shared the status of widowhood. However, size of the friendship network did not differentiate these two groups. Apparently, then, it is not the overall number of friends but, rather, the composition of the network that makes a difference to the process of peer support provision. Density of the friendship network and reachability of network associates also failed to be discriminating morphological characteristics.

The results of the analyses of the interpersonal interaction characteristics of the friendship network suggest that frequency of contact with widowed or otherwise single friends (i.e., peers) and durability of the friendship relationships are factors relevant to the process of peer support provision. However, frequency of contact with other subsets of the friendship network (i.e., married friends and neighbors) and change in frequency of contact with old friends are not relevant factors. That is, while widows with strong peer support had more frequent contact with their widowed or otherwise single friends than did the widows with weak peer support, they did not have more frequent contact with either their married friends or their neighbors. Finally, although the widows with strong peer support had not experienced any greater drop in the frequency with which they see their old friends than the widows with weak peer support, more of their closest friends were new friends (i.e., had been made since being widowed).

Level of involvement with kin apparently has little to do with the peer support process as not a single measure depicting frequency of interaction with family members differed appreciably between widows with strong and weak peer support. That is, the widows with strong peer support had as much contact with their parents, inlaws, children, and other close relatives as did their counterparts with weak peer support. Moreover, they were experiencing no greater change in the frequency of interaction with family members since being widowed than were the widows with weak peer support. These data, therefore, lend support to the notion that family and friends comprise distinct primary groups that perform

Table 2 Comparisons between widows with weak and strong peer support
on structural characteristics

| | Groups | | |
| | Weak peer support ($n = 28$) | Strong peer support ($n = 34$) | |
Dimension of comparison			Significance[a]
Morphological characteristics of friendship network			
Size	5.5	5.8	NS
Reachability	.1	.0	NS
Homogeneity	1.6	2.2	.002
Density	2.4	2.3	NS
Interaction characteristics of friendship network			
Contact with widowed friends	2.1	3.8	.000
Contact with married friends	2.1	2.4	NS
Contact with neighbors	2.1	2.4	NS
Change in contact with old friends	1.5	1.5	NS
Durability	2.4	3.4	.04
Interaction characteristics of kin network			
Contact with parents	1.5	2.1	NS
Contact with inlaws	1.2	1.7	NS
Contact with children	2.7	2.6	NS
Contact with other close relatives	2.2	2.4	NS
Change in contact with kin	2.2	2.1	NS
Interaction characteristics of community network			
Prior participation in community-based organizations	7.4	8.3	NS
Current participation in community-based organizations	6.0	7.9	.05
Participation in self-help widow groups	1.2	1.3	NS
Use of professional help network:			
Clergy, doctor	59%	59%	NS[b]
Psychiatrist, psychologist, counselor	23%	24%	NS[b]

[a]All statistical analyses were calculated using t-tests between group means, unless otherwise indicated.
[b]Fisher's Exact Test.

different and nonsubstitutive support functions (Litwak & Szelenyi, 1969; Weiss, 1969).

Formal and informal help givers also appear to perform distinct and nonsubstitutive support functions for recently widowed women. These data do not support the contention put forth by some investigators that people seek help from professionals as an alternative to inadequate informal network resources (Kadushin, 1969; Kasl, Gore, & Cobb, 1975; Mayer & Timms, 1970). On the contrary, they lend support to the notion, as argued by Kalish (1982), that help from professional service providers is not viewed as a viable alternative to help from friends or family members. Widows with weak peer support were no more likely to seek out professional helpers (i.e., clergy, doctors, psychiatrists, psychologists, counselors) than were their counterparts with strong support from peers.

Although widows with strong peer support are currently more active in community-based organizations than those with weak peer support, they do not appear to inherently be more of the "joiner" type. That is, before being widowed both groups of women joined and participated in such organizations to a comparable extent. Moreover, surprisingly, the widows with strong peer support are not more involved in organizations comprised solely of peers in similar life circumstances—that is, self-help groups for the widowed. Perhaps the explanation for this puzzling set of findings is linked to the different types of friendship relationships formed through participation in these different types of organizations. While friendships formed through widowed self-help groups may tend to revolve around the issues and problems of widowhood, resulting in a more narrow, unidimensional base for the relationships, friendships formed through different types of community groups may afford other (i.e., multiple) dimensions to the relationships. This unidimensional/multidimensional distinction may be the key to the difference in effects on the provision of peer support of participating in self-help versus other community groups. Multidimensional friendship relationships have been shown to lend themselves to more satisfying socializing and more tangible assistance than unidimensional relationships (Hirsch, 1980), ultimately providing stronger and more reliable support in general for the parties involved (Hirsch, 1980, 1979; Kapferer, 1969).

DISCUSSION

Peer support has been consistently shown to be an important mediator of successful adjustment to widowhood. However, despite the increasingly obvious implications of the benefits of fostering the provision of this key support for women suffering conjugal bereavement, little is known about how to best affect this process. Any efforts in this direction are marred by a lack of information as to what factors, contextual as well as personal, serve to ensure peer support for widows. The intent of the study presented here was to begin to gain such information. As no single theory presently exists to guide such an inquiry, the relationship between a host of potentially relevant personal and contextual characteristics and the provision of peer support for a sample of relatively recent and still grieving widows was examined. The results of the ensuing analyses suggested that a number of characteristics are particularly conducive to the provision of this key support for widows. Consequently, inferences can now be drawn as to the identity of widows who are more apt to lack this key support resource. That is, by taking the liberty of extrapolating from these data, a profile of the widows at risk can begin to be sketched.

Who Is at Risk?

In general, recent widows who receive relatively weak peer support are women who were housewives before being widowed, but have since joined the work force. They are also women who, while not having a great need for affiliation, depended on their husbands for social interaction, in general, and for arranging social get togethers with friends, in particular. They are women who are having to deal with a relatively severe drop in their financial status and in their health status since being widowed. They are women who are having difficulty adjusting to their role as a single rather than a married person. Moreover, they also appear to be somewhat resistive to accepting the loss, per se, as exemplified by their level of preoccupation with their husbands' death, the frequency with which they visit their husbands' grave, and by the self-reported length of time it took for their intense grief to subside.

In combination these findings present a common theme. Namely, the women who receive weak peer support have experienced more (apparent) disruptive changes and secondary losses as a result of being widowed than their counterparts who receive strong peer support. For example, these women were more dependent on their husbands for arranging social interactions with friends. Loss of their spouses, therefore, leaves them on their own to perform a social integrative role to which they are less unaccustomed and, perhaps, more ill-equipped to perform— making social overtures to friends. This theme of greater disruption also emerges in the areas of finances and health. That is, the widows with weaker peer support have also experienced greater deteriorative changes in these two important life domains. Moreover, many more of the widows with weak peer support experienced a major shift in employment status since being widowed. In sum, not only do these widows have the primary loss (i.e., the loss of their husbands, per se) to which they must adjust, but they are also faced with having to adjust to a myriad of secondary losses (i.e., financial loss, health deterioration, loss of the homemaker role, loss of their social relations "manager"). As such, it is not surprising that they are also experiencing more difficulties with the adjustment process than their counter-parts with strong peer support. They have more (apparent) disruptive life changes to which they must adjust.

Disentanglement of the direction of effects is not possible in a cross-sectional study such as the present one. That is, for example, these data are inconclusive as to whether these women who are still having adjustment difficulties 2 years or so after being widowed have, consequently, taxed their friendship relationships to the breaking point resulting in a lack of strong peer support, or whether the lack of strong support from peers has added to their burdens, thereby making their adjustment more difficult. Nevertheless, these data do indicate that the widows who have experienced more disruptive life changes consequent to being widowed and who are having more difficulty adjusting to this major life transition are also the ones who receive the least amount of peer support. Put another way, the widows with the greatest (apparent) need for this crucial resource are least apt to have it.

These data also indicate that the provision of strong peer support for relatively recent widows is linked to particular structural characteristics of the networks in which the widows are embedded. Although few contextual factors differentiated between widows with strong versus weak peer support, those that did differentiate serve to enlarge on the developing picture of the situation of widows who are apt to be at risk. That is, compared to their counterparts with strong peer support, the widows with weak peer support are less apt to have developed close friendship relationships since being widowed. Moreover, not only do they have fewer widowed friends, but they also have less contact with those widowed friends they do have. They are also less apt to be actively involved in community-based organizations and, at least by inference, they are less likely to have developed multidimensional friendship relationships.

Future efforts, then, to cultivate the peer support process for recent widows may be well-served by focusing attention on the composition of the widows' friendship networks. That is, as networks that comprise more new friends, more widowed friends, and more multidimensional friendship relationships are more apt to provide strong peer support, the strengthening of these network factors where deficient may serve to promote the process of peer support provision for recent widows. And, as widows with strong peer support are much more active in community-based social groups, such organizations may well be pertinent resources for the development of networks that facilitate the peer support process. One serious question is whether or not widows with weak peer support would be open to social support intervention given their relatively low need for affiliation. However, one hopeful sign is that despite their lower need for affiliation, these women had been as involved in social groups before they were widowed as their counterparts with strong peer support and high need for affiliation.

CONCLUSIONS

In sum, then, these data suggest that the provision of strong peer support for women suffering conjugal bereavement is linked with particular characteristics of both the widows themselves and their social surroundings. Whether strong peer support is provided or not seems to depend on at least two general factors: the amount of disruption incurred by the death of the husband; and the composition of the friendship network. However, the validity of these findings, of course, cannot be assumed without the benefit of confirming research.

Moreover, due to the exploratory nature of this study, extensive and detailed information regarding the nature of any one particular aspect of the widows' personal and social environs was sacrificed in service of casting a wider net of possible characteristics that might facilitate the peer support process. However, the findings of this initial study do indicate that specific characteristics are especially relevant to this important process. Future research can now focus more attention on these specific factors, studying them in much more depth and detail. The development of such a line of research may move us closer to the identification of women who are especially at risk once confronted with the major life transition of widowhood. Concomitantly, such research promises to provide some leverage on what it might require to help augment the peer support process, thereby facilitating positive psychosocial adaptation to widowhood.

REFERENCES

Adams, B. N. (1968). *Kinship in an urban setting*. Chicago: Markham.
Arling, G. (1976). The elderly widow and her family, neighbors, and friends. *Journal of Marriage and the Family, 27*, 757–776.
Arth, M. (1962). American culture and the phenomenon of friendship in the aged. In C. Tibbits & W. Donahue (Eds.), *Social and psychological aspects of aging*. New York: Columbia University Press.
Aspects of the aging national population. (1981, October). *Information on Aging, 23*(6).
Axelrod, M. (1956). Urban structure and social participation. *American Sociological Review, 21*, 13–18.
Babchuck, N. (1965). Primary friends and kin: A study of the associations of middle-class couples. *Social Forces, 43*, 483–493.
Bankoff, E. A. (1981). *The informal social network and adaptation to widowhood*. Unpublished Doctoral Dissertation, University of Chicago.

Bankoff, E. A. (1983). Aged parents and their widowed daughters: A support relationship. *Journal of Gerontology, 38*(2), 226–230.

Bankoff, E. A. (1983). Social support and adaptation to widowhood. *Journal of Marriage and the Family, 45*, 827–839.

Barrett, C. J. (1978). Effectiveness of widows' groups in facilitating change. *Journal of Consulting and Clinical Psychology, 46*, 20–31.

Bell, R. R. (1981). *Worlds of friendship*. Beverly Hills: Sage.

Blau, Z. (1961). Structural constraints on friendships in old age. *American Sociological Review, 26*, 429–439.

Bott, E. (1957). *Family and social networks*. London: Tavistock.

Brown, B. B. (1981). The relation of age to friendship. In H. Z. Lopata & D. Maines (Eds.), *Research on the interweave of social roles, Vol. II*. Greenwich, CT: J.A.I. Press.

Caplan, G. (1964). *Principles of preventive psychiatry*. New York: Basic.

Cassel, J. (1974). Psychosocial processes and "stress": Theoretical formulations. *International Journal of Health Services, 4*, 471–482.

Craven, P. & Wellman, B. (1974). The network city. In M. P. Effrat (Ed.), *The community: Approaches and applications*. New York: Free Press.

Dotson, F. (1951). Patterns of voluntary association among working class families. *American Sociological Review, 16*, 687–693.

Eckenrode, J. & Gore, S. (1981). Stressful events and social supports: The significance of context. In B. H. Gottlieb (Ed.), *Social networks and social supports*. Beverly Hills: Sage.

Gans, H. J. (1962). *The urban villagers*. New York: Free Press.

George, L. K. (1982). Models of transitions in middle and later life. *The Annals of the American Academy of Political and Social Science, 464*, 22–37.

Gerard, H. B. (1963). Emotional uncertainty and social comparison. *Journal of Abnormal and Social Psychology, 66*, 568–573.

Gottlieb, B. H. (1981). Preventive interventions involving social networks and social support. In B. H. Gottlieb (Ed.), *Social networks and social supports*. Beverly Hills: Sage.

Harvey, C. D., & Bahr, H. M. (1974). Widowhood, morale and affiliation. *Journal of Marriage and the Family, 36*, 97–106.

Hess, B. (1972). Friendship. In M. W. Riley, M. Johnson, & A. Foner (Eds.), *Aging and society, Vol. III*. New York: Sage.

Hirsch, B. J. (1979). Psychological dimensions of social networks: A multimethod analysis. *American Journal of Community Psychology, 7*, 263–277.

Hirsch, B. J. (1980). Natural support systems and coping with major life changes. *American Journal of Community Psychology, 8*(2), 159–172.

Hirsch, B. J. (1981). Social networks and the coping process: Creating personal communities. In B. H. Gottlieb (Ed.), *Social networks and social supports*. Beverly Hills: Sage.

Hyman, H. H. (1942). The psychology of status. *Archives of Psychology*, no. 269.

Kadushin, C. (1969). *Why people go to psychiatrists*. New York: Atherton.

Kalish, R. A. (1982). Death and survivorship: The final transition. *The Annals of the American Academy of Political and Social Science, 464*, 163–173.

Kapferer, B. (1969). Norms and the manipulation of relationships in a work context. In J. C. Mitchell (Ed.), *Social networks in urban situations*. New York: Humanities.

Kasl, S. V., Gore, S., & Cobb, S. (1975). The experience of losing a job: Reported changes in health symptoms and illness behaviors. *Psychosomatic Medicine, 37*, 106–121.

Komarovsky, M. (1964). *Blue collar marriage*. New York: Random House.

Laumann, E. O. (1973). *Bounds of pluralism: The form and substance of urban social networks*. New York: Wiley.

Lieberman, M. A. & Borman, L. D. (Eds.). (1979). *Self-help groups for coping with crisis*. San Francisco: Jossey-Bass.

Lieberman, M. A., & Pearlin, L. D. (1977). *Everyday life experiences*. A study conducted at the University of Chicago.

Litwak, E., & Szelenyi, I. (1969). Primary group structures and their functions: Kin, neighbors and friends. *American Sociological Review, 34*, 465–481.

Lopata, H. Z. (1970). The social involvement of American widows. *American Behavioural Scientist, 14*, 41–50.

Lopata, H. Z. (1973). *Widowhood in an American City*. Cambridge, MA: Schenkman.

Lopata, H. Z. (1979). *Women as widows: Support systems*. New York: Elsevier.

Lopata, H. Z. (1981). Preface. In H. Z. Lopata & D. Maines (Eds.), *Research in the interweave of social roles: Friendship.* Greenwich, CT: J.A.I. Press.

Lowenthal, M. F., & Haven, C. (1968). Interaction and adaptation: Intimacy as a critical variable. *American Sociological Review, 33,* 20–30.

Mayer, J., & Timms, N. (1970). *The client speaks: Working-class impressions of casework.* Chicago: Aldine.

Mitchell, J. C. (1969). The concept and use of social networks. In J. C. Mitchell (Ed.), *Social networks in urban situations.* Manchester: Manchester University Press.

Mitchell, R. E., & Trickett, E. J. (1980). Social-network and psychosocial adaptation: Implications for community mental health practice. In P. Insel (Ed.), *Environmental variables and the prevention of mental health illness.* Lexington, MA: Heath.

National Opinion Research Center (1974). National data program for the social sciences, Codebook for the spring 1974 general social survey. Chicago (mimeographed).

Parkes, C. M. (1972). *Bereavement: Studies of grief in adult life.* New York: International Universities.

Parkes, C. M. (1975). Unexpected and untimely bereavement: A statistical study of young Boston widows and widowers. In B. S. Schoenberg, I. Gerber, A. Weiner, A. H. Kutcher, D. Peretz, & A. C. Carr (Eds.), *Bereavement: Its psychosocial aspects.* New York: Columbia University Press.

Pearlin, L. D., & Schooler, C. (1978). The structure of coping. *Journal of Health and Social Behavior, 19,* 2–21.

Philbad, C., & Adams, D. (1972). Widowhood, social participation and life satisfaction. *Aging and Human Development, 3,* 323–330.

Rose, A. (1965). Age and social integration among the lower classes in Rome. *Journal of Gerontology, 20,* 250–253.

Rosenberg, M. (1965). *Society and the adolescent self-image.* Princeton, NJ: Princeton University Press.

Rosow, I. (1967). *Social integration of the aged.* New York: Free Press.

Schachter, S. (1959). *The psychology of affiliation.* Stanford, CA: Stanford University Press.

Silverman, P. R. (1967). Services to the widowed: First steps in a program of preventative intervention. *Community Mental Health Journal, 3*(1), 37–44.

Silverman, P. R. (1970). The widow as caregiver in a program of preventive intervention with other widows. *Mental Hygiene, 54*(4), 540–547.

Silverman, P. R. (1972). Widowhood and preventative intervention. *Family Life Coordinator, 21,* 95–104.

Silverman, P. R. (1982). Transitions and models of intervention. *The Annals of the American Academy of Political and Social Science, 464,* 174–187.

Tolsdorf, C. (1976). Social networks, support and coping: An exploratory study. *Family Process, 15,* 407–418.

Walker, K. N., MacBride, A., & Vachon, M. L. S. (1977). Social support networks and the crisis of bereavement. *Social Science and Medicine, 2,* 35–41.

Wan, T. T. H. (1982). *Stressful life events, social-support networks and gerontological health.* Lexington, MA: Heath.

Wellman, B. (1981). Applying network analysis to the study of support. In B. H. Gottlieb (Ed.), *Social networks and social supports.* Beverly Hills: Sage.

Weiss, R. (1969). The fund of sociability. *Trans-action, 6,* 36–43.

Williams, R. M. (1959). Friendship and social values in a suburban community: An exploratory study. *Pacific Sociological Review, 10,* 3–15.

14

Elderly Women's Health and Psychological Adjustment: Life Stressors and Social Support

Margaret W. Linn
VA Hospital and
University of Miami School of Medicine

Many studies have examined stressful life events (stressors) and their effect (strain) on psychological and physical health. The role of women has changed considerably over the past few decades, and change is known to be associated with stress (the balance between demand and resources). Yet, few studies have focused on stressors as they apply to women in general, and even fewer have studied the older woman. This paper discusses the role of the older woman today, the interaction of stress and social support, and the results of a comparison of physical and mental health between elderly women with high and low stress and high or low perceived support.

ROLE OF THE OLDER WOMAN

Perhaps the women affected most by stressors are those who have lived under two life styles. The woman of 65 today was a high school graduate at the time of the depression in 1928. These are the women pictured in the background of popular cigarette ads proclaiming "you've come a long way baby." Many of the social changes cited above have taken place during their adult lives. The older woman today is very different from the older woman only a few decades ago. There are more affluent retired elderly today. Condominium living has become a popular way of life. Instead of being part of the extended family, older people are likely to live by themselves and have more time for their own pursuits than ever before. Labor-saving devices have decreased the time involved in housekeeping. There are fewer family members nearby to turn to for social support. Although the proportion of more affluent and retired older women has increased, this does not imply that there are still not large numbers of the elderly poor, the frail, and they physically incapacitated who may be the most stressed and in need of support of any age group. Since women live longer than men, most nursing homes and rest homes are populated by more very old women than men.

It has been said that the social pathologies of old age are social isolation and loneliness (Neugarten, 1977). In the last several years, gerontologists have focused on the social networks of the elderly (Snow & Gordon, 1980), recognizing the importance of social support for continued functioning, especially in times of stress and crises (Caplan, 1974).

Although it seems rather obvious that social support would be beneficial for well-being, studies have produced mixed findings (Liang, Dvorkin, Kahana, & Mazian, 1980). This has occurred partly because social integration has been variously defined. Lowenthal and Robinson (1976) pointed out that any attempt to measure social interaction should include a subjective dimension of the quality of the interaction. Having a friend is said to help diminish the impact of role loss, since people can still feel needed and influence others (Blau, 1973). Cantor (1975) found that most important neighboring activity of elderly in inner city New York was that of emergency assistance or crisis intervention. Reviewing 30 years of research, Larson (1978) found that when the actual tabulation of visits from family, friends, and neighbors was taken, a positive association was found with well-being. In fact, some studies (Shanas, Townsend, & Wedderburn, 1968; Edwards & Klemmack, 1973) indicated that morale in older age may be more highly associated with having friends than with having children. Still, for major needs people are more likely to turn first to family, then to friends and neighbors, and last to social agencies (Shanas, 1979).

Among studies of the impact of stressors on psychological adjustment of the elderly, retirement has been found to produce strain, as evidenced by decreased self-esteem, satisfaction, and activity in men and women (Atchley, 1971). On the other hand, Streib and Schneider (1971) found little or no evidence of such effects. In another study (Heyman & Jeffers, 1968), about half of the wives of retirees were sorry that their husbands retired, especially if they were from lower socio-economic groups, and Kerckhoff (1964) found wives of retirees had less satisfaction than their retiring husbands. Departure of the last child from home is also believed to be stressful (Lowenthal & Chiriboga, 1972). However, Glenn (1975) concluded that the empty nest syndrome did not typically have an enduring negative effect. In a report of life stressors (Linn, Linn, & Harris, 1981), elderly with high-stress scores differed from those with low stress scores on symptoms of somatization, depression, and anxiety. Cultural groups of Anglo, Black, and Cuban elderly differed on social participation and dysfunction. Controlling for social class diminished some of the differences between cultures, and holding locus of control constant diminished differences between high and low stress groups. The fact that symptoms differentiated high and low stress groups similarly in each culture suggested that reactions to stresses, such as death and illness, which occurred frequently among these older persons, may be a common response that transcends cultural differences.

Many believe that widowhood is the most disruptive of all stressors (Parkes, 1973). The Holmes and Rahe Schedule of Life Events assigns "death of a spouse" the highest weight of any life change in regard to its potential strain (Holmes & Rahe, 1967). However, no long-term detrimental effects were found for those widowed during a longitudinal study (Heyman & Gianturco, 1973). Elderly women are the most likely to be widowed, and their adjustment depends to a great extent on their ability to cope with this event and its consequences.

In summary, the older woman today has seen and been a part of more social change in regard to the role of women than any other age group. Since men die earlier than women, she is often widowed or alone in old age. On the other hand, she more readily seeks out friends and social support networks than older men and thus may have more insulation from the strain produced by stress.

INTERACTION OF SOCIAL STRESS
AND SUPPORT

Social stress can be separated into its source (stressors), its mediators, and its manifestations (strain). The occurrence of undesirable life events is assumed to produce stress (demand on personal resources) because they usually require life change and readjustment. Individuals are assumed to be intolerant of change, as the work of Cannon (1935) and Selye (1956) demonstrated. Life events may create strains or intensify old problems and, thus, may produce chronic wear and tear.

Stressors impact differently on different people. Some of the mediators of stress are whether persons see the events as desirable or not (Mueller, 1980), whether they have control over the events (Fairbank & Hough, 1979), and whether they are on time in regard to the life cycle (Pearlin, 1980). Pearlin, Menaghan, Lieberman, & Mullan (1981) suggested that stressors were more likely to produce stress when they resulted in reduced self-esteem. Whether the person anticipates an event happening or not or whether there has been prior experience with the stressor also seems to determine degree of perceived stress. Social support from family and friends in coping with stressors is another mediator of stress. Social support has variously been defined as social bonds (Henderson, 1977), social networks (Mueller, 1980), meaningful social contact (Cassel, 1976), availability of social confidants (Brown, Bhrolchain, & Harris, 1975), and human companionship (Lynch, 1977). Cobb (1976) described social support as consisting of three elements: information leading the person to believe that he or she is cared for and loved, is esteemed and valued, and belongs to a network of communication and mutual obligation in which others can be counted on should the need arise. Although many have found that social support is a mediator of stress, others (Williams, Ware, & Donald, 1981) have found that social support acted independently in its effect on psychological health.

The manifestations of stress can be viewed as the strain, whether it is the response of a single cell or the total system, as evidenced by physical disease or psychiatric disorders. Studies examining stressors have reported associations between the occurrence of stressors and such physical disorders as myocardial infarction (Rahe & Paasikivi, 1971), chronic asthma (Araujo, Van Arsdel, Holmes, & Dudley, 1973), respiratory illness (Jacobs, Spilken, Norman, & Anderson, 1970), and general physical conditions (Wyler, Masuda, & Holmes, 1971). Psychological impairment, including depression (Paykel et al., 1969), anxiety (Lauer, 1973), psychiatric hospitalization (Fontana, Marcus, Noel, & Rakusin, 1972), schizophrenia (Brown & Birley, 1968), and general psychiatric symptoms (Myers, Lindenthal, & Pepper, 1971) have also been shown to moderately, but consistently, relate to experience with life stressors.

To better understand how stress and social support relate to physical and psychological health of older women, a study was conducted in 1980-1981, and the findings are reported in what follows.

THE STUDY

Women age 65 and over were contacted within three large housing complexes for the elderly in Miami, Florida. All were Anglo women and lived in similar type housing. They were asked to participate in a study regarding stressful life events and health. Out of a total of 209 women contacted in a meeting of the residents of the homes, 166 (80%) volunteered to be seen individually in their apartments for two interviews. In the first interview, recent life events, degree of social support, and levels of physical and psychological function were collected. The second interview was completed 6 months later and assessed these same variables. Interviews took about one hour and were conducted by a research social worker trained to collect the data.

Demographic information included age, marital status, last grade completed in school, social class, and persons in the household. The independent variables in the study were stressful life events and social support.

Recent Stressors

Women rated 41 items of the Holmes and Rahe (1967) Social Readjustment Rating Scale (SRRS), with Christmas and vacation events deleted. At the initial interview, occurrence of any of the life events was based on a time period covering the prior 12 months. Women also provided an estimate of the amount of life change or stress associated with each event on a 0-9 scale. Weights developed for the items in regard to normative estimates of degree of life change, called life change units (LCU), were also computed. The LCUs were used as the criterion of high and low experiences with stress, since the perceived stress scores provided by each person might overlap with their perception of support from family and friends. However, the correlation between the person's perceived stress score and the LCU method was high ($r = .86$), indicating there was considerable agreement between the weighted system and personal estimates of stressfulness. At the second interview, the information on occurrence of stressors was updated to cover the 6 intervening months. The median LCU scores for 18 months was then used to assign the women to either a high or low experience with stress groups.

Social Support

For each event that happened, the woman also provided an estimate on a 0-9 scale of the amount of support from family and friends that she had in dealing with it. Since a total score on support would be influenced by the number of events endorsed, the average amount of support was taken for all events as an indicator of the usual level of support. It was reasoned that families and friends could probably be characterized generally by being more or less supportive; therefore, the median of the averaged support scores from the two interviews was used to place the women into one of two groups indicating their perception of high or low degrees of social support. Those scoring the median were placed into the high-support group.

The dependent variables were physical and psychological functioning. The same tests were administered twice in order to assess changes in health status over the 6 months in relationship to amount of stressfulness and degree of social support.

Physical Function

Data were collected on number of visits to the physician, number of days in bed, and self-assessed health (1 = excellent to 5 = very poor) over the prior 6 months. Total number of medications and number of current illnesses were also obtained. Previous research (Linn, Hunter, & Linn, 1980) has shown that a person's perception of health relates to their physical function and to more objective health evaluations, such as physician ratings. Independent activities of daily living were assessed to determine the person's ability to carry out basic tasks of everyday living. The Instrumental Activities of Daily Living Scale of Lawton and Brody (1969) was used with higher scores indicating more disability.

Psychological Functioning

Symptoms were measured using the 45-item (4-point scales) Hopkin's Symptom Checklist (Derogatis, Lipman, Rickels, Uhlenhuth, & Covi, 1974). Five factor scores are provided by this scale: somatization, anxiety, depression, interpersonal sensitivity, and obsessive-compulsiveness. Life satisfaction was measured using a 12-item (4-point) scale described by Adams (1969) to contain the most discriminating items from the original Neugarten, Havighurst, & Tobin (1961) scale. A 9-item Social Participation Scale (Graney, 1975) was used to determine the extent of social interaction in the environment. Lastly, self-esteem was determined by responses to a 10-item scale developed by Rosenberg (1973). All of the psychological scales were self-rated and higher scores always indicated less favorable responses.

Data Analysis

Data were analyzed in a 2 X 2 factorial design for multivariate analysis of covariance. One factor was high versus low stress and the other was high versus low social support. The questions addressed were whether women with high stress scores over the previous 18 months differed significantly from those with less stress scores on physical and psychological function. Likewise, women with high versus low perceived support from family and friends were compared on these same variables. The analysis also tested whether there was a significant interaction between stress and support that would indicate that support acted in a differential manner in the two stress groups. As recommended by Bancroft (1968), prescores on the physical and psychological variables were held constant in examining levels of these variables at the 6 month follow-up.

Sample Characteristics

Of the 166 women interviewed initially, all but 8 were seen on follow-up. This represented a 6% loss of follow-up data. Those lost to follow-up were compared with those who completed the study on personal characteristics. No significant differences were found between the two groups. Thus, the 158 women followed for 6 months appeared to be a representative sample of the original group.

Average age of the women was 77 years with a standard deviation of 9 years. Only a small percentage (12%) were currently married and living with their husbands. On the average, they had completed the tenth grade of high school. Their social class was 3.7 on the 5-point scale, which indicated lower middle class. The women had lived in their present residence an average of 4 years. Most had moved to Miami from other areas of the country, but about half had relatives in the area.

The homes were in an urban beach area, near to shopping, in a high crime area, and populated by retirees and vacationers as well. Minimal staff related to rental and operation of the facilities was on site; however, residents have access to a senior center nearby and to various community programs where they can form friendships outside the bounds of their apartments and building. No formal security, other than by staff, was provided.

STRESS AND SUPPORT

Ratings of stress by the LCU method ranged from 0 for one woman who reported no stressors to 329 for one individual. The mean score was 156 ($SD = 77$), and the median was 159 (with no person scoring the median). Therefore, 76 women were placed in the high-stress group and 76 in the low-stress group.

The median for perceived support was 3.5 on the 9-point scale, with eight persons scoring the median. Those scoring the median were placed into the high support group; therefore, there were 68 in the low support and 84 in the high support groups. In the high-stress experience group, 40% of the women perceived low support and 60% high support from family and friends. In the low stress experience group, 44% perceived low support as compared with high support (56%).

There were no significant differences between these groups in regard to personal characteristics of the women. Slightly, but not significantly, more of those with high support than those with low support were married.

Table 1 shows the stressors endorsed most frequently by the sample along with the average degree of social support for each. Events endorsed by less than 5% of the sample were not included in the table. Only eight stressors were reported as never occurring, and 19 more were mentioned as occurring for less than 5% of the group. The most frequent stressors were personal illness and injury, changes in sleeping habits, changes in eating habits, changes in recreation, changes in

Table 1   Most frequent stressful events and their levels of support

Events	(%)	Degree of support
Personal illness/injury	42	4.4
Change of sleeping habits	34	1.3
Change in financial circumstances	31	1.5
Change in health of family member	28	4.2
Eating habits changed	27	4.0
Change in recreation	24	2.5
Death of close friend	20	4.0
Change in family get-togethers	19	3.8
Change in social activities	16	4.5
Injury/illness of close friend	14	4.4
Revision of personal habits	12	2.8
Change in church activities	10	4.2
Change in living conditions	8	4.5
Death of family member	7	4.0
Changed residences	6	3.0

financial status, and changes in health of family members. Social support usually came from neighbors and close friends, since most of the elderly women did not have close family members in the geographic area. More social support in dealing with events was perceived for changes in social activities, living conditions, and injury or illness of self or friends. The least amount of support was perceived from changes in sleeping habits, revision of personal habits, and changes in financial circumstances.

Physical Health, Stress, and Support

Table 2 shows comparison of physical health variables between the high and low stress groups and those with high and low-social support. Reported differences were significant at $p < .05$. With the prescores held constant, the main effect of stress at the multivariate level was statistically significant, and the main effect of support was statistically significant. The interaction of stress with support was not statistically significant at the multivariate level.

Two health variables discriminated between high and low stress groups at univariate levels. Those with high stress had more days in bed from illness during the 6-month follow-up than those with low stress. Those with high stress, as compared with low stress, were more disabled in performance of everyday activities of living at the time of follow-up.

Only one variable discriminated between high and low support groups. Those with low support had more days in bed from illness than did the high support group. Although the overall interaction between stress and support was not statistically significant, indicating that high and low support groups discriminated similarly within the two stress groups, self-assessed health showed a significant interaction effect at a univariate level. Those women with high stress and low support rated their health worse than any other group.

Thus, during low stress, the amount of social support did not seem to influence self-assessed health, but in high stressful times, lack of social support was associated significantly with worse evaluations of health.

Psychological Function, Stress, and Support

Table 3 shows psychological function of the women in relationship to stress and support. The overall main effects for stress and support were statistically significant. The overall interaction effect was not significant statistically.

In regard to the main effect of stress, those women with high stressful life events had more depression and less favorable ratings on social participation, life satisfaction, and self-esteem than did the low stress group. Somatization and anxiety also discriminated between high and low stress groups.

Depression differed between high and low support groups, with more depression associated with less social support. Social participation and life satisfaction was significantly lower for those with low versus high support, and self-esteem was less favorable for the low than for the high support group.

Again, although the multivariate F-ratio was not statistically significant for the interaction effect, self-esteem showed a significant univariate interaction effect. Those women with high stress and low support had the lowest self-esteem; whereas

Table 2 Adjusted means for comparison of physical functioning among elderly women with high low stress and high low support

| Variables | High stress | | Low stress | | F-Ratios | | |
| | | | | | | Main effect | |
	Low support ($N = 30$)	High support ($N = 46$)	Low support ($N = 34$)	High support ($N = 42$)	Stress	Support	Interaction
Number of visits to MD last 6 mos.	4.3	4.2	3.9	3.2	2.02	.20	.11
Number of days in bed last 6 mos.	4.5	3.8	3.7	2.7	3.88*	3.67*	.03
Number of medications (current)	2.9	2.8	2.5	2.4	.91	.60	.14
Number of illnesses (current)	3.6	3.4	2.4	2.1	2.11	.22	.05
Self-assessed health	3.8	2.5	2.4	2.6	2.98	2.99	3.96*
Instrumental activities	12.5	11.4	10.4	10.2	5.30**	2.05	1.96
Multivariate Fs					2.72**	1.98*	.77

Note. Self-assessed health rated on 1–5 scale with higher scores being worse.
*$p < .05$; **$p < .01$.

Table 3 Adjusted means for comparison of psychological functioning among elderly women with high low stress and high low support

| | High stress | | Low stress | | F-Ratios | | |
| | | | | | Main effect | | |
Variables	Low support (N = 30)	High support (N = 46)	Low support (N = 34)	High support (N = 42)	Stress	Support	Interaction
Hopkin's Symptoms Checklist							
Somatization (range 12–48)	18.5	17.3	15.7	15.3	2.99*	.66	.07
Anxiety (range 7–28)	9.8	9.6	8.4	8.0	3.11*	.03	.12
Depression (range 11–44)	18.2	16.3	15.0	14.5	6.24**	3.82*	.60
Interpersonal sensitivity (range 7–28)	9.2	9.1	8.9	8.8	1.60	.90	.58
Obsessive-compulsive (range 8–32)	11.1	10.8	10.3	10.7	.23	.44	.76
Social participation (range 9–29)	23.2	21.4	20.4	20.1	5.52**	3.94**	1.04
Life satisfaction (range 15–60)	38.7	35.8	36.6	35.2	5.63**	4.03**	.41
Self-esteem (range 10–40)	22.6	20.4	19.1	18.8	5.49***	3.07*	2.97*
Multivariate Fs					3.89**	2.92*	1.06

Note. Variables are scored so that a higher score is a less favorable response.
*$p < .05$; **$p < .01$.

self-esteem in the low stress women was not significantly different between high and low support.

DISCUSSION

It is obvious that women have accepted new and different roles over the past half century. Along with these changes, they are exposed to more opportunities for occurrence of stressors. Conflicts also arise in assimilation of role conflicts in what is still largely a man's world professionally. Although older women are not involved as much in the dual roles demanded by career and homeworker, they have lived through changes in the images of women's roles. Since they live longer than men on the average, they are faced more often than men with widowhood and loneliness. The changing family roles have also led to more older women being on their own rather than in being a part of the extended family as in the past. Coping with stressors in a changing world might be expected to present problems for the older woman. Although women are more active in regard to social participation than men, this fact alone does not mean that social supports are available. Feeling esteemed and valued, cared for, and most importantly, feeling that there is someone that can be counted on are essential for social support. With loss of peer support through illness and death of family and friends being more frequent in old age, there are fewer sources of social support in old age, and these can not always be counted on for continued help.

In the study just described, more differences in health and psychological well being were found between high and low stress than between high and low support. Those older women who experienced more stressful events over an 18-month period of time had more days in bed from illness, poorer ability to perform everyday activities of living, more somatization, anxiety, depression, less social participation, less life satisfaction, and lower self-esteem on follow-up than those with lower stress. Those with more social support had fewer days in bed from illness, less depression, more social participation, more life satisfaction, and more self-esteem on follow-up than those with less support. Thus, both stress and social support are associated with differences in health status.

Overall, stress and social support did not interact significantly. This indicated that social support was effective in reducing days in bed and depression, or in enhancing social participation and life satisfaction in older women who had experienced high stress as well as those who had lower stress. However, the magnitude of differences was always greater under high stress than low, but only in two instances were the differences great enough to produce significant interaction effects. Those with lower social support had significantly worse perceptions of their health when they had been under high stress. Social support did not produce this effect when stress had been low. Secondly, social support tended to enhance self-esteem more during high stress than it did during low stress. Therefore, social support, in itself, was associated with more positive health, but particularly when stress was high, producing a better evaluation of one's health and self-esteem.

The effects of stress and social support were greater in areas of psychological than in physical health. This is perhaps understandable since such variables as depression and anxiety could be precursors to changes in physical health as well. Depression scores were high in this group of elderly women living independently in the community. They were especially high for the high stress group, and even higher for those with both high stress and little support. Depression is common in old age and could signal the need for intervention. Perhaps ways of increasing social support through encouraging a network of friends or through supportive therapy might help to alleviate or counteract some of the long-range detrimental effects of stress. Support might be activated through volunteer visiting programs where some members of the building visit others or offer assistance in shopping or transportation. Women in this study represent those who attended meetings in the buildings; thus, our study may not have included the social isolates or those, perhaps, in the most need of assistance and support. Social agencies may also be effective in surveying needs of the elderly and in developing groups that could lead to a support network, although mutual help networks appear to be more helpful to the members when they develop by spontaneous and natural methods.

Although the SRRS identified women with high and low stress, it also appeared limited in covering certain areas of stress currently felt by these women. For example, worry and concern about events that have not happened, or in some cases did happen but were not included on the scale, were common. Most of the women worried about crime in the neighborhood. Many feared to go out shopping or even to be alone in their rooms. They isolated themselves behind locked doors, and the stress of possibly being robbed or assaulted was ever present. Although changes in finances may not have occurred, many worried about having enough money to take care of themselves should a crisis arise. Thus, worry, concern, apprehension, and anticipation of problems or events that might occur seemed particularly important to creation of stress in the elderly. A scale that captures concerns about crime, finances, health, and other problems may help to more accurately describe stress in many older persons. An event does not have to happen in order to change a person's life style. The concern about crime, for example, drastically alters the older person's way of life. Concern about money, even though finances may be adequate at the present time, can lead to extreme social readjustment in order to do more saving and prepare for what is feared.

In summary, rather high levels of stress were identified in this group of older women. Almost half perceived social support to be low in dealing with the stress. If social support is effective in enhancing physical and psychological function, as seems to be indicated, then efforts to increase social support could help older women cope better with stress. It is probable that social support buffers the individual from unfavorable effects of stress and change by facilitating coping and adaptation. Women who have support from families, friends, or professionals tend to be better psychologically adjusted, and have fewer health problems. To improve the health and well-being of a large number of elderly women, it may be more feasible to foster social supports than to try to reduce stressors. Different ways of fostering support and their effectiveness should be tested in alleviating health and psychological problems of the elderly.

REFERENCES

Adams, D. L. (1969). Analysis of a life satisfaction index. *Journal of Gerontology, 24,* 470–474.

Araujo, G., Van Arsdel, P., Holmes, T. L., & Dudley, D. (1973). Life change, coping ability, and chronic intrinsic asthma. *Journal of Psychosomatic Research, 17,* 359–363.

Atchley, R. C. (1971). Retirement and leisure participation: Continuity or crises? *Gerontologist, 11,* 13–17.

Bancroft, T. A. (1968). *Topics in intermediate statistics.* Ames, IA: Iowa State University Press.

Blau, Z. S. (1973). *Old age in a changing society: New viewpoints.* New York: Watts.

Brown, G. W., Bhrolchain, M. N., & Harris, T. (1975). Social class and psychiatric disturbance among women in an urban population. *Sociology, 9,* 225–254.

Brown, G. W., & Birley, J. L. (1968). Crises and life changes and the onset of schizophrenia. *Journal of Health and Social Behavior, 9,* 203–214.

Cannon, W. B. (1935). Stresses and strains of homeostasis. *American Journal of Medicine, 189,* 1–14.

Cantor, M. H. (1975). Life space and the social support system of the inner city elderly of New York. *Gerontologist, 15,* 23–27.

Caplan, G. (1974). *Support systems and community mental health.* New York: Behavioral.

Cassel, J. (1976). The contribution of the social environment to host resistance. *American Journal of Epidemiology, 104,* 107–123.

Cobb, S. (1976). Social support as a moderator of life stress. *Psychosomatic Medicine, 38,* 300–314.

Derogatis, L. R., Lipman, R. S., Rickels, K., Uhlenhuth, E. H., & Covi, L. The Hopkins symptom checklist: A self-report inventory. *Behavioral Science, 19,* 1–15.

Edwards, J. N., & Klemmack, D. L. (1973). Correlates of life satisfaction: A reexamination. *Journal of Gerontology, 28,* 499–502.

Fairbank, D. T., & Hough, R. L. (1979). Life event classifications and the event-illness relationship. *Journal of Human Stress, 5,* 41–47.

Fontana, F., Marcus, J., Noel, B., & Rakusin, J. (1972). Prehospitalization coping styles of psychiatric patients: The goal directedness of life events. *Journal of Nervous and Mental Diseases, 155,* 311–321.

Glenn, N. (1975). Psychological well-being in the post-parental stage. *Journal of Marriage and the Family, 37,* 105–110.

Graney, M. J. (1975). Happiness and social participation in aging. *Journal of Gerontology, 30,* 701–706.

Henderson, S. (1977). The social network, support and neurosis: The function of attachment in adult life. *British Journal of Psychiatry, 131,* 185–191.

Heyman, D., & Gianturco, D. (1973). Long-term adaptation by the elderly to bereavement. *Journal of Gerontology, 28,* 359–362.

Heyman, D., & Jeffers, F. (1968). Wives and retirement. *Journal of Gerontology, 23,* 488–496.

Holmes, T., & Rahe, R. (1967). The social readjustment scale. *Journal of Psychosomatic Research, 11,* 213–218.

Jacobs, M., Spilken, A., Norman, M., & Anderson, L. (1970). Life stress and respiratory illness. *Psychosomatic Medicine, 32,* 233–242.

Kerckhoff, A. (1964). Husband-wife expectations and reactions to retirement. *Journal of Gerontology, 19,* 510–516.

Larson, R. (1978). Thirty years of research on the subjective well-being of older Americans. *Journal of Gerontology, 33,* 109–125.

Lauer, R. (1973). The social readjustment scale and anxiety: A cross-cultural study. *Journal of Psychosomatic Research, 17,* 171–174.

Lawton, M. P., & Brody, E. M. (1969). Assessment of older people: Self-maintaining and instrumental activities of daily living. *Gerontologist, 9,* 179–186.

Liang, J., Dvorkin, F., Kahana, E., & Mazian, F. (1980). Social integration and morale: A re-examination. *Journal of Gerontology, 35,* 746–757.

Linn, M. W., Hunter, K. I., & Linn, B. S. (1980). Self-assessed health, impairment, and disability in Anglo, Black, and Cuban elderly. *Medical Care, 18,* 282–288.

Linn, M. W., Linn, B. S., & Harris, R. (1981). Stressful life events, psychological symptoms, and psychosocial adjustment in Anglo, Black, and Cuban elderly. *Social Science & Medicine, 15E,* 282–287.

Lowenthal, M. F., & Chiriboga, D. (1972). Transition to empty nest: Crisis, challenge, or relief? *Archives of General Psychiatry, 26,* 8–14.

Lowenthal, M. F., & Robinson, B. (1976). Social network and isolation. In R. Binstock & E. Shanas (Eds.), *Handbook of aging and the social sciences.* New York: Van Nostrand Reinhold, pp. 432–456.

Lynch, J. (1977). *The broken heart.* New York: Basic.
Mueller, D. P. (1980). Social networks: A promising direction for research on the relationship of the social environment to psychiatric disorder. *Social Science & Medicine, 14A,* 147–161.
Myers, J., Lindenthal, J., & Pepper, M. (1971). Life events and psychiatric impairment. *Journal of Nervous and Mental Diseases, 152,* 149–157.
Neugarten, B. L. (1977). Personality and aging. In J. Birren, & K. W. Schaie (Eds.), *Handbook of the psychology of aging.* New York: Van Nostrand Reinhold.
Neugarten, B. L., Havighurst, R. J., & Tobin, S. S. (1961). The measurement of life satisfaction. *Journal of Gerontology, 16,* 134–143.
Parkes, C. (1973). *Bereavement.* London: Tavistock.
Paykel, E., Myers, J., Dienelt, M., Klerman, J., Lindenthal, J., & Pepper, M. (1969). Life events and depression: A controlled study. *Archives of General Psychiatry, 21,* 753–760.
Pearlin, L. I. (1980). Life strains and psychological distress among adults. In N. J. Smelser & E. H. Erikson (Eds.), *Themes of love and work in adulthood.* Cambridge: Harvard University Press, pp. 174–192.
Pearlin, L. I., Menaghan, E. G., Lieberman, M. A., & Mullan, J. T. (1981). The stress process. *Journal of Health and Social Behavior, 22,* 337–356.
Rahe, R., & Paasikivi, J. (1971). Psychosocial factors and myocardial infarction, II. An outpatient study in Sweden. *Journal of Psychosomatic Research, 15,* 33–39.
Rosenberg, M. (1973). *Measures of social psychological attitudes.* Ann Arbor, MI: Institute for Social Research.
Selye, H. (1956). *The stress of life.* New York: McGraw-Hill.
Shanas, E. (1979). The family as a social support system in old age. *Gerontologist, 19,* 169–174.
Shanas, E., Townsend, P., & Wedderburn, D. (1968). *Old people in three industrial societies.* New York: Atherton.
Snow, D. L., & Gordon, J. B. (1980). Social network analysis and intervention with the elderly. *Gerontologist, 20,* 463–467.
Streib, G., & Schneider, C. (1971). *Retirement in American society.* Ithaca, NY: Cornell University Press.
Williams, A. W., Ware, J. E., Jr., & Donald, C. A. (1981). A model of mental health, life events, and social supports applicable to general populations. *Journal of Health and Social Behavior, 22,* 324–336.
Wyler, A., Masuda, M., & Holmes, T. (1971). Magnitude of life events and seriousness of illness. *Psychosomatic Medicine, 33,* 115–122.

CONCLUSION

15

Social Support: Research, Theory, and Applications from Research on Women

Stevan E. Hobfoll
Tel Aviv University

The chapters contained in this volume focused on coping of women through much of the life span. While social support resources were considered in each of the chapters the authors consistently employed multidimensional models to explain women's coping. A number of common themes emerge across chapters. Some important questions are answered, some relevant questions remain and new issues with new questions develop. This chapter will attempt to organize the contents of the volume by addressing some of the issues that were repeatedly raised regarding methodology, theory, and applications.

Methodological issues will be considered first, including problems of experimental design, interactional effects of social support with other resources, problems with study of the buffering effect question, the use of laboratory analogs, and discussion of behavioral dependent variables. Implications for theory and intervention will then be raised. Attention will be focused on development of a cognitive framework for understanding the role of social support in the stress process. This cognitive framework will then be applied to developing intervention strategies adopting social support as one key "therapeutic" ingredient. Thoughts concerning the limitations and potential negative effects of social support will also be presented. Finally, social support as it effects the needs of women will be addressed. The importance of seeing social support as one of a network of resources will be stressed.

MERGING METHODOLOGY WITH THEORY

Confounding of Life Events and Social Support

The recent stressful life event paradigm has frequently been adapted to the study of social support. Such studies link arrays of events that are different in terms of intensity, type, degree of transition required, time since the event and direction of the potential effect (i.e., good or bad). In the related social support literature, high

I would like to thank Perry London and Yona Teichman for their suggestions regarding the development of this chapter.

and low stress groups are compared as to the effect social support has on resultant strain. In a typical study, for example, high versus low life event groups are divided and compared as to the extent to which these two groups are differentially affected by some parameter of social support. If the high versus low social support groups differ on some measure of strain (e.g., depression, physical illness) to a greater extent when under high stress than when under low stress, the experimenter argues in favor of a "stress buffering" effect. If instead the high social support group experiences less strain both in the high and low stress conditions in comparison to the low social support group, with no interaction of stressor and social support, then the experimenter argues in favor of a "direct effect."

There are a number of assumptions here that may be called into question. First, it is assumed that if the high stressor group were to experience less events during another hypothetical period that they would behave as do the low stressor group and vice versa. A similar assumption is made for social support, i.e., if the low social support group were to receive more support, they would behave as does the high social support group. There are reasons to believe that neither of these assumptions are valid. There is strong evidence to argue that life events and social support do not randomly fall to groups as in a true experiment. Rather, both are characteristics linked to people's sociopsychological life space.

So, for example, persons who experience few stressful life events tend to feel more in control of their environment (Dohrenwend & Martin, 1979), tend to have greater economic resources (Dohrenwend & Dohrenwend, 1981), tend to be physically healthier, and tend not to have experienced a significant loss of a loved one (Thoits, 1983). Persons who differ on social support also tend to differ in other meaningful ways. Perhaps most important if life events and social support are to be studied together, it should be pointed out that life events affect and are affected by social support (Thoits, 1983; Vachon, Chap. 12; Wilcox, Chap. 8).

This interrelatedness is important not only for a theoretical understanding of the effects of social support, but also for applied reasons. Whether there is a buffering or direct effect of social support there are implications for attempting to bolster social networks and consequent support among those who lack this resource, especially if they have a high risk for stressful life events. However, if people who have many stressful events and who are without social support also lack other competencies or social advantages, there is a strong chance that the same factors that put them in that group also prevent their diminishing such events or benefiting from social support. Having social support may be related to preferences for styles of coping, lack of related resources, or the prior occurrence of certain life events (e.g., death of spouse). While the life events-social support research appears to suggest that intervention to lessen stressors or increase social support would be beneficial, it is probable that the tendency to have stressful events or possess social support are trait characteristics linked to a complex chain of social and sociological variables. Stated in another way the recent life event-social support literature allows us to make statements as to how high or low stressful life events groups are differentially affected by high or low amount of social support, not how they *would be* affected if their social support or number of life events were altered.

Confounding of Personality, Social Support, and Life Events

Recent work also included personality characteristics in the study of the stress-social support process. These variables are not independent. Understanding how they are related may help researchers and clinicians arrive at more meaningful experiments and interventions. Their potential confounding may be illustrated in this example.

In a careful series of studies on affiliation behavior Teichman (1973, 1978) has shown that persons who are high in trait anxiety avoid affiliation if they feel their situation is an embarrassing one. Many life events, including those related to health, failure, job loss, divorce, battering, rape, and domestic squabbles cause great embarrassment (Hobfoll, 1985). The request for help in western society, moreover, is in itself perceived by many as embarrassing and demeaning and has repercussions on individuals' self-esteem (Fischer, Nadler, & Whitcher-Alagna, 1982; Nadler, Fischer, & Streufer, 1974). Since high trait anxious individuals are generally more likely to experience failure (Spielberger, 1962; Anson, Bernstein, & Hobfoll, 1984) and also tend to be poorer at interpersonal relations (Hartup, 1970) it can be seen that events, personality, and support are interrelated in a complex and meaningful fashion.

Alternative Design Perspectives

Longitudinal Designs

A number of the studies in this volume and many others in the literature have recommended longitudinal study of social support in particular and the stress process in general, and an increasing number of studies have utilized these costly designs (Aneshensel & Frerichs, 1982; Hobfoll & Walfisch, 1984; Holohan & Moos, 1981). Longitudinal designs have a number of advantages for addressing the issue of cause and effect in correlational research. Such designs allow pre-post-comparison and time series analysis.

Longitudinal designs do not control, however for selection into comparison groups, which may be a considerable thorn in experimenters' methodological side when decoding cause and effect. Because selection is a problem, the interaction of selection with mediating and dependent variables also becomes a problem (Campbell & Stanley, 1963). Thus longitudinal designs do not in and of themselves correct the problem of the interrelatedness of key variables. So, for example Coyne, Aldwin, & Lazarus (1981) and Dohrenwend & Dohrenwend (1981) have shown that individuals who differ on demographic and personality variables also differ in number of life events and the evaluation of the effect of resources on coping with these stressors. Longitudinal studies have typically addressed this problem by controlling statistically for selection at time one, relying on change scores between time one and time two. However, change in number of life events is just as likely to be related to personality and social support as were the original life events score.

Consequently, longitudinal designs do provide more reliable information on cause and effect within groups, but do not of themselves add information as to whether the cause and effect for one group applies to another group. Those who receive social support over time are likely to be the same individuals who possessed supportive social networks at the start. That persons with supportive social networks are aided by this support does not imply that those who do not possess such a network would be aided if they had. The results may be suggestive, but they are not persuasive.

Time since the event is considered to be an integral factor in the degree of stress experienced, recall of events, and suitability of social support and other resources (Andrews, 1981; Eaton, 1978). The model of ecological congruence (Hobfoll, Chap. 1; 1985), which relates to the fit of individuals' perceptions, values, and resources to the circumstances of the stressor event, suggests that time since event occurrence is a central factor in determining the social support requirements. Studies on social support need to consider this key variable, which has been underutilized in this area of research.

The failure to evaluate time since the events may have confounded the study of the stress buffering effect in particular. Why should we expect a stress buffering effect 10 months after an event? By this time emotional support has waned, other resources have had time to come into play, and instrumental support may no longer be congruent with needs. Individuals who differ in the amount of stress in their lives may be differentially affected by social support, but such a process is more likely at an earlier stage.

During the immediate stage following an event, those who have supportive networks might be expected to receive a flood of instrumental assistance, information, love and affection, and direct attempts by social network members to help them solve their problems or prevent a chain of related life events (Wilcox, Chap. 8; Thoits, 1983). They would also at this time be able to apply other resources—personal, financial, constitutional—to battle the negative consequences of the event.

Longitudinal research may be valuable in this regard. Also, in true cross-sectional designs the relation in time since the event may be evaluated either retrospectively or concurrently. Concurrent analysis is possible because individuals are in different stages in terms of events. Some are not experiencing major stressors, some have just experienced them, while others have experienced them many months prior. Such quasi-experimental designs are preferable to the method of aggregating different life events that have occurred at different times as has been done in most research on this topic.

For similar reasons examining individuals who experience a common single event and not an aggregate of many different events may allow for clearer analysis of the buffering effect in particular and the social support process in general (Hobfoll & Walfisch, 1984). Events which are less likely to be related to personal variables may also be chosen to limit the confounding effect discussed earlier. Such designs also limit the possibility of mixing different types of events which require different resources—some actually being incongruent with social support (Hobfoll, 1985).

Instruments for examining social support that include a time perspective may also be helpful, especially if they consider the state-trait distinction in the support process. That is, they should consider if the individual has usually received such support in the past (trait support) and is currently receiving such support (state support). Only effects of state support could produce buffering effects, as supportive social networks (trait support) not providing support at the time of the incident could only contribute to general well-being (e.g. an individual has greater self-esteem because she feels loved). This well-being, in turn could produce a buffering effect. Simply put, if you're not currently receiving aid, you can't be buffered by the aid you didn't receive! In fact, the buffering hypothesis has intuitive appeal because it has been assumed that during stressful periods persons with social networks that have certain qualities receive supportive efforts (state support) from their networks (Caplan, 1974; Cobb, 1976; Dean & Lin, 1977).

Laboratory Analogs may supply another avenue for testing out the nature of the effects of social support in stressful life situations. Such analogs have already been employed successfully and have provided valuable information about social support (Sarason, 1979). The laboratory can provide a setting in which types of support can be varied by situation, and individuals can be randomly placed in high and low stress conditions. Nadler et al. (1974) have also utilized this paradigm in order to study the effects of help seeking, finding important and complex differences among persons who differ in self-esteem.

Such studies can be faulted for not being comparable to "real life" stressor events. Models developed in the laboratory can and should be tested in applied settings. Such studies are valuable, nevertheless, because they allow researchers to clarify their research direction in more controlled conditions before venturing into the more expensive, time consuming, and less controllable realm of field research. Variables that are interrelated in nature may thus be examined in order to disentangle their effects.

Model intervention studies are still another direction that can aid researchers in clarifying theory and developing intervention strategies. Such studies may vary from laboratory analogs to actual efforts to intervene among clinical or at-risk populations. Comparison groups who do not receive the intervention as in the studies by Vachon (Chap. 12) among widows and breast cancer groups provide convincing arguments and avoid many of the problems of confounding variables discussed above.

A word of caution should be added, however. Little is known about the effect of social support on those who normally don't have it. Not having social networks may indicate a preference for the use of other resources. There is also indication from research on loneliness that suggests that such individuals don't possess social skills necessary to exploit supportive efforts even if they were available (Perlman & Peplau, 1981). Depressed individuals have also been shown to demean supportive efforts. Their satisfaction with support offered them is lower than that of non-depressed individuals (Coyne et al., 1981). Attempts to give them more support may be doomed to failure.

Process Analysis is another tool which may be utilized to better understand the mechanics of social support during stressful periods. Hobfoll and Walfisch (1982) presented one process model of social support, which was revised in a later paper (Hobfoll, 1985). In this volume Hirsch and Renders (Chap. 2) and Stein and Rappaport (Chap. 4) also present avenues for evaluating the qualitative aspects of building friendships, expectations from peers and family, and the effect of these on outcome. These will be especially important methodologies if social support based interventions are to be attempted.

Multidimensional Models of Resource Utilization

A number of the studies in this volume have suggested the investigation of multidimensional models of resource utilization. This would also be in line with the work of Kobasa and her colleagues (Kobasa, Maddi, & Courington, 1981) whose concept of "hardiness" is in itself a multidimensional resource consisting of personality trait and cognitive perspective. Antonovsky's (1979) model of general resistance resources and his formulation of "sense of coherence" also emphasizes the need to examine more than a unidimensional stressor-resource fit.

One criticism of these perspectives, however, is that by combining multidimensional factors into a single concept they may lose the ability to differentiate which aspects of the concept contribute to what and how they interact. Antonovsky's (1979) sense of coherence is less likely to lead to this problem. In his attempts to develop measures of sense of coherence, he has developed subscales which can be examined separately in addition to the global score.

Studying a variety of resources in the same research has already proved fruitful (Hobfoll & Walfisch, 1984; Pearlin, Lieberman, Menaghan, & Mullan, 1981; Sandler & Lakey, 1982). If studied in different situations, questions of "which resource is most effective when," can be answered. This may also lead to the development of research trends in addition to the buffering versus direct effect question, which has dominated the literature (Hobfoll & Leiberman, in press).

Multidimensional models allow investigation of many other questions related to social support, including those pertaining to interaction effects among resources, substitution of resource effects and complementation of resource effects. Interaction effect questions include: If you have social support and self-esteem, is it different than not having self-esteem? Will individuals high in self-esteem choose to utilize potential support in all types or stages of stress? Persons high in mastery, say, may choose to utilize support selectively, as they have a preference to control their own lives.

The substitution effect may be investigated in multidimensional research by evaluating if less preferable resources can be substituted when the desired resource is unavailable. Is social support the best thing for women following violent trauma? If it is not available what is the next best thing? How do individuals choose which of a number of potential resources to utilize? Can such patterns if ineffective be changed? There should also be interest in determining if there are certain styles or combinations of resource utilization. If individuals employ social support are they likely to employ other resources before, simultaneously, after? In this sense substitution of resources may not follow a particular sequence. To borrow a term from recent military experience that found the use of a single type of force ineffective, we may also find that "integration of forces" in different combinations of resources is the ideal coping strategy.

Behavioral Measures of Strain

Research on social support has generally focused on psychological and physical health variables for determining the effects of social support on the individual. There has been an absence of employment of behavioral measures of strain, despite the obvious value these would have. Functioning, for instance, is not solely determined by health factors. Research that provided information on work performance, drug taking (legal and illegal), alcohol consumption, smoking, exercising, use of leisure time, sexual activity, household activity, child care, and other behaviors would be very valuable. Such dependent variables speak to the issue of the effect of social support on quality of one's life.

Following rape, for example, there are important behavioral questions to ask. We expect the individual to be very upset, anxious, and depressed. But does the support of intimates, peers, and others result in her going to movies, bathing and attending her infant, or continuing her research at the university? Does she avoid going out at night? Does she choose not to have sex with her husband? What is the effect of the event and the help that she is getting on her life?

In a recent study of women whose loved ones were suddenly called to war, where little information was available about casualties, and where state depression and state anxiety were found to be extremely high, we were startled upon debriefing to find that not one of the women had stopped her normal course of duties (Hobfoll & London, in press). However, many women complained of having been so disorganized as to have forgotten to buy groceries, not wanted to clean their house, stood by their test tubes or typewriter staring into space until someone spoke to them, and other behavioral manifestations of their relative dysfunction. Two points should be gleaned from this. The first is how well these women performed under this massive threat. The second is that there was some performance deficit, which is a measure of strain, and if allowed to continue it would be an additional stressor. The tendency of researchers to focus on psychological and health variables reflects our distance as investigators from a major area of these people's concerns.

IMPLICATIONS FOR THEORY AND APPLICATIONS

Cognition in the Social Support-Stress Interaction

Cognitions take place throughout the utilization of social support and other resources and an understanding of this factor may be integral to an understanding of the "nuts and bolts" of how these resource "potentials" are transferred into "kinetic" effects on the psychological level. In Table 1 the role of cognitive factors throughout the process of social support is presented. Beginning with the stressor event individuals have to become aware of the threat that confronts them. The properties of the stressor must be *considered* (Lazarus, 1977). Following this awareness individuals must *consider* what resources are available to them. They may then *imagine* what the benefit and side effects would be of meeting the threat with a given resource or combination of resources.

Assuming that social support is *decided* upon as one of the resources which may be effective they must *decide* from whom to request support. "Cognitive rehearsal" may be used here to practice how to ask, as left to their own devices such rehearsal may backfire.* This is illustrated in the folk tale of the man who

---

*Fischer, Nadler, & Whitcher-Alagna (1982) have found that requesting help may be avoided as it is viewed by many as demeaning and is often interpreted as causing a lowering of status vis-à-vis the helper.

Table 1 Cognitions in the stress-social support process

Objective events	Related cognitions
Stressor	Perception of threat
	Perceptions and decisions regarding resources
Request support	Perceptions regarding support
	Availability
	Efficacy
	Requesting/receiving aid
Response of network	Perception of response
	Is it supportive?
	Is it enough?
	Integration of information
	Decisions about additional support
Benefit	Evaluation of received support and its effect
Intermediary processes	Perceptions toward friendship
	Decisions to help others

walks to borrow a mule from an old friend. At first he tells himself, "of course Yenkle will give me the mule we're old friends." After another kilometer he hesitates (cognitively) and says to himself, "but he may not give me the mule . . . no he wouldn't do that." After still another kilometer he has thoroughly "rehearsed" how he will ask and "imagined" his embarrassment when Yenkle refuses him in his moment of need. When Yenkle opens the door he receives a severe blow to the head accompanied by the words, "You can keep your broken down mule, how could you treat me this way after all our years of friendship!" The role of cognitive rehearsal for the tale's protagonist is self-evident.

After the network responds, moreoever, new decisions must be made about the adequacy of the support received. These decisions are based on *evaluations* of the efforts carried out in our behalf (see Table 1). These may be concrete evaluations, such as "do I feel better?" or "are my children receiving the kind of loving care from my neighbor who babysits them that I expect?" Dean and Lin (1977) wrote that social support supplies us with information that we are loved, needed, and members of caring networks. Cognitive processes such as attribution and social comparison are the avenues individuals follow to digest this information.

Once supportive efforts have been received their meaning must be *evaluated* (Table 1). "If my husband was present at childbirth does this mean I'm loved?" Such evaluations are essential for translating help into other than instrumental hollow acts. Coyne et al. (1981) has illustrated, for example, how depressed individuals can evaluate a great deal of support as something of little value. We know nothing about how tendencies to evaluate the meaning of support are developed or what variables are related to them. Since so much of the research on social support entails subjective perceptions by people of what kind of help they were given, we may essentially be studying differences in evaluation and not differences in amount or type of help.

When no longer in the heat of coping following a major life event or series of hassles, attitudes and perceptions toward friendships and helping others may be decisive in the building and maintaining of social networks. Women's attitudes and expectations toward what they can glean from peer support will tend to result in a self-fulfilling prophesy. Women who believe that benefit can be derived from peers will nurture and utilize such relations, while those not possessing positive expectations will not make this kind of investment.

If intervention efforts are to be effective, attention must be paid to how individuals perceive help, friendship, family, and support. Certainly, noncognitive factors also play a role in social support. Being loved may be appreciated because it meets our needs and desires, provides satisfaction, and makes us feel cared for and safe. Cognitions are important in these processes too, and affecting them may be easier than affecting needs or personality traits. Cognitive therapies may be helpful toward this end (Michenbaum & Navaco, 1978), as might educational efforts suggested by Ruch and Leon (Chap. 9).

When and If to Intervene

The question at this point needs to be raised as to when and if to intervene to affect social networks, social support, and evaluation of supportive efforts both on our behalf and those we do on the behalf of others. In the following paragraphs the topics of when to intervene, if intervention will help, and how to affect social networks will be addressed.

In recent papers I have discussed the importance of seeing social support as a process which has a continuum of related behaviors that may be divided into stages (Hobfoll, 1985; Hobfoll & Walfisch, 1982). These phases are *perception of need, recruitment of support, support response, integration of support,* and *reciprocation of support.* Consideration of these stages is necessary to address the decision as to when to intervene. The answer is that it depends on which stage one wishes to affect and what the practical and theoretical chances are of effecting change.

Viewing social support in this way, for example, it can be seen that the building of supportive social networks is consistent with the "reciprocation of support" phase which occurs after the crisis related demands have diminished. When a woman loses a spouse, is raped, gives birth, or decides about divorce, she will be feeling highly stressed and may need to give all her attention to the problem. As Bankoff (Chap. 13) argues, peers have a tremendous contribution to make, but we establish such relationships prior to the crisis event. During crises people are preoccupied with their own distress. This makes it unlikely that at this time they can begin to build the kind of intimate networks that they might require. Absorbed in their suffering, they are able only to receive and not to give. Even if we can imagine situations in which during crisis individuals may find some new friends or reinforce ties with family, it is doubtful that they will translate helpful efforts to messages of being loved and cared for if these relationships have not previously been meaningful for them.

During crisis some things can be done. At the recruitment phase professionals may encourage individuals to activate what support they have. They may encourage positive cognitive rehearsal of how the individual would respond if they were asked for help. They may help individuals clarify which type of support to mobilize from whom. While new social networks cannot at this time be built, existing ones may be exploited. After receiving support in the integration phase individuals can be encouraged to positively evaluate what was received. A simple statement such as "your son wouldn't have flown to see you in the hospital if he didn't love you very much," may cue an elderly mother to the meaning of his efforts.

Organized self-help groups may also have beneficial effects during crises. Such groups may be seen as intact supportive networks—a kind of social M.A.S.H. unit. Many such groups are composed of members who have positive attitudes toward the target group, are often well trained in basic counseling techniques, and don't expect an immediate return for their investment. They may be effective even with individuals who lack natural supportive networks (Hobfoll, 1980; Vachon, Chap. 12).

Police, physicians, attorneys, and others who are commonly active during crisis periods may also act as supports during the immediate stages of the crisis when even intimate friends and family are unavailable. Such nonmental health professionals may be especially effective if they are selected and trained with social-psychological needs of their clients in mind (Cowen, McKim, & Weissberg, 1981; Cowen, Zax, & Laird, 1966; Hobfoll & Benor, 1984).

Building Support Systems

Building social networks which provide active, appropriate, quality supportive efforts (other social networks are not "support systems") is a task that is most ecologically congruent with the period in which the individual is experiencing everyday stressors, not major life events. The motivation for doing so may, in fact, be derived from the experience of prior stressful events or difficulties in coping with daily events.

As the chapters by Aneshensel (Chap. 7) and Vanfossen (Chap. 5) clearly indicate, everyday challenges facing women may be motivation enough to seek the support of others. This may take a task oriented form such as car pools, childcare, study groups, or professional training or may be more general such as women's "consciousness raising" groups, sports clubs, or joining lecture or concert series with others. Activities for women alone, families, and couples may each fulfill different needs.

Change agents may catalyze the formation of these groups, seek their financing, and push for local legislation that makes them available. High risk individuals may be identified by professionals or lay groups based on key informants or advertising. The insightful work of George Brown and his colleagues (Brown, Bhrolchain, & Harris, 1975) suggests, however, that those individuals most in need may have difficulty exploiting these activities even if they are readily available. So, for example, women with young children and few economic resources may require intervention that offers combinations of supportive efforts, such as childcare, so that they may exploit activities that are made available for them. Similarly, elderly women may be provided both with transportation and safe escort so that they feel able to take advantage of social support opportunities.

Enhancing Social Competencies

Many individuals may not have the social skills needed to exploit supportive social efforts made available to them (see Bankoff, Chap. 13; Hirsch & Renders, Chap. 2; and Mitchell & Hodson, Chap. 10). Lonely individuals, for instance, lack the skills necessary to utilize affiliative coping opportunities and even arouse rejection in others (Perlan & Peplau, 1981).

Individuals who have natural support systems may reap the benefits such networks have to offer. So too may people who are circumstantially cut off from social support, such as mothers with young children. For the former group the interventionist should leave well enough alone. For the latter group community action and organizational interventions are desirable. However, there is still another category of individuals who lack the social competencies that are necessary to enjoy the products of social relationships, even if friends or professionals avail them to such support. For these people other kinds of interventions must be developed.

The question immediately arises as to which skills need to be developed. The answer to this follows from the model of ecological congruence and from the subsequently derived process model of social support mentioned above. Individuals who ineffectively use social relationships may be lacking in skills which may be deduced from the phases of the social support process detailed above. So, they may incorrectly evaluate who in their social network might offer them support (perception of need). Or they may be too unassertive to request help (recruitment phase). Upon requesting help, or if they are offered help from someone, they may react inappropriately such as by responding overdependently, by responding angrily, or simply by not providing continued social cues as to what their needs may be (response phase).

As many such persons have by preference or by lack of alternative adjusted to social isolation, they may also live a life style that physically distances them from others. They are not necessarily stereotypical social isolates. They may be housewives who have depended on "soap operas" and conversations with six-year-olds for social contact, or an executive woman who climbed the executive ladder without a female mentor or female colleagues and who has felt unwelcomed or welcomed for what she felt were the wrong reasons at the 5 o'clock "happy hours."

A later stage presented in the model (reciprocation of support) is the everyday stress period in which friendships and family relationships may be created, maintained, and strengthened. Again there are a number of social skills that are related to meeting new people, offering help to others, and setting social contacts as one of the priorities of a busy week. This may be difficult for both the housewife and the married career woman. Both roles are extremely demanding (Vanfossen, Chap. 5) and may limit the opportunities to practice social skills. Similarly divorced women may have long forgotten dating skills and the etiquette of social tête-à-tête, as well as how to establish female friendships (Wilcox, Chap. 8). Having had a spouse and children, her life may have been fulfilled (and if not fulfilled, certainly filled) without such friendships. Her social skills may work better with couples than with single men or women.

Women who have experienced a major transitional life event may need to acquire new skills or reinforce previously obtained social competencies. This also follows from the model of ecological congruence if the individual is seen as having skills that are consistent with a given ecosystem and that do not necessarily represent strengths in other ecosystems. In studies of a subarctic skid row it was found, for example, that the skid row members were for the most part successfully utilizing their ecology to survive, obtain food, shelter, entertainment, and medical attention (Hobfoll, Kelso, & Peterson, 1980; 1981; in press). While these goals may not be shared by society in general they do represent successful coping within a chosen ecological niche.

Ostrow, Paul, Dark, and Behrman (Chap. 3) in this light discuss the plight of women returning to university studies at a comparatively later age than most students, often following divorce and having rejected a strong religious milieu. Similarly women following divorce (Wilcox, Chap. 8), cancer therapy (Vachon, Chap. 12), rape (Ruch & Leon, Chap. 9), or battering (Mitchell & Hodson, Chap. 10) may benefit from social competency interventions to restore a loss of trust in their own social skills and abilities. Practice and feedback from trained laypersons and professionals in the relatively guarded helping setting may, as a byproduct, help them increase their sense of mastery and self-esteem, as it may provide them with a feeling of increased control over an important aspect of their lives.

The studies of Aneshensel (Chap. 7), Stein & Rappaport (Chap. 4), Vanfossen (Chap. 5) and Linn (Chap. 14) also suggest that women at different developmental stages might benefit from social competency training to acquire skills that are congruent with the requirement of their new developmental stage. Executives and academics might learn how to utilize a mentor and how to react to employees or unwanted sexual advances. Elderly women who never thought of using public social services may need not only information about such services, but may (unfortunately) need to learn a style of behavior that is effective with social workers and bureaucrats. Many of these skills may be learned in peer groups and female psychologists, psychiatrists, and social workers may be natural organizers, initiators, and expert participants in such groups.

There is, however, some danger here of blaming the victim as Mitchell and Hodson (Chap. 10) note. The problem of how to react to unwanted sexual advances in work and academic settings may require women to be armed with certain social competencies. Cognitive rehearsal of how to react may also help individuals feel more competent and respond as they would like to imagine they would when the need arises. However, this implies that women are part of the problem and that the solutions depend on their "acting appropriately." If the sexual pressures placed on women students and young women academics at an institution like Harvard is so widespread as shown in a recent study ("Fair Harvard," 1983), then what about the situation on the factory shop floor (Barret, 1979). Reacting appropriately is helpful, but it is also a "social band-aid" and not a remedy.

Change must be instituted on the level of those persons who control the sanctions. However, as some persons of senior position were perceived as sexually exploiting persons of more junior status the problem is a complex one indeed. Still the solution and certainly the blame does not lie with the social competencies of women.

In a similar vein the behavior of battered women has also been used to blame them for inviting beatings. For most battered women their apparent acquiescence is a learned behavior that is reactive to a particular situation where there are few viable alternatives (Mitchell & Hodson, Chap. 10). Again building social competencies may be an important intervention strategy for these women. However, such intervention must be instituted in conjunction with provision of safe shelter, legal assistance, police protection, court intervention, financial assistance, and occupational training. In such instances instrumental support is the vital component and affecting social competencies is a much warranted addendum.

Affecting Sense of Obligation

One neglected area of social support research concerns the study of the effect of family values and sense of obligation toward family members. Stein and

Rappaport (Chap. 4) discuss the potential detrimental effect sense of obligation toward family may have on some women. This seems to be the case when individuals place obligation over actual intimacy. We are probably obligated to many more people than we can include on an intimate level. Obligation to family and friends has many positive functions. It helps strengthen our social networks and provides social pressure toward helping and accepting help from others in times of need.

Research is needed to clarify what constitutes a healthy balance between obligation and intimacy. To what extent are the two related? However, there is already some support for the contention that women are benefited by the presence of social ties outside of dense family networks (Hirsch, 1980; Wilcox, Chap. 8). This may especially be the case when a woman needs support for feelings or behaviors which are not acceptable within the family or which threaten shared relationships, such as in the case of divorce, battering, or simply returning to studies against a spouse's wishes (Hirsch, 1980; Mitchell & Hodson, Chap. 10; Wilcox, Chap. 8). This may also be the case when persons within the set of obligated individuals are not perceived as having the tools or understanding to help, such as in the case of breast cancer or grief (Bankoff, Chap. 13; Vachon, Chap. 12).

Another area in which change may need to be affected is in the expectations individuals place on obligated relationships. Family members may be expected to make all kinds of sacrifices that they are unwilling or unable to make. In many situations it is actually more distant social ties that provide us with the necessary support (Wellman, 1981). In this respect there is also a need for research to clarify to what extent our expectations toward the support that is potentially available to us is accurate, and to what extent the benefit we believe will be derived from such efforts is actually gained. To what degree are individuals realistic estimators of their resources and how may we help individuals to improve their judgment?

Returning to the model of ecological congruence we can see the potential problem of involvement in obligated relationships if it is to the detriment of benefit derived relationships. Obligated relationships are actually likely to increase strain as even those obligated ties which we find stressful remain intact. A poor relationship with an inlaw or boss, for example, may have to be tolerated. Obligated relationships may also increase strain by acting as sources of expressed values and taboos which restrict individuals meeting their needs. This is the case because such persons are not only obligated to us, but also to the family, business, or club. In cases where a woman may need support that in some way threatens or even merely causes discomfort to other members, beliefs or creeds of the family, or other social unit, she may be encouraged by her supporters to compromise, back down or "be realistic." While messages that support the group or spouse have their positive side both to the individual and the social unit, women may need more one-sided support when such value clashes occur. Stated another way, we need individuals biased in our favor—intimate advocates!

SUMMARY

This chapter set out to discuss problems in methodology of research on social support and to integrate methodology with theory. Investigation of specific events and attention to time that has transpired since event occurrence was advocated in order to move toward a disentanglement of the stressor—social support—strain interrelationship. Longitudinal and time-series designs, laboratory analogs, model intervention studies, and process analysis were discussed as avenues for future research. The importance of multidimensional research on social support was emphasized as social support was seen as just one among many related resources. In addition, the discussion of merging theory with methodology suggested a need for inclusion of behavioral variables as measures of strain, as social support often is directed at helping the supportee function more effectively in the face of stressors.

Implications for theory and applications from current research, especially as they concern women, were also presented. The importance of cognitions throughout the social support process was examined. A process model of social support was cited and adapted to an evaluation of when and if to intervene, as successful intervention was seen as conditional on an understanding of the ecology of help requesting, giving, and receiving. The concept of ecology was also applied to a discussion of the need to assist women in the development of social competencies. Finally, the relationship of family values and obligations to the development of effective social networks was discussed.

CONCLUSIONS

This volume has made a case for the special needs of women in dealing with life stressor events that confront them from adolescence to old age. The resources that women use to aid their adjustment to these events—both the everyday and the tragic—across such a broad time span, with such disparate samples by researchers from many different disciplines and perspectives, provide a dynamic picture of the stress process. While emphasis has been placed on social support, this volume illustrates that this is but one key resource among a broad array of coping aids.

Looking across studies it is apparent that social support's first source is the family and especially one's spouse or partner. Whether because of time constraints, social norms, or western life style, spouse or partner can be the greatest contributor to our feeling of being valued and our central provider of love, affection, and esteem. Because of their importance this same partner may in strained relationships become one of the most painful contributors to stress. This delicate balance between the partner's role as stress alleviator or stress creator begs the intervention question "what about him?"

Interventions with social networks, if they are to be effective, will have to work with men as well as women. Much of the stress in the life of the housewife or working woman involves work overload that stems from the household. Men need to take greater initiative in this regard. While it may be argued that cooking is a skill that takes years to develop, this argument cannot be applied to those lower art forms such as cleaning, diaper changing, being "on call" for the night bottle, getting the kids dressed and out on time, and the host of other chores left as women's work. Even cooking (if not haute cuisine) is no more difficult than following instructions that are no more complex than those for the car and workshop.

Such cooperation is essential if women are to pursue a career effectively and may be accompanied by a changed evaluation by men of what their partners are doing. More effective at work, new esteem may also be felt by and towards wives.

Such attitude change by men seems essential, because if only women change, this will place new stressors on both them and their relationship. These everyday hassles should not be underestimated either, as for most individuals coping with the everyday mundane is a principal cause of distress (London & Spielberger, 1983).

Following partners, peers seem to be the next most potent ingredient in the social network. In fact peer support has many advantages over spouse support, and it is especially important where spouse support is unavailable or where one's partner is part of the problem. Development of such relationships is an important goal both for the individual and for interventionists interested in enhancing social networks. Having a diverse peer group will insure that varying needs can be met and that help of the type required will be available when it is required. This implies the establishment and maintenance of both close intimate ties as well as looser social or task oriented relationships.

One criticism of this volume is the inevitable focus on the microsocial space at the expense of the macro-social space. Building strong social bonds and sharpening interpersonal skills has a potential contribution in combatting the stressors that will always be a part of the human experience. However, this should not detract from the case for macro-social change.

In this regard change must be instituted at the workplace to insure women equal rights and opportunities. Such innovations as flexitime may ease the stressors impinging on families as well as the environment. Education must encourage women to study subjects that will make them competitive in the marketplace and positive attitudes toward women need to be demonstrated in texts and curricula.

Similarly, combating such problems as rape and battering will require the back up of law enforcement agencies, the courts, and city officials. Statistics that indicate that a woman has a 10% chance of being raped represent a most tragic commentary on our society (Rape, 1983). Institutional change is also called for in the medical world. While the advances of medicine have been significant there is still a need to address problems of concern to female patients (Rand, Chap. 11) whether in the joyous process of childbirth or the life threatening grip of cancer.

The lack of provision of quality childcare is conspicuous in North America. That parents, especially those who do not have the economic resources, must rely on inconvenient, unsupervised, unlicensed nurseries or after-school providers who often have had no education concerning the care of young children, is intolerable. Mothers must either remain home (which may not be economically feasible) or go to work feeling worried and guilty about their child's welfare. In poorer neighborhoods many children are simply left unsupervised from a very young age.

It follows from this volume that intervention strategies should offer a "menu" of resources, resource catalyzers, and means of encouraging skills development for target groups. Community action is also warranted and greater efforts should be made toward affecting the workplace, the courts, and legislation. Supportive human environments will act not only as coping resources, but will also reduce a major cause of stressors. Nor does it follow that social support is only something that "natural," i.e. nonprofessional networks can provide. Indeed instrumental and emotional support by professional networks is valuable, especially where "natural" support is unavailable or ecologically incongruent with individuals' needs. This further implies that professionals must move toward networking their services to provide a broader array of services. Just providing social support is as illogical in this sense as just providing psychotherapy. Each of these services can be effective, but they are likely to be enhanced when offered in appropriate combinations. "Appropriate" needs to be defined by the consumer as well as be the provider, especially if we are to reach the best stressor-individual-resource fit. As the contexts and needs discussed in this volume are relevant to "normal" women it is consistent that such populations be offered choices as to with which intervention they feel comfortable and find relevant for themselves. This of course places professionals in the role of facilitators and requires that they share much of their decision making power with client-consumers, rather than deciding what "they need best."

It was the goal of this volume to provide a comprehensive picture of the role of social support and other resources in the lives of women in combatting the stressors that they undergo across the life span. Hopefully it will encourage further research, catalyze discussion and criticism, and motivate attempts at intervention. The numbers of stressors and personal and social tragedies that such a volume inevitably presents can encourage pessimism and despair. However, that so many women are healthy, functioning, and receiving and providing support speaks to the strength of these women. This volume in that sense is about health, coping, and the most positive aspects of the human experience.

REFERENCES

Andrews, G. (1981). A prospective study of life events and psychological symptoms. *Psychological Medicine, 11,* 795-801.

Aneshensel, C. S., & Frerichs, R. R. (1982). Stress, support and depression: A longitudinal causal model. *Journal of Community Psychology, 10,* 363-376.

Anson, O., Bernstein, J., & Hobfoll, S. E. (1984). Anxiety and performance in two ego threatening situations. *Journal of Personality Assessment, 48,* 168-172.

Antonovsky, A. (1979). *Health, stress and coping.* San Francisco: Jossey-Bass.

Barret, N. S. (1979). Women in the job market: Occupations, earnings and career opportunities. In R. E. Smith (Ed.), *The subtle revolution* (pp. 31-61). Washington, DC: The Urban Institute.

Brown, G., Brholchrain, M., & Harris, T. (1975). Social class and psychiatric disturbances among women in an urban population. *Sociology, 9,* 225-254.

Campbell, D. T., & Stanley, J. C. (1963). *Experimental and quasiexperimental designs for research.* Chicago: Rand McNally.

Caplan, G. (1974). Support systems and community mental health: Lectures on concept development. New York: *Behavioral.*

Cobb, J. (1976). Social support as a moderator of life stress. *Psychosomatic Medicine, 38,* 300-314.

Cowen, E. L., McKim, B. J., & Weissberg, R. P. (1981). Bartenders as informal, interpersonal help agents. *American Journal of Community Psychology, 9,* 715-730.

Cowen, E. L., Zax, M., & Laird, J. D. (1966). A college student volunteer program in the elementary school setting. *Community Mental Health Journal, 2,* 319-328.

Coyne, J. C., Aldwin, C., & Lazarus, R. S. (1981). Depression and coping in stressful episodes. *Journal of Abnormal Psychology, 90,* 439-447.

Dean, A., & Lin, N. (1977). The stress buffering role of social support: Problems and prospects for future investigation. *Journal of Nervous and Mental Disease, 165,* 403-417.

Dohrenwend, B. S., & Dohrenwend, B. P. (1981). Socioenvironmental factors, stress, and psychopathology. *American Journal of Community Psychology, 9,* 128-165.

Dohrenwend, B. S., & Martin, J. L. (1979). Personal versus situational determination of anticipation and control of the occurrence of recent life events. *American Journal of Community Psychology, 7,* 453-468.

Eaton, W. W. (1978). Life events, social supports and psychiatric symptoms. A reanalysis of the New Haven data. *Journal of Health and Social Behavior, 19*, 230–234.

Fair Harvard: Are you fair? (1983, November). *Time*, p. 54.

Fischer, J. D., Nadler, A. S., & Whitcher-Alagna, S. (1982). Recipient reactions to aid. *Psychological Bulletin, 91*, 27–54.

Hartup, W. W. (1970). Peer interaction and social organization. In R. H. Mussen (Ed.), *Carmichael's manual of child psychology, Vol. 2*. (361–456). New York: Wiley.

Hirsch, B. J. (1980). Natural support systems and coping with recent life changes. *American Journal of Community Psychology, 8*, 159–179.

Hobfoll, S. E. (1980). Interracial commitment and involvement in undergraduate tutors in an inner-city preschool. *Journal of Community Psychology, 8*, 80–87.

Hobfoll, S. E. (1985). The limitations of social support in the stress process. In I. G. Sarason & B. R. Sarason (Eds.), *Social support: Research, theory and application*. (pp. 391–414). The Hague: Martinus Nijhof.

Hobfoll, S. E., & Benor, D. E. (1984). Selection of medical students with emphasis on interpersonal intervention potential. *Journal of Community Psychology, 12*, 74–80.

Hobfoll, S. E., Kelso, D., & Peterson, W. J. (1980). The Anchorage skid row. *Journal of Studies on Alcohol, 41*, 94–99.

Hobfoll, S. E., Kelso, D., & Peterson, W. J. (1981). Agency usage of skid row persons. *Journal of Alcohol and Drug Education, 26*, 832–838.

Hobfoll, S. E., Kelso, D., & Peterson, W. J. (in press). When are support systems, support systems? A study of skid row. In S. Einstein (Ed.), *Drug and alcohol use: Issues and factors*. New York: Plenum.

Hobfoll, S. E., & Leiberman, J. (in press). Personality and social resources in immediate and continued stress resistance among women. *Journal of Personality and Social Psychology*.

Hobfoll, S. E., & London, P. (in press). The relationship of self concept and social support to emotional distress among women during war. *Journal of Social and Clinical Psychology*.

Hobfoll, S. E., & Walfisch, S. (1982). *Observations on the mechanics and process of social support*. Paper presented at the annual meeting of the American Psychological Association, Washington, DC.

Hobfoll, S. E., & Walfisch, S. (1984). Coping with a threat to life: A longitudinal study of self-concept, social support and psychological distress. *American Journal of Community Psychology, 12*, 87–100.

Holhohan, C., & Moos, R. (1981). Social support and psychological distress, a longitudinal analysis. *Journal of Abnormal Psychology, 90*, 365–370.

Kobasa, S. C., Maddi, S. R., & Courington, S. (1981). Personality and constitution as mediators in the stress-illness relationship. *Journal of Health and Social Behavior, 22*, 368–378.

Lazarus, R. S. (1977). Cognitive and coping processes in emotion. In A. Monat & R. S. Lazarus (Eds.), *Stress and coping* (pp. 145–158). New York: Columbia University Press.

London, P., & Spielberger, C. D. (1983). Job stress, hassles and medical risk. *American Health*, March/April.

Meichenbaum, D. H., & Navaco, R. (1978). Stress inoculation: A preventive approach. In C. D. Spielberger & I. G. Sarason (Eds.), *Stress and Anxiety, Vol. 5*. (pp. 317–328). Washington, DC: Hemisphere.

Nadler, A., Fisher, J. D., & Streufert, S. (1974). The donor's dilemma: Recipients reaction to aid from friend or foe. *Journal of Applied Social Psychology, 4*, 275–285.

Pearlin, L. I., Lieberman, M. A., Menaghan, E. G., & Mullan, J. T. (1981). The stress process. *Journal of Health and Social Behavior, 22*, 337–356.

Perlman, D., & Peplau, L. A. (1981). Toward a social psychology of loneliness. In R. Gilmour & S. Duck (Eds.), *Personal relationships 3: Personal relationships in disorder* (pp. 31–56). London: Academic.

Rape: The sexual weapon. (1983, September 5). *Time*, p. 37–39.

Sandler, I. N., & Lakey, B. (1982). Locus of control as a stress moderator: The role of control perceptions and social support. *American Journal of Community Psychology, 10*, 65–80.

Sarason, I. G. (1979). *Life stress, self preoccupation and social support* (Report No. SCS-LS-008). Seattle, WA: Office of Naval Research.

Speilberger, C. D. (1962). The effects of manifest anxiety on academic performance of college students. *Mental Hygiene, 46*, 420–426.

Teichman, Y. (1973). Emotional arousal and affiliation. *Journal of Personality and Social Psychology, 9*, 591–605.

Teichman, Y. (1978). Affiliative reactions in different kinds of threat situations. In C. D. Spielberger & I. G. Sarason (Eds.), *Stress and anxiety, Vol. 5* (pp. 131–144). Washington, DC:
Hemisphere.

Thoits, P. A. (1983). Conceptual, methodological and theoretical problems in studying social
support as a buffer against life stress. *Journal of Health and Social Behavior, 23,* 145–159.

Wellman, B. (1981). Applying network analysis to the study of support. In B. H. Gottlieb (Ed.),
Social networks and social support (pp. 171–200). Beverly Hills: Sage.

Author Index

Gottman, J. M., 27
Gould, M. S., 43
Gove, W. R., 69, 83, 99, 100, 103, 105,
    113, 148, 151
Graney, M. J., 227, 234
Greenley, J., 30, 44
Greenley, J. R., 151
Greer, S., 193, 202
Gross, A., 30, 32, 35, 36, 44
Groth, A. N., 144, 151
Gruenbaum, H., 203
Gruenberg, E. M., 174, 184
Gullahorn, J. E., 132
Gundarson, E. K., 141, 151
Gurin, G., 69, 83
Guttentag, M., 83
Guttentlag, S., 44
Guttmacher, A., 184
Gutwirth, L., 94, 96

Halikas, J. A., 199, 202
Hamburg, D. A., 31, 43
Hammer, M., 94, 96
Hampton, R., 117, 132
Hanford, J., 175, 184
Hannon, N., 193, 202
Harris, R., 224, 234
Harris, T., 6, 13, 47, 64, 85, 95, 108, 113,
    189, 202, 225, 234, 248, 254
Harter, R. A., 141, 151
Hartup, W., 17, 27, 241, 255
Harvey, C. O., 208, 221
Haven, C., 94, 96, 207, 222
Havighurst, R. J., 227, 235
Haw, M. A., 104, 113
Hawson, D. M., 31, 43, 92, 95, 108, 112,
    189, 202
Heinstein, M., 174, 184
Heller, K., 41, 44
Helmreich, R., 53, 65, 121, 132
Helmreich, R. L., 160, 163, 169
Helsing, K. J., 99, 113
Henderson, S., 47, 65, 70, 83, 86, 87, 93,
    95, 96, 189, 203, 225, 234
Hennessey, M., 138, 151
Hesbacker, P., 89, 96
Hess, B., 209, 221
Hetherington, E. M., 115, 117, 132
Hetzel, B., 174, 184
Heyman, D., 224, 234
Hilberman, E., 154, 161, 168
Hirsch, B. J., 6, 13, 17, 18, 26, 27, 31, 40,
    42, 44, 47, 51, 65, 118, 130, 210,
    218, 221, 243, 248, 251, 255

Hoberman, U. M., 130, 132
Hobfoll, S. E., 7-9, 11-13, 87, 94, 96, 144,
    151, 183, 184, 189, 203, 241-245,
    247-249, 255
Hodges, W. F., 156, 168
Hodson, C. A., 153, 155, 156, 158, 169,
    248, 250, 251
Hollingshead, A., 191, 203
Holmes, K. A., 1, 37, 145, 146, 152
Holmes, T. H., 141, 151, 174, 175, 184,
    224-226, 233, 234
Holmstrom, L. L., 137, 140-142, 144, 145,
    147, 151
Holohan, C., 241, 255
Horner, M. S., 39, 44
Hotaling, G. T., 169
Hough, R. L., 225, 234
House, J. S., 108, 113
Houstan, B. K., 40, 44
Huba, G. J., 18, 27, 102, 109, 113
Hughes, M., 103, 113
Hunt, J., 4, 14
Huttel, F., 176, 184
Hyman, H. H., 207, 221

Ingersol, B., 49, 65
Ingham, J. G., 86, 93, 96
Insel, P., 221, 222

Jacklin, C. N., 5-7, 14
Jacobs, M., 225, 234
Jamieson, K. R., 196, 203, 204
Janes, C., 155, 169
Jeffers, F., 224, 234
Johnson, J., 71, 74, 84, 181, 184
Johnson, J. H., 53, 66
Johnson, J. S., 100, 113
Johnson, M., 31, 44, 221
Joss, R., 30, 45
Jourard, S., 6, 14

Kadushin, C., 217, 221
Kahana, E., 224, 234
Kalish, R. A., 211, 217, 221
Kanner, A. D., 121, 133
Kapferer, B., 218, 221
Kaplan, B., 69, 70, 83, 84, 142, 151, 174,
    185
Kaplan, B. H., 14, 93, 96, 109, 113, 189,
    203
Kasl, S. V., 217, 221
Katz, S., 138, 140, 151

Subject Index

Demands:
adaptational, 120
emotional, 173
financial, 173
Dependency, 213, 215
Depression, 9, 11, 32, 53, 69, 70, 71, 73,
77, 80–82, 85, 89–94, 99–112, 121,
124, 125, 127, 129–131, 143, 149,
156, 160, 189, 192, 196, 225, 229,
231–233, 240
post-partum, 176
Development:
adolescent, 26
cognitive, 26
sexual, 5
social, 26
Difficulty:
academic, 35, 39, 41
financial, 35, 82
psychological, 141
work, 36, 37
Disorder:
affective, 85–87, 90
depressive, 86
emotional, 85
neutral, 85
psychiatric, 85, 86, 89, 91, 93, 225
psychological, 142, 157
Distress, 157
emotional, 208
psychological, 11, 13, 103, 111, 142,
144, 149, 150, 153, 253
Divorce, 7–9, 34, 35, 37, 39–41, 115–132,
147, 187, 241
Domestic violence, 153–168

Ecological approach, 4, 13
(*See also* Ecological perspective)
Ecological congruence, 8–13
Ecological model, 4
Ecological perspective, 4, 5, 154, 158, 166,
167
(*See also* Ecological approach)
Ecology, 5, 6
of human development, 26
social, 26
Elderly women, 223–233
Emotional trauma, 116
Empathy, 8, 129
Employment, 105, 107, 111
Equity, 106
Event:
battering, 166
life-threatening, 85

Family, 33, 34, 36, 40, 70, 117, 118, 126,
127, 129, 140, 144–146, 149, 150,
154–156, 164, 165, 173, 180, 181,
192, 213, 224–226, 233, 247, 250,
251
Family loss, 142
Friends, 50, 51, 70, 117, 118, 126, 127,
129, 140, 144–146, 148, 154–156,
160, 165, 177, 181, 192, 196,
207–209, 213, 214, 224–226, 229,
233
making, process of, 25
Friendship, 17–27, 33, 36, 155, 162, 208,
216, 243, 246, 249
stages of, 20, 21
Functioning:
physical, 226, 227, 229, 233
psychological, 226, 227, 229, 233

Grief, 212, 215

Hassles, 121, 253
Health, 37, 42, 226, 241, 245, 254
emotional, 174
mental, 6, 17, 31, 89, 103, 142, 148,
174
physical, 6, 53, 106, 157, 198, 213, 229,
230, 232
psychological, 100, 157, 225, 232
Help:
informal sources of, 40, 41, 60
professional, 37
Help giving, 158
Help seeking, 29, 31, 37, 39, 40, 118, 122,
127–129, 155, 156, 158, 209
Helpfulness, 73, 76, 78, 79
Helping, 155
informal, 64
informational, 54, 56
instrumental, 54, 56
(*See also* Support; Aid; Assistance)
Homemaker, 34, 72, 77, 219
Housewife, 218
Husband, 106, 112, 177, 180
participation during birth, 176
violent, 154

Identity, 29
social, 40–42
Illness:
mental, 93
physical, 47, 88, 94, 106, 224, 227, 228,
230, 240